MY PEOPLE

The Story
of
Those Christians
Sometimes Called
Plymouth Brethren

*For he said, Surely they are my people, sons who will not deal falsely;
and he became their Savior.*
Isaiah63:8(RSV)

By Robert H. Baylis

Harold Shaw Publishers
Wheaton, Illinois

ISBN 0-87788-577-X

Cover design by David LaPlaca

Library of Congress Cataloging-in-Publication Data

Baylis, Robert H., 1924-

My people: the story of those Christians sometimes called Plymouth Brethren / by Robert H. Baylis.

Includes bibliographical references and index.

ISBN 0-87788-577-X

1. Plymouth Brethren—History. 2. Plymouth Brethren—Doctrines.

I. Title.

BX8800.B38 1995

289.9—dc20   95-41247

---

99   98   97

10   9   8   7   6   5   4   3   2

TABLE OF CONTENTS

I. BRITISH ORIGINS 1825-1882

The Story Opens
The First Companies
Ebrington Street and Bethesda: Eyewitness Accounts
Whatever Became of the First Brethren Meeting Places?
Early Brethren Hymnody

Ten Cardinal Principles of the Brethren
Which Branch Continued the Original Principles?
A Definition of the Brethren By F.F. Bruce

The Rise of John Nelson Darby
The Greatness of J.N.D.
The Teachings of J.N.D.
The Contribution of A.N. Groves

The Brethren Movement Divides
Bethesda as a Model of Independent Brethrenism
The Beginning of Worldwide Missions

II. PIONEERING DAYS IN NORTH AMERICA
1871-1920

III. THE GOLDEN AGE OF INDEPENDENT BRETHRENISM 1920-1960

IV. THE BRETHREN IN THE SPACE AGE 1960 -

3

APPENDICES

PREFACE

This book has been some five or six years in the making. These years have been momentous ones for the Brethren in North America. In fact, the events of the period from 1980 onward have brought about changes so vast that anything like the unified movement of the thirties, forties and fifties no longer exists.

The appearance of My People at this particular time may thus be somewhat significant. It is possibly a kind of obituary to a life that was, a life like that of a faithful minister of the Word who serves his generation well, and whom God uses for good over many years. But who, like all life on this earth, eventually passes away.

The ebb and flow of human associations, however, does not frustrate our God. The church is built upon the Rock, Christ Jesus, and the changes that come with the passing generations do not prevail against it. The principles upon which the Brethren movement were founded, insofar as they rest on the truth that is in Christ, will continue to be practiced by believers everywhere regardless of historical identities. Change is not only inevitable, it is vital if each generation is to be reached with the Gospel.

While this book may be in a sense an obituary to a way of life that was but is no more, it is not a lament. Exciting things are still happening to and through the Christians sometimes called Plymouth Brethren. There is grass roots outreach going on among both adults and children in the mushrooming suburbs, in the teeming inner cities, and in the numerous communities of non-English speaking peoples. Creative skills are being put to work in preparation of attractive gospel materials for mass distribution. Correspondence Bible courses are being diligently pursued by thousands of prison inmates. And Brethren missionary forces literally circle the globe.

The Brethren are my people. Through a lifetime of association with the assemblies, I know them well, both their strengths and their weaknesses. My purpose in this history is to tell their story in a positive way. Despite disagreements in methodology, all the different branches and splinters have played their part in letting the Light of the Truth shine in a dark world. My sincere hope is that we all will learn through the events of our past what is really important in God's eyes, and to take His agenda more seriously and ours a little less so.

ROBERT H. BAYLIS

Dedicated to the memory of my father
Harry J. Baylis 1892-1968

Acknowledgments

Most of the many kind friends who contributed information or materials to this book have been recognized by name therein. A few contributors played a part so vital that I doubt that the book could have been produced without them. These include John Hozack, who not only copied and printed hundreds of historical photos at his own cost, but also provided from his late father's library books unavailable from any other source; Don Tinder, a more knowledgeable Brethren historian than myself whose advice helped me to avoid some serious pitfalls; John Rush, librarian at Emmaus Bible College, who reproduced for my use copies of many rare materials not available elsewhere; Delbert Maifeld, who provided hundreds of original copies of Brethren periodicals which he had collected over many years; Virginia Hearn, who literally transformed the book through her professional editing skills; and my wife, Naomi, who accompanied me on research expeditions all over the U.S, Canada, England, and Ireland and faithfully supported and encouraged me.

Ed McCulley, Pete Fleming, and Jim Elliot pose with the Piper Cub aircraft used to communicate with the Auca People, 1956.

INTRODUCTION:
WHO ARE
THESE PEOPLE,
ANYWAY?

On January 9, 1956, the news was flashed around the world by radio station HCJB in Quito, Ecuador. Five young American missionaries were missing in the territory of the fierce Auca Indians. Soon the account of their martyrdom was being told by major newspapers everywhere. Later, LIFE Magazine carried a special feature with photographs by the famous Cornell Capa. Today, the names of Jim Elliot, Pete Fleming, Ed McCully, Nate Saint and Roger Youdarian are well known to church historians, and their story is legendary in the annals of evangelical missions. A virtually unknown fact, however, is that three of the five young men named above were not "professional" missionaries at all. They were independent workers, "commended to the Lord for missionary service" by their local churches, with no mission board behind them and no guaranteed means of support.

The Christians with whom Jim Elliot, Peter Fleming and Ed McCully associated hold rather radical views for this day and age. They believe that only God ordains workers to serve in his vineyard, and that the distinction between clergy and laity is a false one, contrary to the New Testament. They have no creeds, operate no theological seminaries and reject all denominational structures and religious hierarchy. Though called "Plymouth Brethren" by others, they themselves recognize no name other than Christians. For convenience, this book will refer to them simply as the "Brethren," or, when necessary to distinguish between branches, as Independent (or "Open") Brethren.[1] From time to time reference will also be made to the "Exclusive" Brethren.

They are not large in numbers, these Brethren, perhaps totaling 1,200 churches in all of North America. But they have had considerable influence on this continent in evangelical circles through their grass-roots gospel outreach at home and their widespread missionary endeavors abroad. Their people are to be found in places of leadership in numerous para-church organizations. Because of the emphasis on the autonomy of the local fellowship, many who are active in Brethren churches (usually, but not always, called "assemblies") know nothing whatever of their history. Or even that they have a history. Others, who have some knowledge of Brethren history, may know only a small part of the story. The task of this book, therefore, is to tackle five major questions about the people called Plymouth Brethren:

1. Where do they fit into the larger scheme of Christian history?

2. How did this particular stream of Christian history get its start and acquire its distinctives?

3. What were the foundations of the movement on this continent?

4. What developments brought into being the rather complex structures that make up the Brethren movement today?

5. What opportunities, problems, and challenges face the Brethren as they look toward the twenty-first century?

Looking back over time to the first century, we see little companies of disciples springing up all over the Roman Empire following the coming of the Holy Spirit at Pentecost. These local congregations were made up of believers only, and are addressed as such by the apostles in the New Testament letters. They had no organization beyond their local leaders, most of whom would have been ordinary working people, or perhaps wealthier merchants. Their gatherings, mostly in homes or public places, had the simplicity of the Last Supper combined with the

---

1 The designation "Open Brethren" means that they practice "open" communion—all believers who truly know Christ are welcome —in contrast to the "Exclusive Brethren" whose communion is closed to all who are not identified with them. These terms, however, are not completely accurate, first because some Exclusive groups may welcome some Christians not members of their circle, and second because, although all Independent Brethren assemblies are "open" in theory, some are more open than others.

teaching aspect of Jewish synagogues. By the second century this simplicity was already beginning to erode, and by the fourth we see a state religion with a priest-class and a ritual very much like the paganism that preceded it. With Pope Gregory I at the end of the sixth century, the Roman Catholic Church emerged as a mighty religious empire with kings and rulers as vassals of the pope.

A thousand years passed, and in the sixteenth century reform swept over Europe. Justification by faith was rediscovered and the Bible was restored as the final authority in all matters of faith ("Sola Scriptura"). But in the centuries to follow, up to our own time, the Protestant churches became either state institutions, as in the British Isles, Germany, and Scandinavia, or organized denominations with a formal structure and hierarchy of clergy. Today official Christendom, whether Catholic, Protestant, or Orthodox, is pretty much the mixture of belief and unbelief, spirituality and worldliness, that it has always been since at least the fourth century.

Historians have tended to look at the progress of the church as a linear development, with one period growing out of the previous one as part of the evolution of Western civilization. In recent years, however, new research has brought to light the fact that the apostolic-type church of the New Testament never has completely died out, even in the darkest days following the fall of the Roman Empire. To quote Leonard Verduin, author of the brilliant *The Reformers and Their Stepchildren:*

> In the twelve centuries that went before the Reformation [Christianity] has never lacked for attempts to get away from the State-Church Priest's Church and to re-institute the apostolic congregational structuralization.

Another book significant to the historic identification of the Brethren is *The Believers' Church* by Donald F. Durnbaugh.

Building on a quotation from Martin Luther, Durnbaugh points out seven distinctives of a believers' church in contrast to mainstream Protestantism, Catholicism, or Orthodoxy:

1. It consists of a "voluntary membership of those confessing Jesus Christ as Lord."

2. It rejects a mixed assembly of believers and unbelievers; members "attempt to live by the high standard of the New Testament."

3. Members perform Christian works, "confident that even their halting and stumbling efforts will be blessed by God."

4. They accept the necessity of discipline in the assembly.

5. They distribute gifts to the poor and share with their brethren in need.

6. Ordinances (baptism and the Lord's Supper) are neither completely formal nor completely spontaneous.

7. "The Word given in the Scriptures and apprehended through the Holy Spirit provides the sole authority."

Durnbaugh includes the "Plymouth Brethren" as "New Testament Restorationists" who emerged out of the political and religious turmoil taking place in Great Britain in the early nineteenth century.

One of the first books to identify the Brethren as a "believers' church" movement arising in the wake of many other such movements over the centuries is *The Pilgrim Church* by E.H. Broadbent. Edmund Broadbent spent nearly fifty years traveling in Central and Eastern Europe, searching out Christian groups past and present that gathered in separation from the established churches. He found that many bodies labeled by historians as heretics, who had been persecuted by official Christendom, were often merely simple Bible-believing Christians. Their "heresy" was to resist the pressure to conform. The Brethren are given considerable space at the end of the book, following the account of the Mennonites and Lutheran believers in Russia, the Campbellites in America, and the revival churches of the Wesleys, George Whitefield and the Haldane brothers.

We close this historic perspective of the Brethren with what Broadbent calls "certain salient points" that "turn the experience of the way that lies behind into guidance for the track that stretches before." By "certain salient points" he means the three most important characteristics of the Brethren or of any "Pilgrim Church" at any time in history:

One is that the Pilgrim Church has possessed in the Scriptures a safe and sufficient guide for all the way from Pentecost to the present time . . .

A second is that the Pilgrim Church is separate from the world; though in it, is not of it. It never becomes an earthly institution . . .

A third is that the church is one. In so far as we know ourselves to be members of the Pilgrim Church we acknowledge as our fellow-pilgrims all who tread the Way of Life. Passing differences, however keen at the time, grow dim as we view the whole pilgrimage spread out before us. In deepest humility as we think of the littleness of our own part, and with heartfelt delight in our fellows, we claim them as such. Their sufferings are ours, their testimony ours, because their Savior, Leader, Lord and Hope is ours . . .

PART I

BRITISH
ORIGINS

1825-1882

English Brethren selling Bibles from a traveling book stall, circa 1885.

1

The Formative Period
1825-1848

The Story Opens

If you go to Dublin today you will find not far from the city center a fenced-in park called Fitzwilliam Square. It is surrounded by fashionable Georgian town houses, many with colorful front doors replete with shiny brass fittings. At one end of Fitzwilliam Square is West Pembroke Street, which ends where it runs at right angles into Baggot Street. A ten-minute walk from Fitzwilliam Square, right on Pembroke Street, left on Baggot Street and right again on Kildare Street will bring you to Trinity College, [See Figure 1] Ireland's equivalent of Oxford. It was in these environs in the 1820s, through the spiritual convictions of a handful of gifted and well-educated young men (and a few women as well) that the Brethren movement was born.

The 1820s in Great Britain was a decade of significance from a religious point of view. The French Revolution with its Reign of Terror, followed by the Napoleonic Wars, had awakened a considerable interest in the books of Daniel and Revelation, as well as in the role of the Holy Spirit in Christian experience. From 1826 to 1830 the eminent banker and politician Henry Drummond invited to Albury Park, his estate in Surrey, numerous prominent evangelicals for a series of Bible prophecy conferences. A popular Scottish clergyman, Edward Irving, took a leading part. Irving's charisma both in End Time speculations and in the exercise of the "sign gifts" attracted a large number of followers, later known as "Irvingites." But his excesses ultimately led to his being defrocked by the Church of Scotland. The interest aroused in the second coming of Christ, however, was real and widespread in Britain.

In 1828 the Corporation and Test Acts (repressive measures against Nonconformists—Baptists, Wesleyans, etc.) were repealed, followed in 1829 by the passing of the Catholic Emancipation Act. Thus both Nonconformists and Catholics were eligible to sit in Parliament. This triggered a strong reaction from several conservative leaders of the Anglican Church at Oxford, notably John Henry Newman, vicar of St. Mary's The University Church; John Keble, editor of The Christian Year; and Edward B. Pusey, regius professor of Hebrew at Oriel College. This group believed that the Church of England was the true descendent of the ancient Catholic Church, and that Anglican bishops were in the line of authority given by Christ to the apostles. They propagated their views through short papers or tracts, and thus were called "Tractarians." Their campaign, which revived high church formalism in the Church of England, was called the "Oxford Movement." In a sense it was the opposite extreme from the Brethren.

* In Ireland the majority of the land was owned by Protestants, who also made up the majority of the middle and upper classes. The masses of people, on the other hand, were Catholic. There were fears of a Catholic uprising, and very little was done by the established church to preach the gospel to the working classes or to encourage Bible reading. Even the Catholic Emancipation Act did not bring complete suffrage, as anyone elected to Parliament had to renounce loyalty to the pope and declare allegiance to the English sovereign. Priests were not eligible for Parliament at all. These religious conditions prevailed at about the time the Brethren movement began, and to some extent influenced it.

As might be expected, evangelical Protestants who were doing graduate work at Trinity College or who were training for a profession in Dublin tended to know one another. So it was in the years 1825-29, when three small groups of young people began to meet for prayer and study of the Bible, eventually they discovered one another. Probably the first of these was formed around an Irish dental student, Edward Cronin, [Fig. 2] who left one of the local churches in protest against its membership policy. He was twenty-five years old at the time. A second group developed from a circle of friends of a Trinity College law student, John Gifford Bellett. [Fig. 3] Two who were friends of Bellett turned out to be the early movement's most original thinkers. One was John Nelson Darby, [Fig. 5] a Church of Ireland curate in the rural district of County Wicklow; the other was Anthony Norris Groves, [Fig. 6] a young English dentist heading for the mission field. A third group included a wealthy young man named John Vesey Parnell, later Lord Congleton, [Fig. 4] and William Stokes, only eighteen years old in 1826. Bellett was born in 1795, Darby in 1800, Groves in 1795 and Lord Congleton in 1805.

The various accounts describing these three groups are not unanimous in all details, but those differences are unimportant. What is important is the formative thinking that was expressed by Groves and Darby. A letter written by Bellett to a friend in 1844 tells of an incident that illustrates this:

> Walking one day with him [Groves], as we were passing down Lower Pembroke Street, he said to me, "This I doubt not is the mind concerning us; we should come together in all simplicity as Disciples, not waiting on any Minister, but trusting that the Lord would edify us together by ministering as he pleased and saw good from the midst of ourselves." At the moment he spoke these words, I was assured my soul had got the right idea.

The editor of Groves's Memoir (1857) tells us that J.G. Bellett and others of the early Brethren "have spoken of Mr. Groves as the father of these principles to their minds." He cites an occasion at which Groves was asked if there were not some principles in the Word of God that would unite all believers in worship. Groves replied:

> Yes, there are: we are evidently called to know nothing among our fellow-Christians but this one fact—Do they belong to Christ? Has Christ received them? Then may we receive them, to the glory of God.

At about the same time that Groves was drawing his radical ideas about Christian unity from Scripture, the young curate J.N. Darby was laid up in Dublin because of an injury,[1] and steeping himself in Bible

---

1 Darby recuperated at the home of his cousin Serjeant Pennefather, a leading Dublin lawyer later to become Lord Chief Justice of Ireland. During this period of formative thinking Darby became acquainted with another remarkable young man who was also a houseguest, Francis Newman, brother of Cardinal Newman of the Oxford Movement. Francis was fascinated with Darby's intense devotion to Christ and won over by his magnetic personality. He became a disciple of the Lord and eventually followed Groves to Baghdad and at one point barely

study. Like his friend Bellett, Darby had studied for the bar, but abandoned that career to become a deacon and later a priest in the Church of Ireland. The young man poured himself into ministry to the Catholic peasants of County Wicklow, and was seeing many turn to Christ when disaster struck. The Archbishop of Dublin issued a declaration requiring all converts from Catholicism to take the British oaths of Allegiance and Supremacy. Reacting with remarkable boldness for a churchman of only two years' experience, Darby wrote and circulated among the clergy a petition protesting this action. His accident (he was thrown against a post by his horse) occurred a short time later.

The result of this time to think and study, he says, was that the Word of God gained "complete ascendancy over me." Out of this experience came his first tract written the following year, 1828, "On the Nature and Unity of the Church of Christ". Although the subject is the one that Groves also addressed, the emphasis is fundamentally different. Darby argues that true Christian unity is achieved only by believers being separated from the world and gathered around Christ:

> The children of God can but follow one thing—the glory of the Lord's name, and that according to the way marked in the Word . . . as he, "that he might sanctify the people with his own blood, suffered without the gate" . . . [we must] go forth to him "without the camp, bearing his reproach."

In the face of the superficial unity of Christendom, a Christian's duty is:

> . . . to meet together and break bread . . . not leaning upon ministry, or assuming anything, or pretending to set up churches, but simply (upon the ground that "where two or three are gathered together, there is Christ in the midst of them") as individuals . . .

It appears that in the winter of 1827-28 Bellett and some friends including J.N. Darby began to break bread informally. This was while Darby was still recuperating and developing his insights that were so significantly to influence the new movement, and before he had written the tract referred to above. Groves also made further application of his new understanding of Scripture at this time by quitting the Church Mission-

---

escaped martyrdom. However, returning to England in 1833 to collect funds for the mission, he found out that rumors of his "unsoundness" had preceded him. When finally forced out of the movement after an attack by Darby he suffered great mental anguish, eventually lost his faith altogether and became a leading anti-Christian writer.

ary Society. He had been informed that, as a layman, he could not administer communion, and he therefore decided to go abroad, depending upon the Lord alone for support. Thus by the end of 1829 Groves and his party had departed, while Darby had returned to his country parish. But shortly thereafter he resigned and returned to Dublin. Invited by Francis Hutchinson, a mutual friend, to meet at his house at No. 9 Fitzwilliam Square, on a more regular basis, Bellett, Darby, Cronin, Hutchinson and a man named Brooke made up the founders of the first "Brethren" meeting.

The First Companies

One of the important factors to keep in mind about the birth of the Brethren movement is that, unlike the Waldensian, Mennonite, Lutheran, Wesleyan and other Protestant beginnings, it happened collectively. Very near the beginning, A.N. Groves and J.N. Darby both formulated in writing some of the original principles drawn from Scripture, but they were not the founders. Those same principles were perceived by a number of others.[1] Keep in mind also that originally this was an independent movement; that is, at least four groups of godly individuals (in Dublin, Plymouth, Bristol, and Barnstaple) recognized truths in the New Testament which they felt should be restored or recovered for the church in their own day, and then formed congregations independently from one another. Later, however, when John Darby's authority was accepted by a large number of the new assemblies, that part of the movement became interdependent. That is, Darby's views on the church emphasized that those who gather in the name of Christ alone (i.e., the Brethren) constitute the visible body of Christ here on earth. Whatever affects one part of the body affects the whole body, and thus each congregation is obligated to become involved in any disputes arising in any one of them. (See chapter 6 for a more complete explanation of Darby's doctrine of the church).

The assembly in Plymouth got its start through some visits made by Darby to Oxford in 1830 and 1831, where he met and impressed by his

---

[1] A book by T.W. Carron, *Christian Testimony Through the Ages* (Pickering and Inglis), traces a number of instances of groups similar to the early Brethren that appeared prior to 1825.

insights into Biblical prophecy two graduate students, Benjamin W. Newton, aged twenty-three, and George V. Wigram, aged twenty-five. Newton lived in Plymouth, where Wigram, who was quite wealthy, kept a house. Invited by Newton in 1831 to spend some time in this historic seaport, Darby met another gifted young man, Capt. Percy Hall, aged twenty-seven, commander of the coast guards. Hall was an effective preacher whose emphasis on prophetic themes drew sizable crowds, and about this time he resigned his commission to give full time to ministry. Toward the end of 1831 Wigram rented an empty chapel on Raleigh Street, and the four friends began to meet for the Lord's Supper on Sunday nights, with Hall preaching on Monday nights.

Although everyone knows of the famous orphanages of George Müller [Fig. 7] at Bristol, many do not know that it was actually the invitation to become co-pastor of an independent chapel that brought Müller to this thriving commercial city. Müller, converted while a student at Halle University in his native Germany, came to London intending to become a missionary to the Jews, but ended up as pastor of a small independent chapel at the south coast resort of Teignmouth. He went here to be near his new friend Henry Craik, [Fig. 8] a young Scot converted while a student at St. Andrews. Both were born in 1805, and both were keen Bible scholars. Craik had been tutor to the sons of Anthony Groves. When Craik was invited to minister at Gideon Chapel in Bristol he accepted only on condition that Müller join him as co-pastor. By this time both had reached many of the same conclusions about the New Testament teachings as those in Dublin and Plymouth, and when they took over another chapel, Bethesda, they incorporated these principles into the life of the church.

Interestingly, at the same time that events were developing in Dublin that led to the meeting on Fitzwilliam Square. A godly, self-educated tradesman was laying the foundation for the new movement in North Devon. Robert Gribble was in the drapery business, and a volunteer Sunday school teacher. He experienced spiritual conversion some time in the 1820s and set out to establish Sunday schools in other villages. His work led to the founding of a chapel, and when his business failed in 1829 he began spending full time in ministry. In 1832 a twenty-nine year-old former lawyer, Robert Chapman, came to Barnstaple to preach, and as Chapman began to be aware of the same New Testament truths as Darby, Groves, Bellett and the others, he in turn influenced Gribble.

A lasting friendship had also begun between Chapman and Müller. Chapman lived to be nearly a hundred and, as Roy Coad says, his "long life and the simple holiness of his character made him the outstanding patriarch and counsellor of the nineteenth century . . . Brethren." [Figs. 21, 22] Although Chapman did not actually put Brethren principles fully into practice at the church in Barnstaple until somewhat later, he was an extremely important influence on the early movement.

Thus were established the first companies of Brethren. It really had nothing to do with organization or any kind of long- range strategy. Nothing bound these congregations together except a recognition that they all agreed regarding the teachings of the New Testament. They soon found that by following these teachings they were viewed as extremists and even fanatics or heretics in the wider Christian community. It was a position that required discipline and self-denial. But many believers were ready for such a step in that day,[1] and their ranks grew rapidly.

At Plymouth, the impact on the community was such that their early meeting places could not hold the people, and a new chapel was built on Ebrington Street that could seat 700 or more. In Bristol the same thing was happening under the ministry of Craik and Müller (Craik being the more effective preacher):

> From the tiny original membership of seven in 1832, the church had grown to about 500. In the years immediately ahead, growth was to prove steady and rapid; most years about seventy-five were added to the fellowship and the monthly church meetings were kept busy enrolling new members.

New assemblies were also springing up in other places. George Wigram began to minister in London and a meeting was started on Rawstorne Street, Camden Town. Captain Hall went off to work with a group in Hereford where there was already considerable interest, and a very

---

1 Of course, a number of factors contributed to the growth of the Brethren in those days. Their energetic preaching of the gospel was another, especially in Plymouth and Hereford where many went out to the country places to evangelize. Prophetic teaching drew many people from the churches, especially in Plymouth. In Bristol a tremendous impact was made by various forms of community service—care for the victims of cholera, of the poor and needy and, of course, of orphans. Another factor was the quality of their leadership, most of whom were aristocrats, highly educated with the ability to read the original languages of the Bible, and some with titles and very extensive means (which they dedicated to the Lord).

large work grew up there. Others were started at about the same time at Torquay, Exeter, Bath, and Salcombe in the south, in several places in Ireland and the north of England, and at Welback Street in London.

We end this section with another quote from the long letter by Edward Bellett describing the early movement and written in July 1848, (but not found until 1936). He says in one place:

> I like to trace these circumstances for they help to assure us that the Lord's hand was independently at work designing to raise another testimony in the midst of his saints. I feel that I have great evidence at command for the existence of this independent energy of His Spirit. Among other witnesses of this nearer home, I mention that dear Groves revisited Ireland after an absence of two or three years and I remember well his telling me of a very important movement in the southern part of India which indicated a mind quite in harmony with that which had been leading us in our position in England and Ireland. The English brethren year after year visited Ireland, not only Dublin, but the country places. J. Harris, once a clergyman near Plymouth, was one of the number. J. Wigram for a long continued time was in Cork, and all this time J. Darby was in the two countries by turns, occasionally with us in Dublin but more generally either in Plymouth or in Cork, and the gatherings multiplying so in England a very great number became known by the name of the Plymouth Brethren, and in this country were called Darbyites.
>
> I do not know that I need follow the history beyond this, dear J, as your inquiry was rather about our beginnings. I would not doubt but a fresh purpose of God, and a fresh work of the Spirit, were put forth in the call of the Brethren . . .

Ebrington Street and Bethesda: Eyewitness Accounts

W.H. Cole

What were the original "Plymouth Brethren" meetings like? A brother named W.H. Cole, well known and esteemed among the Independent Brethren in later life, who joined the meeting in Ebrington Street in 1843, wrote an extensive eyewitness account, from which we quote:

> Through the great mercy of our God, I was converted to him in early youth in Plymouth, my native town, soon after which I was led to see the blessed truth of the personal coming again of our Lord from heaven to take his

church to himself and personally reign over the millennial earth. And [I] was brought into fellowship with those, who I learnt, assembled upon principles taught in the Word of God, where no sectarian wall of division was acknowledged, and where there was the liberty of the Spirit of God, to minister the truths of Scripture by those who were gifted by him for that purpose.

At that time all was happiness and peace, unruffled by personal questions, undisturbed by jealousies or ambitions. The distinctions between poor and rich were lessened by holy, loving fellowship and unity which characterized their intercourse. Their social meetings, where rich and poor alike were welcomed guests, were for the study of the Word, and religious converse. The homes of the wealthy were plainly furnished, presenting an air of unworldliness and making them more homely for their poorer brethren and sisters. Their dress was plain, their habits simple, and their walk distinguished by separation from the world.

The meetings of the assembly were calm, peaceful and hallowed; their singing soft, slow and thoughtful; their worship evinced the nearness of their communion with the Lord; their prayers were earnest for an increased knowledge of God, and for the spread of his truth. Their teaching showed their deep searching of the scriptures under the guidance of the Holy Spirit, whilst the exercise of the varied ministry, under the power of the Spirit, testified to the blessedness of the teaching of God's word on each important subject

. . .

The leading ministering brethren were Mr. W.B. Newton, Mr. J.L. Harris, Mr. H.W. Soltau, Mr. J.E. Batten, and Mr. W. Dyer. Dr. Tregelles, Mr. Clulow, Mr. McLean, and others ministered occasionally, while several others, qualified for leading in worship and prayer, took part in the gatherings. Mr. Newton, who in King Street could only at first speak with diffidence to a small number for a few minutes, could afterwards hold, for two hours at a time, the interested attention of a mixed audience of from 1200 to 1400 persons from the sects around.[1]

---

1 Taking all four original companies into account, at Dublin, Plymouth, Bristol, and Barnstaple, as well as the testimony of Edward Cronin and J.G. Bellett, there is good reason to believe that most of the early Brethren had found these principles in Scripture before coming under the powerful influence of John Darby's unique views. In his well-known letter to Professor Tholuck written in the 1850s, Darby recalls that he, personally, came to an understanding of what later became known as "Plymouth Brethrenism" or "Darbyism" before the meeting on Fitzwilliam Square. About this meeting he says:
Four persons, who were pretty much in the same state of soul as myself, came together to my lodging; we spoke together about these things; and I proposed to them to break bread the

He was the principal teacher of the church. His leading subjects were prophetic, yet by no means confined to these, for he had a large grasp of scripture, and seemed deeply acquainted with every part of that mighty volume of truth. He always dealt with high subjects, momentous to the mind, and sacred to the heart. His delivery was calm, orderly, lucid, captivating, such as became a great scholar, one deeply taught in the Word, and anxious to lead others on in the knowledge of that which he had himself learned from its close study. . .

[Mr. Cole continues for another long paragraph describing the ministry of each of the leading brethren.] The exhortation of these several teachers was to a holy life in fellowship with the Lord Jesus Christ, to the cultivation of love, to a walk worthy of our heavenly calling, and to animate the blessed hope of our Lord's return; that, in short, as we were called heavenly, and made heavenly, we should seek grace to walk in responsibility as heavenly.

I breathed what appeared to me the pure element of love; I was in the enjoyment of the liberty of home; I was enlightened by its teachings, cheered by its joys, comforted by its hallowed fellowship, strengthened by godly companionship, and encouraged by those who were over me in the Lord. Those were delightful times, so sweet for their simplicity. The fruits of the Spirit (Galatians 5:22) were in evidence. Whatever undercurrents were at work they threw nothing to the surface. But it was too fair a scene for Satan to contemplate, and he must by some means mar its beauties and desolate its loveliness.

(Condensed from Cole's complete paper found in the Appendix of the biography, Anthony Norris Groves, by G.H. Lang.)

Mary Ann Evans

Mary Ann Evans was a Christian lady who was a member of a Baptist church in London before being introduced to the Brethren in 1840 during a visit to Bristol. She associated with them for the rest of her life, serving for a time on the staff at Müller's orphanage:

It was in 1840 that I first became acquainted with the "Brethren." I had only once even heard of them before, and then it was in connection with the Second Coming of the Lord, and I had from that time a desire to know more about them. In that year I went to Bristol, and soon after my arrival, my friend Mrs. R.S., asked me where I would go on Sunday. I replied, "I am a Baptist, but where do you go?" She answered, "I belong to the people called Plymouth Brethren." "Then," said I, "they are the very people I

---

following Sunday, which we did. Others then joined us. I left Dublin soon after . . .

want to know something about, for I hear they hold the doctrine of the Second Coming and so do I." "Indeed they do," she replied. I made up my mind to go with her on the following Sunday.

[She describes her fashionable chapel in London with the minister wearing knee breeches, fancy shirt front and a silk scarf on his shoulders.] From such a scene as this I entered Bethesda. A large bare chapel, with scarcely a cushion in it, and half empty. A few very grave-looking men and women came in and knelt down for a few moments, then rising, sat with closed eyes till the service began.

The Brethren were dressed much like other men, but the Sisters' dress was grotesquely ugly. The dress of 'the Friends' is beautiful, if plain, but that of these Sisters was simply hideous. A coarse brown woolen dress and a drab shawl, a straight speckled straw bonnet with drab or brown ribbon straight across, its only trimming, a long thick, brown veil—servants and mistresses alike...

The service began by someone reading the notices: then a pause—soon a Brother rose and prayed. Now we were at once taken up into the presence of God. It was real, earnest Spirit-led prayer, and I forgot the dress and all else.

Another pause and then a hymn sung like a funeral dirge, with closed eyes and all sitting, very badly sung too. But this was all changed shortly after, when Mr. James Wright came into fellowship, and took the management of the singing. Another prayer, and then the bread and wine were passed round. Pause again, and then prayer, now Mr. Craik stood up to speak. Every one had their Bible, and used it. His exposition of Scripture was quite a new feature of worship to me, and it was indeed "marrow and fatness." The meaning of the passage read was brought out as I never heard it before, and I found myself feeding truly in green pastures. [Mr. Craik's] knowledge of the original language was beyond that of most men of learning, and his insight into the meaning of Scripture also . . .

To me it was like a new conversion. I had often heard people pray that "they might be able to give an answer for the hope that was in them," and I pondered what answer I should give. Now I heard a clear [message] that I could understand. The Bible became a new book to me. The brotherly love shown was such as I had never seen before. The godly and simple lives of even wealthy people, who had moved in the highest society, was such as to carry one back to the days of the Apostles, and I felt this was indeed Christianity of a high type.

(Condensed from The Brethren: As I Knew Them From 1840 to 1902 by A.E., "A booklet for private circulation only.")

Whatever became of the first Brethren meeting places?

No. 9 Fitzwilliam Square

The first meeting place, according to Mr. Darby's account, was No. 9 Fitzwilliam Square, Dublin. It is still a fashionable town house and may be the original building; modernized early nineteenth century town houses are not at all uncommon. We simply don't know for sure.

The Upstairs Auction Room On Aungier St. [Fig. 9]

The upstairs auction room on Aungier Street, Dublin, rented by John Parnell, where the enlarged assembly moved from Fitzwilliam Square, apparently survived to the early twentieth century. The assembly itself, however, had died out by 1859 when the revival known as the "Second Great Evangelical Awakening" began (chapter 5). Following the revival, one of the largest chapels in the movement, Merrion Hall, was built in downtown Dublin in 1863. By the late 1980s the congregation had dwindled to a handful, and the building was sold in 1988. It was badly damaged by fire in 1991, but is currently being restored for secular purposes.

Raleigh Chapel [Fig. 10]

In Plymouth the first meeting place is in some doubt. There is much evidence that it was a derelict chapel, Providence, on Raleigh Street in the center of town. This was purchased by George Wigram in 1831 and remained his property after the large hall was built on Ebrington Street. But there is also evidence that the meeting began "in a small house in King Street." When J.N. Darby clashed with B.W. Newton in 1845, he and Wigram started a rival meeting in the Raleigh Street chapel. It was renamed the Raleigh Street Hall following the revival. Although the building survived a bombing raid in 1941, everything else around it was destroyed and the old chapel was torn down to facilitate reconstructing the entire block.

The Ebrington Street Chapel

The following description of the new chapel built by the Brethren on Ebrington Street in 1840 appeared in a 1949 Plymouth newspaper account:

> . . . it was a plain building with no gallery, erected to the society's own plans. The Brethren set apart every Lord's Day for the "breaking of bread" in remembrance of Christ. So a large table occupied the most prominent position in the center, and around it seats were placed on a gentle incline so that everyone could look upon it . . . The acoustics of the hall were said to be so poor that apart from those with unusually strong voices all who spoke had to stand near the table to be heard.

This seating arrangement is said to have been repeated in other buildings erected by the Brethren. The Ebrington Street Hall was sold to the Methodists in 1857 and another building erected in 1897.

The Teignmouth and Shaldon Chapels [Figs. 11, 12]

Both George Müller and Henry Craik pastored small Baptist congregations on the South Coast in the late 1820s and early 1830s, Müller in Teignmouth and Craik in Shaldon across the river. The Teignmouth chapel is in use today as the meeting place of a Brethren assembly. The Shaldon building is now a Catholic chapel.

Bethesda Chapel

Bethesda Chapel in Bristol seems to have been built perhaps ten years before Craik and Müller came to preach in 1832. It was located on George Street just off Park Street, a fashionable part of town. It survived until World War II, when it became a victim of German bombs in 1941.

Early Brethren Hymnody

One of the many characteristics that distinguished the early Brethren from the Protestant denominations was their hymnody, in particular their emphasis on the communion table rather than on the pulpit, on the collective body of the Lord's people rather than on the individual. This collective worship centering on Christ himself found its best and most meaningful expression in hymn singing. In all the early Brethren hymnbooks one finds an understanding of the depths of suffering that our Lord endured for our sake; thanksgiving to God the Father for his grace, mercy, and love; thoughts of identity with the lonely life of Christ in a world that was not his home; and a looking forward to that glorious morning when Jesus will return for his own, and being present where he sits enthroned at the right hand of the Father.

Very early in the Brethren movement hymns of this nature were selected from the hymnbooks of their day. A number written by Isaac Watts, Charles Wesley and other eighteenth century composers were chosen. A few came from even earlier sources in the devotional poetry of Medieval churchmen such as Bernard of Clairvaux and the German pietist Gerhard Tersteegen. Others were borrowed from contemporaries in other closely related movements, such as those of the Irish composer Thomas Kelly. But almost from the beginning, talented men and women from within their own ranks began to compose poems that specifically expressed these emphases. (The tunes were generally borrowed from extant hymns or secular music. Most Brethren hymns can be sung to more than one tune.)

Below are some samples (first stanzas only) of this devotional poetry written or translated by early members of the Brethren movement. These examples are all to be found in the Independent Brethren hymnbook *Hymns of Worship* still in print and available today:

The person and work of Christ:(p.137)

> *What grace, O Lord, and beauty shone*
> *Around Thy steps below!*
> *What patient love was seen in all*
> *Thy life and death of woe.*
>
> > Edward Denny

Praise to God the Father:(p.66)

> *Gracious God, we worship Thee,*
> *Rev'rently we bow the knee;*
> *Jesus Christ our only plea:*
> *Father, we adore Thee.*
>
> > Trevor Francis

The Cross:(p.180)

> *The Lamb of God to slaughter led,*
> *The King of Glory see!*
> *The crown of thorns upon His head,*
> *They nail Him to the tree!*
>
> > Robert Chapman

Worship:(p.135)

> *We'll praise Thee, glorious Lord,*
> *Who died to set us free,*
> *No earthly songs can joy afford*
> *Like heav'nly melody.*

J.N. Darby

Our appreciation of Christ:(p.263)

> *Of Thee, Lord, we would never tire;*
> *This new and living food*
> *Can satisfy our hearts' desire,*
> *For life is in Thy blood.*

Mary Bowley Peters

Our life in this world:(p.299)

> *This world is a wilderness wide—*
> *I have nothing to seek or to choose;*
> *I've no thought in the waste to abide:*
> *I've naught to regret or to lose.*

J.N. Darby

Looking forward to Glory:(p.207)

> *'Midst the darkness, storm and sorrow,*
> *One bright gleam I see;*
> *Well I know the blessed morrow*
> *Christ will come for me.*
> *'Midst the light, and peace and glory*
> *Of the Father's home,*
> *Christ for me is waiting, watching,*
> *Waiting 'till I come.*

Gerhard Tersteegen (translated by Mrs. Frances Bevan)

An illustration of the remarkable versatility of gift among the early Brethren is seen in the first five hymnbooks of the movement, published prior to the great division of 1848:

J.L. Harris, *A Collection of Hymns,* 1834

R.C. Chapman, *Hymns for Use of the Church of Christ,* 1837

G.V. Wigram, *Hymns for the Poor of the Flock,* 1838

Edward Denny, *A Selection of Hymns,* 1839

J.G. Deck, Psalms, *Hymns, and Spiritual Songs,* 1842

Of the above, Deck, Denny, and Chapman were not only compilers, but hymn writers par excellence. Deck, a retired army officer (who moved to New Zealand after 1848 and pioneered numerous Exclusive assemblies), was perhaps the most prolific. Next in output was an Irishman of the upper class, Sir Edward Denny. Robert Chapman, the beloved "apostle of Barnstaple," we have already met in chapter 2. All Brethren hymnbooks contain numerous contributions by each. A fourth prolific composer was J. Denham Smith, an Irish clergyman who later served the Lord among Open Brethren in London as a colleague of C. Russell Hurditch (also a composer of some thirty hymns).

Of the more than thirty Brethren hymnbooks, none has enjoyed more popularity than the so-called *Little Flock*. [Fig. 13] This diminutive, black-bound volume was used extensively by both Exclusives and Open Brethren in North America prior to the 1950s. It was actually the successor to Wigram's *Hymns for the Poor of the Flock*, revised anonymously by Wigram in 1856 and republished as *A Few Hymns* and *Some Spiritual Songs, Selected 1856 for the Little Flock*. In 1881 Darby revised it again, with various additions and deletions, and added a preface. This is the edition most commonly to be found today, though there were several later editions revised by Exclusive parties. The *Little Flock* was generally used at the Lord's Supper, while either song sheets or gospel song books were handed out at the meeting. It contains no music, only the words, and the hymns were (and still are in many places) sung without instrumental accompaniment, the tune set by a precentor or "starter."

All Brethren hymnbooks contain a considerable number of hymns by women. Names that appear quite often in many of the collections are:

Mrs. Frances Bevan (1827-1909)
Lucy Bennett ((1850-1927)
Anne Ross Cousin (1824-1906)
Elizabeth Rundle Charles (1828-96)
Fanny Crosby (1829-1915)
Ada Habershon (1861-1918)
Mary Bowly Peters (1813-56)
Mrs. Beothia Thompson (dates unknown)
Ruth Tracy (1870-1970)

Mrs. Bevan also translated some beautiful hymns from the German, including those of Gerhard Tersteegen. Lucy Bennett's composition,

I am the Lord's!
O joy beyond expression

is familiar to many as a wedding hymn.

Despite the high quality of this unique heritage of hymns and devotional poetry, very few Brethren hymns have found their way into more popular hymnbooks. One major reason is that they tend to be very doctrinal and thus difficult for "ordinary" believers to understand. Another is that they are cast in a language that, like Elizabethan English, is quite foreign to most people today. John Williams suggests that:

> . . . it would probably help enormously if someone would recast a lot of our old hymns in contemporary idioms and set them to reasonable modern music. If we are concerned about what the early Brethren would think about our altering their words, we can set our minds at rest. They, like those before them, evidently had little compunction about "word fixing."

Finally, we should point out that there are a few outstanding exceptions to the obscurity of Brethren hymns. They include:
"What A Friend We Have in Jesus" by Joseph Scriven,
"O the Deep, Deep Love of Jesus" by Trevor Francis,
"Praise the Savior, Ye Who Know Him" by Thomas Kelly,
and one of the best known of all,
"How Great Thou Art" translated by Stuart K. Hine.

(Much of the material in this section is abstracted from the following papers presented at the Course in Brethren History, Regent College, Vancouver, 1990:
Andrews, John: *Brethren Hymnology* and Williams, John: *Early Brethren Hymnology*)

2

First Principles and a Definition

Ten Cardinal Principles of the Brethren

It is important for us to know, as we try to look back through the mists of time to the beginning of the movement, what the original principles were that drew these young, gifted, well educated and in some cases very wealthy young men and women to give up all their advantages in this world in order to follow Jesus. Although there may be some slight difference in opinion, historians would generally agree on the following:

Centrality of the Lord's Supper

From the evidence presented in chapter 1, we have seen that all the originators of the movement at Dublin, Plymouth, and Bristol agreed that the Lord's Supper was at the heart of their fellowship. It was Christ around whom they gathered (Matt. 18:20), and it was the remembrance of his death that occupied them when they met in worship. And so it is still wherever assemblies of the Brethren are found throughout the world. Though some have accused them of morbidly dwelling too much on the death of Christ rather than on his risen life, the Brethren see in this weekly observance nothing legalistic or even ritualistic. For them, remembering the Lord in his death is a basic principle in the New Testament; namely, that a seed in order to live and bear fruit must die. It is precisely out of the death of Christ that flows all we know and experience of eternal life.

Unity

This is also one of the earliest principles to be recognized among the first gatherings. In John 17:20-21 Jesus expressed the deepest desire of his heart when he prayed

> that they all may be one; even as thou, Father, art in me, and I in thee, that they also may be in us, so that the world may believe that thou hast sent me.

The early Brethren perceived that in the Christian world of their day each sect had set up barriers to divide themselves from others, while an even more formidable wall separated the denominations from the established church. They would have those walls down by the simple act of sitting down together on the basis of all belonging to Christ, and expressing their true unity by obeying the Lord's command, "This do in remembrance of Me."

Despite historic problems with their own unity, the Brethren still place this desire of the Lord Jesus at the top of their priorities.

Authority of Scripture

One of the main factors that caused the first Brethren in all four of the communities described in chapter 1 to take radical action was their habit of studying the Bible and of obeying it as God's Word. Thus, as Darby said, the Scriptures "gained ascendancy" over them, and like the Bereans "they received the word with all eagerness, examining the scriptures daily to see if these things were so." The result of this was a movement that has been consistently Bible-centered down though the years. This does not necessarily mean that the Brethren know more about the Bible than other Christians, but rather that they tend more to look to the Scriptures as the basis of authority. Thus the statement that in Britain the Brethren alone were unaffected by nineteenth century biblical criticism is probably accurate.

Church Truth

The Brethren movement came into existence at a time when the Protestant societies born a century or two earlier had become highly organized, formal in their services, and jealous of their membership. The early Brethren in their study of Scripture, especially 1 Timothy, and chapters 10-12, and 14 of 1 Corinthians, rediscovered that the local church is not an organization but a living organism, a body of which Christ is the head. For this reason they refused any name except that of "Christian," and their leaders took the place, not of titled lords but of trusted servants who must be "above reproach." These and other truths about the church have given the assemblies a close-knit "family" character with exceptional "rank and file" involvement, a character whose value is now recognized widely among evangelical churches. In theory at least, the assemblies base their way of meeting, recognizing leadership, etc., solely on the Scriptures.

Devotion to Christ
One of the books that played a vital part in the formative thinking of the early Brethren was Christian Devotedness written by A.N. Groves in 1825. In this little work Groves argues that the Lord's command to the rich young ruler ("Sell all that you have and give to the poor, and you shall have treasure in heaven; and come, follow me,") was put into practice by the apostles and is meant for all Christians. Groves and his wife did this literally, and so did most of those who identified with the Brethren in the first few decades. Auction records still exist of hundreds of items disposed of by some of the Plymouth congregation. An aspect of this personal devotion to the Lord was separation from the world. Brethren gave up public office, refused to vote, to own property, to preoccupy themselves with music, art or entertainment, in order to "gain the prize of the high calling of God in Christ Jesus." Though perhaps not so severe as their forebears, Brethren today still tend to view many of the world's values as worthless vanity.

The Priesthood of All Believers
In a sense the Brethren perhaps more than any other evangelical body brought the Reformation to its logical conclusion by their insistence that all believers are priests. As we have seen in chapter 2, Edward Cronin and his friends discovered very early that there was no basis in Scripture for limiting the administration of the Lord's Supper to ordained ministers, as also did Anthony Norris Groves at the time of his resignation from the Church Missionary Society. The teaching of Hebrews 10:19-25, that "we have confidence to enter the Most Holy Place by the blood of Jesus," has been practiced every Lord's Day by the assemblies

since their inception, and has also inspired a high level of personal devotion and worship in the movement.

Freedom to Exercise Gifts

When A.N. Groves first met Bellett and Darby in Dublin, he was there for the purpose of taking periodic exams leading to a divinity degree and ordination. He felt this to be a necessary preparation for missionary work. Both Bible study and advice from an experienced missionary, however, convinced him, as he says in his journal, "that ordination of any kind to preach the gospel is no requirement of Scripture." J.N. Darby, too, very early came to the conclusion that God's gifts to the church are given by the Spirit, not by human systems. This principle does not mean that the Brethren have no pastors, teachers, or evangelists, but rather that they recognize the gift by its exercise rather than by a title conferred by some organization. In general, the Brethren reject the concept that there are two classes of Christians, clergy and laity, not finding it taught or practiced in the New Testament.

Dependence upon God for Financial Needs

Most Brethren assemblies even today do not take collections in meetings where there may be non-Christians present. Their basis for this is found in the teachings of Jesus and of Paul, and illustrated in the Acts, that on the one hand the children of God can trust their heavenly Father to supply their needs, and on the other hand that Christians should look after the needs of one another. George Müller is the most famous of the Brethren to prove that through prayer and faith God can provide necessary funds without public fund-raising campaigns. Generally it has been a principle from the beginning of the Brethren that God is glorified, the saints blessed, and non-Christians favorably impressed when we make as little public show as possible about finances.

Expectation of the Soon Return of Christ

One of the greatest contributions of the Brethren to the church in the nineteenth and twentieth centuries has been their revival of the truth that Jesus is going to return. "Behold, I come quickly!" Revelation 22:7. So convinced were the Brethren that they might expect the Lord at any time that the customary Christian qualification about future plans, "Lord willing," was replaced by, "If the Lord be not come." Not all Brethren are agreed on the details of the End Times, but most are "pre-millennialists"—that is, they believe that Christ will come to take to heaven all his own, whether living or dead, before the thousand-year reign spoken of in Revelation 20:1-6. Many Brethren believe that especially since World War II there have been numerous and increasing signs of the Lord's coming, especially the role of Israel in world affairs.

Imperative of the Gospel

Several examples have already been given to illustrate the fact that the Brethren, especially the Independent branch after 1848, have continually been motivated by the imperative of the gospel. Records exist to show that in Plymouth, Bristol, Hereford, Barnstaple, and elsewhere where assemblies sprang up, the neighborhood and the villages round about were evangelized and souls saved. For example, as early as 1834 George Müller records in his journal:

> This evening we had again, from six to half-past ten, a meeting with inquirers. The work of the Lord is going on among us as much as ever ... Even after we were worn out to the utmost, we could not see all, but had to send away several individuals.

The Brethren were much affected by the revivals of the 1860s and 1870s (chapter 5), and, in the wake of this, Brethren evangelists planted little assemblies all over North America. It is no accident that they called their meeting places " halls." In our own day the number of Brethren missionaries is far out of proportion to the size of the movement. In Africa, Latin America, Eastern Europe, and elsewhere the Brethren are rapidly growing by evangelization.

Which Branch Continued the Original Principles?

An important question as the Brethren movement nears the end of the twentieth century (to historians, at least) is, Which branch most truly carried on the original principles established in the first decade or two? Who should the Independent Brethren look to as the model for Brethren leadership today: Mr. Darby with his worldwide federation of Exclusives, or Anthony Groves, whose ideas were put into practice at Bethesda in Bristol, at Barnstaple under Robert Chapman, and in the growing circle of Independent assemblies in nineteenth century England and Ireland? In the appendix to his biography of A. N. Groves, G.H. Lang answers this question:

In ch. XIII of this book, written before Mr. Cole's paper came to me, I had said that Open Brethren are the real continuators of the first principles and practice of the Brethren, and that Exclusivism was a surrender of most of them.

It is important that these two views are confirmed by Mr. Cole, seeing that he had personal knowledge of the meetings before the strife arose, that he went through the conflict at its center, and then watched the outcome for over fifty years.

Mr. William Collingwood of Bristol bore personal testimony to the same effect. He united with the Brethren in 1844, before the first disruption, and after fifty-five years wrote in 1899 as follows regarding those who followed Mr. Darby:

"They have taken a position as far removed from the original ground as they are separated from actual fellowship. As to either, they retain nothing in common with those they have left, except that they still have the same custom of breaking bread on the Lord's Day . . ."

A Definition of the Brethren by F.F. Bruce

The following is a definition of the Brethren written by the renowned biblical scholar and prolific author, the late Professor F.F. Bruce. It was composed for the foreword to *Turning the World Upside Down*, the story of Brethren missionary endeavor, and is used with the permission of the publishers, Echoes of Service, Bath, England. It has been slightly adapted for application to North America:

The people called Brethren are often so described because they prefer to be known by a designation comprehensive enough to embrace all their fellow-Christians along with themselves. Those with whom this book is primarily concerned are sometimes distinguished as Open Brethren because their church order differs from that of their friends who are known as Exclusive Brethren.

The Open Brethren have no central organization. They belong to a large number of local churches or assemblies, spread throughout the world. Each of these local churches is independent in its administration; there is no federation or union linking them together. Yet there is a recognizable family likeness between them, and their sense of a spiritual bond is strong.

The Brethren movement originated around the year 1825, although the Brethren commonly insist that their roots are really in the apostolic age, for they aim as far as possible at maintaining the simple and flexible church order of New Testament times. The founders of the movement were a group of young men, many of them associated with Trinity College, Dublin, who tried to find a way in which they could come together for worship and communion simply as fellow-Christians, in disregard of denominational barriers. They had no idea that they were starting a movement; still less had they any thought of founding a new denomination, for that would have defeated the very purpose for which they came together.

From Dublin the movement spread to England. In England the first meeting of Brethren was established at Plymouth in 1831; hence arose the popular term "Plymouth Brethren." Another important meeting of Brethren was Bethesda Chapel, Bristol, which had as one of its pastors the German-born George Müller, best known for the orphanages which he founded in Bristol in 1836 and which survive to the present day. Müller provided a personal link between the movement in the British Isles and similar movements in Europe.

Müller married the sister of Anthony Norris Groves. Groves was a man of large-hearted sympathies, who never forgot that the things which unite Christians are immeasurably more important than the things which divide them. "I would infinitely rather bear with all their evil," he said of some people with whom he seriously disagreed, "than separate from their good." Whether those features which he thought to be "evil" were so, or not, his words express the attitude which Open Brethren acknowledge as their ideal.

The Open Brethren have no doctrinal peculiarities. They hold the historic Christian faith, because they find it plainly taught in the Bible, which is to them, as to other heirs of the Reformation, "the only infallible rule of faith and practice." They are wholeheartedly evangelical in their understanding and presentation of Christianity, proclaiming Jesus Christ, the Son of God, as the all-sufficient Savior of those who put their trust in him and as the only hope for mankind. For this reason they find it especially easy to cooperate in Christian witness with others who share this evangelical emphasis and in many interdenominational causes their influence is greater than their numbers might lead one to expect.

It is practice rather than doctrine that marks them out. Among Open Brethren, baptism is administered only to people who make a personal confession of faith in Christ, and the mode of baptism is immersion. Normally they observe the Lord's Supper every Sunday and hold that the Lord's Table is for all the Lord's people. This is their most distinctive gathering. When they meet for communion, together with any Christians who care to join them for this occasion, their devotions are conducted by no presiding minister and follow no predetermined sequence, but are marked nevertheless by a reverent spontaneity and orderliness. Various brethren contribute to the worship by suggesting suitable hymns to be sung, by leading the congregation in prayer and thanksgiving, or by reading and expounding a passage from the Bible.

The Brethren have no ordained ministry, set apart for functions which others cannot discharge. A considerable number do give their whole time to evangelism and Bible teaching but are not regarded as being in clerical orders. The various local churches are administered by responsible brethren called elders or overseers. These have no jurisdiction outside their local churches, and inside them they try to guide by example rather than rule by decree.

The Brethren have always manifested a supreme lack of interest in their numerical strength. Their numbers are difficult to assess, partly because no precise statistics are available and partly because there is no hard-and-fast line of demarcation between Brethren meetings and other independent evangelical churches. [An estimate of their strength in North America is 80,000, but this is at best approximate.] They are to be found in all grades of society and all walks of life.   F.F. BRUCE

3

The Two Great Originators:
J.N. Darby and A.N. Groves

The Rise of J.N. Darby

After the founding of the three original Brethren assemblies in Dublin, Plymouth, and Bristol, the movement grew steadily in the British Isles, at first primarily in southwest England. By 1835 around eleven meetings had been established. Although accurate statistics are non-existent, the census of 1851 shows 132 Plymouth Brethren congregations in England, forty-eight in Ireland, and seventy-five in Scotland, which gives some idea of the growth pattern. The movement continued to attract men of education, intellect, and good breeding some of whom became notable preachers, teachers, and pastors. In many cases their wives also contributed much talent and energy. Here and there, meeting places were built or taken over, as Raleigh Street Chapel and the new Ebrington Street Chapel in Plymouth, and Bethesda in Bristol. But generally the early Brethren met in rented halls above shops. The furnishings were plain to the point of austerity. Because their focal point was Jesus himself in their midst, they took as their model the upper room where the Lord met with his disciples. It became customary to refer to their meeting places as "the Room."

We should briefly mention in passing some of those who were prominent in those early days. At Plymouth there was Samuel Prideaux Tregelles, later a distinguished Bible scholar; Richard Hill, a former Church of England clergyman, and his brother-in-law Henry Soltau, a lawyer; James Harris, another ex-clergyman, who shared much of the preaching with B.W. Newton; and Henry Borlase, the first editor of the Brethren magazine The Christian Witness. In London the minister of Islington Chapel, W.H. Dorman, joined the Brethren, as well as John Eliot Howard, a member of the manufacturing firm of Howard and Sons. A friend of Groves, Mr. Caldecott, resigned from the Anglican ministry to found a work at Sidmouth; John Parnell returned from India to minister at Müller's old Baptist Church at Teignmouth which had become a Brethren assembly; and the Irish hymn writer, Sir James Denny, associated with them in Somerset. A wealthy businessman, William Yapp, built a chapel onto his house to accommodate the growing congregation at Hereford. In Bristol the work at Bethesda was enriched by the coming of James Ireland Wright, who later was Müller's successor.

Rich though the early Brethren were in talented leaders, speakers, writers, and scholars, one name stands out from all the rest when historians view the movement in perspective, that of John Nelson Darby. Darby [Fig. 14] was the foremost founder of new assemblies, the most respected teacher, and the source of a whole system of Biblical interpretation peculiar to the Brethren. After leaving the ministry of the Church of Ireland he spent his entire life as a kind of apostle, traveling extensively all over the world, shepherding new gatherings through visits and correspondence and writing numerous books and articles including commentaries on the entire Bible. As mentioned earlier, part of the movement under Darby's influence became interdependent and answerable to a central authority. Darby also turned a large portion of the movement from a Restorationist position (striving to restore New Testament church principles) to that of a Patternist, the position that God has revealed in the New Testament a single pattern of truth (previously undiscovered) which every godly believer is called to follow.

From the beginning of 1832, when Darby left the newly founded assembly in Plymouth to continue his itinerant ministry in Ireland, until 1845 when he returned there from the Continent to deal with certain problems, his output and achievements were astounding. The foundation for an entire theology now known as Dispensationalism was laid during this period, along with an almost uncanny mastery of the Bible. The prophetic aspect of his system appears to have been brought into focus by three conferences on prophecy held at Powerscourt Castle south of Dublin in 1831, '32 and '33. Lady Powerscourt was a devout young widow whose interest in unfulfilled prophecy had been stimulated by Edward Irving, the charismatic Scottish preacher mentioned in chapter 1. While Darby attended all three conferences (and Newton attended the first two but boycotted the third), the gathering in 1833 was attended by a number of the other leading Brethren, including George Müller and Henry Craik. Here Darby made clear his position on the apostasy of Christendom. He came out strongly for believers to separate from all religious systems and to gather with those who awaited the "secret rapture" when Christ would come for his own prior to the Great Tribulation.

Another significant development in J.N. Darby's growing influence occurred in 1838 when George Wigram, his most ardent disciple, proposed "one central meeting, the common responsibility of all within reach, and as many meetings subordinate to it as grace might vouchsafe." This proposal was acted upon, presumably with Darby's approval, and resulted in a Saturday evening gathering of leaders from a number of meetings in London and environs. The intent, as Wigram suggested, was to aid smaller assemblies in administration and to ensure harmony among them in matters of policy. But in fact it was the birth of a federation of Brethren assemblies with a controlling body that not only determined if anyone needed discipline in any given meeting, but had the power to bar an individual from communion at any assembly in the network. As later events will show, the basis for discipline became ever more finely defined, and excommunication was levied against even some of the original leaders for petty or imagined infractions. Indirectly, as it acted to reinforce his principles, this central meeting greatly added to Darby's personal power.

A third development in John Darby's rise to preeminence was his missionary endeavors on the Continent between 1839 and 1845. Among his many gifts was a mastery of the three main Continental languages, French, German, and Italian, making it possible for him to move among the churches there almost as a native. In 1837 he made an exploratory visit to Geneva, finding many evangelical Protestants who had broken away from the State Church. He returned toward the end of 1839 and at first ministered in churches in Geneva and Neuchatel, where his help was appreciated. In March 1840 he was invited to Lausanne to assist in resolving a controversy over Wesleyan-type perfectionism. By spring 1841, with the aid of a very effective tract, he was able to restore peace, gaining the confidence of the pastor. During this period he also began to lecture on prophecy, which drew large audiences, and through his new and challenging views on the Bible (together with his magnetic personality) won over a number of key people. From among these he chose disciples whom he taught in a kind of Bible school at his residence.

The success of this campaign is still evident in French Switzerland, where 150 years later there remain a number of Brethren (or "Darbyite") assemblies. Naturally this activity caused great consternation among the evangelical pastors, who in 1842 called a "conference fraternelle" to try and negotiate with him. Nothing was resolved, however. Leaving his newly trained followers to continue teaching his unique doctrines, Darby began a period of intense travel throughout Western Europe. Everywhere he went—Southern France, Germany, The Netherlands—little assemblies were planted,[1] often led by a disciple such as Carl Brockhaus in Germany, whom Darby had taught personally. As in Switzerland, many of these assemblies still exist and Darby's influence remains strong. (A case in point: a new biography of Darby appeared in 1990 written by Max Weremchuk, a German.) In spring 1844 Darby returned once again to Lausanne, staying in the area to teach until the following year, when Jesuit-inspired riots directed against the Brethren made it advisable for him to leave the country.

The Greatness of J.N. Darby

The following paragraphs are quoted from A History of the Plymouth Brethren by William Blair Neatby. William Blair's father was an Exclusive Brethren preacher, and the author himself knew many who had been friends and associates of Darby:

> I have often heard people who were not blind to Darby's faults say with immense emphasis, "He was a great man." If a magnanimous simplicity

---

1 In Robert Louis Stevenson's *Travels with a Donkey in the Cevennes*, the author, who made this trek through the mountains in the south of France in 1878, is approaching the tiny village of LaVernede when he is overtaken by a clear-eyed old man and a young girl. After some conversation about the area the old man asks, "Connaissez-vous le Seigneur?" (Do you know the Lord?) Stevenson, who was a syncretist and embraced all religions—and none—answers in the affirmative, and the old man is delighted. He explains that "They call us Moravians here, but down in the department of Gard where there are a good number, they are called Derbists [i.e., Darbyites] after an English pastor."

makes a man great, they were right. He might be a scholar, but he wore none of a scholar's trappings; he might be supreme in his own little world, but his habitual bearing showed no trace of self-consciousness. To his social inferiors and to young men he was genial and hearty, and he kept his well-known brusquerie for more influential people, and especially for his sycophants— who were many. If he was ruthless in his ecclesiastical conflicts, he had at other times a singularly kindly and sympathetic nature. In the act of addressing a meeting he would roll up his greatcoat as a pillow for a sleeping child whose uncomfortable attitude had struck him. I have heard that, on one of his numerous voyages, he might have been seen pacing the deck all night with a restless child in his arms, in order to afford the worn-out mother an opportunity of rest; and I doubt whether many children were more tenderly nursed that night . . .

In the hills of Eastern France or Switzerland he would often on his pastoral tours receive the hospitality of humble mountaineers. When the materfamilias went out to work in the fields, half his active mind would suffice for his studies, and with the other half he would help the children that sat about him either with their work or their play. We may cease to wonder that the Continental poor accustomed to resent the hauteur of the Englishman abroad, should have idolized the great man who was among them so genially "as one that serveth."

Indeed no one ever took fewer airs. The following anecdote I can vouch for. A certain couple had just joined the Exclusive fraternity, and were receiving their first visit from the great man. They had risen from the supper table, and Darby, kneeling close beside it, was offering a prayer with which his hearers were greatly impressed. But whatever the excellence of the prayer, the lady of the house, an old-fashioned housekeeper, was painfully distracted by the unmistakable sound of the cat feasting on the remains of the supper. Nothing but awe of her distinguished guest could have restrained her from interfering. As they rose from their knees she cast a glance towards the remains of the cold fowl. His eyes followed hers. "It's all right," he said reassuringly; "I took care that she got nothing but the bones."

Another story, which I can relate with equal confidence, illustrates not only this fine simplicity of character, but also the readiness of resource by which he was no less distinguished. He had arrived at the railway station of a Continental town where he was expected to make some little stay, and found himself, as he stepped from the train, face to face with a formidable contingent of the local Brethren. Several ladies of good position were there, all zealous for the honor of becoming his host. It was a delicate situation, but Solomon could not have been more equal to it. "Qui est-ce qui loge les freres?" (Who generally puts up the [ministering] brothers?) said Darby. All eyes turned upon a very humble-looking brother, who had hitherto kept modestly in the background. Darby immediately went up to him, saying, "Je logerai ou logent les freres" (I will stay where the [ministering] brothers are in the habit of staying). And the entertainer of obscure itinerants became the host of the great man himself.

(From Chapter IX, "The Supremacy of Darby")

The Teachings of J.N. Darby

At this point we need to examine some of the major teachings of J.N. Darby. Darby's Collected Writings consist of thirty-four volumes divided into nine categories: apologetic, critical, doctrinal, ecclesiastical, evangelic, expository, miscellaneous, practical, and prophetic. The contents are mainly addresses given by Darby (from which notes were taken), tracts, and letters. This material was collected by William Kelly, one of Darby's most gifted associates.

In terms of their impact upon the thinking of the Independent Brethren, one can discern two major categories of "Darbyite" ideas. Category one consists of teachings regarding God's overall plan from Creation to the return of Christ in judgment. Category II consists of teachings regarding how Christians ought to conduct their affairs at the present time, especially in relation to the local assembly (please see chapter 6 for a more complete explanation of Darby's doctrine of the church). The attempt to summarize these teachings should not be taken as a substitute for reading the original materials. What we give below is much simplified for popular understanding.

Category I
Dispensationalism
The best known definition of "dispensation" was not given by Darby, but by C.I. Scofield, editor of the Scofield Reference Bible:

> A dispensation is a period of time during which man is tested in respect of obedience to some specific revelation of the will of God.

Darby in his intense study of the Bible perceived that in the revealed history of mankind since Creation, God has, in various ways, offered the opportunity for the human race to obey him and enjoy his fellowship. Although salvation ultimately was purchased by the death of Christ on the cross, God has chosen to draw near to those who obeyed him under the particular terms of that period, or dispensation. (The word "dispensation," by the way, appears in the New Testament in 1 Corinthians 9:17, Ephesians 1:10, and Colossians 1:25, and means "economy" or "administration"—in other words, a block of time under God's providence.) In the First Dispensation, Adam and Eve had the opportunity to obey God by keeping hands off the Tree of the Knowledge of Good and Evil. In the Dispensation of Conscience, from Adam to Noah, the human race had the opportunity to obey God through the prompting of their consciences, awakened through the disobedience of their first parents. After Noah came the Dispensation of Human Government, until Abraham; then the Dispensation of Promise, until Moses; and the Dispensation of Law, from Moses to Christ. We are presently in the Dispensation of Grace. The seventh and final dispensation will be the Millennium, when Christ will reign on earth for a thousand years. That, too, will be marred by disobedience. The specific titles above were conferred by C.I. Scofield, but the basic concept originated with Darby.

The Church in Ruins

The key element that characterizes every dispensation, Darby taught, is that mankind fails the test very near the beginning of any particular age. For example, God had hardly finished revealing the Law to Moses when the people of Israel led by Aaron hastened to break the First Commandment (Exodus 32). And despite periodic repentance they continued to disobey God right up to the coming of Christ. The same principle applies in the present dispensation. We see disobedience and sin invading the church even in the days of the apostles. By the fourth century the church as God intended it to be, the pure Bride of Christ, had become a mixture of believers and unbelievers, good and evil. It was in a sense, in ruins, just as the ancient system of worship under the Law was in ruins. And this applies to any body of people calling itself "the church," which is set up as an earthly organization with a priesthood or clergy and a mixed membership. It is merely perpetuating a ruined condition that can never be restored.

Rightly Dividing Scripture

Consistent with his view that Bible history consists of a series of dispensations, Darby also recognized in Scripture three classes of people who are addressed: Jews, Gentiles, and the church. Jews are God's earthly people, whose history is told in the Old Testament. To them, beginning with Abraham, God made various promises having to do with blessing on earth: "I will make you into a great nation and I will bless you; I will make your name great," etc. The church, on the other hand, had its beginning on the Day of Pentecost following the ascension of Christ, when the Holy Spirit came on the disciples with power. Jesus made many promises to the church, and these all have to do with spiritual and heavenly blessings. For example: "In my Father's house are many mansions . . . I go to prepare a place for you." Gentiles are those who inherit neither earthly nor heavenly blessings—"having no hope, and without God in the world." To them the gospel was brought by Paul and others:

> [God] now commandeth all men everywhere to repent, because he hath appointed a day, in which he will judge the world in righteousness by that man whom he hath ordained: whereof he hath given assurance unto all men, in that he hath raised him from the dead. (KJV)

To rightly divide Scripture is to recognize which parts of Scripture are addressed to each class of people.

The Future of Israel

A right division of Scripture in terms of its intended audience requires that we do not confuse material directed toward the Jews, God's earthly people, with material directed toward the church, God's heavenly people. It follows logically, Darby taught, that many of the Old Testament prophecies must therefore be as yet unfulfilled. Numerous oracles declare that Israel will be regathered in the Promised Land, that they will dwell there in peace and prosperity, and that a righteous king, a descendent of David, will reign over them. The church, Darby pointed out, is totally unknown and unpredicted in the Old Testament, so these passages must refer to literal events to take place after the church has left this scene. As Darby taught these things in the mid-nineteenth century when Palestine was still part of the Ottoman Empire, the amazing birth of the State of Israel after World War II has aroused a great deal of interest in Dispensationalism among evangelicals, especially in America.

The Literal Day Position

Darby and others who followed him developed an interpretation of the "seventy weeks" (mentioned in Daniel 9:24), that is called the "Literal

Day Position." This is based on the significance of the number seven in God's dealings with the human race and Israel in particular. God rested on the seventh day following creation. He laid out a schedule for Israel that consisted of a day of rest on every seventh day and seven special feasts during the year. Every seventh year was to be a jubilee year. Thus Darby perceived that the seventy weeks in Daniel 9:24 were to be seen as 70 x 7 or 490 years between the date of the prophecy and the millennial reign of Christ, and worked out the following timetable:

7 weeks = 49 years from the order by Artaxerxes in 445 B.C. to rebuild the temple in Jerusalem until its completion under Ezra and Nehemiah.

62 weeks = 434 years between the rebuilding of the temple and the coming of Messiah; fulfilled in Christ. After the Messiah is crucified or "cut off," Jerusalem and the temple will be destroyed; fulfilled under Titus in 70 A.D. The clock now stops until the rebuilding of the temple at the end of an indefinite period which we know as the Christian era.

> Then follows 1 week = 7 years (Daniel 9:25), at the halfway point of which "the prince" will cause the temple sacrifices to cease and the temple to become desolate until "the Consummation" when Christ shall come in glory, completing 490 years.

The Secret Rapture

Darby's "literal day" interpretation was also applied to Revelation 11:2-3, when the "Gentiles" will tread the Holy City under foot for "forty and two months." If this is viewed as forty-two literal months of thirty days each, we get 1,260 days or three and a half years. Remember that Darby saw three classes of people in the Scriptures: Jews, Gentiles, and the church. Gentiles represent those opposed both to the Jews and the church, which in the context of the Gospels meant the Romans. So the prophecy is saying that the Romans will destroy the temple and stop the sacrifices, which they did in 70 A.D. But Darby argued that the prophecy was only partially fulfilled. There will be a period of time after the Roman invasion in the first century not envisioned by the Hebrew prophets, when the gospel of God's grace will go forth to all nations. At the end of that time the temple will be rebuilt under a false Messiah (the "Antichrist") and sacrifices will be resumed. When that happens, the final "week" of Daniel has begun. In the middle of that seven-year period Christ will come quietly to take all true believers, past and present, to heaven. This is called the "secret rapture." Then will come upon Jerusalem and the whole world a three and a half year period—42 months or 1,260 days—of horrible oppression called "the times of the Gentiles" or the "Great Tribulation." This will be brought to a close by the return of Christ in judgment. [See example in Fig. 15]

Category II
The Principle of Gathering
A familiar Bible passage, Hebrews 13:12-13, quoted by Darby in his first published paper, reads:

> Wherefore Jesus also, that he might sanctify the people with his own blood, suffered without the gate. Let us go forth therefore unto him without the camp, bearing his reproach.

In Darby's view, this is a picture of the ground that a truly committed Christian should occupy in relation to the "ruined" church. As indicated above, the "camp" is Christendom, which like the Israelite encampment in the desert embraces both believers and the world in its form of worship. The Christ of Calvary is outside this system, and those who are his own will gather to him and share his reproach. Thus the Brethren assemblies, especially those loyal to Darby, refused any formal name (including "Plymouth Brethren") and referred to themselves as "Christians gathered in the Name of the Lord Jesus Christ" in such and such a place. The Lord's Supper was the principal meeting of the week, usually held during normal church services elsewhere. Here only those who were truly saved and known to be walking with the Lord were allowed to participate. Within this "circle of fellowship" purity was maintained by a strict discipline, and was enforced in extreme cases by excommunication.

The Activity of the Holy Spirit
The excesses of the Irvingite Movement in terms of the gifts of the Holy Spirit were familiar to the early Brethren, and one or two of those well known to Darby and the others had become caught up with this movement. Apparently there was much discussion of these matters, but the exercise of "sign gifts" came to be viewed as a phenomenon of the infant church. In the assemblies influenced by Darby, however, there came to be much reliance on the Holy Spirit for exercise of the gifts of preaching and teaching, and also of administration. In the breaking of bread meetings there was no evident structure; the Spirit led various

brothers to pray, give out hymns, comment on Scripture, etc. Often a theme developed spontaneously in quite a remarkable way. In time the preaching and even services such as funerals were carried on without anyone in the chair, those present expecting the Spirit to lead.

Unity through Separation from Sin

As we pointed out in chapter 1, one of the first principles that drew the early Brethren together was their recognition of the unity that is to be found in Christ, contrasted with the divisions in the churches. But while Groves, Müller, and Craik emphasized the positive aspect of this, by being willing to keep the door of fellowship open to all Christians on the basis of their common faith in Christ, Darby emphasized rejection of all religious systems. His position was that unity could be achieved only by separating from sin (including the sinful condition of the churches). By implication, this included any who were members of churches or (especially) of the assemblies that were in fellowship with Bethesda. This in time caused the assemblies that followed him to be more preoccupied with ferreting out evil than with reaching out with the gospel. As A.N. Groves, who very early saw this coming, said to Darby in a letter of 1836:

> I ever understood our principle of communion to be the possession of the common life or common blood of the family of God (for the life is in the blood); these were our early thoughts, and are my most matured ones. The transition your little bodies have undergone, in no longer standing forth the witnesses for the glorious and simple truth so much as standing forth witness against all that they judge error, have lowered them in my apprehension from heaven to earth in the position of witnesses.

The Ground of the One Body

As the assemblies that followed Darby were linked together in a network with a central authority (chapter 2), and as they came to refer to themselves as "Christians gathered in the Name of the Lord Jesus Christ," it was easy for them to believe that they alone were meeting in a way approved by the Lord. They thus extended Darby's reasoning to mean that, if they constituted the body of Christ in any particular place, no other Christian group could also be the body of Christ in that place as there is only one body (1 Corinthians 12:12; Ephesians 4:4). Moreover, as Darby wrote regarding a case of excommunication, a person put out of one of their assemblies is in effect "put out of the church of God on earth." Later events proved that this grandiose claim eventually became the means of destroying the oneness which they claimed.

We should now be able to see how J.N. Darby's interpretation of Scripture created a whole new way of looking at past history, at the present position of Christians, and of the future of the world before Christ comes in judgment. These teachings have gone far beyond the Brethren, and especially in America are widely accepted among the more Bible-oriented churches. In general, Darby and a number of other Brethren writers have contributed to evangelical Christianity a heightened awareness that Jesus has promised to return, and that the Bible gives us many clues of what the times before his coming will be like. Equally important, they have made sense of the Old Testament prophecies, recognizing that God will indeed keep his promises to his people in a future time. On the other hand, certain of Darby's teachings about how Christians should conduct themselves now, especially his doctrine of unity through separation from sin, has proved (especially in the hands of his zealous disciples) to be not only unworkable but disastrous.

The Contribution of A.N. Groves

It is only in fairly recent times that the part played by Anthony Norris Groves in the formation of ideas among the early Brethren has come to light.[1]

Earlier historians like Andrew Miller "damned him with faint praise"; writing from the Exclusive perspective, they gave all the credit for founding and shaping the doctrines of the Brethren to J.N. Darby. This is quite justified to the degree that Darby's thinking and particularly Darby's attitude toward the visible church has been carried out in practice, not only by the Exclusive Brethren, but also by much of the Independent branch as well. But the importance of Anthony Norris Groves should not be underestimated.

---

[1] In the 1960s, two histories of the Brethren from a non-Exclusive perspective appeared: Harold Rowdon's *Origins of the Brethren* (Pickering and Inglis, 1967) and *A History of the Brethren Movement* by Roy Coad (Paternoster, 1968).

The Brethren movement arose out of a reaction to sectarianism in the Protestant evangelical churches. It was founded on the principle of the unity of all believers. Darby's first public paper was on the subject of unity (chapter 1). By a most ironic twist, however, the "unity" that Darby conceived of, when carried to extremes, created a sect that has become a by-word for dis-unity. As Dr. James Brookes, a friend and admirer of Darby, said years ago:

The result has been from that day [that is, the division of 1848] to this a most painful and humiliating scene of strife, bitterness, and factional disputation.

The significance of A.N. Groves's contribution is that he, too, saw that sectarianism was fragmenting the body of Christ in the world of his day, and addressed the subject in a paper that he had printed on request of his friends—but his position is at the opposite end of the scale. While Darby argues for unity through separation, Groves holds for a unity that is as broad as the love of Christ. It is true that Groves presented no unique theological system as did Darby, and founded no churches. Yet his views on how enlightened Christians ought to regard their less enlightened brethren, in contrast to Darby's, would if put into action result in a peaceful relationship among Christians of all persuasions.

Groves's primary work on the subject is called "On the Principles of Union and Communion in the Church of Christ." In this paper he frankly admits that there is a problem posed by "the rocks and quicksands of the unnumbered sects and systems that surround us." As far as fellowship with individual Christians is concerned, he says, our principle of communion here on earth should be the same as it will be in heaven. That is, we should "meet the all but dying request of our Lord to manifest our love one toward another, so that all men might know we were his disciples . . . ." In other words, the principle of heavenly communion that we should practice here on earth is, "loving all whom Christ loves, because they bear his impress."

Anticipating the question, "Suppose the other person holds errors that I object to," Groves gently suggests that we might not be perfect ourselves. But the principle is, "so long as we judge Christ to be dwelling with a man, that is our warrant for receiving him." As for his errors, "though we bear them weeping, still we must bear them." It is quite possible that "while we were bearing his burdens, he also was bearing ours, and thus we were mutually fulfilling the law of Christ in bearing them for each other."

As far as congregations are concerned, he says, we have a duty to ourselves and a duty to the church universal. Our duty to ourselves is that we need to find a place to worship on a regular basis, and that place should be

> where the form is most scriptural . . . and the ministrations most spiritual; where there is the sweetest savor of Christ . . . where the Lord is most manifestly present.

Regarding duty or attitude toward the church universal, the principle is complete liberty to worship in any place where the Lord is present. If the Lord should say,

> Didst thou not see . . . an admixture of that which was unscriptural, and the absence of that which was scriptural and in some points error? my answer would be, "Yea, Lord, but I dared not call that place unholy where Thou wert present."

In the case of completely apostate bodies, our duty is to stand on the outside and cry, "Come out of her, my people, come out of her!"

In his conclusion Groves directly addresses the position of "Exclusivism" which, unhappily, is what traditional Brethrenism stands for in the eyes of so many other Christians:

> To the question, Are we not countenancing error by this plan? our answer is, that if we must appear to countenance error, or discountenance brotherly love, and the visible union of the Church of God, we prefer the former, hoping that our lives and our tongues may be allowed by the Lord so intelligibly to speak that at last our righteousness shall be allowed to appear; but if not, still we may feel we have chosen the better part.

The letter (actually written as part of his journal) which contains the above material was composed on board a French brig between Madras and Calcutta in 1834, and is, in fact, a response to what Groves had heard directly from Darby. He begins by saying, "Dear [Darby's] letter, which left on my mind the impression of a Jehu-like zeal which neither pitied nor spared, led me to write the brief [paper] which will, I hope, accompany this." Groves was well aware of the fundamental differences in outlook between himself and Darby that existed almost from the beginning, and was deeply concerned about what he perceived would be the consequences if Darby's position on unity prevailed. Some months earlier he had written:

> I was almost forgetting, till a letter from Mr. Bellett of Dublin reminded me, that I was the first to propose that simple principle of union, the love of Jesus, instead of oneness of judgment in minor things, things that may consist [i.e., co-exist] with a true love to Jesus. Little did I then think to see that dear brother, and many others, united in a holy, loving fellowship on these blessed principles . . .

Two years later, in March 1836, Groves was on his way back to India after a stay in England. During this visit he had seen the damage already being done by Darby's system of exclusivism. While waiting on the south coast for a storm to pass, he took the opportunity to write to Darby and warn him of where this system might take the movement if continued. He begins this "prophetic letter" by assuring Darby "that nothing has estranged my heart from you, nor lowered my confidence in your still being animated by the same enlarged and generous purposes that once so won and rivetted me . . ." Quickly, however, he gets to the point:

> I feel you have departed from those principles by which you once hoped to have effected [these purposes], and are in principle returning to the city from whence you departed . . .

If you continue on this course, he says:

> . . . you will see all the evils of the systems from which you profess to be separated, to spring up among yourselves. You will not discover this so much from the workings of your own soul, as by the spirit of those who have been nurtured up from the beginning, in the system they are taught to feel the only tolerable one; that not having been led like you, and some of those earliest connected with you, through deep experimental suffering and sorrow, they are little acquainted with the real truth that may exist amidst inconceivable darkness: there will be little pity and little sympathy with such, and your union daily becoming one of doctrine and opinion more than life and love, your government will become . . . the authority of men; you will be known more by what you witness against than what you witness for, and practically this will prove that you witness against all but yourselves . . .

We need only to read any one of the several histories of the Exclusive Brethren, written by those (like Harry Ironside) who loved them as a people but could not deny their faults, to see that Groves's prediction was almost eerily accurate. After the troubles of the mid-1840s Darby seems to have regarded the leaders at Bethesda—George Müller, Henry Craik and, by extension, Groves—with bitterness (though his correspondence shows some exceptions to this attitude). In 1864, in complete counter-distinction from the facts, he wrote:

> The evil at Bethesda is the most unprincipled admission of blasphemers against Christ: the coldest contempt for him I ever came across.

Three years later, in 1867, he again went on record:

> I reject Bethesda as wickedness, as I ever did . . . When the blasphemous doctrine of Mr. Newton . . . came out, Bethesda deliberately sheltered and accredited it.

Of this Neatby says:

> Now this statement was not merely an incalculable exaggeration; it was absolutely false, root and branch, and an excellent instance of smoke without fire.

4

Bethesda and the Emergence of the Independent Brethren 1848-1859

The Brethren Movement Divides

In 1830, when John Darby visited Oxford for the first time, he met there among a circle of evangelical students Benjamin W. Newton, a candidate for the Church of England ministry. Darby was drawn to Newton because of the young man's interest in prophecy and also by his objection to "clericalism" (i.e., using the ministry for personal power or gain). As we have seen, it was Newton who invited Darby to Plymouth, and the two along with Wigram and Hall were founders of the assembly there. But tension between Darby and Newton arose after Darby left in 1832, rising ironically out of the two subjects of prophecy and anticlericalism.

Newton flatly rejected the "literal day" theory as well as the "secret rapture," and accused Darby of abandoning the orthodox teaching of the church. Apparently he circulated papers in manuscript form among the infant Brethren groups detailing his opposition to Darby's prophetic views. As mentioned earlier, he refused to attend the 1833 Powerscourt conference on prophecy and scheduled his own prophetic conference at that same time. He also disagreed with Darby on the practice of conducting meetings by the "leading of the Spirit" and claimed that Darby had actually suggested that Newton be in the chair during the Lord's

Supper to stop unprofitable participation. By 1840 a kind of ministerial staff had developed, consisting of Newton, James Harris, Henry Soltau, and a man named Batten. Letters of the time indicate that there was much blessing in the church, with numbers in attendance at 700 or so (the capacity of the new building). But, as Roy Coad says, "There is little doubt that Newton's control of the church at Ebrington Street, Plymouth, was severe and autocratic."

So long as there was harmony at Plymouth, Darby made no public objection, though he and Newton exchanged angry words privately. But early in 1845, while still in Switzerland, Darby wrote to Harris indicating his concern and received a letter in return in which Harris, though noncommittal, invited him to visit Plymouth. When Darby left Lausanne in March he went immediately to Plymouth, took up residence and started a Bible study. Accusations and denials flew back and forth, a meeting between the rivals and a group of their supporters was held but failed to resolve anything, and finally in October Darby forced a church investigation by announcing publicly that he was quitting the Ebrington Street meeting. Even this proved fruitless, as the charges against Newton were too vague, and in fact the real problem was a clash of personalities and doctrinal positions.

Toward the end of 1845 the feud was common knowledge throughout the entire Brethren network, and around ten or twelve respected leaders from various places came to Plymouth to try to arbitrate. Some, like Wigram and Soltau, were partisans of either Darby or Newton, but others like John Parnell (now Lord Congleton) were very fair minded. Reports indicate that about half of the group, after lengthy interviews with Newton, were convinced that he had no evil intentions, but in the end the matter was referred back to the Ebrington elders. Soltau and others issued a statement that they believed Newton to be "entirely innocent of the imputations," but the damage had already been done. On the last Sunday of 1845 Darby and Wigram commenced a rival meeting at Raleigh Street Chapel (still owned by Wigram), and they were joined by a sizable number of the Ebrington congregation.

Throughout 1846 there was continued pressure on Newton and his elders, primarily from the leadership at Rawstorne Street in London where George Wigram was prominent. To add to his woes, Newton's wife was terminally ill and died in May. When attempts to get him to appear before the leadership at Rawstorne Street failed, both Darby and Wigram published absurd personal attacks implying that he was a tool of Satan. Newton, on the other hand, though he never changed his opinion that Darby's prophetic views were unorthodox, never resorted to slander and continued to reply courteously (often through Soltau). At last, in December, the Rawstorne Street leaders sent out a note (though all did not sign) barring Newton from communion there. According to the principle of the "one body," this meant that the entire network of assemblies was closed to him.

The final blow to fall on B.W. Newton occurred in the summer of 1847 when the wife of James Harris, Newton's former colleague, received some notes on Psalm 6 hand-written by an auditor from a lecture given by Newton a long while before. In reading them, Harris noted that Newton seemed to be saying that Christ, as an Israelite, was suffering as the penalty of his own national sin. Harris wrote a letter criticizing this position as heresy and had the letter and notes published. This touched off a "pamphlet war" between Newton and Darby, with Newton defending himself and Darby insisting that Newton was seeking to degrade and dishonor the Lord. In all fairness, it must be said that Newton made two or three attempts in writing to retract his questionable teachings, or at least to "withdraw them for reconsideration," but as he seems already to have lost credibility among many of the Brethren, these moves added only confusion instead of clarity. This was too much for Newton's fellow leaders, who resigned and later "confessed" their error in associating with a heretic. In December, Newton left Plymouth and the Brethren for good. Darby, however, was still not satisfied, and insisted that anyone remaining at the Ebrington Street assembly (now moved to Compton Street) was a partaker in Newton's "sin."

During the controversy over Newton, the one church that was not involved was Bethesda at Bristol. [Fig. 16] Müller and Craik had built this work around the eight principles of the primitive Brethren companies, and the spirit of Anthony Groves's generous attitude toward other Christians seems also to have prevailed. Müller and Craik were the regular preachers, but they had introduced "open" participation at the Lord's Supper as early as 1832. They also shared administration and policy decisions with eight other appointed elders. With a large and growing congregation, the two preachers had their hands full with pastoral and counseling duties. Also, by 1847 George Müller's Scriptural Knowledge Institute and orphan homes were both going concerns. Thus they took no sides, and when part of Ebrington Street hived off they simply recognized both groups.

By 1848, however, the leaders in Bristol were most unwillingly made the major protagonists in the controversy once Newton himself was out of the picture. The problem was created by certain individuals at Bethesda who were actually disciples of Darby, and who made an issue out of the acceptance by the elders of some members of Ebrington Street at the breaking of bread meeting. Their intent was to force Bethesda to judge and condemn Newton as a heretic along with anyone associated with him. Instead the ten elders carefully weighed the matter, and, convinced that the Ebrington people were not "tainted" by Newton's particular errors, published a letter giving several very sensible reasons why they could not act as judges. The result was that Darby himself visited Bristol and attempted to persuade Müller and Craik to condemn Newton's tracts, warning them that if they refused they would be cut off from all the other assemblies. When the two friends stood firm, Darby made good his threat, and in August 1848 circulated a letter excommunicating not only Bethesda "but all assemblies who received anyone who went there."

The letter of excommunication of Bethesda, which put a strain on their relationships with the other assemblies, did regrettably force the elders to compromise. Previously it had been their policy not to bar any believer from fellowship on the basis of non-essential doctrinal differences. But after a number of meetings spent in scrutinizing Newton's writings, they announced that anyone holding Newton's views would not be received at the Lord's Table. This satisfied no one and merely made matters worse, and eventually they reverted to their original position. Darby, on the other hand, had second thoughts, and in July 1849 called on Müller at the orphan home. After exchange of greetings he said, "As you have judged Newton's tracts there is no longer any reason why we should be separated." Müller replied, "I have this moment only ten minutes time, having an important engagement before me; and as you have acted so wickedly in this matter, I cannot now enter upon it, as I have no time."[1] Darby rose and left, and the two never saw one another again in this life. [Fig. 17]

---

[1] There are no witnesses to this interview, so we must rely on the testimony of one or the other of these great men. While Darby denied the statements that were made, he seemed to affirm that the meeting did take place. On the other hand, Müller's lifelong habit of recording

The network of assemblies that until 1848 had been united now became two separate streams. Those siding with Darby continued as a cohesive federation with a central authority consisting of the Saturday meeting in London, which ultimately answered to Darby himself. Over the years until the great man's death in 1882 they grew and multiplied, not only in Britain but everywhere Darby traveled, including the United States and Canada, the West Indies, Australia, New Zealand and Western Europe. It is estimated that some 1,500 meetings worldwide looked to him as their chief authority. Among his disciples were many excellent writers, such as C.H. MacIntosh, William Kelly, and Charles Stanley who, through numerous books, periodicals and tracts, developed and popularized Darby's system of Biblical interpretation. While zealous to preach the Gospel they maintained a strict policy of excluding all from their communion except those who were members of the "one body." And all who joined them were required to "judge the question"[1] of Bethesda's offense.

In chapter 4 we will pursue the story of the Independent Brethren, with whose history we are primarily concerned. It is to saints of the early Brethren movement like Anthony Norris Groves, Elizabeth Paget, Henry Craik, George Müller, Robert Chapman, and Lord Congleton that we like to trace our spiritual heritage in terms of ecclesiology, evangelism, world missions, and social concerns. But for Biblical exposition, Old Testament typology and understanding of prophecy we cannot deny the huge debt owed by the movement to J.N. Darby and those

---

facts and events with meticulous precision and the saintliness of his life make any tampering with the truth highly unlikely. No doubt there will always be an element of mystery surrounding this incident.

1 In the view of Brethren historians like Andrew Miller and W.B. Neatby, the Independent Brethren constitute only one of the many branches growing out of a single trunk. As family quarrels tend to run very deep, the Exclusives have maintained a grudge against any and all in the Independent assemblies even down to the present day. The argument goes like this: Bethesda compromised with sin in not condemning B.W. Newton (not true, of course; see chapter 4. They did condemn Newton's errors). Therefore, all who trace their history back to Bethesda identify themselves with that compromise. The only way for fellowship to be restored between the descendants of those who condemned Newton's heresy and those who did not (Bethesda and all who take this independent stand) is for the latter to "judge the question" properly—that is, to agree that Bethesda was wrong. In years gone by (and perhaps even still in some places) it was quite common for an Exclusive brother to refuse acquaintance with someone from an Independent assembly by asking, "Have you judged the question?" (And chances are the person would answer, quite innocently, "What question?")

gifted brethren who followed him, such as J.G. Bellett, William Kelly, C.H. Macintosh and a host of other writers and teachers.

Bethesda as a Model of Independent Brethrenism

While a number of growing assemblies and gifted leaders sided with Bethesda after their condemnation by John Darby, our best model of the "Independent" Brethren form of local church must be Bethesda itself [Fig. 19]. In this chapter we want to take note of several significant factors that went into the development of this work, which has been well documented, both by Craik's and Müller's journals and that of Müller's successor, James Wright. Biographies have been written about all three, and recently a history has been published of Bethesda and its network of churches in the Bristol area. The Müller Foundation is still active as well, and preserves many books, documents, and memorabilia relating to the assembly movement.

First and perhaps most important is the character both of Henry Craik and George Müller, as individuals and as associates. Both men and their wives walked with God and trusted Him completely. Both were singularly gifted. Craik was the superior scholar and preacher, while Müller was the organizer and practical steward (though not far behind as a scholar—his huge library may still be seen at the Müller Foundation.) Both expended themselves fully in pastoral work. Though they delegated responsibility to elders at Bethesda, they were without question the primary leaders. Yet in the thirty-six years of their association there was never a shade of disharmony between them. In Müller's words upon Craik's death in 1866, each was a "beloved fellow worker and intimate friend" to the other.

A second important factor is that Bethesda was a new work into which Müller and Craik put into practice the ten cardinal principles of the early Brethren (chapter 2). It was not, as some have erroneously argued, merely a variation of a denominational church already in existence. The two men had come to see these truths for themselves in Scripture while Müller was serving as pastor of Ebenezer Chapel in Teignmouth (later to become a Brethren assembly, and still in existence), and Craik as pastor of the Baptist chapel at Shaldon across the river. For example, early in 1830 Müller instituted the Lord's Supper every Sunday, following Acts 20:7, and also began to open the worship meetings so that any of the brethren with some spiritual gift could take part. In October 1830 he announced that he would no longer take a regular salary, but would accept only voluntary offerings. [Fig. 20] He also did away with the practice of renting pews. In that same month he married Mary Groves, sister of Anthony Norris Groves, and following the Lord's command in Luke 12:33 the newlyweds literally sold all that they had and gave it to the poor.

Their work at Bristol began with Gideon Chapel, a pre-existing congregation. Bethesda was taken over as an empty building in July 1832. On August 13 Müller recorded in his diary: This evening one brother and four sisters united with Brother Craik and me in church fellowship at Bethesda, without any rules, desiring only to act as the Lord shall be pleased to give us light through His Word.

In the first year (1832-33) 109 people had been added to the two congregations and sixty-five had professed faith in Christ. But there was a distinct difference between the two congregations. At Gideon there came to be an undercurrent of discontent with the weekly celebration of the Lord's Supper and the refusal of the two young pastors to limit membership to those who had been baptized. By 1839 a split seemed imminent and the two leaders went apart for two weeks to seek wisdom from the Lord. The result included a decision to give up Gideon. This was done in April 1840 with an invitation to all at Gideon who wished to "separate from every sectarian system" to meet at Bethesda.

A third factor is the difference in views regarding the place of the Brethren movement in church history. George Müller and Henry Craik thought of Bethesda as a restoration of what the local church was like as seen in the New Testament. Where the New Testament gave evidence of elders and deacons in the local church, they had elders and deacons. Where they saw Timothy and Titus ministering full time to the saints at particular local churches, they were pleased to serve the Lord in the same way. When they found the churches in the Acts baptizing new adult believers, they baptized new adult believers. But when they found no evidence for requiring baptism as a condition for participation in the Lord's Supper, they made no such requirement at Bethesda. Where they could in good conscience agree with their brethren in the Anglican and other churches, they did so gladly. Thus it was that about the same time that J.N. Darby was developing his exclusive principles in Switzerland, "Bethesda moved in precisely the opposite direction."

A fourth thing about Bethesda was its durability. Important as the foundation laid by Craik and Müller was, the work was not built around them and did not cease when they were gone. The two original meetings in Aungier Street, Dublin, and Ebrington Street, Plymouth, had vanished long before the end of the nineteenth century. Bethesda not only remained but gave birth to an entire family of over twenty gatherings in and around Bristol. This was achieved not by splits and schisms, but by mutual agreement and encouragement. The entire network (somewhat diminished since the 1960s) is still in fellowship with each other and shares speakers and other ministry. Among their ranks have been several men who have had an impact upon the entire church, including George Müller himself and his notable successor James Wright; W.E. Vine, author of the well-known Expository Dictionary of New Testament Words; the historian E.H. Broadbent, author of The Pilgrim Church; and more recently, Arthur Rendle Short, known to generations of university students for his Modern Discovery and the Bible and other apologetic works.

This is not to say that Bethesda and its network have not had problems. The split with Darby hurt the work badly, as many found his teachings very convincing and left to associate with Exclusive gatherings. The following is quoted from *I Will Build My Church: 150 Years of Local Church Work in Bristol* by Keith and Allen Linton:

> In Bristol, throughout these unhappy years of hostility and bitterness, Müller and Craik, although greatly pained by the false and slanderous accusations, refused to retaliate but quietly continued their work for God. The losses caused by the turmoil were serious but not disastrous.

Yet neither the death of Henry Craik in 1866 or of George Müller thirty-two years later caused the ministry to falter. The practice of appointing elders created a ready supply of leadership. Two world wars, the second causing catastrophic destruction to the city of Bristol (old Bethesda Chapel being among the casualties), rather than hindering outreach provided new opportunities for service. Only in the past decade or two, with their unprecedented social changes, have the assemblies related to Bethesda been under a rather severe strain to keep up with the times. All indications are that they will cope.

By way of a postscript it should be mentioned that other Independent assemblies associated with Bethesda have also stood the test of time. In Barnstaple a modern chapel now stands on the site of the old hall built by Robert Chapman on Grosvenor Street. The original building of Brooke Street Hall, the Tottingham assembly in North London associated with the Howard brothers (with its burying ground now a children's playground) is still extant, though the area has completely changed its character. Here, in 1851, the young Hudson Taylor met pioneer missionary to China Wilhelm Lobscheid. The former Baptist chapel in Teignmouth, where Müller first preached, still carries on as Bitton Park Hall (chapter 1). Several others whose history goes back to the 1840s are still thriving in new locations.

The Beginning of World-Wide Missions

One of the most important features of Brethren history, and indeed the most exciting aspect of their story, is their worldwide missionary outreach. Allusion was made to this in the Introduction with reference to Jim Elliot and others. Even today, Brethren missionaries are disproportionately numerous compared with the size of their home congregations in the U.S. and Canada. The real success of their endeavors to take the gospel to the world, in fact, cannot be seen in North America at all. Rather, it is evident in far-flung places like Singapore, Romania, Argentina, Central Africa, etc., where the Brethren are among the most numerous and actively growing evangelical bodies. In 1984 a history of Brethren missions edited by Frederick A. Tatford was published by Echoes of Service in Bath, England. It consists of ten large volumes!

For the Brethren, missionary outreach is a logical extension of their commitment to literal obedience of the words of Jesus, "Ye shall be witnesses unto me both in Jerusalem, and in all Judaea, and in Samaria, and unto the uttermost part of the earth" (Acts 1:8). It also squares with their perception of the imperative nature of the gospel, and with their emphasis on the nearness of the return of the Lord. Their first foreign missionary, Anthony Norris Groves, actually went abroad at about the same time that the first assembly in Dublin was established (so technically was not a "Brethren" missionary at all). He followed in the wake of a number of others who had pioneered the modern missionary movement, beginning with Baptist missionary William Carey in 1793. But in certain ways Groves was unique, as he went to the heart of the Muslim world where no others had penetrated, and he went without the support of a society and in dependence upon God alone. His example greatly influenced two later but more famous pioneers, Robert Morrison and James Hudson Taylor.

Groves was away from England the first time from June 1829 to early 1835. His is an amazing story. Pioneering courage, endurance of every unimaginable hardship, suffering and frustration, exercise of exceptional creativity and ingenuity to carve out a ministry where none existed before—all play a part. It took Groves and his party over six months to make the trip to Baghdad. With him were Mary Groves and their two sons and baby daughter, his sister Lydia, a young deaf man named Kitto (later to become a well-known Bible scholar) and a Miss Taylor. Two others joined them in St. Petersburg. They traveled on foot and in wagons or carriages via Moscow and south to the Caucasus Mountains, beyond to Shushee (modern Teheran) and thence to Baghdad, arriving in December. Here Groves started a school, primarily to help himself with Arabic. He also practiced medicine, specializing in diseases of the eye. Attempts were made to evangelize on a small scale, but the Muslims proved as impervious to the gospel then as now.

The most severe trials started in March 1831. A major epidemic of the plague struck the city, followed by a disastrous flood that swept away thousands of dwellings. The waters stopped at the top of the street where Groves and his family lived. Mary Groves died in May and their little girl a few weeks later. Something of the character of the man may be seen in this passage from his diary written shortly after the death of his wife:

> From the day that my dearest Mary and myself deliberately prepared to set out on the work in which we finally embarked, the Lord never allowed us to doubt that it was His work, and that the result to the church of God would be far greater than our remaining quietly at home.

Then came civil war, and bullets whizzed over the house. A relief party made up of F.W. Newman, Edward Cronin with his young daughter, mother and sister, John Parnell and a Mr. Hamilton arrived at Aleppo, but were unable to proceed. Knowing of this, Groves's frustration and anxiety were intense. This party had also suffered greatly; Nancy Cronin, who had married Parnell at Aleppo, was taken sick and died, and Newman nearly succumbed of fever. When, in April 1832, the party made the last stage of the journey, an attempt to distribute Turkish New Testaments caused a riot and the men were stoned. Cronin was left for dead. They finally arrived in Baghdad in June. Cronin's mother died shortly thereafter.

Groves remained in Baghdad less than a year after the arrival of his friends. Advised by a Christian military man, Col. (later Gen.) Cotton, of opportunities in British India, he left for India in May 1833, where he spent the remaining months before returning to England in 1835. Having married again during his brief stay at home, he went back in 1836 to spend another twelve years ministering mainly to Europeans but also making an impact upon certain Indian Christians. Not all of his innovative ideas were successes, and some of his relationships with missionaries caused friction. But, as Harold Rowdon points out in Origins of the Brethren, he was far ahead of his time as a missionary thinker. He maintained that the most scriptural pattern is for missionaries to be supported by one or two churches with whom they can have a close relationship. They might even go with only partial support and earn their own living. He also felt that missionaries should adopt a simple lifestyle similar to those they were serving, and that it was desirable for Indians to evangelize their own people. Now, 150 years later, these ideas have come into their own.

Commitment to missions abroad seems to have been an important part of the world view adopted by all of the early Brethren. As we have seen, Edward Cronin and John Parnell went to Iraq in support of Groves, and it is known that B.W. Newton, G.V. Wigram and Henry Craik all actively considered service overseas. Starting in 1839, John Nelson Darby spent a considerable amount of his long life ministering abroad, including several extended visits to the U.S. and Canada. Robert Chapman of Barnstaple made an evangelistic journey to Spain in 1832, where he distributed large numbers of Scripture portions. Upon his return he described the opportunities there for the gospel, and eventually a number of other Brethren missionaries settled in that country. Two couples from Barnstaple, Mr. and Mrs. George Beer and Mr. and Mrs. William Bowden, also went to labor in India. In British Guiana, a Church of England clergyman, Leonard Strong, became disillusioned by opposition to his efforts to minister to the slaves. Doubting the scriptural ground of the established church, he gave up his living to meet in simplicity in the name of Christ alone. In 1842 George Müller endorsed this work by sending financial aid. Eventually Strong became part of the Brethren movement.

George Müller's financial support of world missions through the Scriptural Knowledge Institute is well known. This support was not limited to missionaries commended by the Brethren, as Müller made his decisions on an individual basis without reference to organization. For example, the Institute assisted Hudson Taylor in the founding of work in China. From 1870 onward some 2,000 pounds annually went to the work of the China Inland Mission. Müller himself went abroad five times between 1835 and 1845 (and of course traveled extensively in his later years after the orphanage work had made him famous). The first trip was to accompany Groves to Germany to recruit missionaries. He made a second journey in 1838, which resulted in two parties going to India. Again in 1840 Müller visited Germany with the same object, and gained another eight volunteers. His 1843-44 trip was a response to an invitation to help combat certain doctrinal errors in the Baptist church in Stuttgart. This time a Brethren assembly was formed, which he visited again in 1845.

The record of early Brethren missions would not be complete without the story of the founding of the work in Italy. Here it originated, not with English missionaries going out, but with an Italian coming to England. Count Piero Guicciardini, [Fig. 23] of an ancient Florentine family, was converted through reading a Bible given to him by an employee, and began meeting with other evangelicals. For a short period during a revolution in 1848-49 there was religious freedom, and in 1849 these believers started a public meeting. But once the revolution was put down, there came severe repression; Guicciardini was imprisoned for some months in 1851, and later was exiled. Certain others were given brutal sentences merely for professing their faith. Mercifully, a deputation from England including the evangelical Earl of Cavan presented a plea to the Grand Duke of Tuscany on their behalf.

Meanwhile Guicciardini had reached England, where he associated with the Brethren. Here he met another Italian exile, Teodoro Rossetti,[1] a cousin of the poets Dante Gabriel and Christina Rossetti. Through Guicciardini, Rossetti became a believer, and in 1871, when the Grand Duke was forced out, the two returned to Florence to commence there a flourishing testimony along Brethren lines that still continues. Eventu-

---

1 Biographies of Count Guicciardini and Teodoro Rossetti have been written by Daisy Ronco, lecturer at University College, Bangor, Wales, and an authority on religious movements in nineteenth century Italy.

ally missionaries came from Britain to assist in the work, the first being two couples, Mr. and Mrs. Cole and Mr. and Mrs. J.S. Anderson. A notable aspect of the Brethren activity in Italy was their interaction with the ancient churches of the Waldensians. Brethren influence in Florence is also indicated by the extensive collection of early Brethren writings in the National Library, a gift of Count Guicciardini.[1]

---

1 During the past twenty-five years, a "key man" in Florence and Italy as a whole has been Stephen Woods, son of Stacey and Yvonne Woods.

5

The Second Great Evangelical Awakening 1859-1870s

The Revival and the Brethren

Starting in the year 1859, a remarkable outpouring of God's Spirit took place all over Britain, characterized by a great response to the preaching of the gospel. In volume three of *Christian England* (1984, Eerdmans), David Edwards gives the following description:

> The revival beginning in the USA in 1857, and reaching England two years later, has been called the "Second Evangelical Awakening." To some extent it deserves that grand title. Many of its gatherings on both sides of the Atlantic were as full of excitement as the congregations of Whitefield and the Wesleys, and its leaders could travel around and address evening meetings far more easily than the pioneers could, thanks to the steamship, the railway, and gas light. Some striking characters became famous in this way— Richard Weaver [Fig. 25] the English miner who had previously been Undaunted Dick the boxer, converted to Christ when he saw blood streaming down the face of his opponent: Reginald Radcliffe, formerly a solicitor, who sent out assistants on to the streets of Liverpool urging men to come to the services . . . The hymn "Stand up, stand up for Jesus" is a lingering echo of the enthusiasm.

The Chicago evangelist Dwight L. Moody himself was converted during the early stages of the revival in America. In 1873, accompanied by his gifted song leader Ira Sankey, he held an extensive campaign in Britain. His meetings in Edinburgh and Glasgow were filled to overflowing, and in London over a course of several weeks some two and a half million people heard the gospel. (This was Moody's third visit to England. He first came with an express desire to visit two men, Charles Spurgeon and George Müller.)

The revival, according to Brethren historian Roy Coad:

> transformed the religious life both of North America and of Britain. Churches of all denominations were filled, and not only churches, but hired halls and theaters and great open-air spaces. Converts were numbered in hundreds of thousand, and great but often eccentric preachers of the gospel, both working men and men from the upper classes of society, began to attract large crowds of hearers throughout the country.

Between 1860 and 1870 the Baptists, Methodists, and Congregationalists experienced an unprecedented harvest of new members, the Baptists adding two-thirds to their numbers through the greatest decade of growth in their history. But the impact upon the Open Brethren was even more substantial, in that the revival not only brought new assemblies into existence, but it gave the movement an altogether different character. Again to quote Roy Coad:

> The independent Brethren received an impetus from the revival movement that within two decades transformed both their character and their influence.

And, as we shall see, it was this new model of Independent Brethren assembly, brought into being by revival preachers, that was exported to North America.

The revival in the British Isles broke out first in Northern Ireland in 1859. A number of important evangelists who had a widespread impact on the movement were associated with the Brethren, at least five in Ireland: James M'Quilkin (who came to faith through a remarkable woman, Mrs. Colville, who herself led many to Christ), Jeremiah Meneely, John Galway M'Vicker, Joseph Denham Smith, and T. Shuldham Henry. In addition to Gordon Furlong and John Hambleton, [Fig. 24] the revival preachers associated with Brethren in England included two other colorful characters: Joshua Poole, known as "Fiddler Joss," who was converted in Wakefield Prison, and Henry Moorhouse, a former card sharper known as the "boy preacher." Equally effective were some men of the upper classes, including Sir Robert Anderson, later head of the criminal investigation department of Scotland Yard, Lord Reginald Radcliffe, Brownlow North and the Earls of Cavan and Carrick. One of Gordon Furlong's converts was a man whose name later became a household word, John Thomas Barnardo of the Barnardo Homes.

Around London the revival was greatly encouraged by John Morley, senior partner of the textile firm of I. and R. Morley, who brought many of the revival preachers to the metropolis. In South London an important acquisition of the Brethren was William Lincoln, former curate at St. George's, Southwark. The Blackdown Hills district on the border of Devon and Somerset saw the beginning of a substantial work lasting many years, both in evangelism and social concerns, through George Brealey and his wife. The revival was also keenly felt in many areas of Scotland, both in the villages and in major towns and cities. Later, in the 1870s, Glasgow became a main center of Independent Brethren activity.

The Brethren congregations that sprang up after 1859 tended to be strongly influenced by the revival preachers. Instead of "meeting rooms" they now assembled in "gospel halls." [Fig. 26] Instead of leaders from the aristocracy their leadership was often self-taught working people, much like many of the evangelists themselves. About this time the Sunday evening gospel meeting came into being as an evangelistic tool, gas lamps having made the streets safer. Often street preaching and tract distribution would precede the gospel meeting.

A number of the later evangelists found the Brethren well suited to their style of reaching out to the unchurched population. Some, like Lord Radstock, joined the Brethren in evangelism while retaining membership elsewhere. Others, like Joseph Denham Smith, a former Congregational minister; Gordon Furlong, an Aberdeen lawyer (mentioned above); John Hambleton, an ex-actor and adventurer; and London YMCA secretary Charles Russell Hurditch identified completely with the movement.

The first gospel halls were established in Northern Ireland through the efforts of the evangelists. (It is of interest to note that in 1990 gospel halls could still be found in almost every village and town throughout Ulster, with tent meetings still a familiar institution.) These men knew about George Müller, and links were established with leaders at Bristol and Barnstaple and elsewhere in England. In Dublin the original Brethren assembly had died out. The revival brought a number of prominent individuals back into Brethren ranks, and one of the largest gospel halls in Ireland, Merrion Hall, [Fig. 27] was built in a central location near Trinity College. From here Richard W. Owens emigrated to New York in 1871 and began a lengthy ministry that resulted in some thirty churches. Thus Owens can be considered the first of the Independent Brethren to spend his entire career in ministry in North America.

Henry Moorhouse

The story of Henry (or Harry) Moorhouse [Fig. 28], sometimes billed as the "boy evangelist" because of his youthful looks, is of particular interest to North Americans because of the spiritual impact of his three visits to this continent, especially on Dwight L. Moody. Moorhouse was born in Manchester in 1840 to workingclass Methodist parents. His education was minimal, and he was put to work at age twelve. He was a bright, outgoing lad, whose slight build made him depend on his wits more than on his muscles. He soon got into trouble entertaining his fellow workers by some daredevil acrobatics. Before long he followed his companions into the gin palaces and card parlors of Manchester, and by age sixteen was a "prince of players," backed by the proprietor against all comers and winning enough to fill his own pockets. Yet he kept up the practice of going to Sunday school, and became so torn between passion for vice and conviction of sin that he took to carrying a loaded pistol with thoughts of suicide. After a short stint in the army he returned to Manchester and once again came under conviction by hearing a revival preacher at a meeting he had entered intending to disrupt it. Later one of his former companions who had been converted in the revival led him to Christ.

Harry Moorhouse began to meet with a congregation of Brethren in Fairfield Street, found employment and married Mary, his childhood sweetheart. Their only child was a little girl, Minnie, paralyzed from birth. His biographer John MacPherson says:

> His "newness of life" was early fostered by holy associations and friendships. His conversion was in all respects a distinct, clear-cut separation from the world. He went clean over to the Lord's side. There was no halting, no reservations in the interest of the flesh, no attempts to mince the matter, or maintain some secret, sly, or slender connection with the world. He started well. He identified himself with the most spiritually-minded men, the most thoroughly-devoted Christians, the most apostolic, self-denying, and disinterested soul-winners, the most decided and outspoken friends of true revival.

The young evangelist made a very shaky start at preaching, which forced him to memorize Scripture texts. He was greatly encouraged by John Hambleton and eventually left his employment and teamed up with Hambleton for a lengthy preaching tour. They used hired halls, theaters, street corners, village greens and other places where people gathered. Their method was to hold up a board with the words (composed by Hambleton),

Christ for me!

Praise the Lord!

Mercy's free!

and to give out tracts and engage in dialogue with the people:

Sirs, it just comes to this in the end: Heaven or Hell? If you don't come to Christ, you won't go to heaven when you die.

When a crowd gathered around, they would preach. This first tour took them to Stratford where the Shakespeare Tercentenary was in progress, and to Epsom where the races were taking place. "Nothing daunted by the rude jostling of the angry crowds, the raillery, the blasphemy, and the ferocious use of the horsewhip and all sorts of missiles, they preached Jesus and left the issue with their Master."

The evangelistic career of Harry Moorhouse took him throughout England, to Ireland, and on nine trips to the United States. As the "boy evangelist" he preached the gospel to great effect. Thousands came to hear him, many out of curiosity, but countless listeners were converted or had their faith restored. But his favorite public ministry was teaching the Bible. Later he devoted much of his time to producing and sending out vehicles expressly for the purpose of selling Bibles, the famous "Bible carriages." He delighted in engaging in this work himself, especially in preaching the Word from the carriage platform, though as the end of his short life neared he was often prevented by frequent coughing spells and weakness (he died in 1880 at the age of forty).

His first encounter with Dwight L. Moody took place in Dublin during Moody's first visit to Great Britain in 1867. Moody himself recorded his impression:

He introduced himself to me and said he would like to come to Chicago to preach. He was a beardless boy—he didn't look more than seventeen—

and I said to myself, "He can't preach." He wanted me to let him know
what boat I was going to America on, as he would like to go on the boat
with me. Well, I thought he couldn't preach, and I didn't let him know.

Moorhouse, twenty-seven at the time, made his first visit to America
the following year. After numerous very effective preaching engage-
ments including many black churches in the South, he wrote to Moody
and asked again if he could preach at his church in Chicago. After an
exchange in correspondence, Moody and his elders reluctantly agreed
to letting him have the pulpit on a Thursday evening when Moody was
to be away. Returning on Saturday, Moody was amazed to hear that the
young man had electrified his audiences twice with messages on John
3:16. Moorhouse was scheduled next on Sunday evening, and Moody
was in the audience—to hear "the most extraordinary sermon"[1] on the
same text. For four more nights Henry Moorhouse preached with
power from John 3:16. From this time onward, Moody himself adopted
Bible exposition as his preaching method.

True to the original Brethren principle of basing all ministry on
God's Word, Harry Moorhouse was a powerful Bible expositor. His
biographer says:

> He could make the Word itself speak. This is, perhaps, the highest function
> of the Christian teacher, the perfection of his art. In his expositions of an
> entire book of scripture, his interpretations were sometimes fanciful, and
> his lessons far-fetched; but even in his conceits and fancies he did not go
> further afield than good old Matthew Henry . . . His lectures and readings
> were often suggestive, and sometimes original; and able pastors were not
> ashamed to acknowledge that under his humble leading they had got
> upon a fresh line of thought. At his Bible-readings could be seen ministers,
> physicians, lawyers and other professional men, persons of education and
> refinement, accustomed from one Lord's-day to another to listen to the
> most elaborate discussions of revealed truth; Christian workers of every
> class; with a crowd of the common church-going people; all deeply inter-
> ested in the lessons of spiritual wisdom drawn from the Word of God, by
> this ingenious but unsophisticated commentator.

---

1 The hymn writer Philip P. Bliss was in the audience, and was greatly impressed by the
young preacher's emphasis on the word "Whosoever." The result was the famous gospel
hymn, "Whosoever Will," in which each stanza begins with the word "Whosoever," and the
chorus reads:"Whosoever will, Whosoever will." Send the proclamation over vale and hill;'Tis
a loving Father calls the wanderer home: "Whosoever will may come." (From *Great Hymns and
Their Stories* by W.J.L. Sheppard, Lutterworth Press, 1985).

In this connection it should be noted that in 1874 Moorhouse preached several times at the Second Presbyterian Church in Princeton. Here the packed audiences included many students and professors, of whom a significant number responded to the gospel.

In the last few years of his short life, Moorhouse concentrated on evangelism through Bible selling and distribution, using his "Bible carriages." [Fig. 29] These were especially constructed horse-drawn wagons something like a Gypsy caravan with a platform on one end for open-air preaching. The carriages were taken to fairs and markets where crowds gathered, and the evangelist would address the multitude from the platform, a helper would play a portable harmonium and volunteers would circulate selling Testaments at two-pence each. In 1878, though in very ill health, he took a Bible carriage to Whitechapel in East London for several weeks. Others took up this ministry until there was a whole fleet, and later this was a successful means of evangelism in North America. Henry Moorhouse carried on his work, often in great weakness and pain, until the last weeks of 1880. He passed from this life on the last day of that year. (Condensed from *Henry Moorhouse: The English Evangelist* by the Rev. John MacPherson, n.d.)

Later Nineteenth Century Missions Pioneers

In the wake of the "Second Great Evangelical Awakening" (chapter 5) there was a considerable increase in Brethren missions activity. Personnel were added to fields like India, already opened by A.N. Groves, and pioneers began work in a number of other countries of the world. Not all of these were "full time," however; in some developed areas like Australia and New Zealand, assemblies were planted by businessmen and their wives, with evangelists and teachers coming from England or from among their own ranks later on. But in places like China, Malay, Central Africa, and Russia, conditions made it necessary for missionaries to be trail-blazers, so to speak, and support from the homeland was essential.

Around 1860 two former Presbyterian ministers, a Mr. Chapman and Alexander Grant, founded missionary work in the Straits and later in the Malay States in line with Brethren principles. William McDonald arrived in Penang in 1866 and continued steadfastly for over forty years. In addition to mission stations, the early work included ministry to lepers, home visitation by the women, and a small orphanage. The latter was established by a Miss B.C. McClay, who later was drowned in the sinking of the Lusitania by the Germans.

Frederick Stanley Arnot [Fig. 30] is, next to David Livingstone himself, the greatest explorer of the then unknown continent of Africa, and a missionary hero not only among the Brethren but of the entire church. As a boy he lived in Hamilton, Scotland, near Livingstone's home town of Blantyre, and knew the Livingstone family. He determined with God's help to follow in the great man's footsteps, and at a young age began to prepare himself for Africa. In 1881, at the age of twenty-two, he took ship for Capetown, and from there to Durban. At this point he disappeared into the interior not to be heard from for four years. Like Livingstone, he faced death from disease, thirst, and hostile natives, and was the prisoner of one chief in the Zambesi Valley for eighteen months.

Reaching the west coast, Arnot again set out for the interior in 1885, and became the first white man to reach the capital of Chief Msiri in Katanga. He returned to Britain in 1888, married, and six months later returned to Africa with a party that included C.A. Swan, Peter Scot, and the Canadian W.L. Faulknor. They were followed by two more parties in 1889, both men and women, many of whom died within a year or two. Ever since those early days, when Brethren missionary graves marked a trail from Katanga to the coast at Benguela, this corridor has been called "The Beloved Strip." Arnot himself died in Johannesburg in 1914 at age fifty-five.

Among the members of the 1889 party was Dan Crawford, who became nearly as famous as Arnot. Crawford labored with the others for a time at Katanga, but in 1891 Chief Msiri was killed by a Belgian army officer and Crawford moved to the area of Lake Mwery, where he established a permanent station at Luanza. Though lacking a formal education, he was an avid reader with a gift for languages. He taught himself Greek and Hebrew and eventually translated the Bible into the Luba language. An individualist with a keen sense of humor, he identified himself closely with the native peoples and thus made himself unpopular with some of the Europeans in the area. Two books, Thinking Black and Back to the Long Grass made him known worldwide. Crawford died in 1926, like Arnot, at age fifty-five.

The first Brethren missionaries to China arrived in the late 1860s, following in the wake of J. Hudson Taylor who had established the China Inland Mission in 1865. From the beginning of Taylor's work, a close relationship existed between the Brethren and the CIM, as Taylor was much influenced in his principles by the Independent Brethren, especially George Müller and A.N. Groves. Before his first trip to China in 1853 he attended an assembly in London. Roger Steer in the latest biography of Hudson Taylor[1] says:

> He spent Sundays happily at Brook[e] Street Chapel, Tottingham, usually entertained by a former Quaker lady, Miss Stacey, who became a lifelong friend.

George Stott, a young Scotsman who had lost a leg at age nineteen, communicated with Taylor and arrived in China in 1866. When asked about his handicap before departing he had replied, "I don't see those with two legs going, so I must." Braving hostility, he established a boys' boarding school in Wenchow and eventually saw some conversions. Grace Ciggie became interested in China through hearing Taylor at a meeting in Glasgow. After working for a time in the Glasgow slums she went to Wenchow in 1870, where she married George Stott the same year.

Mr. and Mrs. Charles H. Judd went to China in 1868, settling for a time in the coastal city of Chinkiang. Charles went on board ships to witness to seamen, and established a ministry that included foreign residents. They moved to Nanking in 1874 accompanied by J. Hudson Taylor, and then again to the province of Hupeh. Robert and Frances White began service in Chinkiang in 1869. They returned to Britain in 1874 to study medicine, leaving the work solely in the charge of Benjamin Bagnal. Upon their return the Whites started a dispensary which treated over five thousand patients annually. Another somewhat later pioneering couple in medical work was Albert and Annie Parrott. Albert began with the China Inland Mission in 1878, returned to England to attend medical school and was commended in 1892. Their work centered in Lao-ho-k'ou on the Han River, where they were joined by George and Fannie Bergin.

One of the most remarkable of the Brethren missionaries of the revival era was Fredrich Wilhelm Baedeker. [Fig. 31] Baedeker was the son of a German naturalist (and cousin of the guidebook author) who had spent many years of his early life wandering about the world

---

1 Roger Steer, *J. Hudson Taylor*, Harold Shaw Publishers, 1990.

before becoming a doctor of philosophy at Freiburg University. He visited England and was married in Weston-super-Mare in 1862. Four years later he attended an evangelistic meeting in the same town sponsored by the Brethren, where Lord Radstock was preaching, and was converted. Shortly after this, Lord Radstock engaged in an evangelistic ministry among the aristocracy of Russia and Eastern Europe, holding Bible readings in the drawing rooms of the great people. (Tolstoy in Resurrection describes these meetings, though somewhat cynically.) Radstock introduced Baedeker to some of his Russian friends in high government posts and through them Baedeker obtained a prison visitor's permit valid throughout Russia. He held this permit for eighteen years, visiting prisons and penal institutions right across Russia to Sakhalin Island and preaching to desperate men and women the good news of a risen Savior. He was also able to visit and encourage various groups of believers when persecution against evangelicals was stepped up later in the century.

By the end of World War I there were over 700 Brethren missionaries on every continent of the world and many of the islands. In a little book called Back to the Beginning, published in 1919, the author Thomas Baird estimates that more than that number had died since Anthony Norris Groves first went out, many of them through sickness. A few suffered martyrdom through violence, like Mr. and Mrs. H.C. Kingham and their tiny daughter Gracie, who in 1900 were beaten to death by an infuriated Chinese mob. We close this chapter with a tribute found in The History of the Plymouth Brethren by W.B. Neatby, published in 1901. This is the story of the Exclusive Brethren, and Neatby on the whole takes a dim view of the Independents. But he ends his comments with the following:

> Both at home and abroad the Open Brethren give themselves to mission work with ardor. Their stations are dotted over the face of the whole earth. They have added at least one, in Mr. F.S. Arnot of Garenganze, to the roll of the great pioneers of the modern missionary movement; and many other names, less famous, but perhaps no less worthy, might easily be mentioned. This is their truest glory.

The Foundations of Brethren Missionary Support

The first organization associated with Brethren that undertook the responsibility of home support for missionaries without performing the functions of a mission board was George Müller's Scriptural Knowledge Institute founded in 1834. It had three stated purposes:

1. To establish new day-schools, Sunday schools, and adult schools "in which instruction is given upon scriptural principles."

2. To circulate Bibles and New Testaments.

3. To aid those missionaries "whose proceedings appear to be most according to the Scriptures."

Over the years the Scriptural Knowledge Institute has aided thousands of missionaries and helped to start schools all over the world. Along with the George Müller Foundation, it continues its good work to this day.

Aside from Müller's work, there was no attempt to make known the needs of Brethren missionaries until 1853 when A.N. Groves returned home from India for the last time. Groves, very ill at this time, was greatly concerned about his fellow workers back on the field, as certain doctrines were circulating among the Brethren in England that discouraged interest in missions. He communicated this to the believers at the Tottingham assembly in London, and one of the men there, James VanSommer, began a newsletter, the Missionary Reporter, not long after. VonSommer's concept of support was "Every church a missionary society." In other words, he believed that missionaries should be supported and cared for by their sending assemblies. He carried on this good work of publishing missionary letters for nine or ten years, most likely at his own expense.

In 1860 two of the great men in the history of Brethren missions in England, John Maclean and William Yapp of Leominster, began to circulate a newsletter in support of the work in Italy. They called it Letters of Interest. Later they included reports from Spain, where workers had followed in the footsteps of Robert Chapman. When Henry Groves, eldest son of A.N. Groves, came home from service in India he assisted with this work. In 1872 Maclean, Henry Groves and another leading brother, Henry Dyer, commenced the foremost Brethren missionary service organization in the world, whose publication was called The

Missionary Echo (in 1885 the name of their publication was changed to the familiar Echoes of Service.) From nearly the beginning, the headquarters of this venerable organization has been at Whitecomb Crescent, Bath.

Back at Leominster, conferences were started in 1874 that had a strong missionary emphasis. Two or three of these were held each year for many years and did a great deal to build up the Brethren missionary force. At Bath, Groves and Maclean, the first editors of Echoes, undertook to distribute gifts to missionaries, and as the overseas force grew and with it all the complexities of keeping track of large amounts of money the organization became very important in dealing with government tax requirements. Until fairly recent times they kept records of all Brethren missionaries regardless of home country. In 1972 these records were compiled into a history of Brethren missions called Turning the World Upside Down.

We noted at the beginning of this book that Jim Elliot and the other martyrs of Ecuador, like all Brethren missionaries, went to the field without guaranteed salaries, trusting the Lord to supply their needs. It would be wrong, however, to believe that the early Brethren reserved the principle of living by faith only for so-called "full time workers." This would be to make a distinction between "clergy" and "laity," which they rejected entirely. The leaders and missionaries may have given up regular salaries by choice or necessity. But those at home who supported them faithfully, while still plodding away at their jobs, trusted God no less. For the Brethren, to "live by faith" is what it means to be a Christian.

6

The Exclusive Brethren and J.N. Darby 1848-1882

The Influence Of The Exclusive Brethren

In 1848 J.N. Darby, as we saw in chapter 4, circulated a letter cutting off Bethesda from fellowship with the other Brethren assemblies, and including also any congregation that sided with Bethesda in the Newton question. Thus with this edict Darby himself unwittingly created a new movement which came to be known as the Independent or Open Brethren. What Mr. Darby thought would happen is difficult to say, but it is certain that it was not the intention of the elders at Bethesda to secede. The new movement included the important congregations of Barnstaple, Hereford and Tottingham and Hackney in London as well as several smaller ones (see map). [Fig. 19]

Nevertheless, the Exclusives remained the main branch, with not only a larger number of assemblies in the United Kingdom but many in French Switzerland, France, Germany, and the Netherlands as well. The majority of the gifted leaders remained loyal to Darby, including the founders Edward Cronin, John Bellett, and George Wigram, and a number more were added. Among these were J.B. Stoney, whose teachings attracted a wide circle, the very influential William Kelly, whose gifts were recognized by Charles Spurgeon, and C.H. Macintosh, whose works on the Pentateuch (still in print) have had a considerable influence far beyond Brethren circles. [Fig. 32]

The Exclusive Brethren experienced much growth during the nineteenth century. Some of this was due to their extensive literature; Roy Coad cites eleven monthly magazines circulating from London, some reaching forty to fifty thousand readers. Many younger people converted in the revivals were attracted by the challenge of Bible teaching that seemed to go deeper than what was to be had elsewhere, especially in the study of the Old Testament. They were also drawn to the call of a highly disciplined lifestyle that seriously rejected the world and all of its attractions to follow Christ.

But the primary factor in the success of the Exclusives was J.N. Darby himself, his personal gifts and the immense influence that he wielded among perhaps 1,500 assemblies worldwide. Despite his great shortcomings, which we have dealt with elsewhere, Darby was a true prophet, mystic and "saint." From the 1820s he never had a settled earthly home. He traveled continuously, visiting America at least seven times for extended periods. His personal devotion to Christ was equal to that of the apostles, and is reflected in his exquisite hymns. He kept up an enormous correspondence, and maintained a personal interest in each of the gatherings loyal to him, regardless of how small. These factors all combined to make the Exclusive Brethren more widely known and influential in the nineteenth century than the Independents.

However, while the Exclusive Brethren made a substantial impact on the Christian church by stirring up renewed interest in congregational worship, in Old Testament prophecy and typology, and in separation from the world, they also gained notoriety by their intolerance, not only of Christians outside their circle but of any among themselves who happened to veer ever so slightly from their narrow line of orthodoxy. As W.H. Griffith Thomas, one of their not unfriendly critics put it, "The Brethren are remarkable people for rightly dividing the Word of Truth and wrongly dividing themselves." As long as J.N. Darby remained the unquestioned final authority there was, as we have pointed out, some thirty-five years of relative harmony and growth. But toward the end of his long life some of his less profitable and more Biblically questionable doctrines began to backfire, and to generate a bitter fragmentation process that, amazingly, is still going on. In one case it produced a bizarre cult that hit the headlines in Great Britain and has made the name "Plymouth Brethren" in Commonwealth countries synonymous with religious extremism. It is, sadly, the fate of the Exclusives (which to some extent the Independents share by association) to be known by the church at large for schism and sectarianism—the very things that Darby dreaded and loathed.

When we tell the story of Independent Brethren history in North America we will have more to say about the Exclusives on a somewhat more positive note. But for the record we will give here a brief summary of their first major division (or second, if you count the Bethesda split as the first), called the Kelly or Ramsgate Division of 1881. In this we have a classical example of how legalistic doctrine can do immense harm to the cause of the gospel.

The Kelly-Ramsgate Division was a direct result of the doctrine of the "Ground of the One Body" (chapter 3). It seems that an Exclusive meeting at Ryde on the Isle of Wight had been wrangling among themselves for many months over the marriage of a brother to his deceased wife's sister. Thus the meeting was considered by the Exclusives generally as out of order or "rotten." A clergyman named Finch had, meanwhile, become convinced of the Biblical manner in which the Brethren met and had left the Church of England to start a small Brethren-type gathering in Ryde. In this he was encouraged by the aged Edward Cronin, now associated with an assembly in Kennington, London. When Cronin in all innocence reported this to his Kennington brethren and also to Darby by letter, instead of rejoicing, there was great consternation. In their eyes Cronin had denied the unity of the body of Christ, as there could be only one body in any given place.

Illogical though it may seem, the Kennington leaders decided to disown the new congregation. But this was not enough for the decision-makers at the Central Meeting, who wanted Cronin (the very man who first "came out" to the new movement in the 1820s) excommunicated. Darby, perhaps reluctantly, concurred with this opinion. The Kennington brethren (to their credit) hesitated for some time, but finally sacrificed the godly old man. He was forced to occupy a place out of the circle of fellowship during the breaking of bread, where he is said to have sat weeping. Because of this hesitation, some hotheads at Ramsgate excommunicated the entire Kennington church. At this point the large-minded William Kelly refused to endorse such foolishness, and in the ensuing debate (which actually lasted for years) many meetings that looked to Kelly rather than Darby as their authority hived off. Eventually the entire movement worldwide was forced to side either with Ramsgate (backed by the Central Meeting and Darby) or Kelly.

As Harry Ironside points out in *A Historical Sketch of the Plymouth Brethren*:

> Kelly like Darby was not strong enough to control the zealots in his party! Soon the same rigid principles were seen in many of the so-called Kelly meetings.

And this was only the beginning! Before many years the Exclusives were divided again in England by the excommunication of the scholarly C.E. Stuart and in America by the major split-off of the followers of F.W. Grant. After Darby's death the main party was led by J.B. Stoney, and after him by F.E. Raven, who was the focal point of another split in 1890.[1]

A division in 1908 created the "Glanton Brethren," and eventually leadership fell to James Taylor, senior, and his son James Taylor, junior. Under the latter's control it left the pathway of orthodoxy altogether and became the cult referred to above.

The tragic record of the various divisions among the Exclusive Brethren—sometimes fragmenting a group of Christians to the point where members of the same family would refuse to eat with one another, and where strife has become so bitter that it has led to suicide and worse—is important to us for at least three reasons. First, it is an example of what can happen to any body of believers when doctrinal correctness becomes more important than love of the brethren. Second, it is the logical result of Exclusivism carried to its extreme. That is, the perfect pattern for the collective life of Christians is not clearly defined in the New Testament, and must therefore become a matter of interpretation. And ultimately believers are bound to disagree on interpretation. Third, the Independent Brethren are historically related to their Exclusive brothers and sisters whether they like it or not—to some degree they also bear the stigma attached to the name "Plymouth Brethren." Their past (and, alas, present too) is not without strife, so it is wise to refrain

---

1 The Raven division was of far-reaching consequences, affecting Brethren not only in Britain but on the Continent and in America. Details are found in the second volume of The History of the Brethren by Napoleon Noel, for scholars who are interested in such intricacies. It is interesting to note that Raven, like Newton and indeed Darby himself, got into trouble by trying to dissect the great mystery of the Incarnation. This, like most if not all central truths of the gospel, must remain for us a paradox until in glory we are permitted to penetrate deeper into the mind of God.

from excessive criticism. Furthermore, the Independent assemblies from time to time are able to welcome families who have left the Exclusives, and on the whole they are both godly and well taught in the Scriptures.

J.N. Darby's View of the Church

Darby's [Fig. 33] view of the church—what it is and what it is not—is central to what might be called "Brethrenism." It is, in fact, the key to the difference between Plymouth Brethren and all other churches. Much good has come from this, in that the Brethren have been one of the forerunners of "ecumenicity"—that is, that no artificial barriers should separate the true followers of Christ. But sadly, many of the misunderstandings and tensions that have plagued the movement in North America during this century have also sprung from differences revolving around this doctrine.

On this continent, Darby's view of the church was followed faithfully by the pioneers and their successors, as far as it was understood, and it is still perpetuated by the more traditional Independent Brethren assemblies.[1] But today, in all probability, few persons in the Independent Brethren assemblies study Darby's original writings on this subject (covered in a number of essays in his Collected Writings in the volumes entitled "Ecclesiastical"). As an aid to those who may know little or nothing about what J.N. Darby taught, the following is an attempt to summarize his doctrine of the church in everyday language.

First, Darby believed that the church as God intended it to be is what is described in Acts chapters 2-6: a visible congregation of believers filled with the Holy Spirit meeting together for teaching in the apostles' doctrine, for fellowship, for the breaking of bread, and for prayers (Acts 2:42). This church truly represented Christ here on earth.

---

1 The early Independent or Open Brethren assemblies in North America were virtually indistinguishable from the Exclusives. The one difference was the question of local independence versus central authority. But even in this matter the Open Brethren in a given area acted as though they were a federation, and held conferences, picnics and other events jointly. Also, anyone from an assembly in the network would be received at the Lord's Table in any other Open Brethren assembly on the continent if they presented a "letter of commendation."

It was a unified entity—there was only one church in Jerusalem in the beginning. It had a decent order with authoritative leadership, the believers shared all they had with one another in love, and overt sin was quickly judged and put away (Acts 5:1-6). But as time went on, the true church in various places became corrupted with sectarianism and immorality, was infiltrated by false teachers and ultimately became part of the world system. In Darby's vocabulary, it became "Christendom." There were still churches, but they were no longer a single unified body with Christ as their head. They were in ruins:

> The church is in a state of ruin; it has ceased to bear testimony to the glory of Christ, as it ought to have done, and as it did indeed at the beginning.

Second, because the church is in ruins, nothing we can do will restore it. True Christians cannot revive the church, cannot return it to what it was like in Acts 2-6. The reason the restoration of the church is impossible is not because there are no true Christians in it, but because it is not a single unity in Christ. Everywhere, the church is fragmented into numerous human organizations, most of which have a long history peculiar to themselves.

> That visible unity, where the Holy Ghost displayed his power, so that the grace and power of Christ, manifested in the body of the church, were seen by the world itself, because the Spirit of the Head dwelt in the body; where is, I say, that unity? It no longer exists.

Any church on earth today (Catholic, Anglican, Orthodox, Lutheran, Reformed, etc.), even though it may be thoroughly evangelical, preach the gospel and teach the Word, is not what God intended, because it still meets as such and such a church and finds its unity in that context. It does not find its true unity in Christ alone.

Third, Darby rejected the concept of the invisible church—that is, the idea that all born-again Christians everywhere constitute the church as God intended it to be. In his view, any visible gathering in the name of Christ, calling itself a church, is a church, though it indeed may misrepresent Christ more than represent him. God intended the church to be the visible body of Christ here on earth, so an "invisible church" is a contradiction in terms:

> I do affirm, that the church has been placed on earth to display, as a body, in a visible unity, the glory of its head, by the Holy Ghost. This it no longer does

. . . although the faithful are sure of being saved in glory.

Fourth, and perhaps most important, is that, in view of the ruined state of the visible, professing church, the only course for a child of God to take is to separate from it, leave it as Abraham left Ur of the Chaldees, and gather simply in the name of Christ alone. The key verse for this is Matthew 18:20:

For where two or three are gathered together in my name,
there am I in the midst of them.

The breaking of bread is such a gathering's outward symbol:

Here [in the breaking of bread] then are found the character and life of the church, that into which it is called . . . and in which alone is true unity.

Fifth, in Darby's view, Christians gathered in this way are a witness to the ruined churches around them of the true unity which God intended, and which could (and should) include all believers in any given place.

Our duty as believers is to be witnesses of what we believe . . . and as Christ is the faithful and true witness, such ought the church to be.[1]

The assemblies are unique in that they are made up of believers who have no other bond (such as a denomination, mission board, etc.) except their relationship to Christ. Those who are in the churches should "come out from among them" and unite with an assembly where Christ is the true head.

Sixth, in the local assembly, Christ is the one to whom each believer is responsible, rather than to the pastor, the elders, the consistory, etc. Therefore each believer ought to exercise his (or her) gift as unto the Lord, regardless of whether he finds everything that goes on in that fellowship to his liking.[2]

We thus see, that the principle of ministry is the active energy of love, of grace, flowing from the faith by which we know God . . . In its essence, ministry flows from individual knowledge of the master's character . . . We see, moreover, that it is the sovereignty of God, who gives, as he sees good,

---

1 When Darby uses the word "church" to refer to a Brethren assembly, he means it in the sense of the Greek term *ekklesia*—that is, simply a gathering or congregation of God's people.
2 This explains why the Brethren traditionally have disdained titles such as "the reverend," "minister," "pastor," "elder," or "deacon."

either natural capacity—as the vessel to contain the gift—or the gift, according to the measure of the gift of Christ . . .

Seventh, the local assembly or gathering of Christians to remember the Lord in the breaking of bread does not constitute a church:

> Plymouth Brethren . . . believe that they alone are assembled upon the true principle of the church of God . . . but they believe that the church is in ruins, and that the pretension to be the church of God in a place would be a false pretension.

Eighth, if the unity of the assembly depends on the relationship to Christ of each member, and evil is somehow introduced into that company, then unity is broken because Christ cannot reign in the presence of sin. Therefore judgment has to take place and the assembly must separate itself from the guilty person unless there is confession and restoration.

The church is to put out from itself the wicked person, and thus maintains its separation from evil. And unity is maintained in the power of the Holy Ghost and a good conscience.[1]

Ninth, and finally, if the sole basis for unity is fellowship with Christ, our universal head, and all assemblies everywhere are witnesses to that unity, then, if one assembly has unjudged sin in its midst it destroys the unity of the body because the aggregate of assemblies constitute the One Body. This doctrine made it right and even necessary for the assemblies as a whole to judge any one of the local congregations.

> . . . unity is the glory of the church; but unity to secure and promote our own interests is not the unity of the church, but [is] confederacy and denial of the nature and hope of the church.[2]

---

1 Darby's logic here seems to be that the assembly, even though gathered out from the visible church, ought to take the church in Acts 2-6 as its model. There, overt sin was quickly judged and put away. Charles Colson, in his excellent book on the church, *The Body*, agrees: "Accountability is a hollow concept unless it is enforced. There must be teeth in a church's demand for orthodoxy and righteous behavior; that is what we call discipline."

But, sadly, putting the papal power of excommunication into the hands of men in local assemblies also led to much abuse.

2 The "one body" concept as the basis for a federation of assemblies where the actions of all would be judged by a few goes back to George Wigram's suggestion to Darby in 1838 regarding a central "oversight" meeting in London (chapter 3). Evidently Darby somehow

(The above material has been abstracted mainly from the essays listed below, which appear in numbers 1 and 4 of "Ecclesiastical" in Darby's *Collected Writings:*
"On the Formation of Churches"
"Considerations on the Nature and Unity of the Church of Christ"
"Separation from Evil God's Principle of Unity"
"What Is the Unity of the Church?"
"Discipline and Unity of the Assembly"
"Churches and the Church"
"Remarks on the State of the Church")

---

failed to see what is plain to others outside the movement: that a network of congregations controlled by or answerable to a central authority constitutes a sect.

PART II

PIONEERING DAYS IN NORTH AMERICA 1871-1920

Brethren conference at Rose Isle, Manitoba, circa 1895.

7

The First Wave of Evangelism 1871-1900

Background of the North American Pioneers

In 1982 a study of Brethren origins in North America was presented as a master's thesis at Vanderbilt University by a young historian, Ross McLaren. In this thesis, titled *The Triple Tradition: The Origin and Development of the Open Brethren in North America*, McLaren documented a fact long suspected by some: the character of the Independent Brethren assemblies on this continent up to World War I was quite different from the network of churches aligned with Bethesda after 1848. Not only was the movement in North America like the gospel halls that sprang up in Britain in the wake of the Second Great Evangelical Awakening (chapter 5), in a number of important ways it followed J.N. Darby rather than Anthony Norris Groves in its principles and world view. How did this came about? With the exception of Richard Owens of Dublin (chapter 5), all of the first generation of Brethren pioneer evangelists in North America were Scotsmen and former Presbyterians. Not only that, but they were all interconnected with one another as missionaries serving the Free Church of Scotland, a split-off from the mainline Presbyterians. The Reformed or Presbyterian Church had been born through the heroic leadership of John Knox in the days of the Catholic Queen Mary of the Scots. It was founded on the Scriptures and the doctrines of John Calvin. In the seventeenth century the Covenanters, those who signed covenants in 1638 and 1643 to resist the establishment of a hierarchy of bishops, were severely persecuted. By the early nineteenth century, however, the Presbyterians had become the established church in Scotland, and were complacent. But their complacency was shattered in 1843 by what has been called "The Disruption."

At that time there were in the Scottish church a number of evangelical ministers, and in 1843, led by Thomas Chalmers, 474 of them seceded and formed the Free Church of Scotland, with Chalmers as moderator. A few years later Chalmers was developing an outreach for the gospel in the slum areas of Edinburgh and put a young man named Donald Ross [Fig. 35] in charge of one of the missions. In 1857, after a time of preaching on Sundays and working in a business during the week, Ross was called to serve God full time among the miners at New Mains, Larnarkshire. He took this step fearfully; he always said afterward that he was "squeezed out" into ministry. He proved himself as an evangelist at New Mains, where a number came to know Christ through his ministry, and later when a superintendent was being sought for the North-East Coast Mission with headquarters in Aberdeen, Donald Ross was chosen.

The work of the North-East Coast Mission was to bring the gospel to sailors, fishermen, and their families. Ross was well suited for this assignment, as God had used him among miners and their families, an equally poor, rough class of society generally neglected by the regular clergy. He moved to Aberdeen and in time gathered a team of some twenty or so evangelists, all of whom he selected personally. One of them, Donald Munro, later wrote:

> All the missionaries were not equal in gifts or graces, but there were in the mission some of the choicest spirits and most devoted men we ever met—godly, self-denying, and successful.

Ross had a struggle raising support to keep the mission going, but his greatest difficulty was the resistance of the ministers.

> As a rule, we could get the people of the coast to hear us, but this aroused the jealousy of the clergy to a fearful extent in some cases. Especially did the established church men dislike it, for they hated everything in the shape of Evangelicalism.

He and all the other evangelists became convinced from these experiences that there was little good in the organized church.

Toward the end of the 1860s Donald Ross was preaching at Aber-
lour, Banffshire, on the text, "Come out from among them and be ye
separate" (1 Corinthians 6:17). At the close of the meeting one of the
elders challenged him with, "But where are we to go?" Ross replied,
"That is what is troubling myself." Later he wrote:

> We were convinced that something was radically wrong with the
> churches. They were made up mostly . . . of unconverted persons; and the
> preachers did not seem to care for that, but, on the contrary, spoke evil of
> those who were converted, and of those whom God was using for conver-
> sions . . . we were beginning to think over the question whether it was not
> our duty to have no more fellowship with the thing that was simply an
> agency for the Devil to deceive souls.

The result was his resignation from the mission and the formation in
early 1870 of an independent fellowship of evangelists, the Northern
Evangelistic Society. At least two of those who joined him, Donald
Munro and James Smith, later became pioneer preachers in North
America.

In forming the new society, Ross makes it clear that he was still
unfamiliar with the Brethren:

> We knew nothing of gathering to the name of the Lord Jesus . . . We had
> heard of "Brethren," but only as bad, bad people, and we resolved to have
> nothing to do with them.[1]

But even as opposition increased against the evangelists, including a
widely circulated slanderous tract written by a certain Mr. M'Intosh of
the Free Church, so the preaching of the gospel drew crowds everywhere (many drawn by curiosity aroused by their enemies). As numbers of persons became soundly converted, the need grew for

---

1 * According to a research paper entitled *Scottish Brethren: Division and Wholeness 1838-1916*
by Neil Dickson, there were only five Brethren assemblies in Scotland before 1860. In this
period in history, Scotland was rapidly becoming industrialized and the population was
expanding. The old established religious order was inadequate to meet this challenge, thereby
providing a climate in which evangelism and inter-church cooperation flourished. Thus the
area was ready for the Second Great Evangelical Awakening, which followed after 1859. The
number of Brethren assemblies increased dramatically after 1860, but in most cases the people
had little or no awareness that they were part of a movement that had started some three
decades before in Dublin.

"believers' churches" that would provide teaching and fellowship built on the Bible. Ross saw only one pathway open to him: to leave the Presbyterian Church altogether, dissolve the mission, and for each evangelist to act independently as led by the Lord.

It should be pointed out that Donald Ross did not take advantage of his position as superintendent of the North-East Coast Mission or of the Northern Evangelistic Society to "steal sheep" from the Presbyterians. Munro writes:

> Neither Mr. Ross nor any of his co-workers had, up to this time, said a word in regard to leaving the churches, or even hinted at such a step. They still hoped for a "purging" of the unconverted ministers and members . . .

Letters from Ross to certain of the evangelists still exist, in which he condemns "unguarded words" that would arouse the wrath of the ministers. But as he and the others studied the New Testament they became more and more convinced of principles recognized and practiced by the Brethren, and also that where the truth about Christ is preached, division is sure to follow. Around 1868 he refrained from taking communion when he realized that the elements were being given indiscriminately to unbelievers. Later he was baptized by immersion in the River Dee. Thus, not by opposition, but by the force of his own convictions he was "squeezed out" of the Presbyterian Church.

At about the same time as the breakup of the short-lived Northern Evangelistic Society, Ross took over an unused chapel in the unsavory Gallowgate district of Aberdeen and began preaching regularly. There was also in Aberdeen at this time a small gathering of Christians associated with Brethren. He joined with them for the Lord's Supper on Sunday mornings, as it corresponded to the pattern he found in the New Testament. In fact, he had been present at a meeting in a joiner's workshop in Old Rayne somewhat earlier when a small company of independent believers had broken bread together for the first time. He was approached by the chief elder, John Ritchie (later well known among Brethren for his publishing ventures), with a proposal to unite the two chapels. At first resisting the move because of his deep distrust of any kind of religious organization, Ross eventually complied. Later he wrote: "Here it is where our link with those known as Brethren was formed."

Also during this period, 1871-72, the men who had had connections with Donald Ross in the Northern Evangelistic Society such as Donald

Munro also "came out"—that is, left the Presbyterian Church—and began to preach independently. Most of them found, as Ross did, that the Brethren model of autonomous local churches, where the Bible was the source of all teaching and Christians gathered simply in the name of Christ alone, met the needs of their converts very adequately. The result was, as Ross reports, that "all over the county and other counties of Scotland, and also in the north of England, meetings of this kind sprang up . . ." Thus it was through a movement quite unrelated to the events in Dublin and the south of England that these Scottish evangelists were prepared by God to be the pioneers of the Independent Brethren in North America. (The above quotes are from *Donald Ross: Pioneer Evangelist* edited by his son, Charles Ross, and *Donald Munro: A Servant of Jesus Christ* by John Ritchie.)

Beginnings in North America

Between 1871 and 1880 six of the Scottish evangelists associated with Donald Ross, as well as Ross himself crossed the Atlantic to do pioneer gospel preaching in North America. All but one eventually settled there. But before looking more closely at how this came about, we need to consider the view of the church that these remarkable men had. Their outlook actually corresponded closely to that of J.N. Darby's doctrine of the "church in ruins" (chapter 6). Ross and his colleagues, though perhaps not using this same terminology in the early days, saw no good in organized Christianity and turned their backs on the churches around them for the rest of their days.

Like Darby, these evangelists had come to their conclusions both through repeatedly butting heads with the clergy, and by exhaustive study of the Bible. Moreover, they were men who had won their right to preach through standing up and doing it in the hardest way possible, in public places, often in the face of ridicule and, occasionally, physical violence. Most were opinionated, absolutely confident of their position, and every one of them as austere and strict as the Pilgrim Fathers. They were not the kind of men one would want to argue with. Yet at the same time they were large-hearted individuals, able to laugh at themselves in the midst of hardship and adversity, and full of kindness. And for the gatherings they founded both in the Old World and in the New, they were the word of authority next to the apostles themselves.

Donald Ross is of first importance to the history of these North American assemblies, not only because he was the original leader under whom the others had labored, but because he was the founder and editor of the first Independent Brethren journals on this continent. It is from the journals that we gain what we know about Brethren theology in those early years. Ross began his journalistic career while still in Aberdeen, where in addition to a heavy preaching and teaching load he published four papers monthly: *The Northern Evangelistic Intelligencer; The Northern Youth*, a children's publication; *The Northern Evangelist*, a gospel journal; and *The Northern Assemblies*, which gave help to newly founded meetings. The first of the above became the *Northern Witness*, and then in 1887 under J.R. Caldwell, *The Witness*, which Roy Coad says "has proved to be one of the most enduring of all Brethren journals" (succeeded by *The Harvester*).

In 1874, Donald Ross moved to Edinburgh. While in Aberdeen he had opened a shop for the distribution of Christian literature, and did the same in Edinburgh, thinking to devote his time more to publishing and selling books and tracts. He also opened a shop in Glasgow. The Glasgow shop became the forerunner of the well-known British publishers Pickering & Inglis, but as Ross was a better evangelist than businessman, the others failed. It also was in Edinburgh that he began an assembly in his own home. During this time he was approached by the Exclusive Brethren, but refused to join them. As his son says:

> . . . his mind ever rejected their pretension to be able to draw a circle in Christendom, inside of which only were meetings that could be recognized, and outside of which nothing was to be owned in the way of assemblies of the Lord's people.

Ironically, Ross and his colleagues came very close to drawing just such a circle in North America.

The first of the Scottish evangelists to preach in North America was Donald Munro, [Fig. 36] who came to Parkhill, Ontario, in the fall of 1871.[1]

---

1 *I am pleased to include the photo of both Mr. and Mrs. Donald Munroe, as the wives of the early workers rarely got much public notice (nor did they particularly want any). But at this point in history we need to remind ourselves that they, too, served the Lord fully as faithfully as their husbands, without any of the esteem enjoyed by the evangelists in those days.

Munro had been conducting gospel campaigns in the villages and working-class districts for about twelve months with no letup, and the purpose of this trip was to visit his brothers who had moved to Canada and get a bit of change and rest. But before long he perceived that the churches in Parkhill were as devoid of spiritual life as those in the Scottish villages. In a letter describing this condition he says: The Methodist minister preached as if all the people were going to heaven, so he called them 'brethren.' The Presbyterian minister preached as if we were all unconverted, but he sent us to Moses for some preparation and improvement before coming to Jesus.

Munro hired a hall himself and began to preach nightly. After ten days he reported in a letter that "over a dozen profess to have closed with the precious Jesus."

While in Canada, Donald Munro had gotten a letter from Ross telling that he had received believers' baptism, a subject Munro had been struggling with himself. After returning in November he was baptized by Donald Ross in Aberdeen on December 31, 1871. Although he had been present at the Lord's table in the joiner's shop in Old Rayne in 1871, he was cautious about starting meetings of this nature. According to his biographer:

> The lack of light, and the fear of doing anything contrary to the will of God, prevented more being done in these early stages of the work of separation of God's people from the world's religion.

In early 1872, little meetings were springing up where the evangelists had been preaching, and these were encouraged by Donald Ross's paper, *The Northern Assemblies*. When Munro and John Smith began a campaign in Huntley it was not long before they, too, "spread the Lord's table" in their lodgings. This continued as a local assembly after they left.

Munro returned to North America in October 1872, making Toronto his home, and was soon followed by James Campbell and John Smith. [Fig. 37] He was joined by Smith at Parkhill in 1873, and the two resumed gospel preaching:

> The Word was again preached in power, the Spirit convicting many of sin, and of these a number were born of God, and set on the way to heaven, confessing Christ as their Lord in personal life. And when the gospel part of their labors had been completed, they taught those who had been saved the truth of believer's baptism, separation from the world's religion, and

gathering unto the name of the Lord Jesus. The result of this was that an assembly of believers was formed in Parkhill, according to the pattern given in the Word of God, which has continued all these years.

John Ritchie wrote that paragraph early in the twentieth century. In 1992 the Parkhill assembly was still in existence, certainly the oldest gathering of its kind in Canada.

Like Donald Munro, John Gill came to America for a visit in 1871 and returned for good the next year, making Boston his base. He did not itinerate like the others, but preached faithfully for most of his life in and around Boston. James Campbell founded assemblies in St. Louis, Missouri, and St. Charles, Minnesota, before going on to evangelize in Ireland in association with James Smith. After the death of Smith he was joined by William Matthews. Once the campaign in Parkhill was completed, John Smith moved to Cleveland, Ohio, which became his center of activity. Donald Munro made a visit to Scotland in 1876 and returned back across the Atlantic to Boston bringing Donald Ross with him. In 1879, Ross moved his family to Chicago. Sometime during this period John M. Carnie also began work in North America. Alexander Marshall, [Fig. 38] whose preaching made such an impact on residents of Ontario that assembly Christians in that area were called "Marshalites," came to Hamilton in 1879, eventually making Orillia his home.

One result of the kind of preaching done by the pioneer evangelists in North America was the making of disciples, both men and women, and the calling of the young men to preach and teach the Word. Munro comments on the remarkable number of young men in Ontario who became "gospellers," carrying on evangelistic meetings in this area. Under Munro's preaching, two outstanding young men were converted during the same week in 1874, William Faulknor [Fig. 39] and T.D.W. Muir.

After preaching for a time in Ontario, Faulknor sailed for Africa in 1887, joining Charles Swan at Mukurru in the kingdom of Garenganze opened up by Frederick Arnot. He thus became one of the first Independent Brethren missionaries commended from North America. Forced by illness to return in 1890, Faulknor faithfully served the Lord in the Los Angeles area until his death in 1906. Muir worked with Munro and Smith during his early ministry, then in 1881 moved to Detroit, which became his permanent home base. In later years he was one of the foremost speakers and writers among the Brethren.

We end this section with a rather amazing story about the beginning of the Independent Brethren work in Toronto, a city that over the years has played a very important role in assembly history. In 1874, in Berlin, Ontario, Donald Munro met a young bank clerk named John Ironside. He was from a place in Scotland, New Deer in Aberdeenshire, very familiar to Munro. Through Munro, Ironside "was led into soul liberty, and out from denominationalism to own Christ as Lord in assembly and in personal life." Shortly thereafter, the young clerk and his wife moved to Toronto, and both became very active in witnessing to their faith—so much so that John became known as "The Eternity Man."

When Munro and John Smith came to Toronto in 1875 to begin a gospel campaign they were unable to find an affordable hall. While walking the streets praying for guidance, they were met by John Ironside, who handed them a letter containing twenty-five dollars, the very amount needed. The five weeks of meetings became the fruitful start of much blessing later. And John Ironside? His and Sophia's first child was born in 1876, a boy named Henry Allan. That boy grew up to become Harry Ironside, one of the most prominent of the Brethren preachers and authors in the early twentieth century, and later the pastor of Moody Church in Chicago. Two years later, John Ironside was dead at the age of twenty-seven.

Pioneering from Coast to Coast

The first few decades in North America were ones of vigorous evangelism coupled with what we might today call "church planting." Often the gospel meetings would be attended by Christians from denominational churches, and these along with any who might have received the Lord for the first time were taught "assembly truths," usually beginning with public baptism by immersion. By the end of the century there were Independent Brethren assemblies, some with just a handful of believers and a few with more substantial numbers, scattered from coast to coast. As there were no "professional" pastors, the little groups depended much on the periodic visits of the traveling evangelists. But in the movement as a whole it is also quite amazing how much gift was exercised by the believers themselves, many becoming much better Bible teachers than the local clergy.

The work of an evangelist in those days was not for faint hearts. The only long distance transportation was by train or steamer, public accommodation in many places was spartan, and communication was limited to the mail (or the telegraph in an emergency). A paragraph from the biography of Alexander Marshall gives a vivid picture (edited slightly for clarity):

> From necessity as well as from choice the preachers were pioneers. Assemblies were few and far between, and if souls were to be won new ground must be broken up. They lived among the people, they lived with the people, shared their hardships, and fared as they fared. Fellowship in the gospel, and with the worker was on apostolic lines, and gifts were more frequently in kind than in coin. The scanty shelter from the rigors of winter meant enduring of much hardship, hair and beard being sometimes frozen when they awoke in the morning. But they were full of the joy of the Lord, and these things were made light of, provided they could carry the message of salvation to the needy, and be the means of pointing some sinner to the Savior.

The ranks of the pioneer evangelists continued to grow through immigration on through the '80s. John Knox McEwen came from Ireland to begin work in New York in 1879. In the early 1880s he pioneered in Nova Scotia, establishing the first assemblies in the Canadian Maritimes. Also from Ireland were William Matthews, the associate of James Campbell, and William J. McClure, who was converted through Campbell. McClure eventually went to the Far West where his base became Oakland, California. Other British evangelists who came in those early days were John Greer, David Rea, Richard Irving, J. Norman Case (a medical doctor who later went on to China) [Fig. 41] and Robert Telfer (see also Appendix III, Roster of Commended Workers). These names mean very little now, even to most people among the Brethren; the few records where they are found are long out of print. But they were great in God's Kingdom, both as faithful preachers of the Word and by giving character to the new network of assemblies through their selfless lifestyle.

Of great importance to both the Independent and Exclusive Brethren in Great Britain was the annual Bible conference, and this soon became true also in North America. [Fig. 45] In Canada, conferences were usually held over the Easter weekend, in May on the Queen's Birthday, over Dominion Day in July, or at Christmas or New Year's. In the U.S., the favorite times were the Fourth of July and Thanksgiving. When

Donald Ross accompanied Donald Munro to the U.S. in 1876 he ministered for a time among a small group in Boston that had been formed
just the year before. At year's end he journeyed to Hamilton, Ontario,
where the first Independent Brethren conference in North America was
held. [Fig. 55] Records indicate that a good number of new believers
were present. Ross and Munro were the speakers.

From Munro's biography comes the following description of those
early conferences: [Fig. 43]

> Most of such conferences continue for several days, giving ample opportu-
> nity for varied ministry to meet all needs, and enabling those who come
> long distances to have opportunity for Christian fellowship and inter-
> course with fellow-saints. There is no chairman, no appointed speakers, no
> time-limit to addresses, no appeals for money, and no collections. The
> offering taken on the morning of the Lord's Day, from those who assemble
> to "show the Lord's death," is devoted to meet the expenses of the meet-
> ings . . .

Simple meals were usually prepared by the women of the host assembly and served at the conference site. [Fig. 42] This made for a time of
relaxation and even a bit of fun, a relief from the intense seriousness of
the preaching. Overnight accommodations were also provided by the
local folk. We are indebted to Ernest Tatham for the following, taken
from an early Brethren conference announcement:

> For sleeping arrangements Bro. G. will provide the usual straw bed and
> bolster only. Therefore each person coming to the meeting will please
> bring his or her own outfit of blankets, sheets & towels. Brethren who
> travel from place to place in the Lord's service having no outfit will be
> provided for.

At the third Hamilton conference in January 1879 there was a visiting
speaker from England, Rice T. Hopkins of Birkenhead. Hopkins had
shared in the ministry with Donald Munro in the Orkney Islands some
years earlier, and was met at the pier in New York by Munro and
Richard Owens, formerly of Dublin. He raised the question why the
evangelists were not making use of tents in their itinerant preaching, as
was being done in Great Britain, and then held a special meeting of
assembly elders to bring this matter to their attention. The elders in turn
set about to alert their congregations to this need. Money was raised,
and within a year John Smith, Alexander Marshall, Donald Ross, John
Bain, J.M. Carnie, T.D.W. Muir, and John Martin were all making use of

tents. [Fig. 44] These temporary shelters served as missions for preaching the gospel and for Bible readings, as meeting halls for new gatherings, and often as living quarters for the preachers. Despite such inconveniences as heat in the summer, winds that occasionally blew them down, pranksters who cut the ropes, rain muddying the ground, and fleas, tents have been used for starting many an assembly right up to the present day.

So it was that in the summer of 1879 a tent was the instrument used for starting the first Independent Brethren gathering in Chicago, probably the most important U.S. city in their history. Here Donald Ross was assisted by James Goodfellow, son of a Canadian farmer and Ross's faithful helper for many years. Aside from this one companion, Ross was without a single friend or contact in this city. But he was undaunted. His son tells us that the rugged Scot actually enjoyed such a challenge:

> His chief delight in aggressive work was a tent. It was to him the symbol of gospel pioneering, and he fairly revelled in it.

The tent was pitched opposite Union Park, then on the west edge of the city, and before long a few believers were gathered to remember the Lord under the canvas. One of these was Caleb J. Baker, an awning manufacturer and dedicated mission worker, who became Ross's closest American friend and supporter. Baker paid a heavy price for this friendship, as he lost the support of many evangelical Christians who thought Ross a troublemaker and heretic. But he was convinced that the truth was on Ross's side. It was Baker who became the chief supplier of tents to evangelists all over the continent. Baker also was the designer of two charts used extensively by the evangelists. "Two Roads; Two Destinies" was a gospel chart. [Fig. 46] "Life or Death; Hades or Sheol" was a dispensational chart used to teach believers. Baker later moved to Kansas City and was a key figure in the development of assembly work in that city.

In early 1887 Donald Ross accompanied by James Goodfellow went west from Chicago to pioneer in California. In those days the train made this trip in a little under a week (because there were no dining cars, the train stopped every so often at trackside catering houses so passengers could get meals). The tent went along with them and was set up in San Francisco. There already was a Brethren assembly in San Francisco, whose primary leader was Charles Montgomery, a prominent businessman and hotelier. This, however, had been a meeting of the Grant Exclusive Brethren (chapter 12), but in 1888 they listed their meeting place as a gospel hall, an Open Brethren designation. The meetings were well attended and some persons were saved. In the summer, Ross and Goodfellow moved the tent to Oakland across the bay. Here there was also encouraging spiritual fruit, and Munro's biography tells us that "fifteen believers were baptized, and an assembly of about thirty was formed, their first meeting place being the canvas tent." In October of that year the combined assemblies held a conference in San Francisco, the first such gathering west of the Rockies, with Ross, Goodfellow and Munro (who had made the journey just for this occasion) as speakers. Thus a network of assemblies now reached from coast to coast.

The Barley Cake and Our Record

In January 1881, *The Barley Cake*, the first Independent Brethren magazine in North America was published in Chicago by Donald Ross. It has been noted that Ross had started four periodicals and two publishing houses in Scotland, so was well equipped for this venture. It was a small (6" x 9") publication of sixteen pages with rust-colored covers. In 1887 the name was changed to *Our Record*. [Fig. 47] Ross did the editing in his inimitable direct style until 1902, a year before his death, when his son Charles Ross took the helm. [Fig. 48] In 1911, T.D.W. Muir, who had long been a contributor, became editor and moved the place of publication to Detroit. He remained editor until publication ceased twenty years later.

The format of these first magazines remained fairly consistent throughout their lifetimes. The front cover sometimes had an editorial, sometimes ads for tracts, Bibles, etc., and in later years a table of contents. Inside were articles by the editor or others, either on Bible exposition along dispensational lines, or exhortations directed specifically toward members of the assemblies. Occasionally there were answers to practical questions (e.g., "Should a Christian be a member of a trades union?") or encouragement to live separately from the world (including denominational churches), to witness, to practice "church truth" such as believer's baptism and the weekly celebration of the Lord's Supper. Frequently there were articles from J.N. Darby, William Lincoln, and other Exclusive writers. Every issue included reports of the activities of various workers, announcements of conferences, sometimes letters from missionaries.

The material for the first twenty years under the editorship of Donald Ross, one of the most colorful characters in Independent Brethren history, contained many reports and observations on his travels that were lively and interesting. There are also concrete examples, poems, anecdotes, etc., that are missing under the later editorship of Charles Ross and Thomas Muir. In the following excerpt from Donald Ross's report on the tent campaign in Santa Cruz, California, July 1887, we see the work of a keen and talented observer:

> This place is a resort for fashionable sea-bathing, and for that purpose, probably, there is no better accommodation of its kind anywhere. About a week before July 4th, there were here thousands of well-to-do people . . . Talk of the "Aristocracy of England," we can assure our readers we have seen nothing anywhere more gaudy and showy; some of the crowd were men of money without the refinement needed, either natural or acquired, and women with painted faces having little delicacy, or feminine sensitiveness . . . On the 4th of July the whole town seemed alive with carriages, bicycles, and all kinds of fashionable turn-outs. Gay ladies accompanied by fashionable gentlemen were promenading everywhere . . . In the bay were all manner of yachts and sailing craft displaying a superabundance of bunting . . . Four or five bullet holes have been left in the tent, besides a tear at the bottom where some fire-works have been exploded while the preaching was in progress. These are our 4th of July tent ornaments.

But what was written in the periodicals was a major source of teaching concerning the particular views of the Independent Brethren on this continent. As McLaren points out, "What Ross printed was what had been and what was being preached and practiced by the evangelists." In the following excerpts from *The Barley Cake* and *Our Record* we illustrate some of those teachings peculiar to the movement during its first two decades:

December 1881 "Kirk Making" by Donald Ross

> At present all evangelistic efforts made inside the sects [i.e., denominational churches], though through them some may be saved, are as far as permanent results are concerned—if the converts are left within—in the shape of reproductive power, like filling up the Atlantic Ocean . . . To lead into, or encourage saints to remain in the sects is not only helping to

perpetuate the thing that is totally unscriptural, but it helps to lull into deeper sleep the unconverted

. . . The best thing that could happen to these sects is, that all saved by grace should turn their backs on them at once, then some at least of the unconverted who are their main supporters would get disgusted and begin to suspect that something is wrong . . .

January 1883 "What Church Should I Join?" by Donald Ross

Dear young believer—this is the Church of God as spoken of in the Scriptures; begun on the day of Pentecost by the descent of the Holy Ghost—at present being gathered out from the nations of the earth through the preaching of the gospel, having no earthly inheritance or potentate—separate alike from Jew and Gentile—One new man—One Holy Church—the Bride of Christ, to be completed and presented to Him when He comes. Of this body—the only one mentioned in the Scriptures—you are already a "member" . . . By the act of God you became a member of the Church which is Christ's body, on the day of your conversion, and you'll continue so, for all eternity. Hallelujah!

January 1886 "The Lost Day" by Donald Ross

That day is lost, in which I have not *learned something from the Word of God!* . . . That day is lost in which I have not done some *act of benevolence!* . . . That day is lost in which I have not gained some *victory over sin!* . . . That day is lost in which I have not enjoyed some *communion with God!* . . . That day is lost in which I have not sought *in prayer* some spiritual blessing for myself and others . . . That day is lost in which I have allowed myself to remain *unreconciled to a brother!* . . That day is lost in which I have not made some *advance* on my way to heaven! . . . The time is short-Christ is coming. Shall I not begin this day to do some of the neglected work for which I was sent into the world?

January 1889 from "Gospel Tent Work" by Donald Ross

We usually find the most flaming profession is like a huge wind bag which collapses instantly [when] it is pricked or probed by God's precious Word; and surely the convert who cannot bear God's Word, is not God's at all. Hence at our meetings at first, usually there is a fair attendance. Then the people ask about our musical organ and "musical conductors," and the other religious tom-foolery they are accustomed to, but there is none—the Word of God preached begins to grip—the audience falls off one by one. There are no sensations or testimony meetings, and the biting Word of God soon sends the chaff to the dust-heap; and afterwards when all of it goes, the very few grains of wheat left will get revived, and the conversions begin . . .

June 1893 "Principles of Gathering" by J.N. Darby

Donald Ross introduces the article with this note: "We reprint the following with pleasure. The practices of those who profess to have believed with J.N.D. show a sad departure from first principles . . . Ed." The entire text of Darby's article is given, the heart of which is as follows:

> The question is as to reception of saints to partake of the table of the Lord with us; whether any can be admitted who are not formally and regularly amongst us . . . Suppose a person, known to be godly, and sound in faith, who has not left some ecclesiastical system—nay, thinks Scripture favors an ordained ministry . . . Is he to be excluded because he is of some system as to which his conscience is not enlightened—nay, which he may think more right? If so, the degree of light is title to communion, and the unity of the body is denied by the assembly which refuses him.

December 1895 "Service" by Donald Ross

> Conduct your service with nothing but God—not with any particular set of persons. You may be comforted by fellowship, and your heart refreshed; but you must work by your own individual faith and energy, without leaning on any one whatever; for if you do you cannot be a faithful servant. Service must ever be measured by faith and one's own communion with God.

November 1900 "Brethrenism-What Is It?" by Donald Ross

This article, too long to give here, consists of extracts from J.N. Darby's paper written in 1828, "The Nature and Unity of the Church of Christ"—see chapter 3. In Donald Ross's introduction he clearly states his position with regard to the teachings of J.N. Darby:

> . . . we believe that Mr. J.N. Darby was in the very forefront of the battle, and hence we naturally turn to his writing to find the workings of the Spirit of God in the hearts of that devoted band whom the Lord called at this time to lift up His banner of truth for the gathering together of His own people scattered among the various parties of Christendom.

And finally—

October 1881 "A Word to the Ladies" by Donald Ross

In answer to a question in connection with 1 Peter 3:3 and 1 Tim. 2:9, we must confess that we are not educated in all the fashions that afflicted ladies for the last 2000 years. Therefore, we are not able to say with trustworthy authority whether the "plaiting," "braiding" and "banging" of the hair at the present time correspond with those of the past. We judge, however, the apostolic object was to check the vanity of Christian sisters, the expensiveness of nonsensical elaborations, and to restrain from ridiculousness in garb and appearance, lest the naturally timid, modest and retiring woman become a prominent object for vulgar gaze, to the injury of all concerned.

8

Tales of the Pioneers

Reaching Ex-Slaves in the Post-War South

James Wharton was somewhat an exception to what has been said earlier about the work of the pioneer evangelists in North America. His aim (from the little information we have about him) was to preach the gospel but not to plant assemblies. He was in the United States from 1880 to 1891. Donald Ross had a rather sour view of Wharton because he cooperated with existing churches. The following is a report from Wharton to the *Missionary Echo* dated December 1880:

> [New Orleans] has been my center of work since I arrived from England, and I am thankful to say that the gospel has been listened to night after night by eager and attentive hearers. Very many have professed conversion, and the unhappy features, telling of deep conviction of sin, have been exchanged for bright and smiling countenances, denoting the perfect peace that has taken possession of their hearts. At Straight, about thirty-eight were received into fellowship on profession of their faith . . . every night several have come forward for prayer . . . I hope that about twenty will be baptized shortly. . . One young man, long anxious, came last night to tell us he was converted. "De old man, de debil, tell me ober and ober again, Dere's plenty ob time for you yet. You's young, and you's only fooling wid dese people, and dey will be sure to laugh at you." But the young man had hearkened to the devil's lie long enough, and he said, "Laugh or no laugh, I'se going to start out for Christ; and thank God for such a mighty good Christmas gift, more dan I expected." This is one of the very many who tell what God has done for them in such simple, childlike words, which could only come from one who had experienced the new birth.

Richard Irving on the Frontier

Richard Irving attended the East London Institute founded by Henry Grattan Guinness, where he met James Norman Case. Case later joined Irving in pioneer work in the north of Ontario before going on to China. Irving continued to serve the Lord in Ontario well into the 1930s.

In the month of April, 1885, I heard from a young convert of a needy section of country about one hundred miles north of Belleville, Ontario, then known as the "backwoods of Ontario." This brother named Colp had just moved there and had taken up land a few miles outside the village of Bancroft. It is a very poor farming country and the settlers had small clearances, log houses, and log barns; everything bore the marks of poverty-so poor in fact that the ordinary preacher could not be supported. Brother Colp had cottage meetings, and the people responded so heartily that he urged me to go and preach the gospel among them.

I left Trenton the same month by rail for the greater part of the distance, but at that time there was no railway into Bancroft, so for the last twenty miles I traveled by stage, and over roads seldom seen now-a-days. I found brother Colp's house in the midst of forest, with perhaps twenty yards of clearance around it. We also found, among these humble settlers, converted people of the old fashioned Methodist type. They listened hungrily to the gospel, preached perhaps in a simpler way than they had previously heard it, with constant reference to the Scriptures.

The Bible became a new book to them. It caused a stir among these people and many were saved; others were established. It was not difficult to teach what the Word of God said about salvation and the "things which accompany salvation." They had a desire to know the will of God and to do it. The ordinances of baptism and the Lord's Supper were quickly understood, as also what the Word said about His coming. Soon *The Table* was spread, and a small company assembled in His name alone and partook of the emblems, bread and wine, showing forth His death, and the Lord's Supper had a new meaning to these simple, humble believers.

Thus in this simple way this first assembly was formed in that locality after what we believe to be the New Testament Pattern, and after fifty years it is still in existence. (From a letter by Richard Irving in *Light and Liberty*, December 1935.)

T.D.W. Muir Remembers His First Visit to Michigan

Muir [Fig. 51], who was born and raised in Canada, resided in Detroit, Michigan, for most of his life, and this area was the center for his extensive ministry. Below is the account of his first visit to Michigan, which took place in 1881:

A sister who had been saved at meetings in Canada and was desirous of having the gospel preached in her native town, elicited from me a promise that I would go there when the way was open. Receiving word that the time was propitious I started out to keep my promise. The trip had to be made partly by train, and the latter half of the journey had to be negotiated by stage-coach, and as it happened on this occasion that my train arrived later than the time of departure of the stage, I had to stay over in a little country town until the next day. My cash in hand was at low ebb and I found I would have to economize to reach my destination, and so I spent most of my capital in renting a room at the station "hotel," purposing to save on my lunch and supper by eating some crackers and cheese that I had brought along with me.

After my first frugal meal I went to spy out the land, and found in the center of the town what looked like a good pulpit for an open air meeting, the covering over a tank which contained a supply of water for use in case of fire. I went to all the houses and stores and left tracts in each with the announcement that a gospel meeting would be held that evening at 7 o'clock. The school teacher also gave me permission to announce the same to the children under her charge and I left a supply of tracts for them to take to their homes.

After canvassing the whole place I returned to my room for a rest, as a severe headache had developed from the want, I suppose, of my accustomed cup of tea, and I lay down and was soon fast asleep. When I awoke with a start my headache had developed in the "splitting" kind, the room was pitch dark, and I began to reason with myself as to the advisability of holding a meeting at all. "It was dark, it was late, the people wouldn't come, my headache was intense; better let it go." But the enemy's advice did not prevail. I sprang up, struck a match, found it was still a quarter of an hour before seven o'clock, and armed with a supply of tracts I started off. There was hardly any light to guide one in the street, only the feeble rays from the lamps in the few store windows, and when I got to my "pulpit," not a soul was to be seen.

However I mounted the platform, began to sing a gospel hymn, and soon I was able to recognize, as my eyes became accustomed to the darkness, that I had quite an audience surrounding me. A second story room just across from the fire-tank was lit up, but after a short time the light there was extinguished, and I began and continued my preaching in the dark. After I had delivered the message of salvation I said to the people, "Now, you have all had tracts already, but I have a fresh supply of different kinds, and if you please accept them, they are yours." They were readily taken and the people dispersed to their home, all but one man who greeted me with these words: "Elder," (I was just then turned twenty years of age), "Elder," he said, "I wish you would come to my house and spend the night with me."

"I am sorry," I said, "that I cannot accept your invitation, as I have engaged a room at the hotel: otherwise I would gladly have gone with you." "Well, elder," he said, "I would like to talk with you and if you don't mind I will walk with you to the hotel." This we did and on the way he unburdened his mind to this effect:

"Some time ago my wife died. At the funeral just as her body was being lowered into the grave, this thought struck me with great force: If that were your body that is being lowered into the grave, where would your soul be?, and that question has haunted me ever since and I have never got it answered. I went to the preacher of one church in town, and he said I should join the church. I joined the church but he was not able to solve the problem that tormented me. I went to another minister and he told me I should be baptized and join his church. I did so, but was no nearer a satisfactory answer to the terrible question. I have drove [driven] to every church within a twenty-five mile radius of this town, and put the question to every preacher, and not one has been able to dispel the darkness of my mind or solve the difficulty. Tonight I was in the lodge-room across from where you were preaching and when you began singing the hymn I got the meeting adjourned to go and hear the preaching. And as I listened to what you had to say I felt and believed that you could help me to get an answer to that awful question that pursues me night and day."

[Muir and the man walked back and forth talking until eleven o'clock that night, and at last the man was able to find peace through believing in the Lord Jesus Christ. Muir kept track of him, and found that he was genuinely saved.]

At last I went into the hotel and being very thirsty I said to the bar tender, "Will you please show me where I can get a glass of water?" "You can't get any water here. You can have beer or whiskey but no water." I discovered that the proprietor of the hotel was out of town and that this man was in charge during his absence. I said to him, "I am a guest in this hotel. If the proprietor were here I am sure he would accommodate me with all the water I want. I request you to show me the water tap so that I may help myself." After a long and persistent refusal he realized that he could not sell me any liquor and at last very reluctantly he showed me where the faucet was and there I was able to quench my thirst. As I was drinking the water, I said "Friend, have you ever had a draught of the water of life?" to which he replied, "I don't know what you are talking about" and so left me.

[Muir retired to his room, but was soon disturbed by loud knocks and kicks on his door, then banging on the piano in the next room and clashing of tin pans. Knowing that this was the bartender and the waitress having fun at his expense, he retired and was soon asleep despite the noise. The next morning the waitress was very sheepish as she served him his breakfast and listened to his brief gospel presentation. While waiting for the stage coach he was approached by another young man who had heard him preach and wanted to ask some questions. He found the young man very interested in salvation.]

Soon I was away on the coach to my destination and found on my arrival that the only place where I could have gospel meetings was a school-house that had no lamps for the necessary illumination in night services. As I distributed tracts in and around the little town I saw a man working in a field of turnips. I accosted him and after inviting him to the meetings I inquired if he would sell me a half dozen of his turnips. He said "You can have them for nothing, but whatever do you want with half a dozen turnips?" My answer was "If you will come to the meeting to-night you will see your turnips." By cutting the turnips in two, and scooping out a hole in the center of each half I was able to fit the turnips into the brackets where the lamps used to be placed, and found the illumination was quite sufficient for the meetings, and the farmer was there that first night and saw his turnips, and the use to which they had been put.

[The meetings were well attended, souls were saved and Christians revived. Muir was given use of the deserted Baptist church, and many came to hear. He also preached in the open air on market days.]

A chair did duty as a pulpit and a kerosene lamp, hung on a post, supplied the needed light for reading the Scriptures, except when some wag would come along and extinguish the light by blowing down through the chimney. This last annoyance occurred several times one evening necessitating relighting, until a somewhat intoxicated Irishman came to my rescue by posting himself at the lamp and announcing to all and sundry that whoever sought to touch that lamp would have to reckon with him. There was no further interference that night.

[The old Baptist man where Muir was staying asked Muir on behalf of the congregation if he would stay and be their pastor. He offered Muir $600 a year. Muir decided to have a little fun with his host.]

"But," I replied, "suppose that I should *need* $1000 a year to carry on my work, what would you say to that?"

"A thousand dollars! What would a young man like you need $1000 for? It is out of the question."

"But," I insisted, "suppose I should *need* $1000?"

"No, $600 is all we can possibly give you and let me tell you we will have a hard struggle to get even that."

"Well, in that case," I answered, "I think I will just continue with my present Master, for He has promised to supply *all* my needs, whether it is $600 or $1000."(From *Assembly Annals*)

John Knox McEwen: The "Umbrella Man"

John Knox McEwen was born in Northern Ireland in 1853 to a family of strict Presbyterian "Covenanters." He received Christ as his personal Savior through the preaching of James Campbell and James Smith in 1874, and before long began to preach—and to go through the "school of hard knocks" that served as boot camp for Brethren evangelists. On more than one occasion he was threatened by a mob with beating or lynching, was the target of rotten eggs, and was even personally assaulted. Once while giving out tracts in a railway carriage a woman pounded him in the face with her fists while the people in the car laughed and cheered. In his early career he concentrated on the city of Belfast, preaching in the open air and under canvas. He adopted the method of John Hambleton (chapter 5) of having Scripture texts printed on large sheets of paper which were fastened to boards and carried about the streets to gather a crowd. At times a thousand or more people would be drawn to hear the message.

McEwen was blessed with a ready wit, a trumpet-like singing voice, and plenty of courage. He felt burdened for the financial community of Belfast and came up with the idea of having Scripture texts painted on a large umbrella. With this he walked up and down in front of the stock exchange so that the traders could easily read "The wages of sin is death" and "Peace through the blood." McEwen's umbrella became the talk of the city, and the evening paper carried a long editorial about it. He would often appear with the umbrella or a gospel banner in some crowded place and sing hymns. He could be heard for blocks! He even tried displaying his large signs from the open top of a moving two-decker trolley, but was ordered off by the conductor.

After preaching in Edinburgh and in the Orkney and Shetland Islands, McEwen sailed for New York in May 1879 and was met by his brother William who had preceded him. In New York City, entertained by Mr. and Mrs. Richard Owens, he held store-front meetings. One young man who was saved in those meetings was W.P. Douglas, who later served the Lord for over sixty years.

McEwen joined T.D.W. Muir for tent work in Toronto during the summer and later pioneered on his own in Ontario and then in 1882 in Bay City, Michigan. Here on one occasion he was actually given police protection from a mob that planned to tar and feather him. Next he visited Boston, joining John Gill in preaching on the Commons, and then Philadelphia, his brother's new home. Upon his urging, James Campbell came over from Ireland in 1884 to hold meetings, and through this a flourishing assembly was planted in Philadelphia.

It was in the winter of 1883 that John Knox McEwen pioneered in Nova Scotia, the legendary land of Evangeline on the Atlantic seaboard. He arrived in Amhurst on a train from Ontario at a time of freezing cold, alone and without a single contact. The first thing he did was to go into an empty stable and, on his knees on the frozen floor, cry out to God. Then he went along the main street and began to give out tracts. One man looked at the tract he was handed and said, "There was a man here last week giving similar papers away." McEwen inquired and found out that this man lived at Leicester, twelve miles away.

He made arrangements to drive to Leicester with the postman on his sleigh. Drifts from a recent snowstorm made the road dangerous. Several times the sleigh overturned, pitching the two men and the mail sacks into the snow. At last they arrived at the farmhouse where the tract distributor, a young Irishman named Samuel Wallace, was renting a room. McEwen inquired for Wallace, and when the young man appeared he stuck out his hand and said, "I'm going to heaven!"

"Praise God," said Wallace grasping the outstretched hand, "So am I!"

J.K. McEwen and Samuel Wallace began a work for the Lord in Port Howe, which was soon accompanied by a great spiritual response, as well as by much opposition. Before long, thirteen believers were baptized in the river there, and another baptism followed that drew a large crowd. Eventually assemblies were established in Port Howe and at Doherty Creek (later called Pugwash Junction). The converts became known derisively as "McEwenites" and suffered much abuse. Most persisted faithfully, however, and gospel halls are to be found in these two places today (as well as in numerous other towns and cities in this province).

McEwen returned to Britain, married in 1889 and returned to Nova Scotia with his wife. In later life he became an international figure, preaching widely in England, Ireland, and Scotland and crossing a number of times to North America. He died in 1944 in his ninety-first year, active to the end. Two nephews, Sam and Hugh McEwen, later served the Lord among the Brethren in the U.S. and Canada for many years. (From *John Knox McEwen and Pioneer Work In the Maritimes* by John T. Dickson)

9

The Movement Becomes Established 1900-1920

The Independent Brethren as a United People

The evangelists who pioneered in North America were convinced that they were offering a Biblical alternative to the organized church by encouraging the formation of local assemblies to break bread, study the Bible, pray, and evangelize. By 1900 a network of such assemblies had developed throughout the continent. Each assembly was autonomous and governed its own affairs as well as it could. The members in each place saw their gathering as a witness to the true unity that characterized the church in Acts 2-6, and made it clear that they gathered in the name of the Lord Jesus Christ alone. But continent-wide the Independent Brethren assemblies were closely connected with one another (and to no one else) by conferences, by a periodical, by a common system of biblical interpretation (Dispensationalism), by reading the same books, and by supporting the same missionaries. They were, in reality, a united people.

Perhaps the most powerful bond that unified the Independent Brethren in those early days was the relationship of the evangelists to their converts and to members of the assemblies that they started or visited over the years. These congregations quite naturally emulated the ministering brother who pastored them. As Donald Ross says:

> Assemblies of believers take their character largely from their first gospel preachers. The converts generally imitate the preachers, and the more excellent these are, the greater and more general the imitation of them is.

The rejection of any sort of church hierarchy or special class of individuals, set aside to serve local churches as pastors and ministers, meant that the local congregations looked to the traveling evangelists for authoritative Bible teaching and pastoral care. As these servants of the Lord moved from place to place, their teaching welded the network of assemblies together in doctrine and outlook. This applied to interpretation of Scripture and also to any strong opinion the evangelist might have about the Christian life. The influence of certain men like Ross, Munro, and Marshall was especially powerful as these and others endeared themselves to the saints by sharing their homes and their lives, giving counsel to husbands and wives, and becoming fast friends with Christian families all over the country.

Through the evangelists, the early assemblies were taught their unique position as a remnant people, outside the professing church. Below is a lengthy quote from John Ritchie's biography of Donald Munro (slightly edited for clarity) which clearly shows the great degree to which the North American evangelists drew upon Darby's view of the church (chapter 6):

> When Mr. Munro and Mr. Smith began their labors in Ontario, there were very few believers known to be assembling simply in the Lord's name, according to the pattern given in the Word. Now there are very many of such companies, some small, and others large, here and there, in large cities, in country villages, on prairie farms, from the Atlantic to the Pacific Coast. [These have been] brought into existence by means of the gospel faithfully preached to sinners, resulting in conversion, and the truth plainly spoken to saints, resulting in their separation from the world. [Thus they have come] clear out from its religious sects and systems, to assemble as the Word of God commands, according to the pattern given in the Epistles, which is to be our only guide throughout the present dispensation.
>
> Man has no more right to frame his own plan of Church constitution, to devise his way of worship, to set up his systems of ministry and government, than he has to create a new gospel, or make a human way of salvation. The same living Lord in heaven, who gave His gospel to Paul (Gal. 1:6-12) apart from man or his teaching, gave to him the plan and pattern of His Church in all its details—(see 1 Cor. 11:1 to 16:37) and he as a wise master-builder used that plan (1 Cor. 3:16) in the formation of those churches which he, and others, as 'God's fellow-workers' (1 Cor. 3:9, RV)

were permitted to gather. And this pattern has been recorded in the Word, which we are told is all-sufficient for all the days until the Lord shall come, and the testimony of His Churches as lampstands holding forth His light on earth (Rev. 1:20) shall cease.

Two Great Second Generation Pioneers

North America in the early twentieth century was just beginning to feel the effects of modern science and technology. In the cities, streets were being paved, electric trolleys were replacing horse cars, and the main thoroughfares were garnished with a forest of overhead wires. Many homes were getting telephones and replacing gas lamps with electrical fixtures. A network of trains, ferries, and steamboats connected the smaller towns with urban centers. The automobile, in particular the model-T Ford, was successfully competing with the horse and buggy as a popular means of private transportation. But in the more remote places people still lived much as their forefathers had done, and there were many lonely settlements opened up by the railway on the edge of what was still an undeveloped wilderness.

Around the turn of the century one man began to devote his life to bringing the gospel to men and women on the Canadian frontier. His name was J.J. Rouse. Another man began a life of traveling evangelism and ministry that was to take him to nearly all the forty-eight states and many other countries of the world. His name was William J. McClure.

J.J. Rouse

Rouse [Fig. 50] was born in 1869 on a farm in Ontario, Canada, not far from Orillia. His family were staunch Congregationalists, and on one occasion Rouse and his youthful cronies broke up a tent meeting where Alexander Marshall and others were preaching. Later, however, his elder sister associated with a little assembly of "Marshallites," as the Brethren there were called. Saved in his teenage years, Rouse felt called to the mission field, and at the age of twenty-three attended college in preparation for this goal. He encountered Donald Munro at a Brethren conference which he attended out of curiosity, and became convinced that ordination is not taught in the Bible. Not long afterward he was baptized, and joined James Goodfellow in evangelistic work throughout Ontario. Their home was a yellow, horse-drawn Bible carriage with Scripture verses all over it.

In the fall of 1897, Rouse struck out on his own, visiting the Muskoga and Parry Sound districts, where the land is extremely poor and in consequence the people impoverished. As no trains went there he used what he whimsically called his "footmobile," sometimes walking distances of twenty-five or thirty miles to reach a handful of needy folks who were willing to listen to the Good News. On one occasion he took a "short cut" across fourteen miles of frozen lake, the last few miles dragging two tree poles when the ice was beginning to crack beneath him. Of this first winter as a pioneer he says,

> Walking about carrying my Bible, tracts, and some clothing (the latter never increased my burden much), and having meetings in homes and school houses, as the doors were open, although suffering physical privation, yet happy in the Lord, and conscious of the fact I was not building on another man's foundation (Rom. 15:20) helped deepen the joy.

For some eight or nine years Rouse preached the gospel throughout Ontario, seeing assemblies planted in Wyebridge, Bracebridge, Kearny, Huntsville, and an unnamed settlement on the north end of Lake Temiskaming. He was married to Eva Russell during this period, and in 1905 he and his wife moved to Edmonton, Alberta. At this date there were no Brethren assemblies between Brandon, Manitoba, and Vancouver, British Columbia. By the time the Canadian Northern Railway reached Edmonton in 1907 a meeting was established in Edmonton, which soon doubled in size with the rise in immigration.

By 1908, when the Rouses once again moved westward to Vancouver, they left behind in Alberta five new assemblies. From his base at Ladysmith, Vancouver Island, the evangelist worked much of the time during the next dozen years in the northern frontier towns of Vanderhoof, Fort Fraser, Smithers, Myworth and Prince Rupert. Returning to the prairies in 1921, Rouse made his home at Calgary and continued to pioneer in the forgotten backwoods settlements for another several years until his health broke. When unable to pioneer, he continued his public ministry until close to his death in the late 1940s.

J.J. Rouse represents the essence of the way the pioneers viewed the relationship of the church to the world. In one place he says,

> In the Gospels we have the commission or authority to go into all the world and preach the gospel to every creature. In Acts we have the history

of the disciples going, and in the Epistles we have instructions as to how to carry on the work. And I notice in 1 Cor. 12 where you have the local assembly and the gifts, there is no mention of evangelists. I take it to mean that the place for evangelists is out in the world and not in the assembly, but in this day you would think the Scriptures said go ye into all the assemblies . . .

William J. McClure

McClure [Fig. 49] was born to a blacksmith and his wife in Banbridge, County Down, Northern Ireland, on Christmas Day 1857. He was born again in 1874, the year of the Moody-Sankey meetings in Belfast, through reading 1 Peter 2:24 and Isaiah 53:5-6. While working in a foundry in Belfast he attended tent meetings of James Campbell and James Smith and became convinced of the priesthood of all believers and of other truths held by Brethren. Later he said that this was "like a second conversion." McClure started to prepare for the Baptist ministry, but through the preaching of David Rea he began to meet with the Christians at Old Lodge Road. In company with a number of young men who were exercised about serving the Lord in those days of revival, he grew rapidly as a preacher and excelled in the typology of the Old Testament as taught by C.H. Macintosh. In 1881 he left for America and, together with Robert Telfer and Kenneth Muir, associated with Donald Ross in the new work in Chicago.

Like Rouse, William McClure was a pioneer gospel preacher and tent worker, using charts both to evangelize and to teach the saints. He conducted many campaigns in areas where there was no assembly and helped to establish meetings in many places in the U.S. and Canada. He differed from Rouse in that he never married, traveled worldwide, and during his later years ministered at conferences from coast to coast on a more or less regular basis. He was also an accomplished writer, contributing numerous articles to *Our Record* and other periodicals as well as composing a collection of poems. By the time of World War I he was one of the best-known Brethren preachers on both sides of the Atlantic.

In 1883, McClure left his work as a lathe operator in Chicago to serve the Lord full time, commencing with tent work in Ontario. He labored in Ontario for ten years together with W.P. Douglas, Robert Telfer and, later, William Hunter. Accompanied by Andrew Fraser, he went west to Oakland, California, in 1893, meeting for the first time John McIntyre, whose home he called his own for the rest of his days. Joined by Hunter, he held meetings in Portland, Oregon, culminating with the building of a hall on Stark Street. He continued north, holding meetings in Victoria and Vancouver, and then in the fall of that year ministered to a group of believers in Los Angeles. Through this work the West Jefferson meeting was established. With the exception of a preaching trip east with Donald Ross in 1896 and a visit home to Belfast in 1900, he remained in the West until 1902.

From 1902 onward McClure's travels became too extensive even to summarize. He preached in virtually every major population center in North America from Texas to the Maritimes and New England to San Diego. He visited and held meetings in Northern Ireland, England, South Africa, New Zealand, Australia, Palestine, Japan, and China. When World War I broke out he drew large crowds with his messages on prophecy. Year by year he was a greatly welcomed participant in annual conferences in New York, Boston, Philadelphia, Detroit, Los Angeles, Oakland, and an assortment of smaller places. A tall, imposing figure in his prime, McClure always commanded an audience in open-air meetings. Among the saints he was beloved as a wise counselor. The Lord took the elderly veteran home in 1941 shortly before his eighty-fourth birthday, and within a week of the homegoing of his lifelong friend John McIntyre.

Assembly Growth 1871-1920

We have seen how 1871 was the year of beginnings for the Independent Brethren in North America, with Richard Owens of Merrion Hall, Dublin, moving to New York (chapter 7) and Donald Munro beginning to preach at Parkhill, Ontario, while on a visit to his brother. By 1879 at least ten gatherings were established. Two years later, in 1881, Donald Ross started circulating *The Barley Cake* from his home in Chicago, and from this first journal we learn the names of thirty-three pioneer workers. Conferences that year were held in Chicago over Thanksgiving, and at Hamilton, Ontario, over the New Year's holiday. Evangelism and church planting were going forward in thirteen states—Maine, Massachusetts, New York, Pennsylvania, Maryland, Ohio, Indiana, Michigan, Illinois, Iowa, Nebraska, Missouri, and Louisiana—plus some twenty-five places in Ontario, Canada, and in Nova Scotia. There were also gatherings in Minnesota and the Canadian Northwest Territories. A letter from the Northwest reads:

There are thirteen of us who meet in *Jesus Name* alone to break the bread . .
Out of these, eight have been saved within the last three months, and
other three, God brought to see through His word, the Scripturalness and
propriety of gathering to no other name but Jesus. In our great weakness,
isolated and alone, God saved these few dear souls, [some of whom] . . .
walk as much as 12 miles on the Lord's Day morning to meet Jesus.

In the summer of 1881, gospel tents were used for evangelism by various brethren in Ontario, Detroit, New England, and the Chicago area.
Most of the pioneer work was carried out in rented halls and store
fronts. The believers generally met in homes at first, or in temperance
halls and the like above shops. Open-air work was standard, along with
door-to-door visitation and tract distribution. Evangelists continued
coming from the "Old Country," supplementing the ranks of young
men on this side who took up the challenge after their conversion. By
1900, seventy-six brethren were mentioned in the workers' sections of
Our Record. Pioneering and assembly planting had spread to Georgia,
North Dakota, Colorado, New Jersey, New Hampshire, Virginia, Kansas, Oregon, and California in the U.S., and in Canada to Manitoba and
British Columbia.

Early in the twentieth century several of the gallant Scottish pio-
neers finished their earthly journeys and fell asleep in the Lord. Donald
Ross died in 1903, James Campbell in 1904, Donald Munro in 1908. John
Smith lived on into the second decade, until 1913. Their places as "chief
men" in North America were taken by William McClure, Charles Ross,
T.D.W. Muir, William Beers, William Hunter, E.A. Martin, A.N. O'Brien,
John Rae, and others. In 1900, conferences were held in the major cities
of Toronto, Detroit, Philadelphia, Chicago, St. Louis, Kansas City, New
York, Richmond, and San Francisco, and in smaller places in Ontario,
New England, and the Mid-West, at least twenty-four conferences in all.
The use of gospel tents during the summer had also increased dramati-
cally.

Statistics on the growth of the Independent Brethren during the
earliest years are not available, as Walterick began publishing the Assembly *Address Book* in the late 1930s (Loizeaux Bros. published the first
Exclusive address book in 1878). We do have U.S. census figures, however, as follows:

	Groups	Members	Sunday schools
1906	128	4752	93
1916	129	5923	101

The significance of these figures is that the most rapid growth in assembly planting took place between 1871 and 1906, with virtually no new assemblies planted in the next decade. In the ten years between 1906 and 1916, however, the existing gatherings grew in membership by nearly twenty-five percent. Following World War I, as we shall see later, there was another dramatic increase in new assemblies. By 1920 we find over 135 workers in twenty-three states and all six Canadian provinces. Compared to other evangelical groups such as the Baptists, the numbers of Brethren workers and assemblies by 1920 may seem minor. But they were beginning to have, and during the next four decades did achieve, a phenomenal impact for the gospel and Bible teaching in North America far beyond the scope of their own circle of churches.

Life Among the Saints

By the end of World War I (November 11, 1918) and the period of recovery that followed, many of the assemblies that had been started by the evangelists in the U.S. and Canada had become well established, and in some cases fairly large. During the first decade of the twentieth century a number built their own gospel halls (though some of the early evangelists, Donald Ross in particular, were very much against Christians owning property). The old gospel halls seem to have been designed *not* to look like a traditional local church. Most of them vaguely resembled schoolhouses or lodges of fraternal orders, except that they had Scripture verses both on the building itself and sometimes on detached notice boards. The name, *such-and-such gospel hall*, was usually prominent, and the notice board would inform passers-by that this was the meeting place of "Christians Gathered in the Name of the Lord Jesus Christ." Normally the advertised meetings consisted of the Lord's Supper at eleven o'clock on Sunday morning, a gospel meeting on Sunday night, and a prayer and Bible reading some evening during the week. There might also be the meeting times of the Sunday school and sisters' missionary class.

The Brethren avoided anything like a Christian Year calendar. For them every Sunday is Resurrection Day, and the only difference Easter or Christmas made was perhaps a special object lesson in the Sunday school. But this is not to say that the Brethren had no social life. Like a large family, the assembly would often get together for missions fundraisers, receptions for visiting preachers, after-meeting socials during conferences, etc., usually in homes. And anyone who grew up in a Scots-Irish assembly will recall the frequent invitations to "tea" (an "Old Country" tradition meaning a hearty buffet including that most heavenly of creations, butter shortbread).

Generally two special events of a social nature during the year were sponsored by the meeting itself: the annual picnic (often May 30 or July 4 in the U.S. and Dominion Day in Canada) and the Sunday school "Treat." The latter, normally held in December, was *not* exactly a Christmas program but a kind of performance in which each class beginning with the tiny tots sang a gospel song (with motions), recited verses or anecdotes in rhyme, or acted out an incident of sharing the gospel with friends or associates (usually reserved for the high schoolers). Prizes for attendance were then given out, and candy distributed to all. Picnics in the early days were fairly genteel, consisting mainly of an outdoor meal. [Fig. 53] Later there were races and tugs-of-war and perhaps baseball or soccer.

The main event of the week, of course, was the Lord's Supper on Sunday morning. The "morning meeting" found the saints sitting in a circle or semi-circle with the symbols of the Lord's death literally "in their midst." Behind them on seats at the back or sides of the hall would be their unsaved or uncommitted children of age twelve or older and others not yet received into fellowship. [Fig. 54] Any person unknown to them would be met at the door by an elder who would "examine" the individual or individuals in question as to faith and sound doctrine. If the visitors brought a "letter of commendation" from another assembly, however, they would be welcomed immediately and "announced" or introduced to the company.

When the believers entered the hall they were handed a small black hymnbook containing words only. Everyone in the assembly would know the music by heart. This in most cases would have been the *Believers Hymn Book* or the well-known "Little Flock" hymnal (chapter 1). Many assemblies in North America used this even though it was an Exclusive publication. No instrument of any kind was used to accompany the singing.[1]

---

1 J.N. Darby did not deny the beauty of instrumental music, but believed that, like all the

> No instrument can equal in effect (Haydn said so) the human voice. Besides, as I said, it is not true [that is, the claim that playing musical instruments is a gift from God]. It is merely helping the pleasure of fallen nature, not a thing evil in itself, but connecting sensual pleasure with spiritual life. . . Harps and organs down here began in Cain's city, when he had gone out from the presence of the Lord. (From *Letters of J.N.D.*, Vol. III, pp. 475-76)

Hymns were given out by number, a brother sometimes reading the first stanza aloud, and another brother with an ear for music starting the singing on the right note. The meeting would consist of hymns, Scripture reading usually with commentary, and prayers, all spontaneous and all directed toward the worship of the Lord Jesus Christ. The only collection of the week was taken after the elements, a whole loaf of bread and a chalice of wine (no grape juice in those days) had been passed. Women did not take part audibly and did not expect to. Given some reasonable speaking gift among the brothers and a lot of genuine love for the Lord, a Brethren worship meeting could be a wonderful experience of God's presence.

Sunday night was always reserved for the gospel meeting. The precedent for this went back to the days of revival in Great Britain (chapter 5). Here a gospel songbook was used, or sometimes song sheets if the gathering couldn't afford books. Many assemblies held an open-air service beforehand, and the public was invited to come to the hall to hear a more complete presentation of the Good News. The brothers who had a gift for speaking shared in preaching the gospel on Sunday nights, and new (male) converts were urged to give their testimonies at this time. It was a great training ground for young men, some of whom went on to a lifetime of ministry while earning a living at the same time. The interior of the halls reinforced the message with framed texts on the walls, and sometimes a blunt warning to the unconverted, e.g., "Eternity Where—Heaven or Hell?"

The above describes the "traditional" Brethren assembly, though of course even in the early days there were variations. In not a few cases, "traditional" assemblies still exist, though much of the old austerity has disappeared. As far as administration, each gospel hall was strictly independent. As J.N. Darby had taught that only the apostles or their

---

other beautiful things in this world, it posed a danger by its appeal to the natural man:

representatives (such as Timothy) could appoint elders, the assemblies generally recognized no titles of elder or deacon as such. It was, however, urged that responsible brethren ought to *do the work* of elders, and normally several senior men were recognized as "the oversight." In theory at least, decisions of a non-spiritual nature that affected the whole congregation were made by all the brethren in a council called the "business meeting." In earlier times as today, gifts varied from one church to another, and the strongest assemblies were those with effective leadership.

A Treat at Buffalo

The following account describing a typical "Treat" appeared in *Light and Liberty* in February 1940. No doubt many still living today can remember such events:

> The annual Sunday school treat of the assembly hall was held, as has been the custom for over 50 years, on New Year's Day. The boys and girls were entertained with a Bible quiz game in which every correct answer merited a candy stick of assorted flavors and colors. While the children were thus engaged the grownups were invited downstairs to the Sunday school room where they were served a light lunch. At six o'clock the boys and girls were served, and at seven the whole Sunday school with parents and friends gathered in the hall for the event of the evening. The program consisted of exercises, dialogues and recitations, interspersed with hymns of praise led by our efficient song leader, Robert Boggess. Before the program concluded with the awarding of prizes for attendance and memory work, Mr. Edward Fairbairn, a beloved brother now in his 86th year, who has always had a part on the program, brought a message.

10

Strife Weakens the Movement

"Tight" and "Loose" Brethren

One of the unique characteristics of all branches of the Plymouth Brethren is their refusal to embrace any formal creeds or established systems of Biblical interpretation, insisting that the Bible alone is a sufficient guide in all matters of life and faith. This fierce independence, plus the absence of a Brethren theological seminary, no doubt have been major factors in keeping the movement from developing a liberal "left wing."

On the other hand, this stance has created a very strong resistance to change of *any* kind, and a tendency for assemblies to become polarized over matters of form that have little or nothing to do with the essentials of faith. Instead of exercising their liberty as autonomous congregations to "agree to disagree," the Independent Brethren too often have followed the tragic pathway taken by the Exclusives in separating one from another over such things (each using the Scriptures to justify their position).

So, almost from the beginning there have been differences between those who are considered strict or "tight" by others, and those who are viewed by their contemporaries as liberal or "loose." This tension was heightened among the Independent branch by an event that occurred in Great Britain in 1887. A new magazine called *Needed Truth* began to be circulated, which was the expression of a faction in the North of England and Scotland who were convinced that the church was a much more specific gathering than most Christians realized. From 1 Corinthians 5:9-13 they concluded that Paul was instructing a special group "inside" the church to judge their brethren "outside" and, if necessary, to separate from them. This so-called "Needed Truth" faction set up a kind of presbytery or leadership board at local, district, and national levels. Calling themselves "The Fellowship," they proceeded to make the somewhat extravagant claim that they alone made up the Church of God, all other Christian groups being tainted by the world.

From the little information still available, it seems that the "Needed Truth" as a distinct sect (still existing in Britain) never grew very large in North America.[1] The printed material circulated widely on this side of the Atlantic, nonetheless, and even some of the leading evangelists like Donald Munro were caught up with it for a time. The seeds of false doctrine that were sown in early days began to spring up by the second decade of the twentieth century in the form of contention among the leadership over "tightness" and "looseness." We learn that while these problems turned up in a number of places, they had a particularly disastrous effect in Ontario, where the first assemblies were formed and where they were most numerous. Brethren who had known each other and worked together for years were now estranged; certain veteran preachers were now welcome at some assemblies and not at others.

William McClure, the foremost Brethren worker at the time, was a mediating figure in the dispute, which raged from around 1910 for more than a decade. The popular view apparently was that Robert McMurdo was the leading preacher representing the "tight" position while Alexander Marshall the leader of those who taught the "loose" position. In a letter of August 10, 1914, McClure takes issue with this idea:

> An assembly takes the ground that they can receive ministry from Mr. Marshall, and some others of their school, if I may be allowed the term, and also from Mr. Telfer, Mr. Oliver, and others who have become known as "tight." For taking this stand, those who have been opposed to what has been called "loose" teachings have been encouraged to leave and form

---

1 * Dr. Robert Peterson has discovered that a small Needed Truth assembly still exists (1992) in the southern part of Colorado, but it is unknown whether they have survived from earlier times or are a recent import from Great Britain. William Conard reports that there are Needed Truth churches in Ontario, British Columbia, Trinidad, and two in Denver, Colorado.

another assembly. Then Mr. Marshall and Mr. McMurdo are blamed as the ones who made the division. What do you think God will think of that kind of thing?

Since ever I took my place outside to the Name of the Lord, it has been the constant practice to receive those who have held absolutely what Mr. McMurdo holds. It was a constant thing to see on the same platform men belonging to each of the schools, and no trouble growing out of it, and I believe in my inmost being that many troubles have come out of the attempt of some dear brethren to act upon another and less Christlike principle than these dear men.

Some reconciliation took place in the early '20s, but the polarization was never really resolved. Eventually a significant number of meetings broke off from the mainstream because of the "looseness" which they believed had invaded the movement. In their terminology, they wished to continue following the "Old Paths" (Jer. 6:16). In the 1940s and 1950s when most of the mainstream assemblies dropped the name "gospel hall" in favor of "gospel chapel" or "Bible chapel," the "Old Paths" meetings retained their original name—and still do to this day. They are listed in Walterick's *Address Book* and are particularly served by the magazine *Truth and Tidings*, which retains a format much like *Our Record*. "Old Paths" evangelists still preach in the open air and under canvas (chapter 13).

Issues that Divide: 1910-1930

In an excellent article titled "Fundamentals and Secondary Issues," William MacDonald distinguishes between the "non-negotiables" of our faith and two classes of lesser issues. The fundamentals "over which," he says, "there can be no difference of opinion" concern the person and work of Christ, the authority of the Bible as the Word of God, and the basic tenets of the gospel. The non-fundamental issues MacDonald divides into "important" and "secondary." Under "important" he includes divorce and remarriage; the outlines of prophecy; women's head coverings; women's ministry in the church; the gifts of the Spirit; and .. . the five points of Calvinism. In his opinion, "Sooner or later every local assembly must adopt a position on [each] subject." The other class of issues he calls "secondary," and they include wine vs. grape juice for the Lord's Supper, which version of the Bible should be used, the use of musical instruments, etc. Regarding these he suggests that "there has to be a certain amount of give and take for the sake of unity and peace (Eph. 4:1-6)." MacDonald's wisdom in regard to "issues that divide" is significant when we look back at the divisions that took place from around 1910 to 1930.

The dividing issues of those days were practices that certain assemblies felt (rightly or wrongly) had been taught by the pioneer evangelists. They include:

Reception

This had to do with policy about receiving new members into the circle of fellowship. Some assemblies felt that every believer ought to be received upon confession; others insisted that candidates should be examined for godly behavior and purity of doctrine.

The "open" platform

This meant depending on the Spirit to give the Lord's servants a message to preach, rather than having a set program with a chairman and designated preacher. Although this practice seems to have brought blessing in the early days of the Brethren, it had become subject to much abuse.

The use of musical instruments

As has already been noted, it was J.N. Darby's position that the human voice was the best instrument with which to praise God, and that the use of instruments was an imitation of the world. Some assemblies had started to use a piano for meetings other than the Lord's Supper, and there was much emotional debate over the subject both between assemblies and within assemblies.

Fellowship with Christians outside the assembly

In these times it was generally understood that the assemblies did not fellowship with the "sects," but there were wide differences of opinion among the preachers whether or not individual Christians should keep separate from members of other churches.

This narrowing process was viewed with great alarm by some of the leading brethren in a position to know what was happening in the movement as a whole. They recognized that it could lead only to further separation and fragmentation, just like the Exclusives. In 1927 a posthumous article by J.R. Caldwell, dealing with the controversy, appeared in *Armour of Light* magazine:

> The length to which "exclusive" lines of fellowship have been carried, the hardness with which they have been enforced, the plausible arguments

and the mis-applied Scriptures by which they are supported, and the results that have followed upon their being carried out, combine to render a testimony . . . both opportune and needful.

A bit further he states:

How greatly would we rejoice if the principles acted upon in the assemblies in the first half century of their existence were reverted to and true believers heartily welcomed because God had received them. Those were days of liberty, joy and power!

That same year a fifty-six page booklet by the renowned pioneer evangelist Alexander Marshall appeared, with the title *"Holding Fast the Faithful Word: Wither Are We Drifting?"* The preface consisted of the article by J.R. Caldwell just referred to. Marshall gives an eloquent argument in favor of the spirit of openness and liberty. At the end he drew his conclusions:

I. Every believer is in the only "fellowship" Scripture speaks of, viz., fellowship of His Son Jesus Christ our Lord" (1 Cor. 1:9).

II. Because of this fact we are to "receive" or welcome God's people to all their birthright privileges, including the Lord's Supper (Rom. 15:7).

III. We receive Christians, not on account of their connection with a "party," "circle," or "fellowship," but on account of their relation to Christ. If God has received them, and they are not Scripturally disqualified, we are bound to receive them. We don't receive them because of whence they come, but because of what they are (Rom. 14:3; Mark 9:41; Matt. 10:40).

IV. Baptism, being an ordinance of the Lord, should be observed by all Christians. It is, however, a personal act, and is not set forth in Scripture as a condition of fellowship. Baptism is no more essential to fellowship than it is essential to salvation. Any company of professing Christians that insists on baptism as a basis of communion is unscripturally gathered (Matt. 28:19,20; Acts 8:38; 18:8; Rom. 14:3).

V. Denominationalism involves the acceptance of a written, or unwritten, creed [for] membership [in] the party; but Christians known as "Brethren" have strenuously repudiated such a position. In theory at least, they have maintained that difference of judgment on "minor" points should be no barrier to Christian fellowship. Such differences afford opportunities for the exercise of patience and forbearance. The insisting on uniformity where God has permitted liberty and forbidden us to judge one another is the fruitful cause of sorrow and division. Let us not forget that the truth of

God may be used as a wedge to divide, instead of a means to unite the people of God (Phil. 3:15,16).

VI. Many confound separation from sects [institutional churches] with separation from Christians in sects.

VII. Each servant of Christ is directly responsible to the Lord for his service. It is He who calls and qualifies; it is He who commissions to preach and teach; and it is to Him and Him alone that he must give account. Teaching and preaching, and every form of ministry are personal (Mark 13:34; Col. 3:24; 2 Cor. 5:10).

VIII. The sphere of service is described by such expressions as "the world," "every creature," "all saints," "the household of faith," and excludes none (Mark 16:16; Matt. 28:19,20; Gal. 6:10). Although the sheep are scattered, although the unsaved are "members" of this, that, or the other "sect," "mission," or "party," the responsibility of the "Lord's messenger" to carry the "Lord's message" to them is still binding. It is therefore the duty of servants of Christ to carry out their Master's instructions (Luke 24:47; Matt. 21:28; Acts 8:4).

In his concluding paragraph Marshall again quotes from J.R. Caldwell:

The fear of being judged and condemned, preached at, prayed at, separated from and maligned, proves too much for the courage of many. To escape it they lay down their necks under the yoke of men, and surrender the real liberty of seeking only and always to be well pleasing to God. The danger of falling under bondage to the fear of man is most disastrous. We are ever in increasing danger of being slaves to men and their ideas, and the pathway of faith is becoming less and less known. (The quote from William MacDonald is from "Fundamentals and Secondary Issues," *This I Believe* Series, Walterick Publishers, n.d.)

III

THE
GOLDEN AGE
OF
INDEPENDENT
BRETHRENISM
1920-1960

Deffenbaugh family and gospel car, early '30s.

11

Introduction to a Fruitful Period

Momentous Times

In the opening lines of *A Tale of Two Cities*, Charles Dickens'immortal novel about the French Revolution, he spoke of that era as the "best of times" and the "worst of times." For many North Americans, these words also aptly apply to the forty years between 1920 and 1960. How can we portray such a momentous period in a few lines? It begins only a few months after the Armistice and the return of tens of thousands of young men from the trenches and battlefields of World War I. Woodrow Wilson was in the White House with his valiant but unrealistic dream of a League of Nations. It was the era of Prohibition, of Al Capone and the criminal warlords. There was the development of paved highways and emergence of the automobile culture, of skyscrapers and ocean liners, and of mass tourism abroad. There was Lindburgh's solo flight to Paris in 1927, the stock market crash in 1929, the Great Depression and Roosevelt's New Deal, and the rise of the two most notorious tyrants the world has ever known, Adolph Hitler and Joseph Stalin.

And there was much more: Talking motion pictures and the captivation of society by movie stars, the Dustbowl and migrant workers moving westward, bobbed hair, short skirts and beach pajamas, the Spanish Civil War, the beginning of commercial airlines and the China Clipper, the invasion of China by Japan, classical radio programs like Amos 'n' Andy, One Man's Family and Gangbusters, the Big Bands, all steel cars, the abdication of Edward VIII, Pearl Harbor, war on two fronts, gas rationing and gold stars in windows, the Atom Bomb, the return of the troops and the GI Bill, the Iron Curtain, tract homes and the exodus to the suburbs.

During those memorable years the Brethren in North America experienced as a united people their greatest success in gospel outreach, and established their identity as an evangelical movement. It was *outreach* that defined and characterized the Independent Brethren during these years, though other developments closely related to outreach also took place: social concerns, foreign missions support, and formal Biblical teaching, including writing and publishing. A fifth development was openness toward other Christians, especially through para-church organizations, and this too was related to outreach. Finally came a sixth development, the merger of the Grant Exclusives with the Independent Brethren (chapter 12), which also had much to do with outreach. Those who lived through the Great Depression and World War II may not have thought so at the time, but those were great days for the Independent Brethren, the best they were to achieve in the form of a network of gospel halls.

Growth and Expansion at Mid-Century

The last U.S. census that gathered statistics on religious affiliation was reported in 1936. Below are figures for "Plymouth Brethren II," the government's designation for the Independent Brethren, reported in 1906, 1916, 1926, and 1936:

	Groups	Members	Sunday schools
1906	128	4,752	93
1916	129	5,928	101
1926	307	13,497	239
1936	344	15,684	276

These figures show that in the U.S. the number of assemblies reported increased by nearly 138 percent in the ten years between 1916 and 1926. The greatest part of this growth would have taken place in the post-World War I years from 1919 to 1925. Over the next ten years, however, the increase was only about twelve percent, undoubtedly the effect of the Depression and hard times in the early 1930s.

In the late 1930s Lloyd Walterick began publishing a yearly "Address Book of Some Assemblies in the United States, Canada, Bermuda, and British West Indies." The earliest available is 1941. There we find listings for 550 assemblies or correspondents (the latter either holding meetings in a home or otherwise attempting to start a fellowship). These are found in all states including Alaska and Hawaii except Mississippi, Montana, Nevada, and Vermont. In Canada there are 273 listings representing all provinces including New Brunswick, Nova Scotia, and Prince Edward Island, a total in North America of 823.

This increase of about sixty percent in the U.S. probably reflects both assembly planting in the second half of the 1930s and the alignment of many Grant Exclusive assemblies with the Independents. Nine years later, however, in 1950, the Address Book lists 571 in the U.S. and 265 in Canada, a total of 836. Presumably the only slight rise in the U.S. and an actual drop in Canada was due to war conditions with gasoline rationing and other curtailments.

These figures are impressive but not earth-shaking. Considering the population increase as well as the growth of towns and cities in the first half of the twentieth century, the Brethren movement was actually tiny in terms of numbers of churches. In an editorial that appeared on the cover of *Letters of Interest* in October 1949, Bill McCartney reported that there were assemblies in about one-half of one percent of the 124,780 communities in the U.S. This underscores what has already been said in the previous section—that it was not church growth that gave the Brethren their distinctive character at mid-century, but their *outreach*.

During the 1930s, 1940s and 1950s the Brethren were served by five periodicals: *Our Record, Light and Liberty, Letters of Interest, Truth and Tidings,* and *Words in Season*. These publications all carried letters and articles that reflected the amazing scope and variety of evangelistic outreach being carried on during that period. From booths in county fairs to Bible verses on roadside rocks to boat evangelism along isolated coasts to witnessing among chain-gang prisoners to children's meetings in store fronts, barns, and back parlors, the Brethren during this amazing period were reaching out with the gospel. The remainder of Part III will give some details.

12

The Exclusive Brethren in North America

The Grants and Independents Unite

The Exclusive Brethren, as was mentioned earlier, had a history in North America quite different from their history in Great Britain, and ultimately there was an amalgamation with the Independents by a number of assemblies in the Grant party, the largest group. The significance of that development will become evident as we progress. Other groups of Exclusives continued along their own pathways, a few were reconciled to one another after earlier separations and a few hundred of their assemblies are to be found throughout North America today. This chapter will describe some effects of J.N. Darby's early visits to this continent, and then will briefly trace the events that led to the above merger.

Darby made his first visit to North America in 1862, ministering primarily in Ontario in the area between Toronto and London. Some assemblies had already been formed in that area by Darby's followers coming from Great Britain. Over the border in the U.S. there were also some settlements of believers who came originally from the congregations that Darby had founded in the Lausanne area of French-Switzerland and in the south of France. Robert Mojonnier tells of one family, that of Alexandre Tripod of Aubonne, who immigrated in 1849, settling first in Highland, Illinois, [Fig. 56] where many Swiss lived, and later in Sebastopol. His great-grandfather, Frederick Mojonnier, had followed the same route in 1850, by sailing ship to New Orleans and river boat to St. Louis and by wagon to Highland. A chapel was built by these Christians in Sebastopol, which stood until around 1925. Part of Darby's plan in coming across the Atlantic was to visit these people, possibly this very group, and he did indeed leave Ontario to spend some time with them. Later he wrote:

> My object was to visit the French and Swiss brethren, which . . . I through mercy effected, and was out in the prairies living among them as in old times . . .

Between the years 1862 and 1876 or 1877, Darby visited North America several times for extended periods. In 1875 he took the train to San Francisco in company with one of the Exclusive preachers, Robert Grant, and his old friend George Wigram, but for the most part he concentrated on the larger cities of the Midwest and East. There was in America already considerable interest in Bible prophecy, and a sect called the Millerites had gained much notoriety by attempting to predict specific dates for the Lord's return. Darby's own unique system of interpreting Daniel and Revelation, particularly his doctrine of the "secret rapture" (chapter 3) gave him numerous opportunities to expound the Scriptures to prominent churchmen and even to minister in their churches. But few were convinced enough of Darby's position to separate from their denominations and "gather in the Name of Christ alone." An address book of 1878 published by Loizeaux lists eighty-eight Exclusive Brethren gatherings in the U.S., the majority in the states of Massachusetts, New York, New Jersey, Michigan, and Illinois. Of the one hundred or so Canadian gatherings listed, the vast majority are in Ontario.

By 1880 the leading teacher and theologian among the Darbyite network in North America was Frederick W. Grant. Born in London, Frederick and his brother Robert had immigrated to Ontario while in their early twenties. Frederick, who had been educated at King's College School in London, was able to qualify for ordination as an Anglican minister, but left that calling after becoming convinced of the Brethren position through reading their literature. He moved to Toronto and served widely among the Exclusive assemblies, his gifts soon making him prominent among them. He was the author of a number of books and articles that had wide circulation, including the remarkable *Numerical Bible*, and was editor of the Exclusive journal, *Helps by the Way*.

Harry Ironside wrote in later years, "When it comes to theology itself, I owe more to the works of F.W. Grant, I think, than even to Mr. Darby or Mr. Kelly."

Both Frederick and Robert Grant, also an Exclusive preacher, had been with Darby on various occasions and corresponded regularly with him right up to a few weeks before the death of the old warrior in 1882. F.W. Grant, however, was a somewhat impetuous man with a tendency to be argumentative, and there were between him and Darby some disagreements on what to most people would seem minor theological points. These differences and one incident in particular at a conference in England, when Grant was said to have walked out on the aged Darby, were made much of a few years later in a blowup over what was called the "sealing of the Spirit" (Eph. 4:30).

The doctrine in question grew out of the seeming paradox of the believer's condition as Paul described it in Romans 7, contrasted with Romans 8. Darby speculated that a person receives eternal life by believing in Christ, but does not come into *possession* of the Holy Spirit until being "sealed" by apprehending the concept of being raised with Christ, thus receiving the life of the Spirit (Rom. 8:11). The issue came to a head around 1880 in Toronto. Two men from the assembly sent to share the bread and wine with a young convert on his deathbed refused him communion on the ground that, though a believer, he did not fully understand Romans 8. Robert Grant was present at the meeting where this incident was reported, and was so outraged that he wrote an article entitled "When is the believer sealed?" which was subsequently published in his brother's magazine. In this article he pointed out that nowhere does the Bible teach that "sealing" is dependent upon a certain understanding of the gospel, but rather that eternal life and "sealing of the Spirit" occur simultaneously at the point of belief.

Frederick Grant was not certain in his own mind about the "sealing" issue at the time. But shortly after the death of Darby he published an article essentially agreeing with his brother's position, and followed it with a longer piece in a booklet called "Life in Christ and the Sealing of the Spirit." The Exclusive Brethren by this time, as we saw in the case of Edward Cronin and the so-called Kelly or Park Street Division (chapter 6), had come to a place of regarding themselves as the one and only appropriate expression of the "church of God on earth." They considered the slightest disagreement with the doctrines received from Darby a very serious offense against Christ himself. In this case, Frederick

Grant's action was also seen as an attack on the late J.N. Darby. Two Exclusive preachers from Great Britain, Lord Adelbert Cecil and Alfred Mace, [Fig. 57] took up the case against F.W. Grant, and in 1884 at an Exclusive Brethren chapel in Montreal condemned him publicly as a heretic. A letter was drawn up, and those present, even some who did not understand the issue at all, were required to sign it. About a third of the Exclusive assemblies sided with the "Natural History Hall" party (named after the place where the document was signed), excommunicating F.W. Grant. The larger percentage remained loyal to him.

At around the time that these events were taking place, F.W. Grant [Fig. 58] moved to the United States, settling in Plainfield, New Jersey, where there was a large gathering of Brethren. Plainfield, therefore, became the main center for the Grant party in North America. Associated with Grant were a number of well known preachers: his brother, Robert, Paul and Timothy Loizeaux, F.C. Jennings, Samuel Ridout, and B.C. Greenman. In 1890, according to census figures, there were 109 assemblies with 2,289 communicants in this circle. The interesting (and most admirable) feature of the Grant party is that, for the forty-five years or so of their existence, a continuing interfacing process was going on, not only with other Exclusives, but in particular with the Independent Brethren.[1]

The first major move toward reconciliation occurred in 1892, when the Grants invited their own assemblies and also the Independents to a conference at Plainfield to consider the issues that separated them. About a thousand Brethren showed up—but not Donald Ross, Donald Munro, and John Smith, the chief Independents, who were suspicious. Following the deliberations, a letter was circulated, signed by F.W. Grant, B.C. Greenman, and Samuel Ridout, that "looseness does not exist" and that it would "be a joy" to think that we might be able to "welcome them [the Independents] among us." There was considerable objection to this conclusion, especially from Exclusives in Britain, the Bahamas, and New Zealand called the Stuarts (after Bible teacher Clarence E. Stuart) whose assemblies had merged with the Grants.

---

1 Ross McLaren's thesis, *The Triple Tradition*, deals in detail with this period of interfacing. See also *A Historical Sketch of the Brethren Movement* by H.A. Ironside and "Family Matters" by William Conard in *Interest*, July-August 1992.

The three main problems were the "looseness" referred to above, the form of church government (circle of fellowship versus local autonomy) and mode of baptism (some Exclusives favored household baptism). The objectors felt that the Independents in America were still on the same loose ground as Bethesda in the Darby-Newton controversy many years earlier (chapter 4). There was also considerable loyalty to household baptism and to a federation of churches since these were principles taught by Darby. As we have suggested, the pendulum swung back and forth for some forty-five years until, at last, the majority of the Grant teachers became convinced that their traditional position did not align with Scripture.

In the early part of the twentieth century, one of the key figures in this long and painful process of amalgamation between the two branches of Brethren[1] was Henry Allen Ironside, [Fig. 59] whose father's friendship with Donald Munro was important to the founding of the Independent work in Toronto (chapter 7). By 1886, Sophia Ironside and her two boys were living in Los Angeles. Young Harry made a complete commitment to Christ in 1890, and before long joined the Salvation Army. His intelligence and natural gift as a public speaker advanced him quickly, and he went through officer training and became a captain. Disillusioned, however, with failure to attain "holiness" by his own efforts, Ironside found the truth of the finished work of Christ in a Brethren tract. In 1896 he left the Salvationists to associate with the Grant Brethren, an association that lasted until 1930 when he accepted the senior pastorate at Moody Memorial Church in Chicago. Harry Ironside, probably the most ecumenical of all the Grant preachers, moved in both Grant and Independent circles and was a friend of William McClure and other Independent leaders. By his deep grasp of Scripture he made a convincing case for believer's baptism, and his entire life was a powerful witness against the narrow separateness of the Exclusives.

The merger of the Grant Exclusives and the Independents that took place in the 1930s and 1940s seems to have been precipitated by the ministering brethren on both sides beginning to work to-

---

1 This was a painful process because there were bitter conflicts in some Grant assemblies, and certain preachers were ousted. Feelings ran so high that there were even cases of suicide.

gether.[1] Two factors were involved. On the one hand the issues that separated them (see above) were tried and found wanting. A bitter feud between two business partners in a Grant assembly in Philadelphia became a world-wide scandal and proved, ultimately, that it is impossible for a network of churches to judge a local matter. Household baptism simply could not stand up under such examination as given, for example, in Ironside's *Baptism: What Saith the Scripture?* Looseness turned out to be nothing more than criticism leveled by tight members of both Grant and Independent camps at their more open-minded brethren.

The merger opened a new era for the Independent Brethren in North America, changing the character of the movement considerably and creating a shift somewhat away from pioneer evangelism to Bible teaching and missions training. Young men, and women too, with vision and a more generous attitude toward other Christians, were attempting to build, through unity rather than separation, a more effective movement for God. As C. Ernest Tatham, one of those young preachers, said recently in retrospect, "The 'Rapproachment' was accomplished, not by 'Councils,' but by the unifying Holy Spirit who indicated that while walls should be built *around* the city—as in Nehemiah's day —they should not be erected *through* the city!"

Exclusive Principles Impossible to Maintain

Miss Minnie Armerding was commended by a Grant Exclusive assembly in 1925 to labor among the Indians at Winslow, Arizona, and vicinity. The door to this field had been opened by Harry Ironside, who was instrumental in bringing a number of assembly missionaries to this work. Later Miss Armerding was joined by her father, who in 1952 at the age of ninety-one was still active in ministry. Among Mr. Armerding's large family were Henry and Carl, widely known Bible teachers, and Hudson, former president of Wheaton College. In the

---

1 Church historian Donald Tinder points out that this chapter may give the erroneous impression that almost all of the Grant assemblies became Independents, when in fact nearly half remained in the Exclusive camp.

early 1950s, having worked with Christians from many different backgrounds, Miss Armerding and her father felt compelled to issue the following statement:

> In view of the stand that has been taken by a number of the Assemblies in recent months, in respect to *fellowship*, as published in *The Bulletin* [a Grant Brethren publication], we believe that we too should let our brethren know how we do.
>
> During the more than twenty-five years that the Lord has permitted us to serve Him here, we have found it impossible to maintain the *exclusive* principles of our brethren. Here, in the Southwest, we learned to know saintly men and women, outside of our own circle of fellowship, who were wholeheartedly devoted to the Lord, living blameless lives, serving the Lord faithfully, and ministering His Word in all of its purity and power, without compromise; men and women manifestly filled with the Holy Spirit. To refuse to let such remember the Lord with us would, according to our convictions, be dishonoring to the Lord, and a stumbling block to our simple Christian Indians, and a denial of the truth of the *One Body*. There is not one member of the Body of Christ to whom we can say, "I have no need of thee," and while there have been few occasions that we have had such visiting us on the Lord's Day, we have, according to Romans 14:22, been happy in the course that we have followed, and that we would continue to follow.
>
> Affectionately, in Christ Jesus our Lord, (signed) E. Armerding, Minnie Armerding"

(From *Letters of Interest*, May 1952)

13
Pioneering and Assembly Planting in the 1920s and 1930s

Lampstands in Iowa

In Northeastern Iowa a network of fifteen gospel halls still is a witness to the faithful preaching for over one hundred years of numerous brethren of "Old Paths" persuasion. Since 1893 there have been evangelistic campaigns of one sort or another, usually under canvas, in some two hundred places. This is in an area covering about a third of the state. As recently as March 1992 we find *Words in Season* reporting four weeks of gospel meetings by brethren James Webb and James Hanna in West Union, a small town of about 2,700 in the northeast corner of the state. Five weeks of gospel meetings in Willmar, Minnesota, conducted by Iowa brethren Robert Orr and Roy Weber, are also noted.

The story of the planting of these fifteen testimonies, with many remarkable examples of the work of the Spirit in the lives of individuals, has been preserved by evangelist Leonard DeBuhr in *Golden Lampstands of Northern Iowa*, published in 1985. In this valuable record, DeBuhr traces the growth of each assembly from the first efforts to bring the gospel to that particular community to the beginning of regular meetings, and later the opening of a gospel hall. There are few areas in North America where the history of a Brethren network is so complete.[1]

Part of the story is traced back to Northern Ireland in the late nineteenth century. Here a preacher named John Blair had first heard the message of salvation in meetings held by William Matthews and James Campbell (chapter 7). Blair had a sister, Mrs. William Orr, who lived southeast of Dunkerton and, concerned about the condition of her soul, he made the long journey to visit her, arriving in November 1891. He held meetings in a home and in the local schoolhouse, and several were brought to the Lord, including Mrs. Orr.

Blair returned home and visited again in 1893, at which time the new believers were baptized. A small remembrance meeting was started in the home of Tom Dunkerton. This grew and continued over the years. Another assembly was started in Waterloo fifteen miles away, and when automobiles came into general use, the two groups merged in Waterloo. In the early 1970s four brethren held a series of tent meetings in Dunkerton and a few more souls were gathered in. In 1976 nineteen believers began to remember the Lord in Dunkerton again. Today a substantial congregation gathers at a gospel hall in Dunkerton.

In the early days in Waterloo, [Fig. 60] a businessman, E.G. Matthews, had a great interest in reaching others with the gospel. Somehow Matthews was familiar with various Brethren evangelists, whom he invited to hold meetings in Waterloo. Among those who came were John Blair, Charles Ross, James Harcus, A.N. O'Brien, and William McClure. A small remembrance meeting was started in Matthews's home in 1898. This grew over the years into what is now the Western Avenue Gospel Hall.

Some time not long after the turn of the century, Matthews was on a train and sat next to a young farmer named Oliver Smith. This young man had gone forward in a Billy Sunday campaign, but could not answer with certainty Matthews's question, "*How* were you saved?" Later Smith was greatly helped to assurance of salvation by a neighbor, and in 1915 when W.J. McClure held special meetings in Waterloo he put seats in his old hayrack wagon and hauled twenty to thirty people to the services every night. A few years later Oliver Smith was commended by the Waterloo assembly to full-time work.

Of the fifteen gospel halls in northeastern Iowa, nearly all were greatly influenced by the preaching and personal witness of Oliver Smith. This dear brother labored unceasingly in evangelism: in open-air preaching, tent work, and wherever else opportunity arose. [Fig. 61] To quote Leonard DeBuhr:

> He was God's man, for God's time of great visitation in Northern Iowa. Literally thousands were touched by his plain speaking, by his full assurance, as he presented the claims of Christ to the lost souls of men.

Smith had an amazing gift for personal evangelism, and DeBuhr gives numerous examples of people who found Christ through his conversation with them. On one occasion in 1945, Smith was driving with another evangelist through Clear Lake and saw an old man walking on his lawn using a cane. His wife was raking leaves nearby. Smith stopped the car, walked over to the man and said, "Do you know you will have to be born again to go to Heaven?"

The man began to weep and said, "I know I do." Later, both this man and his wife were saved.

Oliver Smith had a Model-T Ford on which he painted the words "Gospel Car" and "Jesus Saves." In 1925, evangelist Tom Olson presented him with the keys to a new Essex "gospel car," saying, "You can use this better than I can." Smith would also paint gospel messages on rocks near the highway and on the sides of underpasses.

The methods of evangelism and assembly planting used by Oliver Smith have been continued to this day by other brethren raised up by God for the work in northern Iowa such as Louis Brandt, William Warke, Henry Wahls, Clifford Smith, Pat Magee, Robert Orr, and Leonard DeBuhr. Primarily it consists simply of preaching the Word in a hall, tent, schoolhouse, store front, or even out of doors. There are no frills like instrumental music, motion pictures, soloists, etc. Very little advertising is used; the local Christians come and bring their neighbors. When people are saved they are baptized by immersion, often outdoors in a river.

When work in the mines ran out, the believers moved to other areas in the region and eventually meetings were established in Forbush, Rathbun, Jerome, Centerville, and elsewhere. No full-time workers were involved in the beginning. Later, tent work was carried on, resulting in several more assemblies. The first gathering to remember the Lord in Des Moines was started in 1912 in the home of J.D. Green, a brother from Centerville. In southwestern Iowa the gospel was first brought by a commended worker, A. Broadfoot, in 1884. The first assembly was started in Berea shortly thereafter. Several other brethren gave assistance, as the report says:

These brethren traveling by horseback, team and buggy over the open prairies carried the gospel to the neighboring towns . . . holding meetings in country schoolhouses.

The Prodigal Returns

In 1910 a young man significantly named Charles Spurgeon Summers left his native Scotland to minister among the little circle of Brethren assemblies in the U.S. and Canada. For thirty years he led the life common to Brethren preachers in those days: tent evangelism in the warm months, ministering in halls and store fronts and anywhere else opportunity afforded at other times, taking funerals when required, and opening the Word at conferences during the holidays. Summers also was a good writer, and committed to paper many of the principles gleaned from Scripture that he felt should guide the Lord's people. Much of this material was published in the periodical *Words in Season* between the years 1919 and 1948.

Summers married Alice Miller, fifteen years younger, in 1924, and eventually there were two daughters, Margaret and Janet, and an only son, Charles B. The going was tough during the Great Depression, believers had little money to support the Lord's servants, but the Lord was faithful and somehow they got by. In 1940, however, Summers decided that he needed to spend more time with his young family, and so retired from the traveling ministry and took work in Tacoma, Washington. Thus he was at home when young Charles grew into his teenage years. But, instead of being drawn to his father's faith, Charles B. involved himself with friends and activities at school and distanced himself from his dad and all that he believed. Shortly after the younger Summers joined the navy in 1957, Charles Spurgeon Summers died of cancer.

In 1990, Charles B. Summers published a book called *Return to Old Paths*. Much of this book is a tribute to his father, including a brief biography, a chronology of his life as an itinerant preacher and a generous selection of the elder Summers's writings, abstracted from manuscripts discovered many years after his father's death. But most significant is Charles B. Summers's own story, the pilgrimage of a modern prodigal. He traces the pathway down which, as a well-read scholar and college instructor, he wandered further and further away from

God. Then he recounts how, like the son in the parable, he began the road back to the Father—driven not by having to eat the husks that the pigs had left, but by the accidental death of his only daughter. In a way it was a return, not only to the heavenly Father, but to his earthly one as well.[1]

Reports from the first *Letters of Interest*

It is fascinating to read the letters and reports from workers in any of the early Brethren magazines—*Our Record, The American Pioneer, Light and Liberty, Assembly Annals,* etc. Here we find the bed-rock foundation of the Independent Brethren movement in North America. The first issue, volume 1 number 1, of *Letters of Interest from the Home Field,* July 1934, illustrates something of the nature of pioneer work still going on in the mid-1930s.

First, a brief quotation from each worker's letter:

William Ingram, Baldwinton, Saskatchewan

In the schoolhouses one gets good audiences. Hardships are plentiful, but God has blessed His work. There are a number of small assemblies bravely holding forth for God in Alberta and Saskatchewan.

William E. Belch, Cascapedia, Quebec

On the Gaspe Coast are eight small assemblies. They are very weak in themselves as there is a lack of local gift . . . During the winter months it is difficult to get about on account of the terrific piles of snow, but in January I rejoiced to see some fifteen saved at Carlisle, and later at the same place five more, and some of these have been added to the small assembly.

Peter J. Pilon, Holland, Michigan

Brother Pilon has labored in the rural districts of Michigan. In 1929 the military hospital at Camp Custer, Michigan, was opened to him

---

1 References above are to the following source: Charles B. Summers, *Return to Old Paths: The Ministry of Charles Spurgeon Summers,* Prodigal Press, 6709 N. 24th St., Tacoma, WA 98406, 1990.

and he labored among its 600 patients with blessing [reported by the Editor].

J.D. Ibbotson, Savannah, Georgia

Have just finished meetings at Guyton, Georgia, thirty-eight miles from Savannah. Meetings were held in school houses holding about forty people. There was blessing among Saints and sinners.

Amos Le Cureaux, Sugar Creek, Michigan

Saints in this section are poor but liberal considering their poverty. There is a desire to know the way of the Lord perfectly.

August Hasse, Hoboken, New Jersey

My home is in Hopatcong, N.J. Have children's meetings there every Sunday. D.V. hope to start a Bible class in my home. Have a Bible class once every week in Newton, N.J.

Harold Jones, Albany, New York

A good number were saved in Key West. The Exclusive Brethren there gladly received them and there is peace and harmony. There is a great need in Florida and in fact in all the Southern States.

Owen Hoffman, Washington, Georgia

In February and March the tent was almost full, about 200 some evenings. So far three have given evidence of being saved. Seven are to be baptized May 13.

O.W. Elder, Yakima, Washington

I have a gospel truck and use a public address amplifier which enables me to speak to people in a whole city block. I have more openings than I can attend to for a whole year.

J.W. Bramhall, Jr., Sumpter, South Carolina

The Spirit of God has led a group of Christians in the denominations to meet once a week for Bible reading and prayer as Christians. There is quite a group of them, and for five weeks I have had much joy in preaching the Word. [So far as we know, J.W. Bramhall is the only one of these pioneers still preaching when this book went to press in 1995.]

James Smith, Ashville, North Carolina

I recently drove 500 miles through Tennessee and in all that distance there is only one small assembly.

F.W. Nugent, Merchantville, New Jersey

About five years ago, being exercised about the need in the South, I was led to Canton, North Carolina, where after laboring with Brother W.G. Foster a number of precious souls were saved.

John F. Miller, Chicago, Illinois

Have had gospel meetings in Henryetta and Atoka, Oklahoma. [In Henryetta] there is a small assembly in a brother's home. In the latter place there was an assembly, but the sheep have been scattered for lack of a shepherd. The people in all these places are so poor that they cannot even buy hymn books.

C.B. Cramer, Louisville, Kentucky

The unfortunate feature of gospel work is that preachers only stay long enough to get people interested, and then off they go to fresh fields. Why is this? It is because preachers are literally compelled to move from needy places because Saints who have the wherewithal do not cooperate with God to meet the need.

Frank Detweiler, Virginia

After three summers of tent effort in Bristol a small assembly of about twenty souls was planted there, and a hall built. After three more seasons of tent work another assembly was planted in Marion, also an assembly at Johnson City.

A.B. Rogers, Omaha, Nebraska

Have worked in the following places: Eastern Colorado (my birth place), the foothills of the Rocky Mountains, Western Ozark Mountain Region, Louisiana, and Eastern Iowa where some twenty-five now remember the Lord, and there are two small gatherings in Louisiana.

Charles Bowen, Vancouver, British Columbia

Have been in mining villages and remote settlements of British Columbia. Visited every house in six settlements, leaving Gospels, also having meetings in homes and schoolhouses. Many homes visited have no knowledge of the gospel.

H.G. Mackay, Bristol, Virginia

We are now in Marion, Virginia. Saints have no regular meeting place in Marion and this hinders the work. During the week nights have attendance of from thirty to forty in private homes and in the open air Saturday evening we get about 100.

William Murray, Matheson, Ontario

We are faced with the problem of getting a hall in Currie. For the sum of $200 we could put up a building that would be plain and cheap but suitable for our purposes.

F.W. Schwartz, Detroit, Michigan

During last summer a gospel trailer was operated in a number of towns in this region and quite an interest was observed in some of them. As a result of tent and schoolhouse work a number were saved. [Fig. 62]

E.K. Bailey, Bell, California

We are in our sixth week of meetings in Bell, California .. . Children's meetings on Monday evenings and Sunday afternoons attract large crowds.

Lawrence London, Colgate, Oklahoma

The Lord has led me to serve Him at Bethel School House near Colgate. As a result of preaching the Word, there is a nice company of saints here.

On the back page of this first *Letters of Interest* is a moving communication from Richard Varder, dated December 27, 1932. Before the magazine was circulated, Varder had passed from this life. We reproduce it below in its entirety, as it powerfully illustrates the character of those workers who deliberately sought out the most difficult fields:

I have no idea as to when or by whom I can get this letter to the nearest post office—Meadow Lake, forty-two miles distant. Since I arrived here, on the 12th inst.,I have had two opportunities of sending mail, and as yet, only one of getting any. So you see we are pretty well isolated.

Everything here is in a primitive state. [People live in] log houses with mud roofs which do not keep out the rains. The settlers, apparently, have yet to learn the way in which to fix a roof with mud and thatch grass. Most of the houses have no flooring—just Mother Earth. About sixteen years ago this was a primeval forest, chiefly of spruce that towered from 100 to probably 150 feet high, with a good sprinkling of very tall white poplar. A bad fire came along, killed everything, and now the once stately spruce lie in a hopeless tangle from three to six feet deep. The cleared patches amount to four, five or six acres, and, as there is very little hay to be obtained, it is estimated that two-thirds of the cattle and horses which were brought into this settlement have died of starvation.

I have kept on continuously in the gospel since my arrival, with congregations of from seven to twelve. But the people are getting interested and I have offers of several homes. At one of these, on the 18th, about twenty grown-ups and thirty children came, and at another, on Christmas Day, we had about eighteen grown-ups, and I was much encouraged by the many offers given to me to hold meetings in different homes. I took the people into my confidence—told them that I was the Lord's servant regarding what I should preach, but that I was willing to be their servant regarding time and place.

The roads are very bad here. Horses make about three miles per hour. Many have no team and some are temporarily absent. Then this is the "dark of the moon."

Episcopalians, Presbyterians, and United have come in and have forsaken the field so I have it all to myself. This would be a splendid place for a young man who could walk and walk and walk some more, and it would be a great blessing if the Lord would stir up the hearts of some young strong fellows to come in here with the gospel, visiting among the homes, and content to live the life which the settlers here, owing to conditions, have to do.—R.F. Varder

Evangelizing French-Speaking Canadians

The province of Ontario in Canada was the first to be evangelized by the Independent Brethren, and by 1920 assemblies had been established across the land from Victoria, British Columbia to Sidney Mines, Nova Scotia. Even in Quebec there was an active meeting in Montreal which by July 1921 gave notice that they were "buying a new tent for this summer's work, and . . . looking to God for seasonable help to work it." This ministry, however, was in English. There were at this time some 3,500,000 French- speaking Canadians who, with a few minor exceptions, were almost totally unreached by the gospel.

In this day, the problem of a "nation within a nation" created by the French-speaking population of Canada is frequently in the news. Behind this vexing situation lie several centuries of history. The French naval explorer Jacques Cartier discovered the mouth of the St. Lawrence River and the site of Quebec City in 1535. The region became a rich source of fish and fur for the French, but was also exploited by the British, who in 1627 besieged Quebec and forced the surrender of its commander, the famous Samuel de Champlain. Quebec was returned to France in 1632 and remained its possession until 1759 when Quebec City was captured by troops of the British General Wolfe (who was killed in the engagement). While technically part of the British Empire (and later the Commonwealth), French-speaking Canada has stead-fastly retained its original heritage in language, culture, education, and religion, and has stood defiantly aloof from everything English.

In the transfer of authority to the English in 1763, the French were allowed to keep their educational and religious systems, and up to fairly recent times all schools and social services were controlled and run by the Roman Catholics. To keep their domination, the priests have assured women that their salvation lies in child-bearing, resulting (1950) in an average of five children in a French-speaking family to not quite two in an English. By and large the Roman Catholic clergy have fostered hatred for the English and contempt for Protestantism, result-ing (at least before Vatican II in the early 1960s) in severe persecution of anyone who became an evangelical Christian. Thus those who would evangelize French Canadians faced a serious challenge. In 1946, accord-ing to Arthur Hill who had a burden for the French Canadians, there were some 25,000 Roman Catholic clergy in the province of Quebec, and only about thirty evangelical workers, including ten associated with Brethren.

One of the earliest Brethren workers among French-speaking Cana-dians was Louis Germain, who reports in *Light and Liberty* in 1935:

> Since Dr. A.C. Hill has gone to Sherbrooke, God has been with him. Not only he and Mrs. Hill are remembering the Lord with a few Christians, but have also a Bible and prayer meeting. Then Dr. and Mrs. Hill are also sending by mail gospels and tracts to their French patients.

Germain reports that he was told by the chief of police of Sherbrooke to leave town or be arrested, so he concentrated on smaller towns. "Not-withstanding the efforts of the enemy, I was enabled to visit hundreds of homes, to give over 600 Gospels, and some thousands of tracts . . ." Before reaching his home in Ottawa, however, he was taken to a police station and warned.

The first substantial breakthrough for evangelism among the "Quebe-coise" was in the early 1930s when, in the village of Girardville some 300 miles north of Quebec City, the priest decided to have a new church building constructed four miles to the north. Knowing that the villagers were opposed to this move, the priest tried to remove the sacramental vessels by stealth, only to be spotted by a local woman when he was handing the stuff through a window. The woman set upon the wretched cleric with a paddle and drove him out of town, and when the church sued, the court decided in favor of the woman.

Meanwhile someone in the village had obtained a New Testament and was finding that what he read contradicted what the church taught. A town meeting resulted in a decision to advertise in a Montreal paper for a French-speaking Protestant minister to preach in the now deserted church building. The ad was seen by brother John Spreeman, who after much prayer and correspondence made a trip to Girardville accompanied by Noah Gratton. After presenting the gospel at a town meeting, which drew a divided response, they spent weeks holding meetings in homes and working alongside the men in the fields until they were kidnapped and forced out of town by armed men, a plan instigated by the exiled priest. They returned to continue the Lord's work in 1934, and the result was a number of baptisms and the start of an assembly. In 1937 a school was built in Girardville, and teachers were supplied by the Brethren.

For many years Dr. and Mrs. Hill sent out a report called "News from Quebec" designed to draw attention to this needy province (still in operation by Marg Robbins and Richard Strout), and actively recruited workers. Around 1938, Arnold Reynolds, who had been evangelizing in the lumber camps with an organization called the Shantyman's Christian Association, became associated with Brethren at the Hills' invitation, and has with his wife served the Lord among French speakers until this day (1989). By 1946, workers included Mr. and Mrs. John Spreeman, Louis Germain, Noah Gratton, Mr. and Mrs. Vincent Davey, Mr. and Mrs. Emmanuel Laganiere, Mr. and Mrs. Joseph Darling, Harold Fryday, and Mrs. Norman Buchanan (schoolteacher). By 1950 they had been joined by Howard Forbes and Paul Boeda.

According to Arnold Reynolds in a 1989 interview, the cause of the gospel in Quebec has been advanced greatly by two major events since 1950. The first was the Second Vatican Council, referred to above, which from the early 1960s encouraged the reading of Scripture and a more liberal attitude toward non-Catholics. The second was the taking over of education and social services by the civil government, stripping the Catholics of a monopoly they had held for some two hundred years. In 1991 there were over fifty French speaking assemblies in Quebec and 116 workers, plus a Bible College, Bethel Bible Institute.

(Special sources for the above were:

Arthur Hill, "Quebec for Christ," *Letters of Interest*, July 1946; "A Whole Community Turns to Christ," *Letters of Interest*, September 1946; Noah Gratton letter in *Letters of Interest*, June 1947;

Howard Forbes, "Quebec, a Roman Catholic Citadel," *Letters of Interest*, March 1950.)

Birth of a New Fellowship

The following account by H.G. McEwen appeared in *Light and Liberty*, October 1940. It is a typical example of the unique way in which Brethren assemblies were founded during the 1930s and 1940s:

> September eighth was a day long to be remembered in Dover [Delaware], the day when the first small company met in the Name of our Lord Jesus Christ alone, giving up all human names . . . and depending upon His promise, "Where two or three are gathered together in My Name, there am I in the midst of them." We began the day with a service at the C.C.C. camp . . . then drove to the Hall . . . Just a store building, a large, though not an upper room, furnished. In the center the table, the loaf of bread and the cup of wine. Soon sixteen people, most of whom had but recently heard and obeyed the call of God, sat down to partake of the remembrance feast, and to worship God through Christ.
>
> It was a beautiful sight, beholding these Christians, without appointed minister, or selected creed, meeting to worship as "they found it written." Beginning with the hymn, "Meeting in the Savior's Name" the Spirit led on in thanksgiving and praise, and as we sang, "Alas and did my Savior bleed, and did my Sovereign die?" many wept . . . There were more tears after meeting, some of the saints actually hugging the others and saying, "What a blessed feast the Lord has brought us to."
>
> In the afternoon we drove out to Moore's Lake, and before a good crowd of witnesses baptized six. . . Then to prison, carrying the gospel to the men behind bars. [In] the evening Mr. McEwen ministered a solemn and faithful message, and presented Christ, the Savior of the lost. As the day closed all were slow to leave, and some felt it to be the happiest day of [their lives]

Planting and Harvesting in North Carolina

One of the more interesting stories from the 1920-1950 period is how the earliest transition occurred from the itinerant ministry of the pioneer evangelists in early days to the way new work is generally opened up today. The story revolves around a man of God named Lester Wilson, although it did not start with him. At the end of World War I a young man named James C. Chappell returned from army service to his home in Raleigh, North Carolina. A Christian, he had learned from a fellow soldier about gathering to the Name of Christ alone. This he shared with his wife and a friend, David Allen. In 1924, when Brethren evangelists Sam McEwen and W.G. Smith held meetings in Raleigh, a small remembrance gathering was started, with at first just Allen, Mr. and Mrs. Chappell and the two workers.

In 1931, Fred Nugent, another Brethren evangelist, was scheduled to hold a five-week gospel campaign at Clayton, seventeen miles southeast of Raleigh, assisted by a young preacher, Lester Wilson. Nugent, however, was forced by circumstances to remain at home and Wilson had to carry on alone. The young man started out with much fear, but soon crowds packed out the building and at the end of the five weeks fifty-one persons had professed faith in Christ. Wilson, who was living with the Chappells at the time, continued in the area for three years, preaching, holding Bible studies, and helping the little assembly there to develop. In 1934 he was invited to work at Winston-Salem. Here Wilson spent five years building and establishing the congregation to about ninety believers meeting in their own chapel. This work was taken over by Harold Mackay in 1939, who in turn stayed four and a half years. By 1946 the assembly was thriving in the hands of local leaders.

Over the years Lester Wilson was used of the Lord to establish six healthy assemblies in North Carolina, at Raleigh, [Fig. 63] Winston-Salem, Greensboro, Burlington, Siler City, and Durham.[1]

---

1 Lester Wilson, of course, could not have succeeded without a number of other gifted brethren of like-mind cooperating with him. In the period we are speaking of these included

It was at Greensboro that Wilson originated the Family Bible Hour concept in 1941, to bring in the eleven o'clock churchgoers. To quote *Interest* in a January 1992 article, "Thousands of believers in the Southeastern U.S. can trace their spiritual heritage to his labors. He is, in fact, one of the most prolific assembly planters in North America in this century." The significance of this is that *Wilson proved that changes were needed from the methods used by earlier workers in order to gain positive results in a changing society.*

In 1944 Lester Wilson shared in *Letters of Interest* the reasons why he believed the outreach in North Carolina was so effective:

> The secret under God that has produced results in North Carolina is—going to a place and staying there until something is done. This will take years. You can't expect people to get saved one summer, and without any teaching or pastoring during the winter, find them going on and ready for an assembly the next summer

> . . . A summer's work must be followed up by a winter's pastoring and teaching, and then another summer's gospel work with another winter like the first one. . .

> If one is satisfied with a half dozen breaking bread in a house or old store building, then little or no gift is required, and the work will never amount to much and will eventually die out. But if one wants a big work, with a large assembly in a fine building, with an energetic gospel work going on which has an influence in the city . . . then gift must be present, and until this appears it is up to the laborer to stay on the job or get a capable substitute when he leaves.

> It is harder to continue in one place than to [keep visiting different] assemblies. In [the same] place one has to keep digging and keep fresh to maintain interest. The same old sermons over and over again will not do.

> . . . what has been related is all to God's glory, and could be duplicated in every state in the union if the same methods were used . . . such as, all means of advertising, especially the radio, good singing, attractive places for meetings, and staying with the work. To do this in no way violates the principles of Scripture for which we stand, nor does it mean a compromise

---

Harold Mackay, Welcome Detweiler, Clarence Low, Joe Giordano, William Bousfield, William Brown, Ernest Gross, Gordon Reager, John Milton Mills, and W.G. Smith.
(For more information on assembly planting, see *Letters of Interest*, January 1944, July 1946, December 1948, January 1951, March 1954, April 1958 and *Interest*, January 1992.)

with, or imitations of, so-called Christendom . . . Our principles will not fail today, but our methods and customs of 50 years ago will.

Pages from an Itinerant Preacher's Diary

The following anonymous article appeared in the October 1935 issue of *Light and Liberty*. While many of the Lord's people during those Great Depression years had no regular income, it was expected of the itinerant preacher and his wife that they would make their needs known only to God.

Aug. 2—First week of tent meetings over in []; many concerned, none saved, pocketbook empty and gas-gauge says two and one-half gallons in tank and fifty-five miles from home. The Lord always got me home before and He will do so now. If not—well there is no "if" to it.

Aug. 3—I coasted down hills and glided in home with two big zeros—one on the gas-tank and the other on the pocketbook. First sight was the old Ford under the "repair tree." Next—news from wife, "On the way to the meeting with the load, it broke a piston." So all day and part of night I was "out and under" to get it ready for hauling passengers to meetings on Lord's day. Made check for new pistons and it left $3.00 in account. Compared balances to see how close we could draw and found a deficit of sixty-seven cents. Wife brought out a two dollar bill, once given her for personal needs and it was put aside for a Monday morning trip to the bank before the deficit showed up.

Aug. 4-Lord's day, after more prayer, wife went to one assembly and I took the last dollars to fill the gas tank for a 200 mile drive to help a small assembly. Praise God (for we didn't know what to do) a sister gave wife four one dollars bills (they looked like ten dollars bills today) and words failed for thanksgiving. A brother passed on 50 cents and again we thanked the Lord. But the tanks were again empty and I must leave for the tent. Room and board must be paid or the gospel would be disgraced. Our children offered their penny banks. We reluctantly took a few dollars on a temporary loan. We parted after earnest supplications and thanksgivings.

Aug. 9—All week I watched that gas-gauge to see if that tank of gas would finish the week and get me home. After paying room and board, had 17 cents and gas was 22 cents. I wanted to visit a babe in Christ but gas-gauge forbade. Wrote some letters to pigeon-hole until stamps could be procured. All the way home the Lord caused me to repeat in the midst of much intercession, "He that spared not His Own Son—*how shall he not* also with Him freely give us all things?" The Lord had blessed the gospel at the tent so that three had confessed Christ. On arriving home wife told of five confessing at the meetings there. Wasn't it better to have souls saved and an empty pocketbook than to have a full pocketbook and no fruit for the Lord? We answered the Lord, "Yes, Lord, give us souls." Asked wife what the Lord had sent in during the week and she said, "Nothing;" but I rather thought that He had sent it but someone whom He wanted to use as His messenger boy had not brought it.

Aug. 10—Mail came and a sister sent $1.00. If she knew what we needed she would have put in ten, but that one was a God-send. Gas, groceries, and baby food reduced all the children's banks to "vacancy." We waited on God—nothing came—BUT O what promises on that daily calendar!— "Your heavenly Father *knoweth* that ye have need of all these things."

Returning on the fifty-five mile trip to the tent, the preacher is terrified to hear loud knocks in the motor, but keeps on driving and reaches his destination. After a soul-stirring meeting, a Christian lady gives him 50 cents, making his total cash on hand $1.00. The Lord speaks to him in his prayers: "My servant, don't you understand? I am wanting to see how much you can stand without your faith faltering . . . "

That night the tent is blown down in a rain storm, ruining lamps and equipment. The extra 50 cents enables him to drive home for things to repair the tent and equipment. The next day, while his wife is in the town getting thread to sew the canvas, she collides with another car and the owner demands damages. But the mail that day brings "the first beam of light from the Lord, Who is faithful and Who will not suffer us to be tempted above that we are able. When that brother learns in glory what the Lord made that gift to His servants, will he not wish that he had spent even more of his money that way?"

14

Widening Horizons in the 1930s and 1940s

Care of Children and the Elderly

Another positive trend of the 1940s and 1950s was social concern, especially for children who needed a foster home, and for the elderly who required more care than a normal household could provide. In 1941 the Christian Home for Children was founded in Colorado Springs, Colorado. [Fig. 64] By 1948 (when the home was featured on the cover of *Letters of Interest*) there were fifty boys and girls and a staff of ten. John Walden was the director there for many years. Though its role has changed, the ministry still exists under the name Family Life Services, now directed by Ron Bennett.

In March 1948, the Adelaide Christian Children's Home in Los Angeles had seventeen boys and girls, either orphans or from broken homes. Dick Matthews was in charge of that work. There was also the Pittsboro Christian Home in North Carolina and Maplemount Home in Quebec, Canada, and some others. However, this ministry was terminated due to laws requiring the placement of children in foster homes.

The first home for the elderly was Rest Haven Homes of Grand Rapids, begun in 1941. A conference in June 1948, for the boards and staffs of six assembly homes for the elderly, was held in Grand Rapids, Michigan. Represented were: Elim Home, Midland, Ontario; Rest Haven Homes, Grand Rapids; Rest Haven Homes, Spring Lake, Michigan; El Nathan Home, Buffalo, New York; Gospel Halls Home, Longport,

New Jersey; Western Assemblies Home, South Pasadena, California. Current addresses of more than fifteen Brethren retirement homes are given in the Directory of North American Missions published yearly by Interest Ministries.

Summer Conferences for the Whole Family

The first summer Bible conferences for the whole family sponsored by Brethren also started in the same era, during the late 1940s, exceptions being the Guelph conference which originally served the Grant Exclusives, Greenwood Hills, and Cedar Lake, all of which date to the 1930s or earlier. Twelve such conferences were advertised in *Letters of Interest* for the summer of 1948: [Fig. 65]

Blue Ridge, North Carolina;
Yosemite National Park, California;
Camp Berea, New Hampshire;
Cannon Beach, Oregon;
Greenwood Hills, Pennsylvania;
Guelph, Ontario;
Lake Geneva, Wisconsin;
Mazama, Washington;
Lake Koronis, Minnesota;
Neerlandia, Alberta;
Pine Bush Camp, New York;
Stony Brook, Long Island, New York.

Fellowship Outside the Assemblies

As was pointed out earlier (chapter 10), some men and women from Brethren assemblies began to associate for gospel outreach with Christians from denominational churches as early as the 1920s, and this brought criticism from the more conservative believers. This openness grew during the 1930s as para-church ministries like the Gideons were formed, and became very widespread during the 1940s during and after World War II. (Apparently this exclusive attitude was not usually transferred to the mission field, where Brethren have tended to work harmoniously with other Christians since the days of Hudson Taylor and Frederick Arnot.) Some of the ministries in which Brethren have been active are:

The Gideons International
This is an association of Christian business and professional men, founded in 1899. They began free distribution of the Scriptures in 1908. Men from Open Brethren assemblies are prominent in the Gideons in many parts of the world—in fact, an assembly brother is current head of the organization in England (1991).

The Christian Businessmen's Committees
CBMC has also had men from the assemblies prominent in their ranks down through the years. In the 1939-40 World's Fair on Treasure Island, San Francisco Bay, the Christian Businessmen's Committees helped to sponsor the Sermons from Science pavilion featuring Irwin Moon of the Moody Institute of Science. The gospel presenter was Brethren evangelist Tom Olson. Some years later, the International CBMC chairman was George Armerding, brother of evangelist Henry Armerding.

The Navigators
During World War II, 1941-45, thousands of Christian young men in uniform were encouraged in their faith through Scripture memory by the "Navs," an organization started in San Diego by Dawson Trotman. Among them were many from the assemblies, who for the first time in their lives found that deeply committed believers existed outside the Brethren. After the war some of the men from the assemblies joined the Navigator staff, and this link continues today.

Youth For Christ
At the end of World War II, Youth for Christ rallies held on Saturday nights in many cities were attracting both young people and adults from the more progressive assemblies. These events, which began in 1943 and resulted in the formation of YFC International in 1945, were another means of breaking down the isolationist attitude inherited from the early Brethren evangelists. People from assemblies continue today to serve on the Youth for Christ staff.

Foreign Missions and Scripture Translation and Distribution

Chapter 4 has already documented how early Brethren missionaries worked closely with Hudson Taylor and the China Inland Mission. A number from the assemblies are members of the Overseas Missionary Fellowship (the current name of this organization) today. Brethren serve with several other foreign missions societies. They are also represented in the ranks of the Wycliffe Translators and various Bible Societies.

Inter-Varsity Christian Fellowship

Of all the so-called "para-church" organizations in North America, however, none has had a closer link with the Brethren than the Inter-Varsity Christian Fellowship. IVCF was founded in Canada in 1927 by Dr. Howard W. Guinness of England, where the Brethren were strong supporters of student work. (The two foremost books on the defense of the faith there were *Modern Science and the Bible* by Professor A. Rendle Short and *Are the New Testament Documents Reliable?* by F.F. Bruce, both among the Brethren.) The successor of Howard Guiness in Canada was Arthur Hill, a medical doctor who, as has been noted in 13, was for many years a leader among English speaking assemblies in Sherbrooke, Quebec. In 1934, at the invitation of Hill, C. Stacey Woods, [Fig. 80c] son of Brethren evangelist Fred Woods of Australia, became general secretary of the IVCF of Canada. In 1941 he and Charles Troutman took over the leadership of the IVCF then beginning in the U.S.

The vision that Stacey Woods had for non-denominational student work was the same as that of the young university men and women who first gathered together in Dublin in the 1820s. He took the Keswick theme, "All One in Christ Jesus," as InterVarsity's motto and doggedly kept the movement free of sectarianism. Something of that unity and oneness in Christ can be seen today in the great Urbana Missionary Convention which was founded under Woods at Toronto in 1946. Around him he gathered a band of gifted young leaders that included a significant number with Brethren backgrounds—Frank Horton,[1] Char-

---

1 Frank Horton, the son of Africa missionary A.E. Horton, went on to become principal of Institut Biblique Emmaus, a Brethren-related school in French Switzerland. Paul Little, son of Brethren worker Robert Little, who became internationally famous for his books *How to Give Away Your Faith* and *Know Why You Believe*, was the organizer of the first Lausanne Conference on Evangelism. Paul died in an auto accident in July 1975, a great loss to the evangelical world.

les Hummel, Anne Begwin, Paul Little, and Herbert Butt. Like George Müller, Woods refused to disclose any specifics about financial needs. The staff were not required to raise their own support, but were expected to depend on the Lord for the needs of the Fellowship. In those days each campus group was autonomous, and the staff came among them to minister, not to direct activities.

15

Biblical Teaching and Publishing

The Emmaus Story

During the weekend of October 10-13, 1991, some 700 alumni and friends from all over the world converged on Dubuque, Iowa, for the fiftieth anniversary of Emmaus Bible College. One of the high points of the celebration was when president Daniel Smith presented plaques to founder Edward Harlow and Faye Smart, widow of founder John Smart (C. Ernest Tatham felt unable to make the trip from his Florida home). Referring to the beginning of Emmaus's history, Mr. Smith stated: "We assure you that Emmaus continues to teach and train students in the same truths of the New Testament that the pioneers of the school taught." This chapter will briefly tell the story of those who had the initial vision for Emmaus and how that vision grew.

Before Emmaus came into existence a number of the ministering brethren including A.P. Gibbs, George Landis, and Harold Harper had attended Moody Bible School or Toronto Bible School. Some pioneer evangelists like J.J. Rouse, however, felt that young men should strike out into the work and learn from experience, an opinion shared by some dear saints even today. Yet formal Bible teaching actually has much deeper roots in the history of the Brethren. While residing in Switzerland in the 1840s, J.N. Darby conducted regular teaching sessions with a view toward training workers who would in turn teach his particular Biblical doctrines. In a January 1840 letter, he argued:

That one teach, or that more than one take part if united in work, is a matter for them to judge of, under the guidance of the Holy Ghost. Paul and Barnabas assembled themselves with the church, and taught much people. He who has the gift of teaching is responsible to Christ for the exercise of his gift; it may be exercised in private; in the meeting together of brethren if so led, on the Lord's day; or he may assemble them to teach them if he has the capacity for it, for he is acting then on the responsibility which lies on him to trade with his talent.

Chapter 12 pointed out how in the 1930s some of the Grant Exclusive preachers began to have fellowship and work together with their counterparts from the Independent assemblies, and that association in time led to an amalgamation. Some of the Grant men had had Bible school training and saw the value of a systematic approach to gaining a knowledge of Scripture. At Guelph, Ontario, the private estate of a Grant brother, George McAllister, had been turned into a conference center, which by 1933 was under the direction of a joint committee of Brethren from both backgrounds. In the summer of 1935 a short-term Bible school, lasting from two to four weeks, was commenced on the grounds. This was held every summer for the next twenty-five years. C. Ernest Tatham was active in this from the beginning.

According to Tatham, a letter was received at the 1940 Guelph summer Bible school from R. Edward Harlow, a young missionary serving in Africa, enclosing a check for $25 and urging the need of "a place where young people can receive systematic Bible training along assembly lines." The next year, 1941, Harlow was forced to return to Canada because World War II had started. He then shared his vision and organizational skills with Tatham and John Smart, serving also on the summer school staff. Smart, a member of the Missionary Service Committee and Christian Missions in Many Lands, Canada, had spent a year and a half in evangelism in the West Indies. He had returned in 1937 to work for the Lord in Toronto. In September 1941, the trio [Fig. 66] announced the commencement of an evening Bible school at the old Central Gospel Hall in Toronto.

In recalling the beginning of those night school classes, Edward Harlow told how the young teachers "hoped for 25 students . . . and ninety-eight showed up! Within weeks we had 144 enrolled. There was no la-di-da about it—just three forty minute sessions of concentrated Bible lectures each night." The subjects were Old Testament Survey, Doctrine and Homiletics, and the Messianic Psalms taught by Tatham; New Testament Survey, Doctrine, and individual book studies taught by Smart; Christian Education taught by Harlow. According to Harlow, the next step quickly became evident: "We soon realized that with evening classes alone we would never get to first base if we were to reach all the young people who wanted to study the Bible. We all agreed that we should launch a correspondence study program. We did this in 1942."

The correspondence courses were soon widely in use all over North America in Sunday schools, camps, and youth groups. The U.S. as well as Canada was now at war, and courses were sent out free to servicemen at home and abroad. By the mid 1940s the mimeographed courses, based on the curriculum taught in Toronto, numbered fifteen, and two thousand copies had been sent out. Then, as the war drew toward an end and the servicemen who had received the correspondence courses began to come home, there was a further development. To quote Harlow, "We found that a lot of these fellows wanted to continue their studies in the Word. Obviously, what we really needed was a full time day school program. By the time we were ready to hold our first classes (1945) a number of these ex-servicemen had enrolled."

Daytime courses in the full-time Emmaus Bible School began in September 1945 (the month after V-J Day) with eighty to eighty-five students. [Fig. 67] No tuition was charged. An Emmaus Bible School corporation was formed and negotiations were opened with the Canadian Christian Missions in Many Lands board for a building on Harcourt Avenue, Toronto. The development into a full-scale school created a need for more instructors. Over the years this need was satisfactorily met in part by experienced traveling teachers who would spend a number of weeks each year at the school. These included August VanRyn, Charles VanRyn, Peter Pell, Harold Harper, Alfred Gibbs, George Landis, and Neil Fraser. The first full-time Emmaus staff member to follow the initial trio of Harlow, Tatham, and Smart was also one of the first day school students. He was William MacDonald, a young naval officer and graduate of Harvard Business School, whose skills included both Bible teaching and administration.

A substantial number of the students attending Emmaus in Toronto were from the United States, and interest began to develop in establishing a branch there, as well as in western Canada. In early 1947, James Humphrey of Stewards Foundation opened correspondence with Edward Harlow, inviting Emmaus to open a school in Chicago in a building they had purchased at 69th and Normal Boulevard. This was commenced in the spring of the same year with William McDonald as administrator. The board of Emmaus was expanded to include six Chicago members, and the new school was incorporated as Emmaus Bible School of Chicago. Control of policy and curricula remained with Toronto, however, and students wishing to go beyond one year were required to go to the Toronto campus for further study.

In the early 1950s several conditions, such as need for increased financial support and enrollment and governmental regulations regarding Americans studying in Canada, made a move to the U.S. attractive to the Emmaus staff. Changes were also imminent within the staff, as John Smart had accepted a position with *The Fields*. At this time a former YMCA building in Oak Park with recreational facilities and a dormitory was located by the Chicago board members, and a decision was made in 1953 to make the move. Ed Harlow took up residence in Oak Park, where he remained as president until 1958. The school in Toronto was subsequently closed.

Harlow's move was also to serve with *The Fields*, and his place as president was taken by William MacDonald. MacDonald made significant contributions to the development of the correspondence courses, which will be discussed in chapter 21. He served for seven years until 1965. At that time John Smart returned to become president, and during his tenure made a number of improvements to the Oak Park property as well as in the curriculum. During this period, C. Donald Cole, who had served the Lord for several years in Angola, came on the staff to head up the missions emphasis. Upon Smart's sudden home call in 1975, a member of the faculty, Daniel Smith, succeeded to the presidency. Under his leadership, Emmaus received accreditation by the American Association of Bible Colleges. The move to Dubuque to occupy the beautiful facilities and spacious grounds of a former Catholic seminary took place in 1984. [Fig. 68]

(Special sources for the above include an Emmaus publication, *Emmaus Bible College: The First 50 Years,* an interview with Daniel Smith in October 1992, and *Letters of Interest* and *Interest* articles in May 1948, November 1972 and January 1992.)

Brethren Writers and Writing

Anyone who wishes to understand the Brethren prior to 1960 must take into account the *literary* nature of the movement. The writing of books, tracts and hymns in many ways defined them, both to themselves and to others outside their circles. One of their worst enemies, the Rev. William Reid who wrote *Plymouth Brethrenism Unveiled and Refuted*, wrote:

> Only those who have sought after their publications, with the view of acquiring a knowledge of their opinions, can form an adequate conception of the extent and variety of their literature.

This subject is so vast as to be a gold mine for scholars and researchers. Indeed, an entire book, *Brethren Writers* by Arnold D. Ehlert, librarian at Talbot Theological Seminary, was published by Baker Book House (no date given). Regarding content, it is probably safe to say that Brethren writers are best known for devotional literature, typology (particularly types of the Lord Jesus Christ in Old Testament ceremonies), in prophecy, and in expository works of the books of the Bible.

The best public collection of Brethren books and periodicals in North America was to be found at the Biola library in La Mirada, California when Ehlert wrote his book; though, that distinction now belongs to the Emmaus Bible College library in Dubuque, Iowa. Emmaus inherited Ehlert's notes and card files, and the school is actively seeking to develop the definitive Brethren archives on this continent. Other collections accessible to the public are to be found in the libraries at Dallas Theological Seminary, Ontario Theological Seminary in Willowdale near Toronto, and Moody Bible Institute in Chicago. Smaller but significant collections are in the libraries of McMaster University in Hamilton, Ontario; Regent College in Vancouver, British Columbia; Hartford Theological Seminary in Hartford, Connecticut; and Interest Ministries in Wheaton, Illinois. Some private collectors in the U.S. and Canada are also said to possess extensive holdings, running into the thousands of items.

It is beyond the scope of this history (not to mention the ability of the author) to describe works by Brethren writers in detail. By the 1930s and 1940s, most Brethren families would be acquainted with the essential titles. Thus a typical home library at that time probably would include some (but not all) of the following:

Sir Robert Anderson, *Daniel in the Critic's Den*

Frederick S. Arnot, *Missionary Travels in Africa*

J.G. Bellett, *On the Moral Glory of the Lord Jesus Christ*

E.H. Broadbent, *The Pilgrim Church*

Dan Crawford, *Thinking Black* and *Back To the Long Grass*

J.N. Darby, *Collected Writings* (34 vols.) and *Letters* (edited by W. Kelly) (3 vols.)

Synopsis of the Books of the Bible (6 vols.)

F.W. Grant, *The Numerical Bible* (7 vols.)

H.A. Ironside, *The Lamp of Prophecy* and one or more commentaries on particular books of the Bible

William Kelly, *The Bible Treasury* (16 vols.)

W.P. Mackay, *Grace and Truth*

W.J. McClure, *Lectures on the Tabernacle*

C.H. Macintosh, *Notes on the Pentateuch* (6 vols.)

George Müller, *Autobiography*

Hy Pickering, *Chief Men Among the Brethren*

Samuel Ridout, *The Church and Its Order*

John Ritchie, *The Feasts of Jehovah*

Finally, a word about tracts and booklets. These fall into three categories, evangelistic, didactic, and polemic. All three kinds were written by numerous Brethren and sent forth, in some cases, by the tens of thousands. Of evangelistic tract writers, Charles Stanley, a Yorkshire businessman, was one of the best known. His numerous leaflets gained fame as the "C.S. Tracts" (Brethren attached only their initials to their writings in those days), with popular titles like "The Live Bird Let Loose," "The Great Supper," "A Sermon of Five Words," and "The Young Convert's Inquiry." Perhaps the most famous gospel tract of all, however, was George Cutting's "Safety, Certainty and Enjoyment," which figured in the conversion of hundreds, perhaps thousands. Another highly effective Brethren gospel tract was "The Reason Why," written by a New Zealand department store owner, Robert Laidlaw.

Didactic (or teaching) tracts and booklets were basic to the Christian education of believers in the days when traveling evangelists were the only source of trained instructors. Tracts by outstanding British teachers like J. Denham Smith, William Lincoln, C.H. Macintosh, and John Ritchie were at first circulated widely in North America by Donald

Ross, Donald Munro, and other booksellers, with titles like "Life in Christ," "The Coming of the Lord," "Eight Lectures on Prophecy," "Should a Christian Go to War?," "The Unequal Yoke," and "What Church Should I Join?" Before long, however, the need on this side of the Atlantic was supplied by W.J. McClure, T.D.W. Muir, John Ferguson, and other gifted North American writers.

The polemic (or disputing) tracts and booklets of the Brethren were the ammunition for the doctrinal battles that occupied too much of their time and energy. Some of those that played an important part in the debate that raged in the ranks of the Grant Exclusives (chapter 12) were:

F.W. Grant, "A Statement for Examination as to Fellowship With Open Brethren (a word of caution against union with them)"

H.P. Barker, "Why I Abandoned Exclusivism"

Hamilton Smith, "Open Brethren: Their Origin, Principles and Practices"

William Hoste, "Rejudging the Question"

John Bloore, "Present Exercise As To Christian Fellowship"

And perhaps the longest title on record:

"An Open Letter to Our Brethren in the United States and Canada Giving Facts and Conditions That Make Necessary Our Withdrawing from Fellowship with the 5717 Chestnut Street Gathering in Philadelphia Because of the Presence of Unjudged Evil" (anonymous)

Ross McLaren quotes F.F. Bruce as saying, "I have a considerable collection of such polemical pamphlets, and I regard it as a great mercy that we see so little of this sort of thing today."

Brethren Publishers and Publishing

The great importance of literature in the life, worship, and ministry of the people called "Plymouth Brethren" can be clearly seen on this side of the Atlantic in the very active history of publishers and publishing, from the 1870s right down to the present day. There have been well over eighty Brethren periodicals, many of them very small operations. Several of the early booksellers also were small-scale publishers, and no one will ever know how many local or regional publishing enterprises

sprang up over the years. Following are accounts of the more prominent ventures.

Loizeaux Brothers

The story of the Loizeaux Brothers Publishers begins with a family of
godly Protestants from Northern France whose heritage went back to
the Reformation of the sixteenth century. The original Loizeaux brothers, Paul and Timothy, were bright young men whose family settled on
a farm near Vinton, Iowa, in 1853. The farm did well, and both boys
were educated and later taught for a time in New York City. Both were
also licensed as Methodist preachers. Paul, who had returned to Vinton,
came to a knowledge of salvation by grace alone through reading Romans 3, a reference pointed out to him by a sick man he was visiting. He
discovered freedom from guilt through reading Colossians 3. Timothy,
who was teaching French at a college in Evanston, also found these
truths by reading Paul's letters. Their association with the Exclusive
Brethren began in 1870 when Paul attended a conference at Guelph and
met J.N. Darby. Paul's famous tract, "The Lord's Dealing with the Con-
vict Daniel Mann," was based on meetings with the condemned man
during the same trip.

Both of the young Loizeaux men threw themselves energetically
into the Lord's work, Paul as an evangelist and Timothy as more of a
pastor. Then, in 1876, Mrs. Paul Loizeaux received a legacy of $1,000,
which she donated for the purpose of starting a "Bible truth depot" (the
Exclusives had a number of these in London, Edinburgh, and elsewhere
in the United Kingdom). A Christian printer and small press were secured, and the operation began to turn out large numbers of the Charles
Stanley tracts as well as the "Daniel Mann" tract and some others. They
also printed the first Exclusive assembly address books. Orders exceeded the press's capacity, and in 1879 the way opened for them to
take over another Bible truth depot in New York City. At this time the
brothers and their families moved to Plainfield, New Jersey, on the rail
line west of the big city.

The Loizeaux Brothers firm remained in New York for eighty-three
years, moving locations within the city in 1881, 1910, and 1930 as the
business grew and space requirements increased. As was noted in the
previous chapter, Plainfield became the home of a number of Exclusive
Brethren leaders, including F.W. Grant himself, and conferences were
held in tents on the spacious grounds of Paul Loizeaux's home.

Loizeaux Brothers from earliest times to the present has specialized in the Brethren "classics" (C.H. Macintosh having been a consistent best-seller), and have added numerous later authors of whom the most popular has been H.A. Ironside. Other well-known Bible expositors and writers include John Ritchie, F.W. Grant, Lewis Sperry Chafer, Arno C. Gaebelein, E. Schuyler English, Charles Ryrie, August VanRyn, T. Ernest Wilson, Alfred Gibbs, William MacDonald, John Phillips, and Alexander Strauch. Ironside, VanRyn, and MacDonald all had roots in the Grant Exclusives.[1]

In 1963 the company left New York for more spacious and safer quarters in Neptune, New Jersey, not far from Ocean Grove and the shores of the Atlantic. Now a not-for-profit corporation, members of the Loizeaux family (fourth generation) are still involved,[2]

(Special sources for the above include a Loizeaux Brothers publication, *A Century of Christian Publishing 1876-1976*, two telephone interviews with John Williams of Walterick in 1991 and 1992, and an article on Everyday Publications in *Interest*, November 1991.) and the company has resisted takeovers in order to retain its unique identity.

Donald Ross

Not only was Donald Ross the editor and publisher of the first Open Brethren magazine, but he was their first book, tract, and songbook publisher as well. The following article appeared in the May 1882, issue of *The Barley Cake*:

> In order to facilitate the study of the Word of God, and the return, at least of some, to the good old ways of a free, full and eternal salvation by grace, without any real or supposed merit whatsoever, and with a view of helping to liberate the Children of God from that wretched mixture called by some "gospel" and the salvation of others who are honestly seeking it but are mistaken as to the way, we have much pleasure in stating that we have begun to publish standard tracts, containing the good old fashioned gos-

---

1 The company aligned with the Independent Brethren in the late 1920s.

2 Succeeding the original Loizeaux brothers were Timothy's sons, P. Daniel, with the business for over sixty years, and Edward for over thirty. Their brothers Arthur and Alfred also had some association. In 1948, Daniel turned the management over to Elie T. Loizeaux, Jr., a grandson of Timothy. In 1976, the 100th anniversary of the company, the fourth generation was represented by Peter I. Bartlett, a great-grandson of Timothy. Bartlett is now president.

pel that saves, clearly and distinctly stated—tracts which in the great North West ought to be scattered in many thousands, and are published at prices which would not provoke competition. Probably we need not tell our readers that this is done, not for any earthly profit.

Gospel Papers

A number of tabloid-type publications were turned out by various Brethren workers as a means of gospel outreach. The first was *The Ram's Horn*, a monthly paper of eight pages produced by the untiring Donald Ross, who in 1881 announced that "Its one theme will be the gospel of the grace of God in its many-sidedness." Next came *The Gospel Herald*, edited and published by Alexander Marshall in Orillia, Ontario. Other known ones include Charles Montgomery's *Gospel Trumpet* of San Francisco, which was distributed free in great numbers, *The Testimony*, also done by Donald Ross, and *The Gospel Monthly*, *Milk of the Word*, *Words of Peace*, and *The Lifeline*, all mentioned elsewhere.

Words in Season

Though not the earliest, *Words in Season* is the longest-running magazine-publishing venture of the Open Brethren in North America. It was started in 1910 by two Philadelphia Brethren and was taken over the following year by E.H. Martin, who was editor for twenty years. Succeeding editors were Charles R. Keller (who, from 1928 to 1932, also edited a periodical on evangelistic work called *The American Pioneer*), Samuel C. Keller, and the well-known William H. Ferguson, who served from 1948 to 1980. The present editor is A.J. Higgins. A similar periodical, *Truth and Tidings*, was started in 1948 by A.W. Joyce of Toronto, especially for Canadians.

The remarkable thing about *Words in Season* is its consistency. For well over fifty years at least it has remained virtually unchanged, including the cover with its title in characteristic Gothic letters reversed on a band of color. The contents include only Biblical-devotional articles, news of conferences and workers, reports of gospel meetings, and a question and answer section. With rare exceptions there are no pictures and no advertising. It serves the "Old Paths" circle of assemblies in the U.S., Canada, and Northern Ireland.

Faithful Words Publishing Company

Faithful Words, a monthly magazine, was edited by Arthur B. Rogers of St. Louis, Missouri, from 1920 to around 1937. The articles are gospel oriented, written by evangelists like Tom Olson and J. Monypenny, and are illustrated with cartoons. Evidently intended for distribution by the assemblies in their Sunday school and gospel meetings, it includes pages for children and young people, and Sunday school lessons prepared by A.P. Gibbs. Faithful Words Publishing Company also produced *The Life Line*, a weekly gospel paper started in 1924, and *Milk of the Word*, [Fig. 70] a monthly paper for young Christians started in 1930, both edited by Rogers.

Light and Liberty Publishing Company

In 1914 a ministering brother named Robert McMurdo started a periodical called *Armor of Light*. The editorship of this was taken over by H.N. O'Brien of St. Louis in 1927. In 1931, O'Brien was joined by James Spink, and the two founded the Light and Liberty Publishing Company of Fort Dodge, Iowa. *Armor of Light* was terminated in favor of a new magazine, *Light and Liberty*. [Fig. 71] They also engaged in other publishing ventures such as A.P. Gibbs's *Gospel Chorus Book* (chapter 15). For its day, *Light and Liberty* was a lively, attractive production that included Biblical-devotional articles by well-known writers past and present, a Bible student's page, current events, a Sunday school corner, and a missionary section with reports from workers both at home and abroad. The editors undertook to distribute funds to workers, and also to send out free tracts.

Walterick Publishers

Walterick Publishers is known by all Independent Brethren assemblies for producing the annual *Address Book of Some Assemblies of Christians* (taking the cue, of course, from Loizeaux's *List of [Exclusive] Gatherings in the United States and Canada*, first published in 1878). Lloyd Walterick, the founder, started printing tracts at his shop in Ft. Dodge, Iowa, some time in the 1930s. He turned out thousands of these, which he supplied to the evangelists at little or no cost. Like Donald Ross, Walterick was both a publisher and editor. In 1937 he took over the editorship of *Light and Liberty*, which he continued for another twenty-three years until expenses forced its discontinuance in 1960. In 1938 he became editor of *The Fields*, a missionary periodical much like the earlier *Voices from the*

Vineyard. Along with lists of funds received for missionaries, it gave reports sent from the field, some illustrated with photos.

As an outgrowth of tract printing, Lloyd Walterick also began publishing books written by and for Brethren workers, notably those of August VanRyn and Alfred P. Gibbs in the earlier years. Lloyd Walterick died in 1975, and the company is now owned and managed by his former assistant, John Williams. Their catalog contains a number of the well-known Brethren titles, plus the Emmaus Bible Study courses, Sunday school and Bible class materials, and also a number of titles published by Loizeaux, Kregel, and others.

Gospel Folio Press
Another publishing house whose roots go back to the early 1920s is the Gospel Folio Press of Grand Rapids. It was started in 1921 by William Pell and Leonard Sheldrake to produce folio size gospel papers. Pell also edited a magazine called *The Uplook*. In 1923 they began to print uniform Sunday school lessons, and in 1927 came out with a missionary newsletter called *Look on the Fields*, which replaced *The Uplook*. *Words of Peace*, edited by F.W. Schwartz from 1928 onward, was printed by Gospel Folio Press.

In 1931, T.D.W. Muir of Detroit, editor of the venerable *Our Record*, died. This magazine was continued for two more years, edited briefly by H.A. Cameron and Charles Ross, and then in 1933 was succeeded by a similar periodical called *Assembly Annals*, [Fig. 88] edited by Peter Pell and published by the Gospel Folio Press. The aged W.J. McClure made it clear that *Annals* was the magazine to inherit his writings from *Our Record*. It ran until 1961. Recently, in 1990, a new and very attractive *Uplook* magazine has been started by the Gospel Folio Press with J. Boyd Nicholson, Jr., as editor.

Letters of Interest from the Home Field
Around the same time that Walterick was getting under way, in July 1934, Mr. and Mrs. Bill McCartney of Chicago began a monthly magazine called *Letters of Interest from the Home Field*, which at first they mimeographed at home. *Letters* was different from all the other Brethren periodicals preceding it, in that it consisted primarily of reports from workers in North America. The editorial staff also took on the task of receiving and distributing funds to the evangelists and pioneer workers on this continent (though they were not the first to undertake

2. Edward Cronin, earliest of the Brethren to "come out."

1. Trinity College, Dublin. The Old Library (center left) was standing in the 1820s and 1830s.

5. John Nelson Darby: Watercolor portrait by Edward Penstone.

3. J.G. Bellett, a friend of A.N. Groves and one of the founders in Dublin.

6. Anthony Norris Groves. He rivals Darby as the originator of "Brethren principles."

4. John Parnell, later Lord Congleton, the first of several peers of the realm who served the Lord among the Brethren.

7. George Müller, whose practical application of faith influenced the entire Christian World.

9. The building on Aungier Street, Dublin, where (in an upstairs auction room) the first Brethren assembly was formed.

11. Chapel in Teignmouth (much restored) where Müller Preached.

8. Henry Craik, Müller's associate and an excellent scholar and preacher.

12. The tiny chapel in Shaldon, across the river from Teignmouth, where Craik preached.

10. Raleigh Gospel Hall, formerly Providence Chapel, Plymouth.

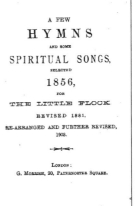

13. *Title page of "Little Flock" hymnbook.*

14. *J.N. Darby. Photo portrait by Alfred Eustace, circa 1850.*

16. *Interior of Bethesda Chapel, Bristol.*

17. *Gravestone of George Müller, Bristol.*

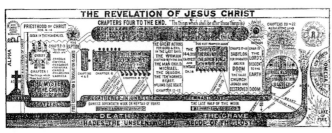

15. *Harry Ironside's chart of Revelation.*

20. *Orphan house No. 1, Ashley Down, Bristol. The Müllers resided here above the main entrance.*

18. *Gravestone of J.N. Darby, Portsmouth.*

21. *Robert Chapman (on right, with white beard) preaching in the open air.*

19. *Map showing Independent Brethren network after Darby's assemblies had separated from them in 1848.*

22. *Betsy Paget, friend of A.N. Groves and co-worker with Robert Chapman, stands outside the humble New Buildings, Barnstaple.*

25. Richard Weaver, colorful Revival preacher and ex-prize fighter.

28. Artist's portrait of Henry Moorhouse, the "boy evangelist."

26. Oldpark Gospel Hall, Belfast, one of many that sprang up in the wake of the Revival.

24. Sketch of John Hambleton, prominent evangelist during the Second Great Evangelical Awakening.

23. Count Guicciardini, founder of the Brethren movement in Italy.

27. Merrion Hall, Dublin, largest and most influential of the gospel halls in Dublin following the Revival.

31. Dr. Fredrich Baedecker, early Brethren missionary who crossed Russia preaching to prisoners.

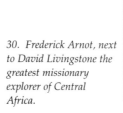

30. Frederick Arnot, next to David Livingstone the greatest missionary explorer of Central Africa.

29. Rare photo of Henry Moorhouse (on left) preaching from a Bible carriage (probably in Manchester).

33. J.N. Darby. Familiar photo taken in later life.

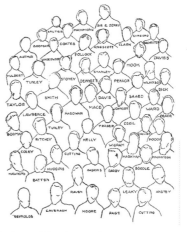

32. Composite photo of prominent Brethren of the nineteenth century.

39. *William Faulknor, first Independent Brethren foreign missionary converted in North America.*

35. *Donald Ross, pioneer evangelist and founder of the first Independent Brethren periodical in North America.*

36. *Mr. & Mrs. Donald Munro. He was the first of the Scots evangelists to preach in North America.*

34. *The venerable Echoes of Service headquarters, over 100 years in Bath, England.*

37. *John Smith, among early pioneers, he eventually made Cleveland, Ohio his base.*

38. Alexander Marshall, the most widely traveled of the first generation pioneer evangelists.

40. The home in Hamilton, Ontario, where an assembly was formed in 1874.

41. Dr. J. Norman Case, who preached in Ontario before going to the mission field in China.

42. Conference meal tent on the grounds of the Paul Loizeaux residence, Plainfield, New Jersey, 1896.

43. Conference speakers John McIntyre, Mr. Poldeman, Robert Telfer, William McClure, and David Oliver, Rose Isle, Manitoba, circa 1895.

44. Gospel Tent with evangelists Mr. Jensen and David D. Jones (grandfather of the author).

45. *Conference at Lyman Iowa (September 1910). Speakers as Follows: First Row Sitting (Left to Right): John Allen, (Berea, Iowa and Long Beach, CA), C. J. Baker (Kansas City, MO), Alex Broadfoot (Berea, Iowa); Second Row Standing (left to right): Jack Charles (Extreme left), John Moffat (Standing Between Mr. Allen and Mr. Baker), C. W. Ross (Kansas City, MO); and D. R. Charles (Behind Mr. Broadfoot). Other men in this group represent some of the local Brethren (Lyman, Iowa) who were present at the beginning of the testimony in Lymon, and some Brethren from nearby assemblies. The testimony in Lyman still continues.*

49. *A poster announcing prophecy meetings by William McClure.*

46. *Caleb Baker's "Two Roads" gospel Chart.*

47. *Title page of* Our Record, *January, 1889.*

48. *Charles Ross, son of the pioneer Donald Ross and a leading second generation preacher and teacher.*

51. *William McClure and T.D.W. Muir, "chief men" among the second generation evangelists.*

54. *Interior of early gospel hall, with chairs set for the Breaking of Bread.*

53. *Gospel hall Sunday school picnic in progress, circa 1900.*

50. *J.J. Rouse, ground-breaking evangelist who pioneered Western Canada.*

52. *A wagon load on the way to the picnic grounds.*

60. Conference group at Waterloo, Iowa, 1923.

58. Frederick Grant (at table in center L, with beard and glasses) during a conference Bible reading, circa 1896.

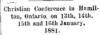

Christian Conference in Hamilton, Ontario, on 13th, 14th, 15th and 16th January, 1881.

The "Larkin Hall," situated on John street, near King street, has been secured for the meetings.

Meetings will be as follows: On Thursday, Friday and Saturday, for prayer, praise and ministry of the Word, at 10 A. M., 2 P. M., and 7 P. M.; on Lord's Day, 16th January, Breaking of Bread at 10 A. M., Ministry of the Word 2 P. M., and Gospel Meeting 7 P. M.

55. Announcement in "The Barley Cake" of 1881 of the annual conference at Hamilton, Ontario.

57. Alfred Mace (on right) with John McIntyre, 1930s.

59. Harry Ironside.

56. First Brethren chapel in the United States, Highland, Illinois.

62. Evangelist Tom Carroll and gospel trailer, circa 1920.

61. Evangelist Oliver Smith (with helpers) and painted rock.

64. Little girls' bedroom, Walden home in Colorado Springs, 1940s.

63. Franklin Street Chapel, Raleigh, North Carolina, the first to be planted by Lester Wilson.

65. Conference grounds ads from the '30s and '50s.

66. *Edward Harlow, Ernest Tatham, and John Smart, the founders of Emmaus Bible College.*

71. *Cover of* Light and Liberty.

70. *Cover of* Milk of the Word.

67. *First daytime class at Emmaus, Toronto, 1945.*

68. *Main building of Emmaus Bible College, Dubuque, Iowa.*

69. *Cover of* Words in Season.

72. *Cover of* Voices from the Vineyard.

75. *Bible camps have provided the Brethren with an effective outreach to children and young people.*

76. *Irene Gallagher's Spanish speaking girls from East Los Angeles departing for camp in the 1950s.*

74. *Evangelist and children's worker Henry Peterson.*

73. *Cover of* The Fields.

77. *Clara Holcomb (at the organ) and Navaho believers in a chapel service.*

79. Crowds at the Harold Wildish campaign in Chicago, 1950s.

80b. Dr. Arthur Hill of Sherbrooke, Quebec.

78. Route of the Gospel Messengers.

80. Stewards Foundation ads from Letters of Interest, 1950s.

80c. C. Stacey Woods, founder of the IVCF, U.S.A.

81. Cover emphasizing U.S. cities as mission fields.

82. Alfred Gibbs

83. T. B. Gilbert

84. Harold Harper

85. William McCartney

86. John Smart

87. August VanRyn

88. Cover of Assembly Annals.

89. First Literature Crusades team to India, 1961.

90. *Hands reach out for Bibles in an Asian city.*

95. *Recently arrived Asian peoples create a new mission field.*

91. *Friendship evangelism in Albania.*

92. *T. Michael Flowers*

94. *Dick Saunders from Great Britain headed a major gospel crusade in Toronto in the '70s.*

93. *African American assemblies witness in the inner cities of North America.*

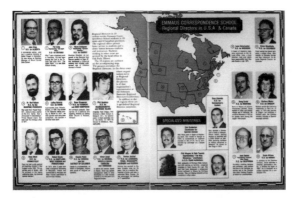

96. Emmaus Correspondence Course Directors in 1976.

100. Participants in the Brethren History Course, Regent College, Vancouver, 1990.

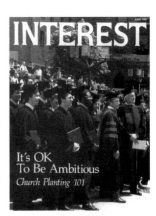

99. In recent years, more and more Brethren leaders have earned scholarly degrees.

97. In the '80s an extensive prison ministry grew out of Emmaus courses.

98. William MacDonald, distinguished Brethren writer and author of Born to Win and Doing Time for Jesus.

101. *A DITP intern conducts an on-campus interview at U. C. Berkeley.*

103. *Cover of the first* Letters of Interest.

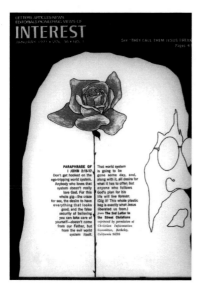

104. *A cover featuring "Jesus Freaks" launches a new style of design for* Interest *magazine.*

102. *Shepherd's Renewal conferences brought elders together for encouragement and training.*

105. *Neil Glass, administrator at Bethesda Hospital in Chicago.*

107. *The emergence of women's ministries in the '80s reflected the needs of a changing society.*

106. *Small group Bible studies are now used by many assemblies.*

108. *Brethren conferences have never lost their importance.*

this responsibility). *Letters of Interest from the Home Field* ran until the end of 1937, and in 1938 the name was shortened to just the first three words. McCartney continued as editor until 1959. It is the forerunner of *Interest*, the major Independent Brethren magazine in North America at the present time (see chapter 23).

The four publishers and distributors below fall into the period from 1960 onward, but we have included them here for consistency:

The Christians Missions Press

In the early 1960s William McCartney had moved to the South for health reasons, and wished to use his retirement to serve the Lord through the production of gospel tracts. He thus became the founder of Christian Missions Press in Waynesboro, Georgia, in 1963. He carried on this work for nineteen years until his death in 1982. The Christian Missions Press is now headquartered in Spartanburg, South Carolina, and carries over 400 titles, including full-sized books.

Everyday Publications

Everyday Publications, Inc., was started in 1964 by R.E. Harlow and his wife Gertrud specifically for the purpose of publishing and distributing easy-to-read English Bible-study aids to Christians in Third World countries where English is understood as a second language. It is based in Scarborough, Ontario, Canada, and is a registered non-profit corporation. Over the years the Harlows themselves have authored more than fifty titles, and sixty other authors have contributed in one way or another. Missionaries in turn have translated EPI books into more than thirty languages around the world. Recently (1991) a decision was made to send books out to Third World Christians free of charge, looking to the Lord for the necessary funds.

DIME Publishers

DIME (Distribuidora Internacional de Materiales Evangélicos), based in Cupertino, California, was started in 1964 by Pedro and Lucy Dillon along with Ed and Connie Lopez and other Spanish speaking believers. DIME (Spanish for "tell me") engages in numerous publishing projects including Emmaus courses, both for Christians and non-Christians, aimed primarily at Latin Americans. Materials are forwarded to over 500 mini-libraries in various countries, to Spanish speaking prison inmates, to radio programs, etc. Recently the Dillons prepared a creative evangelistic booklet called "Up For the Cup," designed to be handed out at the World Cup Soccer Matches. One million seven hundred thousand were printed and distributed by volunteers, with very positive results. They are currently working on another for the 1996 Olympics, to be called "More Than Gold." Five to ten million are projected.

D & K Press
The initials D and K stand for Don and Krista Robertson of San Leandro, California, who describe this company as a "mom and pop operation." Started in the Robertson's home in the late 1980s, D & K specializes in the works of William MacDonald and the discipleship training manuals written by Otis Jean Gibson. Their catalog includes a good selection of books by mostly Brethren authors, Bibles, materials for children, and videos, all at discounted prices.

Brethren Hymnbooks in North America

Even though the pioneer evangelists who came to North America from 1871 onward were at first not directly acquainted with the Brethren, they evidently understood the part that music plays when believers gather at the Lord's Table. From the beginning, unaccompanied hymn singing was an integral part of Independent Brethren assembly life on this continent. For worship hymns, there was plenty of choice, even in the 1870s and 1880s. In addition to the *Little Flock* (chapter 1), there were *Times of Refreshing*, compiled by J. Denham Smith in 1860; the *London Hymn Book*, edited by C. Russell Hurditch in 1865 and revised in 1880 (with twenty-seven of his own hymns); the *Enlarged London Hymn Book*, also by Hurditch, which came out in 1873; *Hymns for Christian Worship and Service*, compiled by J.N. Scobell around 1870; and *Hymns and Spiritual Songs Compiled in Bristol*, brought out by George Müller and Henry Craik, also in 1870.

In Toronto, and probably in Ontario generally, where a large number of assemblies was concentrated, use was made of *The Believer's Hymn Book*, published by Pickering and Inglis in 1884. The following notice appears in *Our Record*, March 1900:

> The fourteenth annual convention of Christians gathered to the Name of the Lord Jesus Christ, in Toronto, Can., will, DV, be held . . . in the Y.W.C.

> Guild Hall, McGill Street (near Yonge) . . . *The Believers Hymn Book* will be
> used at the meeting; please bring one.

This book, like all of the others above, was printed in Britain by Independent Open Brethren publishers, and had to be imported. The same was true of the "Little Flock," which was obtained from G. Morrish, the Exclusive Brethren publisher in London.

It was not until after World War II that Brethren publishers in North America undertook to offer a replacement for the little black hymnbooks so characteristic of the Lord's Supper meeting. *Hymns of Worship and Remembrance*, a collection published by the Gospel Perpetuating Fund of Fort Dodge, Iowa, first appeared in 1950. The Foreword begins with the following "apology":

> The hymns in this book are the result of a real exercise before the Lord on
> the part of many who had felt, for a long time, that a new hymn book was
> needed, which should contain a selection of the most suitable hymns from
> the four or five different hymn books currently used by assemblies of
> Christians who seek to gather in Scriptural simplicity, and also to include
> some other hymns not found in these books.

This is the hymnbook generally used in traditional Breaking of Bread meetings today.

Gospel song books first came into use during the Revival of the 1860s and 1870s. Donald Ross, then editor of *The Barley Cake*, published the first North American Independent Brethren songbook in 1881, not long after his arrival in Chicago. In the December 1881 issue he announced:

> The Gospel Hymn-book is now ready, and supplies of it will be forwarded
> at 5 cts. in paper covers, 10 cts. in limp, and 20 cts. in stiff boards.

In the September 1882 issue he announced a larger edition, "double the size and double the price," which evidently contained both hymns for worship and gospel songs. This would have been of help to many of the little meetings too poor to import books from the Old Country.

Eight years later, in 1890, Ross published yet another gospel songbook because, as he says, "The California Hymn Book is exhausted and there is no other American Gospel Hymn Book clean in all its doctrine known to us." He invites the Lord's servants "to send us at once any good substantial hymns they wish inserted." But not just *any* gospel song was welcome. "Frothy evanescent hymns however inviting the music, we do not wish."

In 1913, James Rae of Vancouver published *The Pacific Gospel Hymn Book*. This little 3" x 5" volume with limp cloth covers contains 200 songs including some hymns suitable for the Breaking of Bread. Anyone raised in a gospel hall Sunday school will recognize many of the memorable selections, including:

A ruler once came to Jesus by night
to ask Him the way of Salvation and light . . .
I will sing of my Redeemer,
and His wondrous love to me . . .
There's a Friend for little children
above the bright blue sky . . .
I am so glad that my Father in Heaven
tells of His love in the book He has given . . .
Into a tent where a Gypsy boy lay,
dying alone at the break of the day . . .

An enlarged edition was brought out by Hector Alves in 1946, with 256 selections, and this is still in print and available from the Western Gospel Publishing Foundation directed by Mrs. Eunice Gorman, Mr. Alves's daughter.

In the April 1920 edition of *Our Record*, edited by T.D.W. Muir of Detroit, we find a brief ad:

SELECTED HYMNS. A Hymn Sheet containing 47 good, singable and Scriptural hymns for gospel and other meetings. Price $2.00 per 100. Only a few hundred left. Order direct from the compiler, Thos. D.W. Muir, 866 Lawton Ave., Detroit, Mich.

Many of the gospel hall Sunday schools used the *CSSM Chorus Book*, a very popular paperback published by the Children's Special Service Mission in Great Britain. This organization, founded in 1867, was one of the first to produce a Christian songbook especially for children and young people. The first Brethren songbook with words and music by a single writer-composer was the *Gospel Chorus Book* by the inimitable Alfred P. Gibbs. It was brought out in 1931 by the Light and Liberty Publishing Company of Ft. Dodge, Iowa, and sold for thirty-five cents each or three for a dollar. Some of the 100 songs in this book have become "classics" of a sort:

Sweet is the story of the Savior's wondrous love . . .
Precious Holy Bible, treasure rich and rare . . .

Remember thy Creator in the days of thy youth . . .
My sheep hear My voice, and I know them and they follow Me . . .
Genesis, Exodus, Leviticus . . . (The Books of the Bible)

Changing times by the early 1940s created a need for a song-book suitable for a variety of meetings in addition to the Breaking of Bread. Headed by T.B. Gilbert, a committee of compilers, including A.P. Gibbs, examined thousands of hymns in an attempt to assemble "a well balanced collection . . . which would give adequate emphasis to the gospel message, the second coming of Christ, children's songs, hymns for worship and prayer, and songs for special occasions." The result was *Choice Hymns of the Faith*, published by the Gospel Perpetuating Fund of Ft. Dodge, Iowa, in 1944. It contains 545 selections.

A modernized and expanded book called *Hymns of Truth and Praise* was published by the same company in 1971. This is a remarkably comprehensive collection. Its 645 selections consist of songs and hymns suitable for every occasion, including the Lord's Supper. Composers range over the entire Christian spectrum from Joseph Addison to Count Nicholas Zinzendorf, and include many of the great Brethren writers such as J.G. Deck, J. Denham Smith, C.R. Hurditch, and J.N. Darby. North American Brethren writer-composers are represented by A.P. Gibbs, John Ferguson, and T.D.W. Muir. All three Brethren hymnbooks are carried by Walterick.

16

Foreign Missions Support

Missionary Service Agencies

The history of Brethren missions parallels that of the Brethren movement itself, both in Britain and North America. We have already seen how two of the early North American evangelists, William Faulknor and J. Norman Case, left for Africa and China respectively before the turn of the century. In many ways the story of Brethren service overseas is a much more uplifting and triumphant story than that of the home assemblies, though God has been glorified in both. It is, however, beyond the scope of this book to tell both stories. A ten-volume history of Brethren missions, organized by fields, was compiled by Frederick Tatford and published by Echoes of Service during the 1980s. It would be grand, however, if we had a suitable record of those who have gone out from North America. In this chapter we will trace the development of *missionary support agencies* in North America.

The earliest reports from missionaries overseas were printed in *The Barley Cake* and *Our Record* from letters received by Donald Ross. Then, early in this century, L.A. Steen began to publish a two-page missionary news sheet called *Voices from the Vineyard*. [Fig. 72] In 1904, Steen was joined in this work by R.J. McLachlan. McLachlan continued to edit *Voices* for many years and became the first president when it was incorporated in 1936. He held that office until his death in 1961. Money sent to the publication office in New York was duly noted in each issue and forwarded to the field, this service being made possible by the incorporation.

The legal aspect of forwarding funds, obtaining visas, etc., had, however, been undertaken by another organization called "Christian Missions in Many Lands" (the name borrowed from Britain), formed and incorporated in 1921 by Charles Bellinger, Richard Hill, Walter Munro, and some other Easterners. CMML has continued to enjoy a good working relationship with the U.S. government, which prefers to deal with a corporation rather than with individual missionaries. In 1938, Bellinger and Hill, along with the former Grant brother John Bloor, formed The Fields, Inc. Their magazine (also called *The Fields*), [Fig. 73] edited by Lloyd Walterick, began with the February 1938 issue. Acknowledgments of funds received were listed along with addresses of missionaries on furlough and other changes. In 1951 this organization began a complete yearly address book of missionaries called *The Missionary Prayer Handbook*.

Another missionary organization, The Missionary Fund, was started in New Jersey by the Grant Brethren in 1925. The founders were Samuel Ridout, P. Daniel Loizeaux, Howard Gillings, and Captain John Barlow. The succeeding merger of the two branches of Brethren led to this work being absorbed by The Fields, Inc. in the 1960s. Barlow moved to Ontario and in 1959 became a very active part of the group that chartered (i.e., incorporated) the Missionary Service Committee, the Canadian counterpart of CMML. The Missionary Service Committee had been formed in 1940 by Stuart Peterson, S.F. Sommacal, John Smart, and R. Gordon Mitchell to cut through Canadian government restrictions on sending funds abroad under wartime conditions. The same men in 1944 incorporated Christian Missions in Many Lands, Canada, as a land- holding and property bequest-receiving organization. Missionaries who are aided by the Missionary Service Committee in Canada are also listed in the CMML Missionary Prayer Handbook.

To complete the record above we have to move ahead to 1971. In that year, initiated by Brethren in metropolitan New York, the four organizations of Voices from the Vineyard, Christian Missions in Many Land, The Fields, along with the Julia Hasse Missionary Home in Union City, New Jersey, were united under a single corporation, CMML, Inc. The two magazines, *Voices from the Vineyard* and *The Fields* were merged into one, called *Missions*, now published ten times a year. Walter Munro was president of CMML for years, followed by Fred MacKenzie, who was called home in 1981. Samuel E. Robinson is the current president (1993).

The role of women in maintaining the Brethren missionary force on the field was formalized in 1949 with the founding of Workers Together by Mrs. Harold Harper. Mrs. Charles VanRyn was also associated with this organization over many years. The purpose of Workers Together is to pinpoint specific needs of missionaries and attempt to meet them—everything from kitchen utensils to motor vehicles. Requests are made known through a quarterly publication.

Important as the service organizations are, the real backbone of Brethren missions is the large number of deeply committed believers in the rank and file of North American assemblies. One good example of this is the Christian Missionary Service Committee in Oakland, California, which assists outgoing workers to pack and prepare for their overseas destinations, provides audio tapes of conference speakers for use on the mission field, and sponsors a missionary conference three times a year. In various other areas on this continent, missionary study classes and inter-assembly missionary meetings and conferences have kept the needs of missionaries before the believers both through hearing missionary speakers and engaging in support projects.

(A special source for the history of missionary organizations in North America is *Turning the World Upside Down*, W.T. Stunt, et al., Echoes of Service, Bath, England, 1972.)

Some Mid-century Missionaries

By 1950, mid-century, the Brethren missionary force from North America had reached perhaps 100 individuals or couples (cf. with 730 individuals listed in 1992). Apparently the only records before 1970 were those kept by the *Echoes of Service* staff in Bath, England. Neither of the magnificent histories of Brethren missions which they have produced give lists by country of commendation. A copy of *Voices from the Vineyard* from 1945 has sixty-six reports or references, many of which represent couples, but this is by no means a complete count. Obtaining life stories of missionaries is even more difficult unless the individual has written an autobiography (as Cyril Brooks did, for example). The five stories below are gleaned from the records as *representative* of that noble band.

William Deans

Bill Deans was born in 1908, the son of Robert and Chrissie Deans. Young Bill took an early interest in printing and layout, and worked in this field for a time after high school. In 1929 the family, including Bill and his sister Ella, were commended to the work in the Congo by Gospel Auditorium of Oakland, California. They joined Gordon and Lois Searle and the Roy Woodham family at Nyankundi. Bill quickly learned the trade language, and in 1930 launched a work among the Babila tribe and also among the pygmies at Lolwa in the Ituri Forest.

A friendship with Piligbo, the chief of the area, gave Bill easy access to the people, and the chief as well as numbers of the tribes people and some pygmies trusted the Lord. The famous explorer Martin Johnson and his wife Osa visited the Ituri Forest in 1932 and wrote a favorable impression of Bill's relationships with the people in his book *Congorilla*. While being treated for rheumatoid arthritis at an Africa Inland Mission station, Bill met Dora Winsor, an AIM missionary. They were married in the Sudan in 1933. Later Bill and Dora returned to Nyankundi, while the work at Lolwa was carried on by his sister Ella and her husband, Bill Spees.

In the latter 1930s and throughout the 1940s, Nyankundi under Bill's supervision became something of a model mission station. Putting his publishing expertise to work, he set up a press and launched two Christian newspapers in native languages. These were followed by magazines for youth and children and literally millions of booklets and tracts. The Emmaus Correspondence Courses were commenced by R.E. Harlow and proved a great success in the area. Around ten assemblies grew up, and before the Congo's independence there was extensive medical work.

With independence and the subsequent lawless rampages of the "Simbas," the missionaries were forced to leave and activities came to a standstill, though many African Christians remained faithful. Work was resumed in 1965. The press now has a staff of over forty, there are schools, orphanages, and a large cooperative medical ministry that, with the aid of Missionary Aviation Fellowship, is able to serve the entire region. There are over one hundred preaching centers providing outlets for forty assemblies. After the home call of Dora in 1979, Bill married Betty Partridge, commended from the U.S. They now (1992) live in Pittsboro, North Carolina, but continue to be heavily involved and return to Nyankundi from time to time. (Condensed from *Turning the World Upside Down* and the Deans' newsletter, *Stacatto Drumbeats from Zaire*, May 8, 1992)

Mr. and Mrs. Cyril Brooks

The Brooks arrived in Manila, the Philippines, in 1922 to join Mr. and Mrs. Wightman, who began work in the old walled city in 1919. They spent a great deal of time in visitation, and also in learning Tagalog, the native language. In 1929 they began a new work in San Juan, a suburb east of Manila. They visited, preached in various halls and in the open air, and held classes for children in various parts of the town. In 1933 a small chapel was built with the help of the Filipino believers. This soon became quite inadequate and a larger building was erected. This, however, was severely damaged during World War II but has since been repaired and enlarged and has [1972] about 150 members with over 200 in the Sunday school.

After liberation from a Japanese internment camp, the Brooks family returned to the U.S. to recover their health and to provide for their children's education. Meanwhile, several Christian G.I.s helped the assembly in San Juan to function again. Cyril and Anna Brooks returned to the Philippines in 1949.

Prior to the war the Brooks had a regular program on the commercial radio in Manila. In 1948 a Christian station, the Far East Broadcasting Company, began to operate and Cyril Brooks was invited to have a program on this station. The Lord led to using the Emmaus course, "What the Bible Teaches," over the radio, and thus from April 1950, the Bible School of the Air was commenced. The response exceeded all expectations. By 1967 over a million requests for Bible courses had been received from all parts of the Philippines.

Leonard Brooks took over as director of the Bible School of the Air when his parents went on furlough in 1963. The senior Brookses celebrated their sixtieth wedding anniversary with the family in Manila in 1982. Presently (1992) the broadcasts are carried on by Filipino brethren while Miss Rose Brooks handles the correspondence work. (Condensed from *Turning the World Upside Down*. An autobiography by Cyril Brooks, *Grace Triumphant*, is available from Walterick Publishers.)

Edwin James Tharp

Edwin Tharp was born in England in 1877, but from 1946 onward became a widely known minister of the Word in North America. He came to full assurance of salvation at age twenty-three through a message on John 5:24 by an American, Charles Wharton. By 1900 he was in fellowship at an assembly at High Wycombe and a partner in a prosperous business. But one day, struck by photos in the newspaper of missionaries massacred in the Chinese "Boxer Rebellion," he heard the Lord say, "Go and take the place of these murdered missionaries." In May 1903 he sailed from Liverpool in company with Edward Eagger, a veteran China missionary.

During the voyage Tharp met a young woman, Margaret Hankey, immigrating with her parents to Canada, and subsequently led her and a friend to Christ. After three months in North America, Tharp sailed for Shanghai, arriving in July 1903. Following a year of language study he opened a new work at K'uan Ch'eng in the north of China. In the meantime Miss Hankey had arrived in China, and they were married in 1905.

After service in K'uan Ch'eng and P'ing Ch'uan, Mr. and Mrs. Tharp moved in 1913 to Lingyuan. This was their home until 1942 when they and their five children were taken prisoner by the Japanese, and later transferred to Japan in 1942. Repatriated later that year, they settled in South Africa, where Margaret died in 1945. Tharp and two of his daughters moved to the U.S., where he married again. For sixteen years he traveled widely, speaking at assemblies and conferences, until the Lord called him home in October 1962. (Condensed from *The Witness*, January 1963.)

Andrew and Nina Stenhouse

Assembly work in Chile virtually commenced in 1927, when Andrew and Nina Stenhouse (commended from Scotland and Canada respectively in 1925), who had spent nearly three years in Argentina, crossed the Andes and settled in Santiago, the capital [population now over 3 million] . . . Within a few months a small assembly had been formed. Two English couples and an American couple and their son, all of whom were already converted, proved a great asset at the beginning of the work. Since then the assembly has grown steadily and a second assembly was subsequently formed on the outskirts of the city. There are also several "annexes" for the preaching of the gospel. There are nearly 400 in fellowship in the two assemblies [1972] and over 300 in the three Sunday schools.

After their marriage in Canada, Mr. and Mrs. Stenhouse first went to Buenos Aires to relieve Mr. and Mrs. Tom Lawrie. While there they were able to acquire a motor Bible coach which had not been used for a number of years. They spent two years using it in Argentina. As the roads at that time were merely dirt tracks with no metal content, they frequently had to dig themselves out of mud holes. Eventually they crossed the mountains and arrived in Chile. A new Bible coach was acquired and they spent nine years using it on the highways and by-ways, distributing vast quantities of gospel literature and Scripture portions. They twice experienced serious earthquakes, when over 40,000 people lost their lives, but were conscious of God's preserving care. They have now retired, but Andrew has told their story in his book, *Counting on God*. (Condensed from *That the World May Know*, Vol. 2, "Dawn Over Latin America", p. 176.)

The Auca Story

Between the river Napo and the river Curaray lies the province of Napo, reaching to the border of Colombia. The capital is Tena, a fast growing city and the main center for the extensive jungle Quechua population. Dr. Wilfred Tidmarsh, commended from U.K. in 1939 and his wife Gwendoline, commended from U.S.A. in 1946, were the senior missionaries in Ecuador at the time of their retirement. At Shandia, in the Oriente, where there has long been an assembly, Dr. Tidmarsh opened a school for Indian children and established a gospel testimony. Later it became a training ground for Jim Elliot, Ed McCully, and Peter Fleming and through their ministry the work developed rapidly and the assembly was built up. In due course, the McCullys hived off to Arajuno, opening a work there, and the Flemings moved to Puyu-pungu, to an outstation earlier opened up by Jim Elliot. The work at Shandia was continued later by Bill and Irene Cathers, Mrs. Elisabeth Elliot, and Miss Mary M. Skinner ...

On returning from furlough in 1956, Dr. and Mrs. Tidmarsh went to Arajuno, to build up the assembly commenced there by the McCullys ... . While their boys were at school, Wilfred and Gwen Tidmarsh lived in Quito, and he devoted himself to the translation of the New Testament into jungle Quechua for the believers of that area, visiting the groups of Christians in the jungles periodically, both for ministry and also for the revision of his translation ... In 1971 Dr. and Mrs. Tidmarsh returned to the U.S.A., but he has continued to visit occasionally ....

Arajuno is a small outpost to the northwest of Shell and is right in the jungle at the edge of Auca territory . . . Wilfred Tidmarsh, who had labored among the Quechua and Colorado Indians, longed to reach the Aucas in this area—Indians who had defied all efforts of traders, administrators, and missionaries to make contact with them.[1] They killed at sight. Primarily because of his wife's ill health, caused by an air crash, he was no longer able to live permanently in this wild eastern area of the Oriente.

In 1952, however, reinforcement arrived from the U.S.A. in the form of Jim and Elisabeth Elliot, Edward and Marilou McCully, and Peter Fleming (and after his marriage in 1954, his wife Olive as well). Initially they worked in the centers of Arajuno, Shandia, and Puyupungu among the Quechua Indians, but their vision was the evangelization of the untamed Aucas. No one knew the language but, from an Auca woman who had fled to live among Quechuas, a limited vocabulary of Auca words and verbs was built up.

The three men teamed up with Roger Youderian of the Gospel Missionary Union . . . and Nate Saint, pilot and missionary of the Missionary Aviation Fellowship. They decided, as a first move, to fly over the Auca compounds and drop gifts. Twelve flights of this nature were made, the gifts consisting of aluminum kettles, shorts, trousers, machetes, combs, and gaudily colored ribbons. The gifts were appropriated by the Indians, who seemed increasingly friendly with each weekly flight. They even returned their own gifts of birds, foodstuffs, and feathers.

Eventually the five men prepared to fly to a beach on the Curaray river, a few miles from the Auca village and attempt to reach the Indians from thence. They flew from Arajuno on January 3, 1956 and made contact with a man and two women on the January 6; the man even flew a short distance in the plane. Nothing more was seen of the Aucas until January 8. Talking to the base camp over the plane's radio, Nate

---

1 "The Waorani Indians of Ecuador's rain forest, once known as the Aucas (who were responsible for the spearing deaths of five missionaries in 1956) now have the New Testament in their own language. Last summer eleven Wycliffe Bible translators presented the first New Testament to the tribe in the remote village of Tiweno. Seventy-five Waorani Christians attended the ceremony, including three of the men who speared the five missionaries. These men are now church leaders." (From *The Church Around the World*, December 1992.)

Saint said, "We are hoping for visitors at about 2:30. I'll call you again at 4:35." He never called back. When his speared body was found in the river by the search party five days later, his watch had stopped at 3:12. Four bodies were later found and buried on the site: the fifth was never found, but an Indian later admitted having seen it and having taken some personal effects from it. Apparently spears were launched at the five missionaries from the jungle and then further injuries caused by machete blows. The men suffered and died, martyrs to the cause of Christ. (Condensed from *That the World May Know*, Vol 2, "Dawn Over Latin America," pp. 233-235.)

17

Outreach to Special Groups

Children's Ministries

Special Children's Campaigns

One type of outreach to boys and girls that no doubt went on much earlier in this century but became widespread during the Depression years and increased even more after World War II was special children's campaigns. All sorts of techniques were used by gifted workers—lantern slides (later replaced by Kodachrome), chalk talks, cartoons, models of various kinds, amateur science experiments—though just plain good story-telling was always effective. Usually Bible stories and the parables of Jesus were the core of the message, though Bunyan's *Pilgrim's Progress* was also used to good effect. Some of the traveling evangelists became specialists in children's campaigns; for example, the witty South African Alfred P. Gibbs (chapter 20), Owen Hoffman with his sensational "black light" and Henry Peterson [Fig. 74] with his stories and *Pilgrim's Progress* slides.

Reports like the following were common in *Letters of Interest* in those days (January 1949):

> Central Gospel Chapel, Des Moines - For about three to four years we used one of the street railway buses to bring boys and girls to Sunday school. The past two years we have used two buses. These buses were employed nightly during the [Owen] Hoffman meetings, and results were outstanding. Our chapel was packed to capacity, with many standing. Some nights in excess of 100 stood. Thirty-five boys and girls professed faith in Christ.

Daily Vacation Bible School

Another form of ministry to children was the Daily Vacation Bible School (DVBS) that became widespread among the assemblies in the 1940s and 1950s. The forerunner of this may have been the Children's Special Service Mission (CSSM), which put on summer programs for children at various beach resorts in Great Britain. This spread to North America in the 1930s, notably in Southern California. DVBS generally consisted then, as now, of a week-long program of crafts, singing, Bible verse memory, and illustrated gospel messages.

Summer Camps

Probably the most effective form of children's ministry, however, has been summer camps. The reason for this is that the camp takes boys and girls out of their familiar environments and creates an atmosphere where, on the one hand they have an ideal parent substitute (the camp counselor), and on the other have the skillful presentation of the gospel under circumstances that gain their maximum attention. Couple that with beautiful natural surroundings, lots of physical activity, good comradeship, and plenty of tasty food, and one can easily see why camp has been the place where innumerable children from Brethren assemblies have met the Lord down through the years.[Fig. 75]

The earliest Brethren Bible camps began in the late 1930s and early 1940s (in 1937 Cedar Lake Conference Grounds in Indiana, possibly the earliest of the camps, advertised their ninth annual boys' camp with Ernest Tatham as speaker). Many congregations joined together to form committees, obtain facilities (usually at an established Christian conference center), and line up speakers and counselors. There was tremendous enthusiasm and vision and lots of hard work, but it was one of the greatest things that ever happened among assemblies on this continent. The July 1949 *Letters of Interest* listed the following thirteen Bible camps:

Bethel Bible Camp, Alberta
Camp Berea, New Hampshire
Camp Hebron, Centerville, Idaho
Upper Peninsula Bible Camp, Forsyth, Michigan
Frontier Lodge, Quebec
Forest Home Camp, Southern California
Greenwood Hills Camp, Pennsylvania
Bay Area Bible Camps, Mt. Hermon, California
Joy Bible Camp, Bancroft, Ontario

"67" Ranch, Cedar Hill, Texas
Stony Brook Lodge, Virginia, Minnesota
Bible Camp, Strasbourg, Saskatchewan
Ocean Beach Bible Camp, Twin Harbors, Washington

By the end of the 1950s camps had more than doubled, and by 1963 had reached thirty-six, several of them under boards made up of assembly people. In 1995 sixty-five camps were listed.

Servicemen's Ministries

While World War II was raging in Europe and the Pacific, many of the people from assemblies participated in one way or another in outreach to servicemen (there were only a few servicewomen in those days). In some places people from the assemblies would go down to city centers where the young men tended to frequent bars and theaters and invite some along to a gospel meeting. A 1944 account in *Letters of Interest* tells of how a young sailor from a Christian home was "picked up" at the USO in Oakland, California, by Ed Baylis (the author's uncle), and then received Christ that evening. In San Diego, the Marlborough Ave assembly used a bus for collecting sailors in that Navy town, with some thirty or more coming along to a hymn sing and special gospel presentation, followed by refreshments. Brethren servicemen's centers and workers were:

Christian Servicemen's Center, Chicago, Illinois - C.E. Bulander
Christian Canteen, New York City
Victory Center, Stelton, New Jersey - Harold Harper
Service Center, San Francisco, California - Tom Olson
Christian Canteen, Kansas City, Missouri - Arthur Rogers
Christian Service Center, New Orleans, Louisiana - VernonSchlief
Hospitality Center, Milwaukee, Wisconsin - Henry Peterson

Since many young men from Brethren homes were serving in the military, the assemblies went out of their way to welcome the "boys in uniform," and announcements like the following would often appear:

Christian servicemen stationed in or around Newport News, VA., will find a warm welcome with the assembly located at 89 Twenty-ninth Street; also at the home of John Millar, Sr., 6928 Huntington Ave.

Outreach to Italian and German Speakers

By the 1940s there were twenty-three Italian-speaking assemblies in the U.S. and Canada. These were located primarily on the eastern seaboard, where immigrants mainly settled in the early part of the century. There were also a few meetings in Canada and on the West Coast. In the east the Italian assemblies were served by five brethren: Frank Pizzulli, Cesare Patrizio, Luigi Rosania, Frank Carboni, and Rocco Cappiello.

The workers concentrated both on helping the believers and in reaching out with Italian language Testaments and tracts to that part of the population who spoke little or no English. Additionally, F.P. Diorio of Brooklyn, New York, published a bi-monthly Italian-English magazine called *La Voce Nel Deserto (The Voice in the Wilderness)* that circulated in the U.S. and Canada and also in Italy and South America. The first Italian-speaking assembly was formed in Hoboken, New Jersey, in 1893. By the 1940s a number had their own buildings, though apparently none of the congregations were very large and opposition was formidable.

In the West a remarkable ministry to Italians was developed by a British businessman, Will Hall, who in 1912 began contacting them in Vancouver and the Fraser Valley. A convert, Mario Scanzano, returned to Italy and eventually started an assembly in his home village. The Italian assembly in Vancouver did gospel work in its own area and also sent great numbers of Italian language Bibles, tracts, and other materials to Italy. Hall traveled up and down the West Coast, scouring telephone books for Italian names and going door to door in Italian neighborhoods (which he scouted out by looking for telltale signs such as olive oil cans). The Italian work on the West Coast by the 1930s included radio broadcasts from Monterey and Oakland, assemblies in Monterey and Portland, and numerous individual contacts.

Outreach to German immigrants was not so widespread in the 1940s, since two wars with Germany had made it expedient for newcomers to learn English quickly. A very fine work, however, was done by a German immigrant, Henry Miller, who came to Chicago in 1913. Miller preached in German on street corners and eventually started a gathering in his home, the beginning of what is now Lakeview Bible Truth Assembly. Miller also knew Lithuanian and preached in that language on the street as well. Later he became a self-supporting worker among Lithuanian immigrants in Wisconsin, Michigan, and the southern states.

Outreach to Spanish Speakers

The work by Brethren among Spanish speaking people—Mexicans, South and Central Americans, Cubans, etc.—began in San Antonio, Texas, with Ervin Dresch in 1918. By 1940 there were three gospel halls, four Sunday schools, plus vacation Bible classes, and gospel outreach to Mexican settlements in Arizona and New Mexico. In New York, with its huge Puerto Rican population, a work was started in 1943 by Paul Bitler in the Bronx and Manhattan, and by Louis Montalvo and Henry Sanchez in Brooklyn about the same time. The first assemblies were in a store front and converted saloon. Eventually there were eight meeting places for Spanish-speaking Christians. Radio and youth ministry were also started in the 1940s, as well as distribution of used clothing.

In New Mexico a small Spanish-speaking assembly was begun by David Metler, which developed into a sizable ministry among boys and girls. John Halliday started in the Lord's work in Florida in the 1940s and in time found an extensive field of service among Cuban immigrants. In East Los Angeles, Irene Gallagher [Fig. 76] began a ministry among Spanish-speaking women and children in 1950 which she carried on faithfully nearly to the end of her life, assisted by various other workers. Spanish-speaking peoples are the largest foreign-speaking minority in the U.S. and occupy extensive districts of New York, Los Angeles, San Antonio, Chicago, and Miami. By the 1970s, the number of Brethren workers in this field made it possible to commence the annual Spanish Workers Conference.

Outreach to Isolated Coastal Dwellers

One of the more unique means of outreach in this remarkable age of grassroots evangelism was that of visiting the remote settlements, lumber camps, and Indian villages of the British Columbia coast by boat. For about thirteen years, from 1943 to 1956, E. Elliot McAllister and his wife Marjorie were skipper and first mate of the M.S. Eagle Wings, a forty-six foot vessel fitted out especially for their use. The B.C. Coast is only about 700 miles long as the crow flies, but in a typical season Eagle Wings would log some 3,000 miles. As the McAllisters wrote in a July 1949 article in *Letters of Interest*:

> Into many an inlet she will poke her prow for a visit of a few hours, or a few days or a week or more while her crew visits loggers, fishermen, canners, Indians and human jetsam cast up on these distant shores by the sea of life, to bring to them the gospel of our Lord Jesus Christ.

The McAllisters knew that this rugged and beautiful coast was home to some 300 logging operations, several thousand fishing vessels, and numerous little settlements often located far from the open sea on the fjords that cut inland for miles. They did their own navigation and piloting, kept the 100 hp engine in repair and constantly faced the challenge of "matching wits with the sea." But their main task was making friends for the sake of the gospel, giving out tracts, visiting homes to read the Scriptures and pray, and in the camps leading community singing and preaching. In some places the Indian people heard them gladly: "In one center we addressed packed audiences seven times in 24 hours because of the death of a 13 year old girl."

By 1960 a boat ministry was also being carried out along the coasts of Newfoundland. In *Letters of Interest* for July-August of that year Herbert Harris gives the following report in the "Pioneering" section:

> We had one of our best seasons with the boat. We anchored at a place called "Daniels Harbour" for about a month. The Lord was working so we put up a portable hall and moved our boat up the shore about fifteen miles. Souls are being saved here so we rented a large house we can use for living quarters as well as a hall. About 200 miles of road has just opened up along this shore so there are many open doors we can now reach by car.

18

Outreach to North American Natives

Indians of the Southwest

One Brethren leader to have a vision for a ministry to the native peoples of the Southwest was Harry Ironside, at that time associated with the Grant Exclusives in Oakland, California.

According to HAI's biography by E. Schuyler English:

> In 1911 a fresh kind of testimony opened up, which occupied Ironside for about two months every autumn for over a decade. This was a ministry to American Indians in their native villages in Arizona, Southern California, and New Mexico—the Mojave, Laguna, Hopi, Walapai and Navajo tribes. He found them a receptive people and looked forward to his visits each year.

During these years Ironside was a speaker at the Southwest Bible and Missionary Conference in Flagstaff, Arizona, for sixteen consecutive summers. Following the conferences he would spend weeks on the reservations, and brought Indians back to Oakland for training. Through Ironside, Mr. and Mrs. Jim Anderson began a lifetime work with the Walapai at Valentine, Arizona, in 1916. Minnie Armerding, sister of Bible teachers Henry and Carl, along with her elderly father also spent many years in this ministry near Winslow, Arizona. Inspired by Harry Ironside, Gordon Fraser eventually left his employment, acquired an advanced degree in anthropology, and in 1958 was invited to head the new Indian Bible Institute (now Indian Bible College), part of the Southwest School of Missions. He was principal for twelve years.

The Southwest School of Missions/Indian Bible College is a positive example of how New Testament principles succeed regardless of the home church affiliation of the missionaries. Although the Brethren have deeply influenced the Southwest School of Missions, this is a cooperative work that represents a number of different Christian bodies. Their united goal is to see an indigenous church develop in every area of North America where there are native peoples. (In 1991 an eleven-member team from the Indian Bible College went north to preach the gospel to the Yakimas of the Northwest. There has also been outreach to a number of other non-Navajo tribes, at least nine of which are represented at the school. In 1992 the college planned an evangelistic campaign in Mongolia where the language is similar, which Navajo believers were able to carry out.)

It was also through Harry Ironside that Horace Holcomb, a "retired" missionary in his seventies, entered the Navajo reservation in 1922 as a commended worker from Gospel Auditorium in Oakland. Holcomb set out across the desert on horseback, accompanied by the then young Carl Armerding, to see if an abandoned trading post he had heard about could be bought cheaply. A deal was made for $400 to acquire the eight-acre parcel that included a few hogans and a native-built stone building. Together with his wife, two daughters and a nurse, Florence Barker, who joined them in 1923, Holcomb began the "Immanuel Mission," the forerunner of the Navajo school that occupies the site today.

Over the next few years Holcomb and another young missionary, Glenn Girdner, built two houses, and with the help of Harry Ironside and Carl Armerding got authorization for the mission from the Bureau of Indian Affairs in Washington. It was Holcomb's daughter Clara, [Fig. 77] however, who managed to learn the difficult Navajo language (one of a very few missionaries who have accomplished this), and after the home call of her parents carried on the work for ten years, often by herself. Acceptance by the native people was very slow, and life on the mission was primitive. But eventually one Navajo woman believed, followed by a man, known as "Yellowhair," who became general handyman. In 1940, Clara was joined by another worker, Howard Montgomery, and two years later by Helen Johnson, who later married Montgomery. Clara died in 1945.

Evelyn Varder, daughter of pioneer evangelist Richard Varder, launched the first school. Later she wrote:

> In the fall of 1948 it was decided to commence an intensive work among the children, so in September we invited seven little Navajo kiddies into our home. These were all either fatherless or motherless. Miss Ruth Valentine came to assist in the children's work at this time . . . The following year it was necessary for the Montgomery family to move into the stone house in order to relieve their larger home for the school work. (Ater forty-eight years of service, Evelyn is still on the job.)

The first fully qualified school teacher at Immanuel Mission School was Alice Huff from Iowa. She came in 1951 and remained for twenty-one years. The first principal was Bob Staley, who came with his family in 1959. By 1977 there was a staff of nineteen, and the facility included a beginners dorm, boys and girls dorms, a dining hall and gym combination, the school, various houses and mobile homes, and the Navajo chapel. An Indian assembly located at the mission uses the chapel, and both school staff and Indians meet together for the Lord's Supper. The school is still functioning today (1992) with W. John Meinzinger as principal. Several Staleys continue on the staff. (The above material was checked for accuracy by Greg Staley.)

Native Americans and the Church

Reduced to 9,000 survivors after the Civil War campaign against the Navajo nation by Kit Carson in 1863-64, there are now approximately 140,000 members of this tribe on three and a half million acres in Arizona. The Navajos, however, are just one tribe. There are 280 tribes and sub-tribes of native peoples in the U.S. and Canada, and, of these eighty-three live within a day's drive of Flagstaff. These consist of Apaches as well as Navajos along the Colorado River, the Pueblo tribes in New Mexico and Arizona, the Missions tribes in Southern California, and the Ute, Shoshonean, and Paiute tribes in the Great Basin area of Nevada, Utah, and Colorado.

According to the late Gordon Fraser, various Christian groups have been trying to convert the native tribes of this continent since the days of the Pilgrims in the early seventeenth century. In the Southwest the Spanish padres began their missions in the late eighteenth century, followed by denominational missions in the nineteenth century, and independent evangelical organizations in this century. But despite all this effort, much of it sincere and earnest, there was still no ongoing, indigenous Native American Christian Church by the mid-1970s. The reason for this, said Fraser, is that these missions always insisted that a white person be in charge of public services and head up the work. Now that era is over; white missionaries are not generally welcomed on the reservations today.

Great changes have occurred in recent years. "Today's Indians are conscious of their identity as a sizable ethnic group" and are trying to revive old tribal rites and cultures. Within this context, "native evangelists and Bible teachers are going to their own people, and to other tribes, with a simple Bible message and with a vigor that would have put white missionaries to shame." The reason for this new approach? "Responsible mission leaders, faced with the failure of conventional patterns, began to rediscover New Testament missionary principles and put them into practice." (Based on information from "Grandmother's Hogan: The Gospel and the Navajo" by Gordon Fraser, founder and chancellor of the Indian Bible Institute, *Interest, September 1975*.)

Ethnic Indian Work in North Carolina

Not all of the native peoples of North America have remained in tribal groups. Here and there, communities of Indians can be found, whose identity is ethnic rather than tribal; they may represent many tribes. In North Carolina one such community is the area in and around the little town of Pembroke near the South Carolina border. Today there are some 40,000 Native Americans in this district, whose members are on all economic, social, and educational levels. Because there is no tribal religion to combat as in the Southwest, Christians working among them find both an open door as well as much resistance or indifference.

Brethren evangelists began to preach among the Native American people in the Pembroke area around 1890. The first to come was Robert Seed, followed by G.F. Cowls, and R.H. Hall. Seed and his family lived in a tent and traveled in a covered wagon, moving down the Eastern Seaboard and apparently crossing into Mexico as well. He used a tent for his meetings at first, later preaching in the Union Chapel northeast of Pembroke. The Brethren evangelists all taught the principle of gathering in the name of Jesus Christ alone, and soon a meeting was started in a temporary location near the Union Chapel crossroads. This moved from place to place until 1914, when a building was constructed on the Preston Locklear farm. It served both as chapel and schoolhouse. As the early evangelists were among the Grant Brethren, the believers here had visits from some of the well-known Grant teachers such as Samuel Ridout, A.E. Booth, and Frederick Grant himself.

The first meeting in Pembroke itself was started in 1929. Not long after this, Lawrence Chambers took up the work of ministry and gospel preaching. During the 1930s a young Indian man, Venus Brooks, was saved, and after college training served the Lord among his own people until the Lord called him home in 1969. In recent years, property on the Preston farm was purchased and a modern auditorium and Sunday school classrooms were constructed. The assembly in Pembroke also built a new auditorium in 1968. A third work was started in the 1950s in Scotland County by Oscar Thompson. Mr. and Mrs. Charles Oxendine, Native Americans, are now serving the Lord among their people in these three assemblies. (Based on a letter from Charles Oxendine, Jr.)

The Shoshone Tribe of the Great Plains

A very different kind of outreach to Native Americans was commenced by Wesley and Gladys Kosin in 1957, when they moved from Wheaton, Illinois, to the Wind River Reservation in Wyoming in order to translate the Bible into the Shoshone language. Kosin had been a chaplain at Cook County Jail and, before that, assistant superintendent at the Pacific Garden Mission in Chicago. He became interested in linguistics because he saw the possibilities of bringing the gospel to those who had no written language. He took two summers of instruction at the Summer Institute of Linguistics, held at the University of North Dakota and sponsored by the Wycliffe Translators, and did so well that in later summers he became the instructor in the same course.

For over twenty years the Kosins lived and worked among the Shoshone, attempting to gain their friendship and enlisting the aid of numerous "informants" to try and reduce this difficult language to written symbols. During the severe winters they lived on the reservation in a tiny cottage; summers were spent in North Dakota at the school of linguistics. A glimpse of their struggles and victories with the

Shoshone language is given in a letter from Wesley in *Letters of Interest*, August 1960:

> I have been having difficulty finding out what the third person singular pronoun is in Shoshone, but the Lord led me to a discovery today as I was getting a phrase written down in Shoshone while eating dinner with our informants.

After several years of hard work, the Kosins had established an alphabet for the sounds in Shoshone and a primer to begin teaching people to read. At that point, permission to publish the primer was sought from the tribal council. This, sadly, was rejected. The answer was a rebuke for the harm done by others: "The white man has taken our land, our people, and now they are going to take our language!" This brought the Bible translation project to a halt, but the Kosins carried on with a weekly radio broadcast and much personal work. In the course of years many of the Shoshone people came to look upon the Kosins as trusted friends, though the actual harvest in souls was few. Eventually the tribal council recognized the value of their efforts. Wesley and Gladys became the first white people to be invited to one of the Shoshone tribe's annual New Year pow-wows, at which they were honored as having made the greatest contribution to the tribe in the previous year. (Condensed from a biography of Wesley and Gladys Kosin by their son, Fred Kosin.)

Indian Life Ministries of Canada

The 1990s have seen a rapidly growing work called Indian Life Ministries develop in Canada through the efforts of Tim and Sue Nielsen of Manitoba. A report in *Interest*, April 1995, states that quantities of an evangelistic book called *The Conquering Indian* have been sent "to every prison, friendship center, native alcohol treatment center and band office in Canada." The Nielsens have had this book translated into French to reach the 63,000 French speaking Indians. *Indian Life* magazine has a circulation of 25,000. "Many have found Christ through its pages and others have grown deeper in their Christian life."

19

Outreach on a Broad Scale

The "Gospel Messengers"

One of the more unique outreach campaigns in the post-war period was developed by a group from Chicago called the "Gospel Messengers." Their strategy (modeled after an English ministry) was to form teams of around six men who would itinerate during the summers with a "gospel car" and sleeping trailer. The teams would target towns and cities along a given route where they would preach in the open air, distribute tracts, and seek for conversations as the Lord led. These campaigns were publicized in *Letters of Interest* so that prayer could be going up from around the country as they moved from place to place. [Fig. 78]

In *Will the Real Plymouth Brethren Please Stand*, Ross McLaren reports that:

> The Gospel Messengers were under the leadership of Arthur Rodgers . . . On the first tour in 1947 eighty cities or towns in the Midwest were visited from May 1 to Sept 5. In 1949 one group evangelized thirty-four Midwest cities . . . All totalled, in the three years from 1947 to 1949 about 400 towns were reached with the gospel in . . . sixteen states.

Radio

During the 1930s, 1940s and 1950s, radio was at its zenith of popularity before television began to crowd it out. Air time was also inexpensive.

By 1948, Brethren evangelists and Bible teachers could be heard on forty stations in seventeen states, four Canadian provinces, as well as Puerto Rico, and Mexico. Broadcasters included Tom Westwood on the West Coast, Ira Eshleman in Florida, Virgil Hollingsworth, Jr., in Georgia, George Leest in Iowa, T.J. Lyttle in New York, H. Welcome Detweiler in North Carolina, J.D. Ibbotson in South Carolina, Walter Nelson in Texas, and George Landis in Greenwood Hills, Pennsylvania. T. Michael Flowers started the Good News Radio Program in the Southeast in the 1950s, and Sam Hart in Pennsylvania began the Grand Old Gospel Hour in 1962. In 1964, Brethren programs were broadcast on 107 stations in North America.

Programs in Canada included "Young Canada Bible Hour" and "Gospel Bells" in Ontario, and a French-speaking broadcast in Quebec. The "Family Bible Hour" started in St. Johns, Newfoundland, in 1951, was heard on thirty-eight stations by 1974. FBH also sponsored a yearly conference.

Evangelistic Crusades

Organized evangelistic campaigns of the D.L. Moody and Billy Sunday type were revived shortly after World War II with the beginning of the Billy Graham Crusades in Los Angeles in 1951. In May and June of 1952, sixteen Brethren assemblies in the Chicago area put on their own crusade, using the gifted evangelist Harold Wildish of Jamaica. [Fig. 79] They rented facilities in two high schools, one on the north side and the other on the south, and advertised widely using billboards, streetcar, and subway posters, and flyers handed out door to door. Neighborhoods were canvassed by the believers in fifty cars with signs on the top. A personal invitation was phoned to 7,600 households. The campaign drew crowds of 1,000 on some nights of the six-week series, and a significant number professed faith in Christ.

During the 1950s and 1960s a number of assemblies also supported the Billy Graham Crusades. Fifteen Toronto meetings got behind the Billy Graham Crusade of 1955, with many of the saints participating as ushers, counselors, and choir members. After the main campaign they held a rally that drew some 550 people who had responded to the gospel message, and offered them follow-up correspondence courses. A number of assemblies in New York cooperated with the 1957 crusade there by bringing bus loads of people and also serving in various ways. Here, too, some assemblies held follow-up rallies. In Chicago there was similar support and participation from assemblies for the 1959 and 1962 crusades. Those fellowships that cooperated received definite benefits in terms of reaching people in their own neighborhoods. (Special sources for the above include *Interest* articles in issues of March 1972 and January 1975.)

Expansion by Chapel Building

The early Brethren gospel halls were nondescript architecturally. Generally they were built at minimum cost and maximum utility, with no thought for aesthetics. Being staunch iconoclasts ("image breakers") these dear saints had no place for artistry in their places of worship. On the one hand, because it was their conviction that believers should come *apart* from the world to worship, they were content to view the Lord himself with eyes of faith rather than have representations of him in religious pictures or symbols. On the other hand, unsaved people who came to their halls were to be *confronted* with solemn warnings of the consequences of rejecting the gospel, not *comforted* with pleasing surroundings.

The younger generation of the 1950s, however, was for the most part in reaction to these convictions, and had little sympathy with the above theological views. Buildings now were becoming an important part of evangelistic outreach. As Stewards board member Robert Mojonnier says in an *Interest* article commemorating Stewards Foundation's thirtieth anniversary, "Across the land assemblies were . . . meeting, witnessing and preaching the gospel in buildings which were no longer adequate for their needs, and sometimes not attractive to the unsaved man or woman needing to be reached with the gospel."

Because of the generous lending policy of Stewards to any assembly that could show fiscal responsibility, a new style of Independent Brethren gathering place began to appear all over the continent. Most were designed for practical concerns: classrooms for Sunday school, carpeting and padded seating in the main auditorium, a fireside room, and kitchen for smaller gatherings and social affairs, etc. Attempts were made to create a pleasing exterior while still avoiding a church-like appearance (the exception being the odd and rather incongruous steeples that sprouted on top of a few). In keeping with the concept that the buildings should *attract* rather than *repel* strangers, the old name "gospel hall" began by the 1950s to be replaced with "gospel chapel" or "Bible chapel" (see 19).

The way Stewards Foundation planned to give aid was through loans at modest rates financed by the sale of bonds to members of Brethren assemblies. [Fig. 80] Bob Mojonnier reported that "the first substantial list of loans which appears in the early minutes totalled $80,700. It included ten loans covering assemblies in seven states and two Canadian provinces." By 1975 these funds had made possible the construction of over 500 chapels with another 320 remodeled or expanded. In short, the vision of the Stewards Foundation founders was a thoroughly sound one for accomplishing the purposes stated in their original charter.

The vision of the Stewards trustees grew as they saw new chapel buildings springing up around the continent, and a campaign developed to encourage assembly planting in all major centers of population. The story is told in the following article from *Letters of Interest*, January 1960:

> In the Chicago area about four years ago the Gospel Expansion Foundation (Stewards) developed for the purpose of planting new assemblies. While the first results have been in and around Chicago, the purpose of G.E.F. is to reach across America, and to work in any and all areas where there is not a local and state-wide or province-wide facility for aiding in the planting of new testimonies. [Fig. 81]

Patterned after the G.E.F. is the Florida Gospel Pioneers, which already has been instrumental in providing buildings for two new assemblies: at West Hollywood and near Cape Canaveral. New Jersey Brethren have discussed a similar organization. New England is in process of setting up P.I.N.E.S. to pioneer in New England. Iowa brethren at the recent worker's conference in Des Moines took the first steps to aid pioneering in that state. California brethren are discussing pioneering there.

The chief purpose of Gospel Expansion Foundation is to provide suitable buildings for pioneering. Incidental to doing this it will help with surveys of cities, housing areas and sites. Then it will go into selected communities, cities, neighborhoods and erect (or purchase if available—though this is rarely the case) a chapel or the first unit of a building. It will carry the financial load of this building, maintaining the monthly mortgage payments, until an assembly has been planted and sufficiently established to take over financial responsibility. Stewards Foundation is in hearty sympathy, and is ready to lend money to G.E.F. for such buildings.

But where will G.E.F. get money with which to service these loans, paying at the rate of $10 per month per $1,000 of loan? By regular contributions of assemblies and individual Christians, and especially the latter.

While cost and site of building will vary widely from place to place, on an average probably about $25,000 will purchase a lot and erect an expandable building entirely suitable for the start of a new effort . . . Now if each family who reads this magazine would give just $1 a month, that would supply $20,000 a month . . . It would permit the erection of about 40 new chapels a year, and the servicing of the monthly payments on the loans to finance them.

Rooms, Halls, Chapels and Churches

In the sixteenth and seventeenth centuries, when most of the Protestant denominations came into being, the Church of England was the only church recognized by the authorities in England and Ireland. Even after nonconformist Christians were allowed to have their own buildings, these were called "chapels" to distinguish them from the Anglican parish churches. Thus when the Brethren movement began in the early nineteenth century, they followed in the same tradition. The buildings they acquired in Plymouth and Bristol were already known as "Providence Chapel" and "Bethesda Chapel." The new places seem to have been called by the streets they were on: Ebrington Street, Rawstorne Street, etc. As mentioned in chapter 1, the believers also referred to their meeting places as the room.

The word *chapel* has an interesting history. It was originally derived from the Latin *capelle* (cape), and can be traced back to the story of St. Martin of Tours, the soldier turned monk who founded a monastery in France (Gaul) in the fourth century. Legend has it that Martin divided his cloak or cape with a supposed beggar on a freezing night, and later the Lord appeared to him wearing the torn piece. The cape was kept in a special sanctuary under the care of *capellani* or chaplains, and gradually *capallani* came to mean the room itself, and then any small place of

Christian worship. Usually it denoted a room inside a building—for example, the side rooms found alongside the nave in Gothic-style churches, or the room or chapel set aside for private worship in the homes of noblemen. In Britain it still means a place of worship other than the Church of England—a Catholic chapel or a Presbyterian chapel, for example; in the U.S. the word has a slightly commercial connotation, as wedding chapel, funeral chapel, etc.

In Victorian England and in North America as well, a hall was a place used for gatherings of any sort, including lectures or concerts. Therefore it was quite proper to call the place where people gathered to hear a gospel message a gospel hall. It communicated meaningfully to the people at that time. In North America, however, the connotation of hall gradually changed, and today it strikes the average person as slightly unsavory, as pool hall, dance hall, union hall, etc., though one still finds concert hall and lecture hall being used in the earlier sense.

The Brethren have traditionally avoided the word *church* for the historical reason given above, and also because the Greek word translated church as used in the New Testament refers to *people*, not to a building. A third reason is because of J.N. Darby's doctrine of the "church in ruins," and his insistence that a local assembly is *not* the church (chapters 3 and 6). The problem with this for many in the movement today, especially younger people not acquainted with traditional Brethrenism, is *communication*. Nonreligious people today cannot comprehend why we use hall or chapel when we *mean* church. Further, the English word *church does*, in fact, come from the Old English word cirice (also, chereche or chirche) and means (according to the Oxford English Dictionary) "A building for public Christian worship." This sort of building did not exist as such when the New Testament was written.

20

Some Well-Known Mid-Century Workers

The next six segments consist of brief biographies of some, but by no means all, of the unforgettable men who served the Lord as Brethren workers in the middle years of the twentieth century:

Alfred P. Gibbs

No one who ever heard Alfred P. Gibbs [Fig. 82] speak, especially in a children's campaign, will ever forget him. He was funny, hilarious at times, but not in a ha-ha sort of way. His humor was straight-faced and was combined with a no-nonsense objectivity in getting the message of the gospel across. He never talked down to kids. He addressed them as though they were small adults, which made his meetings interesting for everyone. He did his own song-leading, and was a master storyteller. He was one of the first evangelists to use lantern slides (later replaced by 35-mm transparencies).

Gibbs was born in Birmingham, England, in 1890, but was raised in Johannesburg, South Africa. He had a twin brother, Edwin, who became a follower of Jesus first and later led Alfred to the Lord (1912). Both boys became actively engaged in Bible study and open-air evangelism. When World War I began, Edwin had already left for Moody Bible School in Chicago, but Alfred served as a military chaplain, preaching to the soldiers in the training camps. In 1919, when Edwin was back in South Africa as a missionary, Alfred set off for Moody himself.

At the Bible school Alfred was not content only to study, but soon threw himself into the work of a rescue mission the Chicago assemblies had started on Madison Street in the Loop. Along with Harold Harper, T.B. Gilbert, James G. Humphrey, and other young men later to be well-known workers, he went through the basic training of street-corner preaching on Skid Row. At Moody, Alfred was befriended by George Landis, who at that time was serving as pastor of a small denominational church. Gibbs continued this relationship after graduating, and often visited Landis and his wife and family. Landis testified many years later that Gibbs never tried to talk him into leaving his denominational connection, but through their many discussions he eventually became persuaded to do so.

Alfred Gibbs never married. Like J.N. Darby he lived out of a suitcase and probably recognized that his calling and marriage would never mix. But he loved children and was "Uncle Alf" to a number of families in whose homes he stayed. Don Cole tells how Gibbs for many years would spend Christmas with them in Kansas City, and it was only when Don became a teenager that he realized that "Uncle Alf" was not his *real* uncle.

> To us children he was utterly fascinating. 'Show me your muscles,' we would shout, and dangle happily from his extended arm. We used to double our fists and beat upon his midriff, only to fall back in breathless astonishment at his rock-like strength.

Most of A.P. Gibbs's numerous books were directed at teaching young believers, including his unique *The Preacher and His Preaching*. Gibbs was a superb instructor and for many years served for part of the year on the staff of Emmaus Bible School (where he is said to have been an unbeatable table tennis champ). He published a gospel songbook in 1931 with words and music of his own composition (chapter 15), and also contributed several hymns to *Choice Hymns of the Faith* and *Hymns of Worship and Remembrance*. "A Thousand, A Thousand Thanksgivings" is one of his most memorable adult hymns, while "Sweet Is the Story" is a children's favorite.

Although Alfred Gibbs was an earnest and effective gospel preacher, he was at his best with kids. "My initials are A.P.G., he would announce. "That stands for 'A Perfect Gentleman!'" He was a marvel at quips, often stated so seriously that they went over the heads of the little ones. Once he was showing slides of Washington, D.C., and came to a time-exposed shot taken in a subway station. "Notice that some people are blurred because they're moving and others are perfectly still," he said with a straight face. "The still ones are government workers!"

When A.P.G. was taken home to glory through an auto accident in 1967, an entire issue of *Letters of Interest* was dedicated to him. A number of well-known Brethren wrote their reminiscences of him, including his brother Edwin, Bill McCartney, Elliot VanRyn, T.B. Gilbert, Lester Wilson, William MacDonald, and Lloyd Walterick. Donald Cole, editor at that time, referring to one of Gibbs's books, *The Dreamer and His Dream*, which tells the story of John Bunyan and *Pilgrim's Progress*, says:

> If there was any one character of Bunyan's he admired above others and sought to emulate, it was Mr. Valiant-for-truth.

T.B. Gilbert

T.B. Gilbert [Fig. 83] is perhaps best known as the founder of the annual Brethren workers' conferences, as well as the originator of the Gospel Perpetuating Fund for producing Brethren hymnbooks. He was the son of Irish immigrants whose parents had received Christ and associated with the Brethren after settling in Chicago in the 1880s. Thus Thomas Bruce, born in 1892, grew up in an atmosphere of dedicated service to the Lord. At age eleven he was saved through the help of evangelist William Buchanan by reading Isaiah 53:5-6. T.B. planned to pursue a business career like his father, and quickly moved up to the position of bookkeeper in a meat-packing plant. He also matured as a Christian, and through his witness led others to Christ, including his brother and sister.

Joining several young men in serving at a rescue mission on Sunday afternoons, T.B. was soon pressed into giving his testimony on street corners, his introduction to a lifetime of preaching. A number of his companions from those days also became preachers, including Harold Harper, Edwin Gibbs, A.E. Horton, Arthur Rodgers, Douglas Ibbotson, and Henry Petersen. Through the influence of Alfred Mace, T.B. began to listen for God to direct his life, and in 1916 told the Lord he would go anywhere to serve him. The next year he left his position at the packing house to begin evangelistic work in Wheatfield, Indiana.

The work of a pioneer evangelist in those times consisted in finding a place to preach, often an empty store front, and then knocking on doors, giving out tracts, and inviting people to attend the meetings. Usually the evangelist would preach six nights a week. Once some persons were saved, a small meeting could be started in a home. Gilbert spent three months in Wheatfield and eventually saw seven converts baptized. For the next four years he repeated similar campaigns in other places in Indiana and in Missouri. In 1921 he purchased his first tent. Like Donald Ross and other early pioneers he loved tent work, and during his career conducted thirty-eight tent campaigns. From time to time he would join Harold Harper and others in preaching at conferences, and once, in 1924, joined evangelist Tom Olson in a preaching tour using a model-T gospel car.

Later in 1924, T.B. moved down to Houston, Texas, for tent work and met Elma Doehring, whom he married in September of that year. The couple remained in Texas until 1927, during which time a daughter, Mary Ann, was born. Then they moved back to Indiana, settling at Knox, where Gilbert convened the first Brethren workers' conference in 1933 to encourage men to enter new fields. Here also his son Bruce was born. The next year they were invited to start work in Champaign, Illinois, but instead were forced to move to Tucson, Arizona, because Elma was found to have tuberculosis. Gilbert was soon teaching a Bible class, conducting a radio program and, in time, carrying on tent campaigns throughout Texas. Disaster struck in 1937 when Brucie died after a short illness, followed not long after by Elma at the age of thirty-one. *Choice Hymns of the Faith*, published in 1941, is dedicated to her.

Gilbert settled his daughter Mary Ann with his sister in Chicago and returned to the life of an itinerant minister, often driving more than 30,000 miles a year. He visited assemblies and did tent evangelism in Indiana, Illinois, Iowa, and Missouri during the warm weather and returned to Tucson in the winter. During this period he saw the need for another hymnbook especially for worship, and with the help of A.P. Gibbs, Harold Harper, George Landis, William Pell, and others brought out *Hymns of Worship and Remembrance* in 1945. In this same year he was remarried to a Tucson widow, Lena Waller Spessard. They remained in Tucson for a few years to see the assembly built up, and in 1952 moved to Shelbyville, Tennessee, for two years, and then to Murfreesboro for ten years. In that area, T.B. first started an assembly through tent evangelism and then concentrated on shepherding, developing leadership, and teaching.

From 1965 onward, T.B. turned his attention to a wider circle of gatherings, holding meetings not only in the southeast states but all through the South and Southwest. In 1966 he was honored at the Mid-South Bible Conference for fifty years in the Lord's work. The Gilberts moved again in 1969, this time to Huntsville, Alabama, where again T.B. planned to throw himself into home meetings, radio work, door to door visitation, etc. But a heart attack in his seventy-seventh year ended his career of vigorous activity. For three years he was confined to home most of the time but was able to see another hymnbook published. He also attended the workers' conference in Chicago in 1971. In April 1972, at the age of seventy-nine, he was called into the presence of his Lord and Savior. [Condensed from *He Loved to Plant* by Donald L. Norbie.]

Harold Harper

Harold Harper [Fig. 84] was ideally suited for helping assemblies get established in a community. He and Mrs. Harper loved to do visitation. They both had a homespun geniality that encouraged even strangers to relax and share confidences. When asked what interested him, Harper would reply "Everything." No doubt this genuine interest in people, their concerns, even their hobbies, opened many doors to him.

Born into a Brethren home in Rochester, New York, and saved at the age of sixteen, Harold was immediately introduced into the Lord's work by giving his testimony at street meetings. At eighteen or so, along with other assembly young people, he spent Saturday afternoons and evenings in gospel outreach in the numerous towns around Rochester, singing and giving testimonies in the open air and distributing tracts from door to door. One Sunday he heard it announced after the Lord's Supper that he was to take the gospel meeting that evening. As he recalled many years later, he studied all day, but upon mounting the platform his mind went completely blank.

One of Harold's early assignments was a mission work in Rochester that later became Congress Avenue Gospel Chapel. It was at this mission that John Bramhall was saved, and later was commended by the assembly for full-time work. Mr. Bramhall is still serving the Lord in the Carolinas. Harold Harper went on to study at Moody Bible Institute, and at the same time began to minister in Irving Park and other districts of Chicago, work that led eventually to the founding of several assemblies. In 1919 he married Margretta Richter, also a Moody graduate, a

marriage that resulted in five children and gained him a lifetime partner in the Lord's service.

Harold and Margretta lived at first in Rochester, but their constant
assistance to various gatherings of the Lord's people took them to Pennsylvania, Minnesota, North Carolina, California, and many other parts
of the continent, and resulted in the founding or strengthening of numerous assemblies. Harold taught part of several years at Emmaus and
also engaged in tent evangelism. Mr. and Mrs. Harper also managed a
servicemen's center near Camp Kilmer, New Jersey, during World War
II, and saw many young men receive Christ.

After the war the Harpers moved to Wheaton, Illinois, where they
served as house parents and counselors at Bethany House near the
Wheaton College campus. They also assisted in the establishment of an
assembly in Wheaton. They kept up a prodigious correspondence with
the young people whose lives their ministry had touched, and at least
twenty-two of those they encouraged went on to serve the Lord in
various fields—living memorials to faithful workers. Harold Harper
finished his life's journey in 1966.

William G. McCartney

If you happened to visit Bethany Chapel in Wheaton during the 1950s,
chances are you would have been greeted by a friendly man with an
Irish accent. That would have been Bill McCartney [Fig. 85]. Bill was an
innovator. That is, he had a gift from the Lord for starting new enterprises. He played a vital part in the birth of some of the most important
institutions that serve the Independent Brethren today, in addition to
helping plant several assemblies.

William George McCartney was born in Portadown, a picturesque
town at the end of the Ards Peninsula in Northern Ireland, the seventh
of ten children. At the age of eighteen, while walking home alone from
a gospel meeting, he passed from death into life. From almost the
beginning of his Christian life, Bill dedicated himself to helping others
to know Christ and to grow in him. The year after his conversion he
immigrated to America and settled in the Chicago area, which became
his home for the next forty-three years.

Before long, the elders at the Laflin Street Gospel Hall, where young
McCartney attended, began to recognize his gift of preaching. In com-
pany with other young men he began pioneer work in various other
Chicago neighborhoods, often with children. The story is told of how he

found a group of boys playing baseball on a Sunday afternoon near the Washington Heights assembly and talked them into going with him to Sunday school (then on Sunday afternoons). Some of these boys later became active Christians at this and other assemblies.

In 1932, Bill McCartney married Mary Gibson of Detroit, and eventually the Lord gave them four children, two boys and two girls. Two years later he and a partner founded Bradshaw and McCartney, Inc., a wholesale furniture company. Unlike some partnerships, Bradshaw and McCartney enjoyed a harmonious relationship for many years. The McCartneys moved to Wheaton in 1946, and started a meeting in their own home. Later Bill helped to found Bethany House, an old mansion fitted out for use by the fledgling assembly as well as for a social center for students from a Brethren background. The present building of Bethany Chapel followed a few years later.

A few years before the Wheaton move, in 1934, Bill and Mary McCartney began turning out a mimeographed sheet with news of pioneer workers in North America, called *Letters of Interest from the Home Field*. This was the humble forerunner of the present *Interest* magazine. A very important part of the work of *Letters of Interest* was (and still is) receiving and forwarding funds to workers on this continent. Eleven years later, in 1945, Bill McCartney and several other men of vision started Stewards Foundation to help assemblies construct suitable buildings (chapter 24).

Again, in 1954, Bill McCartney's vision for helping pioneer workers, in this case with medical services, was an important factor (though not the only factor) in the purchase of Chicago's Belmont Hospital by Stewards Foundation. In time Stewards became owner of five hospitals, two in Chicago and three on the West Coast. These provided not only free medical care for some of the Lord's servants, but each had a Bible-believing chaplain who ministered to the patients.

After many fruitful years in the Chicago area, Bill and Mary McCartney moved to Waynesboro, Georgia, in 1963. Here they began to fulfill another vision, that of supplying tracts to workers wherever they were needed. Thus was born the Christian Missions Press. This work occupied Bill for the last nineteen years of his life, during which time he was able to see the press grow from a tiny back room to the spacious building it occupies today. Following a short illness, he was called home in March 1982.

(Condensed from *W.G. McCartney: His Life and Labors* by Willard Rodgers.)

John Smart

John Smart [Fig. 86] was a man who commanded people's attention. He was tall, statesmanlike, and spoke with confidence and authority. For over thirty-five years he was in a position of leadership among the Brethren. He was born in Scotland of parents who loved the Lord, and since the family moved to Vancouver Island when he was quite young he grew up a Canadian. Part of his teenage years were spent as a farm hand in Alberta, where he resided with Christian friends and had much time to read and think. Here he worked through his own need of a Savior, and one day wrote home to tell his parents he had accepted Christ.

The town of Berry Creek in Alberta and the tiny settlements in the vicinity provided John Smart with early opportunities to preach. Soon he began to work during the winters so he could serve the Lord at his own expense during the summers, usually holding meetings in schoolhouses. Later he teamed up for a time with seasoned evangelists William Wilson and Charles Bowen. Eventually the elders at the Victoria assembly encouraged him to enter the Lord's work full time under their commendation.

In 1932 John teamed up with another young evangelist, Neil Fraser, for an extended preaching visit to the West Indies. Starting at Tobago, British West Indies, their nightly preaching soon resulted in conversions. Their tent, which took many weeks to arrive, was soon filled to capacity with crowds of the curious standing outside, and they were obliged to start special children's meetings as well as sessions for inquirers. After fourteen weeks with the tent, John Smart preached in other parts of the islands before returning to North America. On his return a year later, an assembly was meeting in a wooden building where the tent had been. He returned again for another eight months in 1936-37.

Following his first teaching assignment at the Guelph Summer Bible School in 1937, John was invited to serve in the city of Toronto. He married Faye Surgenor in 1938 and the young couple settled in the east end, where John had his hands full ministering to ten or so assemblies. Shortly after the beginning of World War II in 1939, he joined with several others in founding the Missionary Service Committee (chapter

16). He also began his association with Christian Missions in Many Lands at this time, as well as becoming a contributing editor for *The Fields* magazine in 1940. In 1941 he joined with C. Ernest Tatham and R.E. Harlow to launch the Emmaus Bible School (chapter 15).

By 1948, John Smart was ministering to the Toronto assemblies, teaching at Emmaus and during the summer at the Guelph conference grounds, speaking at conferences in Canada and the U.S., as well as keeping up his responsibilities with the various missions organizations. He now had four children at home, and kept up this heavy pace at considerable sacrifice to his family. Then in 1950 came an invitation from The Fields organization to take charge of their New York office, an offer he accepted somewhat reluctantly, but moved to Plainfield, New Jersey, in 1951. Eventually all four children were baptized and accepted into fellowship at the old Bible Truth Hall.

Editorship of *The Fields* magazine was offered to John in 1953, an assignment that fitted his gift for writing. In connection with *The Fields* he was able to visit missionaries on location in Africa and Europe as well as to speak at missionary conferences in Britain on a number of occasions. He and Faye were both able to attend the Glasgow Missionary Exhibition in 1961, where John was a featured speaker. Then in 1964 he was invited to return to the Emmaus faculty as president. In 1965 the Smarts left Plainfield and took up residence in Oak Park, though John still continued as editor of *The Fields*.

For ten years John Smart gave himself energetically to administrating the Bible school, inspiring the younger faculty as a father and veteran servant of the Lord. A new wing was added in 1968 and other improvements made to the Oak Park property. He brought Angola missionary Don Cole to head the missions department and in 1966 founded an annual missions week at Emmaus. As editor of *The Fields*, he continued to visit missionaries abroad, and in 1970-71 was accompanied by Faye on a trip around the world. It was his great joy to find Emmaus students serving the Lord in many places on the mission field. Vigorous and enthusiastic until the end, he was suddenly called home by the Lord in November 1975. (Condensed from *John Smart: A Life Directed By God* by Faye Smart.)

August VanRyn

One of the most memorable personalities among Brethren workers in the early and middle years of this century was August VanRyn [Fig. 87].

He was number eight in a Dutch family of twelve children whose father was a moderately wealthy pharmaceutical wholesaler. VanRyn Senior was Dutch, but his wife came from Aubonne on the shores of Lake Geneva in French Switzerland. Both were associated with Brethren and Mrs. VanRyn's family knew J.N. Darby. They were in fellowship in an assembly in Arnhem, and on a Sunday morning the entire family would walk the four and a half miles from their home in Oosterbeek. People who knew them would say, "There goes the VanRyn parade!"

August VanRyn's memories of his family and especially of his mother were full of joy and thankfulness:

> My mother ever sought the spiritual welfare of her children and prayed for them daily and often. I can still see her . . . on her knees and hearing her pray

> . . . she brought us daily before the throne of grace *on* her knees; and at other times brought us to terms *across* her knees; all for the same good purpose, to bring us to Christ.

At age seventeen August left the Netherlands for the U.S., where two brothers and a sister had already gone. He never saw his mother again in this life. After three years in Albany, New York, he joined his brothers and sister in Grand Rapids, Michigan, where a large Dutch community resided. He went along to the assembly meetings but was indifferent to the gospel. One night he was buttonholed by a young man who urged him with tears to accept Christ. The young man's obvious concern moved him, and later that evening his brother Louis read the Scriptures to him. As August said, "I was saved—born again—on Sunday, May 1st" [1910].

Not long after his conversion, August joined other young people in open-air preaching on Saturday, a common practice among assemblies on both sides of the Atlantic in those days. They would take the interurban street car to nearby towns and "would preach often to hundreds and give out many tracts . . . we, the beginners, would try to stammer a few words now and then." After a couple of years, August was asked to speak at the Sunday evening meeting. His sermon lasted only a few minutes and another brother had to take up the rest of the time. An older brother told him, "You are not a preacher and you'll never be one." But about two years later this man was among a committee of five who invited him to assist an experienced preacher in a tent campaign.

August felt utterly unfit to begin a public ministry, "but I learned since that the Scriptures teach that God delights to use those who feel they are not fit." He quit his job and began a career of serving the Lord that was to last over sixty years. The first tent campaign was to be in Owasso, Michigan, and for weeks he went door to door with invitations and tracts. At last the actual campaign was to begin:

> I shall never forget the sight that met our eyes when we came to the tent for the first evening meeting. We were amazed to see its 500 capacity crowded to the doors and hundreds more standing on the outside.

The two young workers conducted several campaigns over the following two years. During one of the meetings, VanRyn met a young man named Robert Stratton, originally from New Jersey, who had gone to the Bahamas to preach the gospel. Having married and made the islands his home, he was back in the States only for a visit. Stratton helped in the tent work for a while and then returned. Soon he wrote to August, inviting him to join him in the Lord's work in the Bahamas. On the last day of 1916, August sailed for Nassau where he was met by Stratton and conducted to another island, Abaco. Here at Bob Stratton's home he was introduced to Mrs. Lilah Stratton's sister, Persis. It was love at first sight. A few months later Persis became his wife, a marriage that was to last fifty-six years until her death in 1974.

The VanRyns made their home near the Strattons at March Harbor, and August and his brother-in-law visited towns on Abaco and other islands, preaching the gospel and ministering to the saints. They built two boats, the second of which, called "The Evangel," was fifty-two feet long, fourteen feet wide, and had two sails and a ninety horse power engine. In his memoirs August cites numerous adventures on the sea and also lessons that God taught him through navigation and the ways of sailors. His most harrowing experience was in October 1926, when a tidal wave destroyed their home and nearly took their lives. Their baby girl, in fact, was lost, but the other three children and the parents miraculously survived. This incident followed closely after an amazing revival in which many were saved. A year later the Lord gave them a baby boy, Carroll.

In 1930, after August had been thirteen years in the islands, the VanRyn family moved to Grand Rapids, Michigan, where they lived for three and a half years while August itinerated among the assemblies. During this period, some of the worst years of the Great Depression, he began to send out a monthly newsletter to encourage the Lord's people. He continued this "Letter of Encouragement" for over forty years, and after that it was taken over by others. But Mrs. VanRyn and the children found Michigan weather too severe, and in 1933 the family went south to Florida, where August and Persis resided for the rest of their lives (when not traveling). When Emmaus Bible School started in the 1940s, August was invited to teach, and eventually he wrote a number of Bible commentaries. Both his commentaries and collections of the "Letter of Encouragement" are still carried by Walterick Publishers.

August VanRyn was blessed with a wonderful sense of humor. Even when in pain he could tell a joke. In 1950, while helping to paint the chapel, he fell and broke two vertebrae. After several weeks in a body cast he said to his doctor, "This is the first time I have ever prayed to be an outcast!" The doctor, however, did a one-up on him. After fitting VanRyn with a strong corset he said, "You know, VanRyn, you are no longer an outcast . . . but this thing will make you live an upright life!" Along with his preaching and writing skills, August had an amazing memory— which he attributed to the threat of losing his eyesight. He could actually quote the entire New Testament by memory, as well as large portions of Genesis, Exodus, and Isaiah. One time he quoted all 150 Psalms for a group of young Christians!

(Condensed from *Sixty Years in His Service* by August VanRyn.)

PART IV

THE BRETHREN IN THE SPACE AGE

Dressed as a clown, an International Teams worker reaches children in the inner city.

21
Advances in Outreach and Missions

International Teams: A New Concept of Missions

In 1961 a new dimension was added to Brethren missions with the birth of Literature Crusades, which later became International Teams (I.T.). The story of the first twenty-five years of this remarkable ministry is told by the founder, Kevin Dyer, under the title *Nothing's Too Hard for God*. The title expresses the experience of Dyer, his wife Eloise, and his close associates as they saw this work develop from merely a vision in 1960 (and a rejected one at that) to a world-wide outreach today.

A recent publication of this ministry's magazine, *Teamwork*, lists three major opportunities for service: short-term missions, which includes membership in an evangelism team abroad for two years; Summer Servants teams with two-to-six week projects in many countries; WorldTouch, an opportunity for a church group to serve for a short term abroad. Articles in this issue of *Teamwork* reflect work in Russia, Hungary, Austria, France, the Philippines, Romania, Albania, and at the Olympic games in Spain.

Kevin Dyer was brought up in Tasmania, the son of godly parents associated with Brethren. As a very young lad he was challenged by a missions retreat conducted by his father (a government official and holder of the Order of the British Empire conferred by Queen Elizabeth II). In 1954, not long after finishing high school, he and his brother made their way by ship to London, visiting some of the large cities of

Asia on the way. He was especially moved by seeing a funeral procession in the packed streets of Bombay, and asked God to help him return with the gospel. After working for a time in London the two Dyer boys traveled to Israel and the Middle East and hitchhiked some 20,000 miles throughout Europe. Kevin began studies at Emmaus Bible School in Oak Park, Illinois, in 1956, where he met Eloise, his wife-to-be. They were married in 1957 and, after a year of service with the Emmaus Correspondence School, they returned to Kevin's home in Tasmania.

Kevin and Eloise's first son, Mark, was born in Tasmania, and shortly afterward Kevin received an invitation to head up the Emmaus correspondence work at Oak Park. He still yearned to bring the gospel to the cities of Asia, but he and Eloise believed this call to be the right move for that time. Soon they made the long sea voyage via Singapore and several cities of Asia and Europe back to Chicago. During this transition Kevin conceived the idea of teams of missionaries working together to evangelize large population centers of the world. The start-up strategy called for ten young workers to do mass literature distribution, including an offer of a free correspondence course. Needed was an initial amount of $25,000 for the first year. For starters, Kevin sent a proposal of this plan in writing to five of his trusted friends. After a long wait, however, only two responded, and they were lukewarm to the idea.

Faced with such discouragement, the Dyers were tempted to give up. But in September 1960 they decided to meet every week to pray for Asia with anyone interested. By October there were thirteen in the group, and God began to move in their midst. A decision was made that they would go to India in the summer of 1961 under the name of the Southeast Asia Literature Crusade. Money began to come in, but by spring of 1961 all but one of the original eleven had dropped out. Also, opposition began to increase, in the form of misinformation spread as rumors and criticism from various influential sources within Brethren circles. But against all human odds a team was in place by August 1961. Their boat passage which had been canceled was replaced at the last moment, a sum of $27,700 had been received and the group was on its way. [Fig. 89]

The Lord overcame one obstacle after another as the ship carrying the six-member team made its slow way through the Mediterranean and the Suez Canal to the east coast of Africa, then to Karachi in Pakistan and finally to Bombay. From there it was a grueling forty-hour train ride to Calcutta. Once they reached their destination they found that their order for 80,000 Gospels of Mark was not yet available. They decided to purchase the 20,000 in stock at the Bible Society and push forward, although they were told by the Bible Society that it would be impossible to sell 100,000 gospels in a year, much less in three months. The first three days seemed to confirm that prediction. They averaged less than one hundred sales a day. At the end of day three they decided to stay on the streets until there was a breakthrough. Dragging themselves down the main street of Calcutta at night, they stopped to offer the books and soon a crowd gathered. Hands reached from everywhere, and at the end of the evening they had sold 1,482. At the end of three months all 100,000 were gone. [Fig. 90]

Thus the Calcutta crusade in 1961 taught Kevin and Eloise that nothing is too hard for God. As they expanded the outreach in Asia they learned, too, that short-term missionary service is an excellent intermediate step in introducing young people to a career in missions. Today, hundreds of former team members are commended missionaries on the field. They also found that a period of training before sending young people overseas greatly increases their effectiveness. Upon returning to Chicago they were able, by another set of miracles, to purchase a large old house in suburban Park Ridge. After months of hard work this became the first Literature Crusades training center.

The next crusade was held in Brazil in 1962-63, and Kevin soon discovered that each part of the world has its unique problems for literature teams. For example, in Latin America, sales must be made door-to-door. The Brazil crusade was followed by further expansion in the Orient. Then came another first: literature distribution at the 1964 Olympic games in Japan. For this latter effort Kevin recruited a group of twenty-five Christian businessmen who paid their own way to assist the team. Some 70,000 pieces of literature were passed out each day. Then in 1965, Kevin decided to place four teams in one of each of four cities: Bombay, Manila, Bogota, and Caracas. Thirty-five new team members were needed, so the slogan for that year's recruiting became "35 for 65." By the end of the year, forty-seven had volunteered.

As early as 1964 it became evident that International Teams needed a larger training facility. The present headquarters and training center in Prospect Heights, Illinois, just west of Chicago, was located in November 1964. It consisted of 7.5 acres with a couple of dilapidated buildings. After months of waiting on God for the funds and much hard volunteer labor, the new building was ready for a team of twelve to start training in September 1965. Over the years the property has increased to eleven acres with fourteen large comfortable homes and two well- equipped administrative buildings. (The newest building was subsequently sold, but is available to I.T. on a rental basis).

At the end of December 1966 the first International Teams Missions Congress was held at Wheaton College. Like the triennial student missionary convention sponsored by Inter-Varsity Christian Fellowship at Urbana, the Missions Congress was designed for young people who wanted to investigate the possibilities of serving the Lord overseas. In 1966 some 1,600 came from assemblies all over the U.S. and Canada. The opening and closing addresses were given by Harold Wildish, beloved missionary statesman from Jamaica. Some 400 young people indicated their intention to let God take control of their lives. In 1982 the Congress was moved to the Prospect Heights facility.

In the early 1970s the counterculture and hippie movement were in full swing, and I.T. operated coffee-house ministries in several places, including one called the Catacombs in Prospect Heights. A house-community for young people, the King's Inn, was started in 1972. That year some 200 young people, many of them from broken homes, put their trust in the Lord. Eventually Kevin and Eloise started a new assembly fellowship in their own home, with the idea of building up the church in their own community. It was also in the early 1970s that Kevin, with some of his trusted friends, began their important work of supporting believers then behind the Iron Curtain. [Fig. 91]Ever on the cutting edge of creative trends, Kevin decided in the mid-1980s that it was time for him to move over and make way for young leadership. While he keeps busy as ever for the Lord in a wider sphere, International Teams is now administered by a group of younger leaders headed by Mark Dyer, Kevin's eldest son. (Condensed from *Nothing's Too Hard for God* by Kevin G. Dyer.)

African American Assembly History

The Scotch-Irish influence on the Brethren movement in North America is so firmly established in our minds that it comes as a source of amazement to find that over ten percent of the assemblies in the U.S., and around seven percent in all of North America, do not share this heritage. Moreover, the Lord's work, including active gospel outreach being carried on by black Christians is among the most active and growing on this continent. In 1992 there were eighty-two churches, large and small, made up of about seventy percent African Americans and thirty percent West Indian Americans. Their ministry includes Christian schools, radio programs, foundations, and organizations. Serving these 20,000 believers are 150 full-time workers and several missionaries to Africa and the Caribbean islands. Their radio broadcasts can be heard in all fifty states and Canada.

The origins of this branch of the Brethren in the western hemisphere can be traced to the Caribbean islands, Jamaica in particular, where J.N. Darby and George Wigram visited in 1850 and established at least one Exclusive meeting. Before this there was the work of Leonard Strong, a Church of England clergyman who around 1828 became an independent worker in British Guiana in order to continue his ministry among African slaves (chapter 4). It is possible that some of the black believers might have carried on independent witnesses in the islands, though no evidence of that exists. Jamaican historian Billy Hall also cites the record of Benjamin Shim, an English merchant, who came to Jamaica some time before 1848 and preached the gospel independently.

Following the visit of Darby and Wigram, the Exclusive assemblies in Jamaica and possibly the other islands multiplied over the years, though specific information is not available. The first Independent Brethren meeting was established in Kingstown as a result of a split in the Darbyite group meeting at Hanover Street. The new congregation called their meeting place Assembly Hall. With the arrival of American missionaries Leonard and Irene Bewick in the early 1920s the work went forward, but the first really flourishing Independent assembly, Maranatha, began in 1931 through the efforts of Irish-Canadians William and Grace Gibson. This meeting grew to more than 700 believers, and became a springboard for other gospel outreach throughout the islands.

Meanwhile, in 1910, a sister from what is now Maplewood Bible Chapel in St. Louis, Missouri, started a ministry among black children in the Richmond Heights area. This resulted, in 1912, in the establishment of Richmond Heights Gospel Chapel. At this time a great many West Indians were migrating to the East Coast, including believers from the Bahamas, British Guiana, Barbados, Jamaica, and some smaller islands. Among these were the three Nottage brothers, Whitfield, Talbot, and Berlin, who founded Grace Gospel Chapel in New York City in 1914, the first black assembly on the eastern seaboard. In the next two or three decades similar churches were planted elsewhere in New York, Philadelphia, Chicago, and Detroit. All three of the Nottage brothers became leaders in this growing work.

Following these major cities, black congregations were established over the next few years in Muskegon, Cleveland, St. Louis, Terre Haute, Birmingham, Atlanta, and Los Angeles. Pioneers included Burley Edwards and Theo Williams of Chicago; Brother Carey of Cleveland; William Coleman, Grant Love, Ed Ford and Stanley Lamar of Detroit. Later workers from Southside Bible Chapel in Chicago were Leroy Yates, Melvin Banks, and Harvey Rollerson.

The Good News Radio Program was started by T. Michael Flowers [Fig. 92] to reach the southern U.S. states. Flowers, who was born in the Bahamas, with his wife Ella felt called by God to work in the southeastern states. In 1955 he began pioneering in Savannah, working by himself for many months before he could arrange for his wife and daughter to join him. Over a period of twenty-one years Flowers was used by God to plant churches in Savannah, Augusta, and Atlanta, Georgia, and in Beaufort and Charleston, North Charleston, and St. Helena, South Carolina. In 1966 he formed the Southern Gospel Missions Association, with the goal of establishing a testimony in every major city in the U.S. [Fig. 93] The SGMA has its headquarters in Decatur, Georgia, and holds an annual United Bible Conference over Memorial Day weekend. In 1987, T. Michael Flowers was one of seven men selected to mentor young men for the Billy Graham World Evangelism Team.

Otis Tillman, born in Georgia and raised in Michigan, received Christ at an early age. In the years 1939-41 he was given help to grow in the Lord by Harry Ironside, then pastor of Moody Church in Chicago. He started the Coldspring Bible Chapel in Buffalo, New York, and founded the Gospel Expansion Foundation and also a radio program called The Chapel Hour. He and his wife Geraldine operate an inner-city program that provides food for needy people as well as a special children's ministry.

Born in Harlem but raised in Jamaica by parents who served the Lord, B. Sam Hart preached his first sermon at age fourteen. He desired to reach the black population of America for the gospel and founded his first assembly while attending college in Boston. Later he moved with his wife Joyce to Philadelphia, where he began the Grand Old Gospel

Hour broadcast in 1962. Hart has been used of the Lord to plant twelve churches in the northeastern U.S. and has conducted evangelistic crusades in a number of major U.S. cities as well as the West Indies, South America, Africa, and India. He is vice-president of the National Religious Broadcasters Association.

The National Conference for Pioneering Black America was founded in 1984. Headed by Donovan Case, who was raised in the West Indies and saved through the ministry of Harold Wildish, the NCPBA publishes a daily prayer guide of those working among African Americans. It also sponsors an annual conference of black workers and assembly leaders. Regarding the growth of assemblies among black Americans, Case made this observation in a recent paper:

> In the African American church the culture is so significantly different that if we continue to push traditional "Brethrenism" in terms of order of services, etc., we will only continue to reach a few.

> To have an impact on the thirty million African Americans, we must be creative and adaptable to various cultural comfort zones, and at the same time be biblically sound. We do not have to try to make the Bible relevant. The Bible is relevant all by itself.[1]

Evangelism in the 1970s

Inspired by the Billy Graham crusades, various evangelistic campaigns were conducted by the Brethren in North America through the decade of the 1970s. In 1970 the English ex-boxer Stan Ford made a second visit to this continent. His crusade, called *New Life for You*, took him to eight

---

1 (Sources for the above information:
Donovan Case, "Challenge to a Commitment to the Movement," an address given at the 1992 National Black Worker's Conference;
"Documentary of the Work in Black America," an address given at the 1989 National Black Worker's Conference;
T. Michael Flowers, "Twenty-one Years of Pioneering in Georgia,"
Interest, October 1976;
Billy Hall, "Looking Back Over 68 Years (1920-1988)," A History of the Open Brethren Witness in Jamaica," pp. 21-29, Special Issue on *Assembly Affairs*, January 1989;
"News from North America," *Interest*, July/August 1992.

states (Tennessee, Ohio, Missouri, South Carolina, Florida, Georgia, Illinois, and New York) for fifteen separate campaigns in five months. In Toronto, twenty assemblies joined forces to sponsor a two-week gospel campaign in October 1974, with English evangelist Dick Saunders. [Fig. 94] Thirty trained counselors dealt with those who responded to the invitation to receive Christ, and a one hundred-voice choir from eighteen assemblies sang every evening. The chairman, Sam Thompson, reported "a profound effect on the Christians who worked together in the gospel effort."

On the west coast of Canada the young evangelist Terry Winter, age twenty-seven, commenced a number of crusades that involved Brethren assemblies. In Kitchener, Ontario, Winter conducted an eight-day series of meetings in November 1971 that drew an average of 450 per night. People interested in salvation were invited to come to the front after the meeting for counseling, rather than coming down the aisle during an invitation. Some sixty were counseled in all, and about forty-three of these accepted Christ. No collections were taken during the services. Over the years Winter has become a respected radio and television personality and today, more than twenty years after his first campaigns, his gospel broadcasts are heard across Canada.

Outreach to Immigrants and Refugees

Since the 1960s people from other countries in the world where conditions are unstable have migrated in great numbers to the U.S. and Canada. The following, abstracted from an article called "The 'Eastern' North Americans" by Bill Conard in *Interest*, September 1991, points out the opportunity for outreach among these new residents being exercised by a number of the Brethren assemblies:

> In recent years we have seen Filipinos, Vietnamese, Cambodians, Koreans, and Laotians . . . cross the Pacific. [Fig. 95] Now, with tension in the Philippines, and with Hong Kong scheduled to revert to China in 1997, Asians again seek refuge in North America.[1] During 1989

---

1 It should also be noted that there are in North American a significant number of Christians from India and Pakistan, some of whom have formed their own assemblies.

alone over 200,000 entered the U.S.; other thousands entered Canada. These people have become valuable citizens—many taking top honors in education, science, technology, etc.

Keep in mind that many Asian immigrants believe in Christ. Some statistics experts argue that Canada's Christian population increases in proportion to the influx of Pacific rim people! Also, figure that during the first months of an immigrant's presence in our land he or she needs and welcomes any kind help. This means that these people stand more open to the gospel message at this time than at any previous or subsequent time in their life.

Scores of assemblies in the U.S. and Canada have opened their doors and their hearts to . . . immigrants. This has brought blessing to both the hosts and the guests. In Vancouver, B.C., Heather Bible Chapel and Westminster Bible Chapel sponsor Asian fellowships. In California, Parkside Gospel Chapel (San Francisco) and Laurel Bible Chapel (San Diego) have become multi-lingual and multi-racial as the Christians reach out to immigrants from Asia and Latin America. Evanston (Illinois) Gospel Chapel convenes special meetings to reach and teach Asian children in the neighborhood. Many other assemblies across North America are doing the same.

Believers with [a foreign] background have been fully welcomed into existing North American assemblies, often serving the Lord and His people as ushers, musicians, Bible study and Sunday school teachers, preachers, deacons, and elders. Christ looks for and welcomes all people everywhere. He treats them with love. His followers can do the same.

In the years since 1991, Interest Ministries under the leadership of Andy Holloman has worked diligently to assist various ethnic groups to form their own congregations. New church planting ministries include M.E.S.S.I.A.H. for Spanish-speaking communities; Ecclesia, for the African-American community; Frontline, for the Jewish community; and Vision Ontario, directed toward outreach in the province of Ontario, Canada. In the summer of 1994 a boot camp for ethnic church planters was held in Estes Park, Colorado.

The Amazing Emmaus Correspondences Courses

The first Emmaus correspondence courses were offered in 1942 (chapter 15). Soon these mimeographed lessons were in great demand, not only by servicemen but also by camps, chapel study groups, and the like. As Ross McLaren points out, "the correspondence course have produced a

. . . unity of doctrine and teaching in the assemblies." He refers to such courses as *Bible Prophecy* (a dispensational approach) by Ernest Tatham (1955), *Christ Loved the Church* by William MacDonald (1956) on the doctrine of the church, and *Buried by Baptism*, also by MacDonald (1957), emphasizing believer's baptism. A dispensational classic, *Rightly Dividing the Word of Truth* by C.I. Scofield, was also adapted for an Emmaus course.

An Emmaus publication, *The First 50 Years*, explains how the correspondence courses developed into a global ministry:

> Until 1949 correspondence courses had been designed exclusively to instruct believers in the scripture. It was William MacDonald who first realized the potential of gospel courses for free distribution to non-believers and . . . new believers. The first of these, edited by MacDonald, was *What the Bible Teaches*. It has now been translated into 85 languages, and distribution tops 1.75 million copies.

According to MacDonald, the first missionary to use the new material was Cyril Brooks, who incorporated it as part of his radio ministry in the Philippines. "We had barely finished one course before Mr. Brooks was asking for another," he recalled. Bill MacDonald, in fact, has produced more Emmaus courses than any other writer. [Fig. 98] These include *Lessons in Christian Living, Guide for Christian Growth* and *Romans*.

The amazingly rapid international expansion of the Emmaus courses indicates, first, that a great opportunity was there waiting, and second, that the Brethren missionary force was alive to the possibilities. In the January 1952 edition of *Letters of Interest*, ten years from the birth of the first correspondence courses, a feature article takes the reader on an imaginary trip around the world. Emmaus courses are discovered making an impact in Israel (in the Arab ministry of Harry and Bess Medrow), Irumu in the Belgian Congo (where Ed Harlow was back translating courses into the African tongue, along with Gertrud Koppel, an Emmaus graduate), New Delhi in India; Malaya, Hong Kong; Manila (translated and distributed by Mr. and Mrs. Cyril Brooks), Tokyo (translated and distributed by Paul and Ruth Craig, Emmaus graduates), and Suva in the Fiji Islands (distributed by J. Foster Crane). In 1952 correspondence students totalled 12,984 and 30,162 courses had been sent out.

A Prison Ministry Is Born

The use of Emmaus correspondence courses as a means of evangelism in prisons has had a tremendous impact both in North America and Britain. An article in the March 1973 *Letters of Interest* tells the story of Harold Catlow, director of the Emmaus Correspondence School in Great Britain, where the courses were so successful in changing the lives of young prisoners that prison directors in some places had declared them mandatory educational material. In the U.S., an Assembly prison ministry was started in Cook County Jail, Illinois, by Wesley Kosin in 1952. He carried on faithfully for some five years, for a while with great freedom and later, under a Jewish warden, with extreme difficulty. The work was taken over in 1957 by John Erwin.

In 1975, Phil Wagner and Dale Tweedy, chaplains at Cook County Jail, were appointed as the first distributors of Emmaus courses to penal institutions in North America. [Fig. 97] Ten years later, in 1985, we read that the "work has since spread to hundreds of institutions around the United States as well as the province of Ontario in Canada. Twenty-two penal coordinators are working faithfully to reach inmates with the gospel of Christ." The prison ministry was first coordinated by Gordon Haresign, then became the responsibility of Charles Fizer, former missionary in South Korea. Emmaus correspondence courses are today being used in more than 1,000 institutions, with 1,500,00 courses finding their way behind prison bars by 1991.[1] Of all Emmaus courses completed, sixty-five percent are by prisoners. The most popular are *Born to Win* and *Doing Time With Jesus*.

The prison ministry is currently one of three programs conducted by the Emmaus Correspondence School. The Domestic Ministry, working through regional directors [Fig. 96] and a growing number of associate instructors, provides Bible training for Christians throughout the

---

1 In the 1990s Phil Wagner began to pioneer a prison work in Moscow, and this has grown to a sizable ministry with a team of Russian workers. Resistance by prison authorities has turned into gratitude for the positive effects seen in the prisoners' lives. The team has been featured on television and now has a weekly nation-wide radio spot.

U.S. and Canada. Courses come at two levels, popular and college, and include basic Bible and doctrine studies, special courses directed toward salvation, children and Christian life; plus some newer subjects such as *God's Blueprint for Your Marriage*. The Overseas Ministry involves courses offered in eighty-five countries of the world and in 106 languages, with 100 or more regional directors participating.

The Steve Linscott Story

In 1987 a book appeared by Gordon Haresign, Director of the Emmaus Correspondence School, entitled. *Innocence: The True Story of Steven Linscott.* This relates the account of a young family man attending Emmaus Bible College who on the night of October 4, 1980, had a very realistic dream about a murder. At this very time in an Oak Park Apartment just two houses away, a young woman was brutally killed. Trying to be helpful, Steve later related the dream to detectives, only to find himself charged with the murder and on trial.

The prosecutors, noting some similarities between the dream and the actual crime, claimed the dream was a veiled confession. They also produced physical "evidence" linking Linscott to the murder. His lawyer was unwilling to defend the dream as such, and could not overcome the prosecution's exaggerated claims. There were also irregularities attending the handling of the jury. These factors, according to author Haresign, all led to Linscott's conviction and imprisonment for a crime he did not commit.

Convinced of Linscott's innocence, Haresign resigned from Emmaus to help Steve, Lois, and their family. Other Christians, a new attorney, and Haresign joined to make a successful appeal. Steve was released in November 1985, but in October 1986 the Illinois Supreme Court reinstated the original verdict. Linscott was freed after the book was published, pending an Appeals Court review relating to a new trial. In the end new evidence led to another source and Linscott was released permanently.

(Adapted from an article by Ed Powell, Wheaton, Illinois.)

22

Developments in Education and Training

Schools and Scholars

In the ranks of the men who formed the nucleus of the first Brethren assemblies in Great Britain were several first-rate biblical scholars: Samuel P. Tregelles, Henry Borlaise, George Wigram, B.W. Newton, and of course J.N. Darby. In those days most university graduates knew Greek and Latin, and it is said of Brethren Bible studies that it was common for participants to use their Greek New Testaments. Many of the scholars remained in the Exclusive camp, but the Independent branch in Great Britain had their share: Henry Craik, Lord Congleton, John Eliot Howard, Andrew Jukes, and later W.E. Vine, author of the *Expository Dictionary of New Testament Words*; church historian E.H. Broadbent; apologist Sir Robert Anderson and many others. In North America, the Exclusives in early days produced some scholars of note: the Loizeaux brothers, F.W. Grant, and Samuel Ridout. Among the Independent Brethren on this continent, however, university studies of a formal nature in general and theological studies in particular were considered worldly and inconsistent with the Christian life.

The development of Emmaus Bible College (chapter 15) was the first sign that things were changing. The war years had broadened the spiritual horizons for many young people and Bible school as well as the university were now possibilities. Also, as was pointed out earlier, the merger with the Grant Exclusives brought some formally trained men into the ranks of the Independents. Another influence beginning to impact on academically inclined young people in North America was the scholarly leadership in the more progressive Brethren circles in Great Britain in the early 1950s.

A number of leading British brethren—G.C.D. Howley, editor of *The Witness*, Harold St. John, Montague Goodman, Professor F. F. Bruce, and some others—were concerned about the decline of the assemblies in the United Kingdom after World War II. They believed that the time had come to examine the position of the assemblies in the light of Scripture. To do this they convened an annual meeting for prayer and discussion on the condition of the Brethren assemblies that came to be known as the "High Leigh Conferences." The notes of these very frank messages and discussions dealing with the problems were printed and widely circulated, and made a considerable impact on this side of the Atlantic. Howley visited the U.S. and Canada in 1956, spending much of his time with the younger leadership.

Partly as an outgrowth of High Leigh, a scholarly association was formed in Britain in the early 1960s called the Christian Brethren Research Fellowship (CBRF). Their first journal, published in May 1963, had as its theme, "The Message of the Brethren Today." It contains superb articles by F. Roy Coad, G.C.D. Howley, and James Houston. Meanwhile, back in the U.S., several young men including Walter Liefeld, Donald Tinder, and Carl Armerding were working on their doctorates in areas like theology, church history, and biblical studies. Another young man from the assemblies, Ward Gasque, went across to Manchester, England, to work on his thesis under F.F. Bruce.

In the late 1960s some prominent brethren associated with assemblies in western Canada—among them Brian P. Sutherland, E. Marshall Sheppard, Kenneth O. Smith, and Richard L. Richards— developed a vision for a different kind of Christian educational institution than the Bible-school model. They wanted to provide Bible-related courses by some of the best evangelical scholars in the world for believers with academic degrees who were *not* preparing for the professional clergy. In 1968 this vision became a reality when, upon petition of the above brethren and nine others, the legislative assembly of British Columbia established Regent College as a degree-granting school. Dr. W.J. Martin (U. of Liverpool) and Dr. James Houston (Oxford) were invited from England to become honorary principal and vice-principal.

The first session in the summer of 1969 drew over fifty students from Canada and the U.S., each student taking one or two of the six courses taught by seven faculty members. These students included businessmen, teachers, pastors, professors, Bible-school teachers, graduate students, homemakers, and other Christians from a variety of church affiliations. Over the years Regent has included on its faculty men of God from the highest academic levels, including John R.W. Stott, J.I. Packer, Bruce Waltke, F.F. Bruce, Carl Armerding, Ian Rennie, Clark Pinnock, Paul Stevens, Michael Griffiths, and Samuel Escobar.

It is obvious that if many in Brethren circles considered even Bible school a waste of time and a compromise with the world, Regent's curriculum would be viewed with deep skepticism if not hostility. To try and explain to the skeptics that scholarly studies *could* be the will of God for some Christians, Dr. Stanley Block (who for many years was the InterVarsity faculty sponsor at the University of Minnesota) wrote a paper, "What Is Different about Regent College?" that appeared in the December 1969 issue of *Letters of Interest*. In one place he says:

> Many students, especially those who have had a challenging college edu-
> cation, want to know *why* something is true, and *how* this fact or theory is
> related to other facts, principles and theories . . . These people are not
> satisfied with pat answers and simple solutions to complex problems. Nor
> are they satisfied always to accept the teacher's conclusions and convic-
> tions, no matter how much they respect and value him. This approach can
> be called "depth education."

A sign that more young scholars with a Brethren background are be-coming interested in a serious study of Brethren history, doctrine, music, etc., occurred in July 1990, when a week-long course was held at Regent College called "The Christian Brethren Movement: Its History, Present Status and Future Prospects." [Fig. 100] This was conceived and organized by W. Ward Gasque with F. Roy Coad of England as the main lecturer. The presenters, respondents and seminar leaders numbered nearly forty, and well over a hundred were present. A large delegation came from England and Australia, New Zealand, Malaysia, Germany, and Italy were represented. Plans were laid for a world-wide fellowship of Brethren historians. Another meeting of a somewhat similar nature was held in Singapore in the summer of 1993, and plans call for a third meeting in Italy in 1996.

Finally, there has been since the 1950s some interest in starting a scholarly journal from a Brethren perspective in North America. But, with the possible exception of a Dallas Theological Seminary publication, *Bibliotheca Sacra*, emphasizing Dispensationalism, nothing appeared until December 1989. At that time, a group interested in scholarly research met at the first Decade of Promise conference and agreed to launch a North American Brethren Research Fellowship (NABRF). Rex Koivisto of Multnomah School of the Bible in Portland, Oregon, was appointed secretary. That plan, however, was put on hold after a year or two. Since then, the faculty at Emmaus Bible College in Dubuque has launched a new semiannual publication, *The Emmaus Journal*. It is "devoted to the exposition of the Bible, biblical doctrines, and practical issues from a biblical perspective." The editor is John H. Fish III.

A Gem from High Leigh

One of the great differences between the "traditional" Brethren position and that of the "progressives" is in the attitude toward other bodies of believers, referred to in earlier days as "the sects." The High Leigh conference conveners shocked and angered many of their contemporaries back in the 1950s by suggesting that God has used all the different sections of the Christian church to carry forward the truth of the gospel (thus rejecting the usual interpretation of Darby's doctrine of the "church in ruins"). A message by the saintly Harold St. John addressed this subject:

> We have been facing serious, stern, plain speaking in these past days: we have found that there is so much that we have to confess, and such grave weakness to own, that, as far as we are concerned, we simply dare not pass judgment on our fellow-Christians. There are those with whom our consciences will not allow us to walk in church fellowship. I recognize that. There are many whose consciences will not allow them to walk with us. I recognize that. But have we ever acknowledged the incalculable debt of gratitude which we owe to the great historic churches?
>
> I think of the Church of Rome, scarlet in her sins, supreme in her saints, and strong in the way that she has stood like a rock in early and in medieval history. A score of times she has saved the framework of the Christian society in days of assault by the heathen and by heretics. I recall what we owe to our beloved national Church in this land, for having kept the faith alive for centuries in the towns and villages of England. I thank God for our brethren in the Salvation Army who have reminded us to consider the poor; and for our friends, the Friends, who have poured out their lives, their wealth, and their sympathies in the service of wretched

refugees in scores of darkened lands. Should a man not lay his hand upon his mouth before he criticizes his brethren?

When we pass swift, uninformed, unloving, and ungenerous judgments, surely we have forgotten that if we speak evil of them, at the same time we speak evil of the Lord whose Name they bear. They may be living far closer to Christ than we are, and may be vastly more intelligent in the things of God. Is it not to be expected, by the working of the inexorable law of sowing and reaping, that our friends will sometimes take a leaf from our own book, and utter harsh and censorious criticisms of the meetings with which we are familiar? On the other hand, if we exercise a godly self-restraint in thought and speech, we may yet deserve and win the respect and the regard of our fellow Christians. (Harold St. John, from the closing address of the High Leigh Conference, July 1955.)

Training for Christian Service

As the Brethren movement developed in the years following World War II it became apparent that, in addition to Emmaus, there was a need for more training schools for Christian service. In the period 1950 to 1975 a number of different programs emerged to meet these needs.

Institut Biblique Bethel

The origins of this school actually go back to 1947, when a French Canadian Child Evangelism worker, Dorothy Kenyon, saw that in order for Christian families and congregations to develop, French-speaking evangelists and pastors had to be trained. This vision was shared by Arthur Hill and William Klinck, and with their encouragement a ninety-four-acre farm between Sherbrooke and Lennoxville was purchased in 1948. In 1949, Miss Kenyon was joined by Mr. and Mrs. Walter Angst of the Institut Biblique Emmaus in Lausanne, Switzerland, and a three-year program was launched. The first class of six students graduated in 1952.

A report on Bethel appeared in *Interest* in September 1973; by this time there were fifty-five students, seven full-time faculty, including acting president Sheldon Bard and his wife Catherine, and several part-time faculty. The school had a double curriculum with two student bodies, one to teach Bible courses in French and the other to teach the French language to prospective Christian workers. With Arthur Hill as chairman, the board consisted of members from the two main evangelical groups in Quebec at the time, the Brethren and the Fellowship Baptists.

Discipleship Intern Training Program

The DITP is designed as a kind of "on the job training" for young men heading for assembly leadership, the mission field, or some form of Christian service: evangelism, pioneering, church planting, tent making overseas, etc. Started in 1973 at Fairhaven Bible Chapel, San Leandro, California, by Otis Jean Gibson, Jack Davies, and William MacDonald, the concept was for a hands on program similar to internship for medical students. In approximately 1,500 hours over a period of nine months, some six to twelve young men (all of whom must have had business or trade experience) are immersed in instruction, study, and practical experience.

The "practical experience" consists of open-air witnessing on U.C. Berkeley's Sproul Plaza, [Fig. 101]preaching on a San Francisco street corner, home visitation, personal counseling, leading Bible studies and even helping out in funerals, baptisms, and weddings. Gibson points out that the interns are not merely told *what* to do, but their instructors model *how* to do it and participate in all aspects of the training—which is, in fact, all aspects of the church's ministry.

Now in its eighteenth year, DITP has alumni serving in Israel, Spain, Ireland, Turkey, Brazil, Austria, Pakistan, Honduras, New Zealand, Zaire, and Canada. Several are church planters, elders, or evangelists among assemblies in the U.S. One, Bruce McNicol, is director of Interest Ministries, and another, Barry Mahloy, is chairman of Stewards Foundation. Two, Jim McCarthy and Don Robertson, are now on DITP staff. Gibson is convinced that performing *all* aspects of service is a *necessity*. "In the New Testament," he says, most gifts are to be exercised by *all* Christians."

Mt. Carmel Bible School

Mt. Carmel Bible School started in 1968 in the Bethel Bible Chapel, Edmonton, Alberta, as a program of Bible study and practical Christian learning opportunities. The founding faculty members were Stan King, Robert Taylor, and Bill Gurnett, with Stan serving also as president. Their original slogan was "A Good Place To Start," and the course then, as now, consists of one year's (eight months) class work. Many, but not all, students go on for further training elsewhere. The school quickly grew and in 1973 a building was purchased that was expanded in 1978 to accommodate a student body of nearly fifty. Succeeding presidents were Nelson Annan and Henry Pitman. Although its student enrollment declined along with that in all other Bible schools in the 1980s, Mt. Carmel still carries on an attractive one-year program for around thirty students. The current president is Jay Gurnett.

California Center for Biblical Studies

The Culver City Bible School, later known as the California Center for Biblical Studies, was the brain child of Earl Fries, who had a vision for a one-year Bible training course that would lay a foundation for any other life goal a student might choose. (Eventually this gave rise to the slogan, "One year for life.") For eighteen years Richard and Mary Matthews had worked as house parents for some thirty children at the Adelaide Home in Culver City, California. By 1965, however, new laws had brought this ministry to an end. Using the existing corporate structure of the Adelaide Home as well as the spacious facility with five self-contained homes, Matthews, Fries, and Gary Thompson began CCBS with nineteen students in the fall of 1965.

By 1973 the school had developed to the point where construction on a new classroom and library building was started. In early 1974 work began on a forty-bed men's dorm. That year CCBS began to extend its ministry to the community with a one-day workshop on "the family" in which sixty believers from Los Angeles area assemblies took part. Other workshops and annual lectures open to all Christians were also planned. Staff members during this year included Earl Fries, president, Nathan Smith, formerly of Emmaus, David Gill from the student and street Christian ministry in Berkeley, and Hugo Santucci, former shoe company executive from Orinda, California. Dick Matthews succeeded Earl Fries as president in 1976. The school continued until 1983 when a continent-wide decline in Bible school attendance forced them to close their doors.

Kawartha Lakes Bible College

In 1972 some brethren from assemblies in the area of Peterborough, Ontario, began to lay plans for a school offering intensive Bible studies. Starting with night classes, the school began with a class of full-time day students in 1977 in Edmison Heights Bible Chapel with part-time instructors. A second year program for more advanced biblical studies was opened in 1994, along with a reopening of evening classes. Over 600 students have attended Kawartha Lakes Bible College to date, most of them now serving the Lord as missionaries or leaders in local assemblies. The current president is Dan DeGeer.

His Mansion
This unique training ministry was founded in 1971 by Stan Farmer, Joseph Wagner, and Hal Moore with the goal "to rescue the perishing, disciple and equip them for a life of service, and send them out into the harvest fields where they might reproduce themselves." The work began in a huge Victorian mansion (hence the name), and is now located on a mountainous 360 acre campus near Deering, New Hampshire.

His Mansion students are emotionally and behaviorally dysfunctional young adults. Training consists of counseling, spiritual instruction, and practical work. They are now served by twenty-five experienced staff and forty interns or trainees.

Principles of this ministry are based on those of George Muller of Bristol. No state or federal funds are accepted, no charge is made to the recipients of care, and there is no advertising to solicit money. There are now affiliate ministries in Prospect Heights (Chicago), Ontario, Bahamas, South Africa, Prince Edward Island, and Hungary.

Other Training Ministries
Ministries somewhat similar to His Mansion are Salem-Acres-Beth Haven in Elnora, Alberta, operated by John H. Adams, and Loving Hands, operated by Robert Gilmore at Palm Beach Chapel in North Palm Beach, Florida. Marc Oden in Philadelphia runs a program called Youth Spectacular, which trains young people to put on evangelistic events.

(Special sources for the above include a letter and materials from Jay Gurnett in November 1992, an interview with Otis Jean Gibson in November 1992, a phone interview with Dan DeGeer and materials from Stan Farmer in 1995, and articles from *Interest* in September 1973, February 1974, and September 1976.)

Shepherding Seminars and Assembly Consultations

In addition to publishing *Interest* magazine, the Letters of Interest Associates (since 1988, Interest Ministries) has for several decades sponsored various events to assist the assemblies in their life and growth. Two very successful types of events were Shepherding Seminars and Assembly Consultations.

Shepherding Seminars

Typical of the shepherding seminars was the fourth Shepherds Renewal Seminar held at the Chicago facility of Emmaus Bible College in June 1976. [Fig. 102]It was organized for the benefit of elders in Illinois, Indiana, and Wisconsin, though some came from as far away as Ontario and Colorado. The total attendance of 175 was drawn from forty-two assemblies, and included seasoned leaders and active younger brethren. A manual was given to each participant containing a wealth of materials on topics like "the qualifications of elders," but the seminar itself focused more on subjects like training, counseling, visitation, and ways of keeping watch over the flock.

Jack Davies, O. Jean Gibson, Bill Greenaway, and Mark Porter joined with local leaders Abner Bauman, Bob Ramey, and Dan Smith for this particular event. The first seminar was put on by Fairhaven for elders in the Bay Area in 1972. The idea for taking them to other parts of the country came about at a Letters of Interest Associates conference at Greenwood Hills, Pennsylvania, in 1974, when Gibson was the speaker. The seminars were also conducted at individual assemblies. In later years (1980s and 1990s) Gibson has been taking this service to various foreign countries, including Russia.

Assembly Consultations

Another idea developed at Fairhaven Bible Chapel was the assembly consultation. These, during the 1970s and early 1980s, were conducted by Jean and June Gibson and Mark and Carol Porter. The consultation team visited assemblies upon their request, spending Friday night through Sunday with them. They helped the elders to evaluate the life and growth of the assembly, and on the basis of the needs they observed made suggestions for improvement. This function became a service of Interest Ministries under the direction of Mark Porter in the late 1980s. By 1991 over sixty-five assemblies had taken advantage of an assembly consultation during a four-year period.

23

The Challenge of Change

A "Brave New World" and the Brethren

O brave new world
That has such people in't.
From Shakespeare's *The Tempest*

Aldous Huxley wrote his well-known futuristic novel in 1931, and came amazingly close to the mark in predicting the world that has emerged since then, especially since 1960.[1] The changes in these thirty-plus years have been so immense that they defy any brief description. But for the Lord's people one thing is certain: the truth of God's Word

---

[1] In October 1931, the same year that Huxley's book was published, *Light and Liberty* ran a special edition on the second coming of Christ. In the column on current events the writer, T. Baird, gives "Twelve indications of our Lord's near approach." They are:
 1. Extensive travel, Daniel 12:4
2. Increased knowledge, Daniel 12:4 3. Amazing wealth, James 5:3
4. Human religion, 2 Timothy 3:5
5. Discarded agreements, 2 Timothy 3:3
6. Love of self, 2 Timothy 3:2
7. Love of pleasure, 2 Timothy 3:2
8. Disobedience to parents, 2 Timothy 3:2
9. False Christs, Matthew 24:23
 10. General departure [from truth] 1 Timothy 4:1
 11. Women prominent, Revelation 2:20
 12. Jewish restoration, Matthew 24:32

about the downward course of human history becomes clearer with every passing day. As technology advances with breathtaking rapidity, sin, misery, and woe more than keep pace. A brave new world indeed!

As a church movement in North America, the so-called Plymouth Brethren have not made much impact. Dispensationalism has had a wide acceptance, but mainly through the Baptist, Pentecostal, and other "fundamentalist" bodies, through the influence of the Scofield Bible and through Dallas Theological Seminary under Lewis Sperry Chafer. Contrary to the situation in nineteenth century Britain, Brethren writers are not well known on this continent (Harry Ironside in his day being a possible exception. Paul Little's name is widely known because of his books, but not in connection with the Brethren). There are few if any Brethren preachers of national prominence.

The Independent Brethren have, however, distinguished themselves on this continent in grassroots evangelism. While the other evangelical churches were content to work through a system of ordaining pastors and sending them to fill local pulpits, the Brethren were pioneering gospel outreach anywhere they could get the opportunity. Meetings for adults and children in homes and empty schoolhouses in the backwoods, store-front Sunday schools in the inner cities, tent evangelism in empty lots, prisons, juvenile camps, street corners, gospel cars and trailers, and homely little gospel halls all over the place, this was the way the Brethren worked. It was different, it was revolutionary, it wasn't very dignified. But God used it to make a difference in American and Canadian society.

But by mid-century the Independent Brethren had become an institution. A law that governs any institution is this: "Change or die." We are living in a Brave New World as different from the world of the 1930s and 1940s as that world was different from the Victorian era. Since the 1960s the assemblies everywhere on this continent have been facing a choice—either find new methods of reaching out, or remain stagnant. In some situations, of course, growth is no longer possible, and in that case *faithfulness* is the watchword. But an assembly, capable of change, that refuses to look at the options stands in danger of having its lampstand taken away.

By 1980 a crisis seemed to have been reached. For the progressives in the movement, including a majority of the younger leaders, the Brave New World with its revolutionary impact upon society and individual life-styles was a challenge that had to be met—by a willingness to adapt to the times not their *principles*, but their *practices*. This was succinctly expressed by Kevin Dyer in a message called "The Agony of Change; the Ecstasy of Revival" delivered at the Decade of Promise in 1990. In his opening remarks, Dyer voiced what numerous brethren and sisters in a great many assemblies all over the continent had felt when faced with the problem of decline in their own particular local fellowship:

> It is imperative that we face up to this issue of change, since even a vital, growing church is never free from decay, and often decaying churches have exceedingly vital elements within them. Unless we are very careful, we can be lulled to sleep until it is almost too late.

> Now we must also remember that change is not always a good thing. Death is a form of change, and so is deterioration . . . But we *must* change. Supermarkets have changed over the years. When I was a boy, there were the mom and pop grocery stores where friendly relations, time and personal interest made shopping a joy . . . Today supermarkets . . . are open 24 hours a day. You can find [almost any sort of product] in a single store.

> But church goes on the same. Breaking of Bread at 9:30 and Sunday Family Bible Hour at 11:00—it was and is, and shall be, forever more. No one can fail to see in some segments of assembly life the dry rot produced by apathy, rigidity and spiritual emptiness.

> If you are doing the same thing you were doing 10 years ago, something is wrong . . . People's needs have changed and if the church hasn't moved to meet those needs we have denied the vitality of God's work and the Holy Spirit's power in our generation.

> Apathy and lowered motivation are the most widely noted characteristics of a church on the downward path. If we falter, it will be because of a failure of heart and spirit.

The Unique Role of *Interest Magazine*

One of the clearest indicators of how the Open Brethren movement has responded to the amazing developments of the late twentieth century has been the metamorphosis of *Interest* magazine from its inception in 1934 to the present day. From the beginning, *Interest* has been on the cutting edge of new developments among the Brethren on this continent. Its role has been that of a barometer for change, and as such it has ever been a target for criticism.

The First Letters of Interest

When Bill McCartney, along with J.H. Williamson, R.W. Trotter, and R.W. Stott, started *Letters of Interest from the Home Field* in July 1934, [Fig. 103], it was with a specific purpose in mind. It was one of the worst years of the Great Depression. According to the introductory editorial:

> Many of the Lord's people are out of work and are hardly able to make ends meet, thus the offerings in our assemblies have been greatly reduced and as a result the assemblies are not able to minister to the evangelists as they did when times were better.

Thus the new publication was to be:

> . . . a bulletin giving short accounts of the pioneer and his work and mailing them to every assembly in the United States and Canada and in this way keeping the work before the saints so that they may be exercised to send support to any brother laboring in neglected places.

The first issues were exactly this, a series of bulletins. Volume 1, Number 1, contains one editorial, "Striving Together for the Faith of the Gospel" (Philippians 1:27), and the rest consists of letters from twenty-two pioneer workers (chapter 13).

The 1940s and 1950s

Over the next decade the title was shortened to just the first three words and the bulletin was typeset and printed. The printing was first done in Grand Rapids by the Gospel Folio Press under Will and Peter Pell, and from 1938 by Grover C. Mishler of Elkhart, Indiana. In 1943 it was taken over by Clyde Dennis of Good News Publishing in Chicago, at which time it gained a "new look" with glossy paper, open space, art work, and photographs. Between 1943 and 1947 the same photo appeared on the cover throughout the year.

Taking the December 1945 issue as a sample, we find the magazine expanded from just an editorial and letters to reports on a number of different aspects of ministry and outreach: assembly activities, conferences, Spanish work, children's work, women in the Lord's work, servicemen's news, gospel meetings, radio, the Christian home for children in Colorado—plus an announcement by Edward Harlow on the start-up of Emmaus day classes (with a full-page photo) and a biography of pioneer James Harcus.

With the October 1959 issue the magazine was enlarged from 6 x 8 to the 8-1/2 x 11 format.

The 1960s: A Transitional Decade

Bill McCartney retired in 1961 and his place as editor was taken by Donald Taylor, who had been with *Letters of Interest* since 1949. For most of the turbulent decade of the 1960s the magazine was altered very little. But by 1970 even the more conservative Christian bodies were feeling the impact of the radical storms beating against the accepted traditions in Western society: anti-war and free speech riots on college campuses, the counterculture with its scorn for convention and authority, the sexual revolution, and a general breakdown of traditional moral values.

Furthermore, the assemblies during this period had undergone vast changes, with many of the original chapels in the cities closed or in difficulty, and new ones rising in affluent suburbs. Considerable variety was now being introduced in ministry and evangelism in addition to pioneer preaching in tents and store fronts. Many of the unifying factors such as regional conferences were disappearing, being replaced by local assembly activities. Moreover, now young people were in the forefront of society and were the leaders in technology. The Brethren movement was certainly ready for a new type of periodical.

Beginning the Radical 1970s

C. Donald Cole came on board as associate editor in 1967, became assistant editor in 1969, and when Don Taylor retired to southern California in 1970 (though continuing to write), Cole took over as editor. Taylor and Cole both recognized that the magazine needed to help assembly Christians relate to a vastly different world than that in which *Letters of Interest* had been born and had flourished during the first thirty years of its existence. In January 1969 the name was shortened to *Interest*, thus modifying the emphasis. But the really major changes were yet to come.

January 1971 was a watershed issue. [Fig. 104]To begin with, the art work was startlingly colorful and creative. The front page featured a reverse silhouette of a bearded "flower child" and a paraphrase of 1 John 2:15-17 from "The 2nd Letter to Street Christians." The lead article, "They Call Them Jesus Freaks," told how these young people were making a successful impact with the gospel in the midst of the campus revolution. The article highlights Dan Purkey, an Emmaus graduate and leader of CWLF (Christian World Liberation Front) at Oregon State. Appearing also in this issue was an article Tom Parks called "Needed: Revolution in the Local Church," calling for a major upgrade of assembly Sunday schools, youth ministry, Bible teaching, and gospel outreach.

The new direction of *Interest* was clearly spelled out in the editorial:

> January is as good a time as any for reviewing one's purposes. What is *our* purpose? Put simply, this magazine is an attempt to help each other to live as Christians according to the Word of God. Obviously, we live in the 1970s and truly helpful ministry (i.e. articles, etc.) must reflect an understanding of the times in which we live. It's an ambitious goal, and we have few if any illusions about the success of our work. Nevertheless, we carry on, confident that from time to time we come up with an editorial or article that does indeed speak to the real issues.

Criticism of these changes was not long in coming. For example, one brother wrote:

> What burns me is to read your magazine that tears down everything that I love and respect and treats brethren like myself as fossils who belong to a past generation. We are pitied, scoffed at, ridiculed, while everything that is new or mod is glorified and congratulated. We expect to be misunderstood and criticized by sectarian and denominational publications, but not by those who pose as being our friends and standing for the same things . . . Elders are dropping dead these days, worn out from wrestling with current problems—sisters appearing to break bread hatless, young men to do the same with hair down to their shoulders, women coming in pant suits to the meeting, women with short hair and painted faces and heavy earrings with a flower stuck in their hair at the remembrance supper, brethren coming in very casual clothes or very mod clothes. These are only a few. Your magazine is doing nothing to help in these problems and articles on the Jesus people and how we should welcome and embrace them are driving many a godly elder to distraction . . .

The 1970s Under Jim Stahr

At the end of 1971, Don Cole left to replace Robert Little as radio pastor at Moody Bible School, and the position of editor was filled by another former missionary, eastern Canada pioneer worker James Stahr. Jim Stahr picked up the new direction started by Taylor and Cole and continued on it faithfully for some fifteen years. For example, the contents of the February 1975 issue, in addition to reports from workers, commendations, conferences, etc., included an editorial on evangelicals in the public schools, an article on the schoolbook controversy in Virginia, a photo report on twelve young people from the Northwoods Bible Chapel in Georgia who were attending various colleges, an article by Don Cole on young people called "Wild Oats," an article by commended worker Ross Rainey on "Contentment," an article by Allan Wood on the Holy Spirit called "The Spirit Of Our Lives" and two pages of book reviews.

It is interesting to note the impact of the new youth culture. Of the various new themes of that era—social issues, personal concerns, itinerant verses resident ministry, etc.—the most prominent was that of youth. Articles on teen leadership, teen conferences, "On Campus" and other aspects of college attendance including the Urbana Student Missionary Convention, summer teams for youth to serve abroad, "Young Christians Speak Out," ministry with athletes, youth rallies, etc., were to be found in the majority of issues.

The "Serious Call" Begins a New Era

Jim Stahr's farewell editorial appeared in the May 1986 issue. He was returning to his original preaching and pastoral ministry and the new editor taking over was Bill Conard, returned missionary from Latin America (Peru and Mexico). In his decade and a half tenure Jim was responsible for numerous excellent articles. But he saw his most important contribution to the Brethren assemblies as the period following November 1980:

> Probably the most significant step of these fifteen years was to participate in and publish the "Serious Call To Renewal." That challenge helped stir a concern to see a real spiritual awakening, not only locally but also in the assemblies as a group.

> As the months went by, we began to shift the emphasis somewhat, bringing to the forefront the inevitable result of renewal. That result is growth! "New Testament churches are growing churches," I wrote in an editorial in October 1983. "Growth is one of the trademarks that identify a church that is truly following a New Testament pattern."

> Other editorials, and articles by other writers, dealt with subjects like oppressive leadership, the need of teamwork, the equipping of saints for the ministry, and our need to identify and break through the barriers that keep assemblies from growing . . .

Interest from 1986 Onward

Editor Bill Conard brought out an updated format of the magazine with full-color front cover in mid-1986 and new design inside. The covers from then on usually featured generalized photos that suggested a theme rather than specific people and subjects. By 1983 full color was being used inside as well. Themes often revolved around church planting and new assemblies, training of elders and leaders, ethnic ministries, discipleship and administration, etc., all of which were directed toward bringing renewal to the Brethren movement. There were numerous articles on Bible topics from both Old and New Testaments. Regular features were continued, such as News and Notices (reports from the field), Viewpoint (answers to questions, edited by Walter Liefeld until 1991) and Your Turn (letters from readers). Mark Porter continued to contribute a column regularly on practical assembly matters, and his wife Carol was often featured in the women's column, "Between Us."

In April 1993 Bill Conard announced his resignation to take a post with the Billy Graham Association. For a time the editorials were written by Interest Ministry board members. In April 1994 Mike Hamel took over as editor. Eight months later the December 1994 issue announced the resignation of Mike Hamel, Andy Holloman, and Bruce McNicol. McNicol is now (in 1997) heading Leadership Catalyst, a new service organization in Phoenix, Arizona. The post of editor was assumed temporarily in January 1995 by Ken Botton. In 1996 Botton returned to graduate studies and the magazine was converted to a news sheet featuring fulltime workers. Kevin Dyer became editor in 1997.

Evaluating Growth and Decline

Concern regarding the growth of the "Open" Brethren network in North America was expressed by some of the leadership as early as the post-war period of the late 1940s. In an editorial printed on the front cover of the October 1949 issue of *Letters of Interest,* called "Yet Very Much Land," William McCartney lamented the very small ratio of assemblies to the number of cities and towns in the U.S. (1 for every 222). McCartney's conclusion was that there is a "vast field for pioneering in these United States." It is interesting to note that evangelism was *not* the objective:

> This is not to say . . . that some 124,000 communities do not hear the
> gospel. Doubtless many of them do hear it faithfully preached . . . But it is
> to say that the Scriptural principles which God has laid down for His
> church are being observed in no more than one-half of one percent . . .

Over the next thirty years there was for a time a vigorous chapel-building campaign. Pioneering continued in some places and various older and weaker meetings closed their doors. In the South, the Florida Gospel Pioneers made a concerted effort to develop an assembly-planting strategy, including financing for new chapels and full-time residential workers to serve those chapels. This yielded significant new growth. But compared with other Bible-believing church groups the Brethren lagged behind. The extent of the problem, however, was not discovered until Don Soderquist's investigation of the assemblies nationwide in 1979, leading to the "Serious Call to Renewal" in 1980.

The first attempt to get statistics on the problem of growth (or lack of it) was made by International Crusades (now International Teams) in 1981. Crusades was concerned because they looked to the Brethren churches for short-term workers, particularly young people. They telephoned representatives of 1,100 assemblies throughout the U.S. and Canada and asked questions about size, vitality, and program. The answers yielded the following statistics:

Progressing and growing 23%

Holding steady 25%

Dying or defunct 26%

The remaining twenty-six percent were "Old Paths" assemblies that apparently refused to cooperate with the inquiry. The conclusion reached on the basis of this survey (rightly or wrongly) was that around half of the assemblies in North America were declining or dying.

A somewhat deeper probe into the life of Brethren assemblies in North America was done in 1983-84 by Lois Fleming, daughter of missionaries Ken and Helena Fleming and a graduate student in communications at Wheaton College. Her findings appeared in a two-part article in the April and May 1985 issues of *Interest*. Miss Fleming sent a six-page questionnaire designed to identify areas of concern to 825 assemblies. Her approach was unique in that she asked the respondents what *they* thought were the greatest *needs* of their assembly. These 825 churches had been pre-screened according to the finding of the Crusades survey, so the 825 who got the questionnaire were assumed to be the most responsive to change. Of these, fifty-one percent returned the questionnaire—equal to thirty-six percent of all the assemblies in the 1983 address book. The results quoted in the *Interest* article were as follows:

> Forty percent of the responses dealt with various aspects of leadership.
> Twenty-five percent expressed the need for renewed zeal in evangelism.

It can thus be concluded that in the early 1980s the two most urgently felt concerns among the progressive or open-to-change assemblies were leadership and evangelism. Obviously, no conclusions can be accurately assumed about the meetings that did *not* return the research instrument.

A third study of conditions among the North American assemblies was conducted as a doctoral dissertation in the years prior to 1986 by Nathan D. Smith, formerly an instructor at the California Center for Biblical Studies in Culver City (chapter 22). Smith recognized the limitation of the statistics gathered thus far:

> Percentages and numbers are not leaving the Brethren assemblies; people are. Statistics are not staying in the assemblies; people are . . . I wanted to know the answers to the next logical obvious questions: Why is there a decline in the assemblies? Why are people leaving? What are the sources of disaffection that cause people to leave?

To try to get the most helpful kinds of answers to these questions, Smith decided to do in-depth interviews. As his subjects he selected fifty-two active Christian leaders. All had a long history of association with the Brethren. Thirty-six were second to fourth generation. Even the first-generation people had no less than seven years with a Brethren assembly. Thirty-nine of these individuals had already left and were active in other evangelical churches. The other thirteen were still leaders in the assemblies, including five commended workers. References to these interviews occupy a good part of Smith's very interesting book, *Roots, Renewal and the Brethren*.

Perhaps the most significant chapter in this study is number seven, "The Interviewee's Viewpoints." Here the author lists "three sources of disaffection [which] were by far the most common reasons given as to why people are leaving the Plymouth Brethren assemblies." They are:

Lack of Positive Leadership
Lack of Vitality
Listless Worship Services

Two other sources of dissatisfaction mentioned frequently in the interviews were (in Dr. Smith's words):

Marginalized Women in the Assemblies

Parochialism

All of these topics were supported by numerous actual quotations, Smith acting only as interviewer and editor. They reveal a very strong current of thought running through a large part of the movement that seems to be consistent with the earlier studies. It would be unwise to dismiss it as merely the opinions of malcontents.

Finally, we have facts and figures compiled by Bruce McNicol, president of Interest Ministries, and reported at the course in Brethren History at Regent College, Vancouver, in July 1990. Since the "Serious Call to Renewal" (that is, between 1980 and 1990):

The number of assemblies increased by three percent

The number in fellowship increased by about twenty percent

Attendance at the largest meeting rose twenty-four to twenty-five percent

McNicol estimated that there are about 1,200 congregations in the U.S. and Canada, with around 80,000 in fellowship. The total attendance at the largest congregational meeting would be 128,000 to 130,000. Ninety percent of the congregations are over ten years old. Of those over five years old, five adults or fewer are converted every two years. Those groups one to five years old see five or more conversions a year. Around a dozen Independent Brethren churches are growing at a rapid rate. McNicol also noted that of the five concerns identified in the "Serious Call," the one that is the key to all the others is leadership. Thus Interest Ministries is focusing on equipping leaders to equip the people to do the work of ministry.

"A Serious Call"

The following, entitled "A Serious Call to Renewal" and referred to several times earlier in this history, appeared in the November 1980 issue of Interest:

While there are notable examples of assemblies which are characterized by growth, evangelistic activity, missionary concern, and stimulating Bible teaching, many others are in deep need of renewal. Without being either critical or defensive, we want to bring before concerned Christians the following needs and problems which have been observed among many assemblies in North America:

Lack of Growth

The growth rate of new assemblies is not keeping up with that of the general population or other evangelical groups. Some new assemblies are merely transplants from other locations. Assemblies are often small. New people tend to come from other evangelical churches rather than through conversion. While size and quality are not to be equated, lack of growth usually indicates lack of vitality. Instead of effective evangelism there is complacency in many quarters. Some assemblies go on for years without sending out and supporting new missionaries.

Serious Attrition

Far from growing, many assemblies have died or are gasping for breath. Further, there is a continuing exodus of gifted people who are leaving assemblies and serving as leaders in other churches and para-church groups. We are also losing many of our young people and young married couples who have found life and spiritual stimulation in other churches where they are trained and put to work in areas of responsibility.

Lack of Commitment

There seems to be a malaise of spirit, a lack of enthusiasm, and an embarrassment to be identified as from the brethren assemblies. There is a widespread lack of commitment to New Testament principles. Paradoxically, an increasing number of new groups which do have this commitment are nevertheless reluctant to be linked with existing brethren assemblies.

Most seriously and underlying much of what is observed in these paragraphs, we often lack a deep, realistic commitment to the Lordship of Jesus Christ in our lives and in our assemblies. In place of a responsiveness to Him, there is often an inflexibility which prevents a dynamic church life.

Restrictive Attitudes

A lack of respect for other Christians is sometimes communicated. This can alienate those who would otherwise be attracted to assembly fellowship. We have sometimes communicated a lack of openness to other believers and, while holding New Testament principles without embarrassment or compromise, we often have not been sensitive to the working of God among other groups.

Decline in Leadership

Although we have always stressed the development of gift, we often lack the leadership, vision, and spiritual power to accomplish this. Our cherished reputation for Bible teaching and Bible knowledge has long been fading. Public ministry is often sought from well meaning but ungifted people who may function in a spiritual way as part of the priesthood of all believers, but are not able to teach, preach, counsel, or lead others effectively. There is confusion regarding true spiritual leadership and the development of gifts. We need leaders who are spiritually gifted, well prepared, and fervent in spirit. There is a corresponding need of a humble, gracious, and supportive spirit to welcome such leaders when God provides them.

In deep concern over such needs, we call on each one who reads this to join us in a spirit of prayer and fasting. God has promised, 'Humble yourselves before the Lord and He will lift you up' (James 4:10).

Do you share our concerns? Do you also share our vision and belief that the time has come for renewal among assemblies of Christian brethren? If so, will you tell us your thoughts as to the causes for lack of greater spiritual progress? Can you suggest specific ways in which, with God's help, faults can be corrected and problems solved, so that we can enter the door of opportunity that lies before us? We would like to hear from you.

[Signed by the following brethren]

William F. Anderson, Walter L. Liefeld, Nelson J. Annan, John McCallum, C. Donald Cole, Keith A. Price, Evan C. Davis, Daniel H. Smith, Robert G. Dunlop, Donald G. Soderquist, Kevin G. Dyer, James A. Stahr, Otis Jean Gibson, David Ward

24

Implementing Change

Three Service Organizations

In the U.S. the national service organizations are Stewards Foundation, Stewards Ministries, and Interest Ministries (missionary service organizations are covered in chapter 16). These three organizations (SF, SM, IM) have their roots in the work of William McCartney and his colleagues who founded *Letters of Interest* in 1936 and Stewards Foundation in 1945. It was their intent to serve the Lord as private individuals with no organizational ties. An early Stewards board member, Robert Mojonnier writes:

> They wanted nothing but a self perpetuating board to whom they would add men from time to time.

Starting with private funds (a small loan that was paid back), the Stewards trustees followed a simple but effective plan: to sell bonds to individual Christians in the U.S. and Canada, and then lend that money to any assembly that desired to build a new chapel. This enabled believers to put their savings to work for the Lord at competitive rates, and it made it possible for any responsible gathering, even if unqualified for a conventional loan, to build a new facility without having to make individual guarantees. In the thirty years between 1945 and the end of 1975 some twenty-three million dollars worth of bonds were sold (and twelve million redeemed), and loans to assemblies, camps, retirement homes, etc., totaled about eighteen million. In the early 1950s Stewards Foundation trustees had the opportunity to acquire the assets of Bel-

mont Community Hospital in Chicago, which was in financial difficulty. They saw in this move at least three excellent possibilities: to
minister both to the physical and spiritual needs of people (a chaplain
would be appointed for the latter purpose), to provide medical assistance through free hospital care for commended workers who were in
or could come to Chicago, to gain a valuable asset by getting the facility
into the black. Eventually five hospitals were purchased, in Illinois and
Washington state, all of which offered similar possibilities.

Donald Taylor, a very capable brother formerly with the Le-
Tourneau organization, was appointed business manager of Stewards
Foundation in 1949. In 1961, when William McCartney resigned, Taylor
became president, with James Humphrey as chairman of the board. Not
long after McCartney's retirement Stewards learned that in the eyes of
the IRS the trustees of a not-for-profit corporation are responsible for
any *liabilities* that might have occurred in the past. The *assets*, on the
other hand, belong to the people of the U.S. who granted the tax-ex-
empt status. Stewards was thus obliged to pay some $300,000 to clear
Belmont's back debts.

The IRS also demanded that Stewards have a membership other
than the trustees. At first this was satisfied by declaring as members all
assemblies that had loans from Stewards (a formal association that
already existed). Later, however, the IRS came back claiming that this
provision only created a religious savings and loan company, and demanding open membership. As this threatened to compromise the principle of independence, there was consideration of converting to a
private foundation. But, thinking that the danger of control one way or
the other was remote, the trustees sent a letter out to the assemblies
inviting "voluntary membership."

Through the dedicated business acumen and hard work of men like
Donald Taylor, Wilson McCracken, Neil Glass, Dwight Mattix, Bill
Erickson, and Bob Hanson the hospitals were turned around financially.
[Fig. 105] Each carried its own debt obligations through Stewards and
other lending institutions, then retired the debt through profitable business procedures. The hospitals were not all organized in the same way,
however. Riverton and Centralia in Washington were part of Stewards
Foundation, while Belmont and Bethesda in Illinois and Auburn in
Washington were set up as separate not-for-profit corporations. The
board of directors of each corporation was responsible for the liabilities
of that corporation.

All through the 1960s and 1970s the five hospitals successfully fulfilled the possibilities that the Stewards trustees envisioned. All had chaplains and other Christian staff who shared the Good News with patients, all ministered to the medical needs of commended workers by writing off their hospital costs, and all gained in monetary value. By the early 1980s, however, the operation of health care facilities became much more complex. The directors pondered the problem and prayed about it for over a year, but finally decided that the time had come to sell the hospitals. This was done in 1982, to an organization called Universal Health Services, under very favorable conditions, including the opportunity to retain the chaplains. For several reasons the timing turned out to be precisely right, and no doubt was of the Lord.

The proceeds of the sale of Centralia and Riverton went directly to Stewards Foundation. The three corporations of Belmont, Bethesda, and Auburn were consolidated into one, Bethesda Ministries, which received the proceeds ($24,570,000) from these three hospitals. In 1985 this corporation changed its name to Stewards Ministries. Thus the original concept of serving the assemblies by providing loans for new buildings expanded forty years later into two organizations, Stewards Foundation and Stewards Ministries, with many millions at their disposal to help the Lord's people in many areas—all at no cost whatever to the assemblies.

Chapter 23 described how Stewards Foundation and the Letters of Interest Associates had from the 1940s been exercised about the growth and development of the assemblies on this continent. As related in that chapter, the chairman of the Stewards Foundation Development Committee, Don Soderquist, decided in the late 1970s to research the concern of many that the assembly movement in North America was not growing. Soderquist spent several months on this project and traveled to a number of areas throughout the continent. His findings led to the formation of a Committee on Assembly Life and Leadership (CALL Committee). In 1980 it issued a *Serious Call To Renewal* (23d). Growing out of *A Serious Call* was a vision to take decisive action toward renewal within the Independent Brethren Movement. In November 1983 the directors of Letters of Interest Associates agreed to spearhead this action, and began a search for someone capable of directing the church planting and renewal programs. Bruce McNicol, a teaching elder and commended worker at Laurel Park Chapel in Portland, Oregon, was appointed to the position in October 1985, with the title of president. In

1988 the name of the Letters of Interest Associates was changed to Interest Ministries, with McNicol continuing as president.

The purpose, organization, and support structure of each of the three Brethren service groups is as follows:

Stewards Foundation

This not-for-profit corporation fulfills a., 1/2 of d. and f. of the seven purposes stated in the Stewards Foundation Charter of 1964, revised in 1973 (see 24b following). It manages the mortgage loan program, it provides medical insurance for commended workers, and it acts as trustee for trusts and wills. Currently, financing is derived from interest on capital. Decisions related to the operation of Stewards Foundation are made by its board of elected trustees, headed by officers. Members (the assemblies) vote only to elect trustees, to amend the articles of incorporation, and to approve of a merger or dissolution of the corporation and its assets. The money does not belong to the assemblies, nor do member assemblies have any direct say in how the money is spent.

Stewards Ministries

This is a not-for-profit corporation governed by a self-perpetuating board of trustees. Its status is approved by the IRS. Its purpose is to provide funding in two areas: current programs and gifts and grants. *Current* programs include scholarships to children of commended workers and to workers themselves for advanced training, church planting, needs of retired workers (including widows), and fellowship for commended workers and hospital chaplains. *Gifts and grants* are used to help individuals, assemblies, and assembly-related organizations in their service for the Lord. Among those helped are the sixty-five camps in the U.S. and Canada, Emmaus Bible College, Mt. Carmel Bible School, Discipleship Intern Training Program, International Teams, His Mansion, the Lighthouse Ministry in Vancouver, Conference for Pioneering Black America, MESSIAH, Christian Missions in Many Lands, Workers Together, Family Life Ministries in Colorado Springs, Christian Ministries for the Deaf in Flint, Michigan, etc. This money comes from interest on capital received from the sale of the three hospitals, plus more recent investments. Since 1982, Stewards Ministries has invested over $21,000,000 in the Lord's work, and their current net worth is in excess of $28,000,000.

Interest Ministries

Interest Ministries is a privately directed service organization responsible to a self-perpetuating board of directors.[1] It serves the Brethren assemblies through the publication of *Interest* magazine and financial assistance to commended workers (over $10,000,000 distributed in the decade prior to 1991). Until the end of 1994 it provided the operation of a resource center, church planting, and consultation programs (chapter 22), and sponsored conferences and seminars including Decade of Promise in December, 1989 and 1992. It is funded largely through Stewards Ministries.[2]

The Purposes of Stewards Foundation

In order to prove to the IRS that they were not just in the religious savings and loan business, Stewards had to show by the following article that they were fulfilling a number of purposes which the assemblies individually could not undertake. This inadvertently created a national organization indistinguishable from a religious denomination. The only way the trustees could avoid the implications of this violation of Brethren principles was to *act* in a manner independent from assembly control, according to the intention of the founders.

Article 4, Purposes

This organization is organized and shall be operated exclusively for the purpose of serving and assisting churches or assemblies organized in the pattern outlined in the New Testament and to perform the scriptural ministries and functions of the churches or assemblies which they can not effectively perform when acting alone, including, but not limited to, the following:

---

[1] Vision Ontario (VO) is the Canadian equivalent to Interest Ministries. It started around 1990 as a volunteer organization and is now a full fledged service ministry. According to a report in the *Partnership International Newsletter*, summer 1992,
VO is seeking to enhance evangelism in the assemblies through church planting efforts, leadership training, and networking. An executive director has been appointed and an office established in Waterloo, Ontario.

[2] A major source for the preceding section was Robert Mojonnier, who served on the Stewards Foundation Board during the critical years when the IRS was making its demands. Mr. Mojonnier provided the information in letters both for circulation and privately to the author written in 1992, 1993, and 1994.

a. To finance and support churches or assemblies of Christians gathered in the name of our Lord Jesus Christ and related organizations including without limitation schools, camps, and missions.

b. To promote and encourage pioneer gospel work and teaching throughout the United States and elsewhere to advance the cause of our Lord Jesus Christ by and through various means of communications, including, but not limited to, the use of radio, television, telephone, correspondence, and by and through the publication and/or distribution of papers, books, leaflets, magazines, and periodicals.

c. To finance, lease, own, aid or operate hospitals, skilled nursing homes, communities of retirement homes and/or nursing homes, and extended care or other health care facilities in furtherance of the purposes heretofore set forth.

d. To advise and counsel with churches or assemblies or individual members thereof in the management and expenditure of their funds and to act as trustee in the administration of funds held by this corporation or by churches or assemblies.

e. To make gifts, grants and contributions to churches, assemblies and other qualified religious, charitable or educational organizations, to encourage new or pioneer activities for general religious or charitable or educational purposes.

f. To provide and administer medical, surgical and hospital expense assistance to "commended workers" associated with churches or assemblies.

g. To provide assistance, including scholarships, to enable qualified students to prepare for service in the furtherance of one or more of the purposes herein stated.

A New Emphasis on Church Planting

From the mid-1980s, in an effort to offset the decline in numbers of the Brethren network in North America, Interest Ministries has attempted to encourage the planting of new churches. From about 1984, conferences on church-planting have been held with the encouragement and cooperation of Interest Ministries together with area assemblies. Topics covered include the following:
How New Testament Churches Grow
How Do Small Assemblies Grow?

Planning for a Balanced and Dynamic Church
Vision: How to Get It and How to Share It
Developing a Life-Changing Preaching Ministry
How to Develop Godly and Skillful Leaders
Effectively Reaching Your Community For Christ
The Elder's Lifestyle
Developing Effective Elders' Teams
Men's and Women's Ministries [Fig. 107]
Building Christian Community Through Small Groups Christian Education and Youth Ministry
The Ministry of Worship and Music

By 1992, this encouragement had resulted in the birth of over fifty new assemblies.

The main difference between pioneering and what we refer to today as church planting is the itinerant nature of the pioneer's ministry. There were just a handful of them in the very early days and a whole continent to cover. Today the needs are different. The late Lester Wilson commented on the role of the resident worker like this:

> Sometimes the pioneer or the one who lays the foundation has to remain long enough to build the framework of the superstructure before leaving it . . . In a building, the finishing work takes longest and is the most tedious. Elders and overseers are not produced overnight. Since they should not be novices, it often takes from ten to fifteen years to develop them. Many a work that had a good start faltered because it was left to local or inexperienced men too soon.

How does church planting take place in the late twentieth century? Lester Wilson in the same article gives eight ways of getting started:

1. Hive off from another assembly
2. A couple moving to a city (Acts 18:20)
3. Bible class in a home [Fig. 106]
4. Children's meetings
5. Open-air meetings
6. Exercise of several from churches
7. Gospel campaigns
8. Buying a lot in a new development and starting with a new building

Another difference between pioneering and modern church planting is the strategy of a team approach. Although the pioneer evangelists often started work in a new community by themselves or with one teammate, the church-planting team is made up of the people who plan to form the nucleus of the new assembly. In some cases the team approach involves using statistics and techniques found to be successful by other Bible-believing churches in reaching out to the unchurched. The church-planting team may also project the need for one or more full-time workers with different gifts: Bible exposition, administration, youth work, music, etc. The team may or may not include a full-time worker, at least in the beginning, but will be made up of those who are committed to leadership.

A Visit to a "New Style" Brethren Church

The Mountain View Bible Church (not its real name) meets for two services on Sunday mornings in a high school gym. We plan to attend the second service at eleven a.m. To get to this location we drive for perhaps half a mile through average suburban neighborhoods. We see a sign with the name we are looking for on the curb, and a couple of others clearly identifying the entrance as we drive in. People are leaving, others coming, and the parking lot has only a few spaces open. Two men (greeters) are at the door. They have name tags, seem genuinely glad to see us (we are unknown to them). They hand us what turns out to be a bulletin with four half-sheets stuffed inside. *Lots going on here,* we think.

Inside, fifty to sixty people are milling around talking and scurrying here and there. On one side is a row of tables with people seated behind signs announcing, "Tape Sale," "Lost and Found," "Missionary Information," etc. Cold drinks and coffee are available in another spot. It looks a little like a convention or trade show. We are directed to a table where a young woman makes name badges for us.

We are just a bit late and the second service has already started. It takes place behind a wall of portable screens where perhaps 200 chairs are set up in a semicircle facing the platform in one corner of the gym. We can hear the singing, along with the sound of drums and other musical instruments, and can see over the screens the words projected on the wall.

This is the smaller of the two identical services, and about 100 people occupy the chairs. On the platform are four young women singers each holding portable mikes, two young men singers, two young men with electric guitars, a young man with a set of drums, and another young man playing an electronic keyboard. All are obviously skilled, and play and sing with practiced ease. The keyboard player turns out to be the music director, and we find that he has written and composed some of the songs himself.

The songs are mostly contemporary, consisting basically of Scripture set to rhythmic music. One hymn, by Fanny Crosby, "Blessed Assurance," is included. The music is loud and exciting, but it enhances the worship as the emphasis is on extending the love of Christ to others. One of the young men with a rich baritone voice sings "People Need the Lord."

A little later four people probably in their twenties, the "drama team," do a skit on "Learning to Love the Unlovable." They enter into a lively discussion on whether or not they could love somebody with a repulsive disease. One fellow insists that he hated his little sister when she broke out with the measles. Under pressure he concedes that he *thought* he hated her at the time. They conclude by saying, "Well, let's see what's going on in Sunday school this morning."

The message of the morning is given by a brother in his late forties. We learn that he is a scientist with a graduate degree, but has left his employment to serve the Lord full time. His message is well constructed and obviously rehearsed; he has already given it once before in the earlier service. As he talks he moves around the platform, microphone in one hand and Bible (and notes) in the other. He begins by telling the story of a young woman who served as an American spy during the Japanese occupation of the Philippines during World War II. She moved freely though enemy lines collecting information that enabled our air force to bomb with pinpoint accuracy, thus saving thousands of lives that otherwise would have been lost in an invasion. At this point he puts a picture of the young woman on the overhead projector. You can hear a gasp as the audience sees that she is a horribly disfigured leper.

One of the handouts given at the door is message notes, punched for insertion into a notebook. The message is based on four Scripture readings in Mark 3, Mark 9, Mark 10, and John 13. The readings are printed on the four sides of the folded sheet, and below are blanks to fill out as the speaker covers these points and puts transparencies of them on the overhead projector. The audience, many of them non-Christians (referred to as seekers) or new believers with no religious background, learn that (1) Jesus loved and chose the twelve disciples despite their vast differences, (2) Jesus taught that in order to be *first* they had to be *last*, (3) Jesus showed love to the most demanding and unlovable, and (4) by washing their feet Jesus *demonstrated* His new commandment: "Love one another."

Surprisingly, the message takes a fairly long time, thirty-five minutes or more. Throughout, the presenter uses the overhead projector to show the audience what to write in their notes, and also to punctuate his points with cartoons. (The best teachers, we are reminded, always use concrete illustrations to communicate abstract ideas.) At the end he calls two young men to the platform, one of whom had invited the other to a small group Bible study a couple of years earlier. Through this means the second young man eventually was saved. The young men tell their stories, reinforcing the idea that people can help one another to learn to love others.

This assembly has numerous activities throughout the week, including several Bible studies and prayer groups. The Lord's Supper is held Sunday evenings in a Baptist church social hall, and also includes Bible exposition. Responsibility for the various aspects of this work is borne by a group of elders, including two full-time workers. Looking at the bulletin and the inserts, and at the number of people visibly engaged in various functions, we conclude that a fair number of people are exercising their gifts here.

The Mountain View Bible Church began as an amicable hive-off from another assembly about five years before. The leaders do not see this work as a model for other assemblies to imitate. It is simply the pathway they believe God wants *them* to follow. At the moment they are reaching about 900 people in one way or another, and expect to grow at a yearly rate of something over forty percent. Part of their Philosophy of Ministry printed in the bulletin reads:

> We believe the greatest way we can love people is to introduce them to the Savior, whom to know is life eternal. MVBC seeks to nurture all in a personal relationship with Christ and in a growing faith in His Word and promises. We are committed to helping you discover and develop your gifts in His service.

Brethren Conferences in the 1970s, 1980s, and 1990s

Although the annual Bible conferences in many areas were abandoned after the 1950s and 1960s because of relocation of the chapels and the focus on local assembly activities, the importance of conferences among the Independent Brethren certainly did not diminish in the next three decades. Following are various types of conferences listed in *Interest*, *The Uplook*, and *Words in Season*: [Fig. 108]

Summer conferences at conference centers like Lake Geneva (WI), Guelph (ONT), Camp Berea (NH), Greenwood Hills (PA), etc., and also at Yosemite National Park (CA)

Annual area conferences such as the Mid-South

Workers' conferences in various areas, including

Black workers' conferences (chapter 21)

Pastors' conferences (sponsored by the Grand Old Gospel Hour)

Women's missionary conferences

Area missionary conferences

Prison coordinator's conferences

Men's conferences

Assembly leadership conferences

College and career conferences

Renewal and enrichment conferences

And undoubtedly there were others.

Besides the above, a number of conferences were held annually at various chapels in such places as Limon, Colorado; Oak Forest, Illinois; Omaha, Nebraska; and Flint, Michigan. *Words in Season* listed conferences to be held in gospel halls around the continent throughout the year. Labor Day, Thanksgiving, and Easter were still favorite times for Brethren conferences in a number of places.

In recent years the missionary service organization CMML (Christian Missions in Many Lands) has collaborated with the Greenwood Hills (Pennsylvania) conference organizers to sponsor events emphasizing preparation for serving the Lord overseas as well as prayer and support for missionaries on the field. The first Missionary Orientation Program was a five-day event in September 1992. It covered such topics as a history of Brethren missions, biblical basis for missions, language training, cross- cultural relationships, methods of evangelism, etc. Leaders included Sam Robinson, John Jeffers, Bill Coffey, Ken Fleming, T. Ernest Wilson, and others. A second such program was held in June 1993.

Other CMML conferences at Greenwood Hills in 1993 included a Spring Men's Retreat in March and a summer conference in July-August (speakers included Jim Cochrane from the Dominican Republic, Floyd Schneider from Austria, and Stan Warren of Echoes of Service, England). CMML Saturday conferences were also held in Grand Rapids, Michigan, in October and Duncanville, Texas, in November.

Chapter 21 pointed out that International Teams held a triennial Missions Congress in the Chicago area for a number of years, drawing a very large number of young people. Up until the late 1980s, International Teams sponsored SCOPE, which brought together elders and commended workers in May for a week of lectures, discussions, and prayer at their facility in Prospect Heights, Illinois. This was superseded in December 1989 by Decade of Promise, an elders, leaders and commended workers convention held in Dearborn, Michigan, between Christmas and New Year's.

Original plans for the Decade of Promise by Interest Ministries projected 300 participants. This figure grew to 800 as excitement across the continent grew, and plans were made to hold all meetings in the spacious Dearborn Hyatt Regency. In the end, attendance reached 1,200, and another 1,000 had to be turned away because of lack of space. The overall theme was "The Investment of a Lifetime," with each of the four daily themes entitled "Think biblically," "Act Wisely," "Work Cooperatively" and "Live Confidently." Daily Bible expositions were led by Tom Taylor, and nine general sessions and some ninety afternoon seminars were available.

Reaction by the participants indicated renewed interest in applying assembly (i.e., New Testament) principles to the contemporary world. This was well expressed by Clifford Ice, an assembly member and city inspector in Atlanta, Georgia:

> Decade of Promise has shown me that many people are sincerely concerned that the assemblies be relevant and effective in the coming years. I've been in the assemblies 13 years, and at times I've questioned whether they were prepared to face the future, to chart a biblical course that would reach people . . . I can't express how encouraging this has been for me, as a black believer who associates with a group that is predominately white.

Here I find openness, a receptibility that says, "Everybody is welcome!" I see that there's a place for me!

Another Decade of Promise was held at the end of 1992 at the Hyatt Regency, O'Hare Airport, Chicago. An additional feature was a special Youth Track designed for youth leaders with four nationally known speakers. Attendance ran around 1,800.

The Dangers of a Changing Climate

A first for Christian Missions in Many Lands was the very large (1,200 registrants) Missions 1993 Conference entitled "God's Work God's Way." This took place December 27-30 at the Hyatt Regency in Cincinnati, Ohio. Featured speakers were William MacDonald and David Gooding. There were numerous seminars and a very stimulating music program.

The "challenge of change" which was addressed so eloquently by Kevin Dyer at the Decade of Promise in December 1989 (chapter 23) was also a major concern at Missions 1993. As part of a seminar called "Doctrinal Trends," J.B. Nicholson, Jr., editor of *Uplook* magazine, gave a message called "The Changing Climate," which dealt with the sweeping changes facing Brethren assemblies in the late twentieth century. Nicholson identified and commented on nine indications of change:

"Intellectual Mobility"
Growing Ignorance of the Bible
Family Altars on the Endangered List
Increasing Secularization
The Missing Generation
Retreating Evangelistic Zeal
Lack of Discernment Among Overseers
Increasing Fragmentation
Loss of Assembly Distinctives

Discussing "intellectual mobility," Nicholson referred to "'Christian' radio, television, literature, and music [that] flows freely into the homes and minds of assembly believers." He expressed concern that "young believers especially should be protected from [such] damaging influences" because men "speaking perverse (truth with a twist) things" are a mark of the end times. He suggested that the influence of doctrines that cause divisions and offense (Romans 16:17-18) may be offset by the counsel of "godly men in each assembly who will be able to discern not only error but also unprofitable ministry . . . "

To underscore the point that there is widespread ignorance of the Bible among members of Brethren assemblies, Nicholson cited what was offered at the assembly he attended as a child: a "two-week gospel campaign each year," "a two-week ministry series," "a weekly ministry meeting," "Sunday School—through the Bible in five years," "a weekly young people's Bible study," and "conferences on Easter and Thanksgiving weekends."

The family altar, Nicholson said, is rare in this day and age. "I have traveled widely . . . and stayed in the finest Christian homes, yet I rarely see the family gathered around the Word, praying or singing together." He also noted that Christian homes today are "filled with the sights and sounds of Egypt: 'rock music' instead of Christian songs, questionable videos and TV programs, etc." He contended that the standards of Christians are dropping only a little behind the world's standards, and that a "slow but steady erosion" of the biblical principle of separation is taking place in the Christian community.

Nicholson also noted that the post-World War II generation, now in their fifties and sixties, is largely missing from Brethren assemblies in North America, and those who have remained "have not applied themselves to the Word and are not ready to take serious responsibility in local churches." He thus challenged even older men to be willing to continue standing for the truth in the face of opposition until such a time as men just now getting started can take up responsibility for the life of the assembly.

Regarding evangelism, Nicholson said, "In many assemblies, gospel outreach is pathetic. At one end of the spectrum, some proclaim the message but with no sinners present. At the other end, some use an array of methods to entice a crowd and forget the message." He acknowledged "a resurgence of evangelism in some quarters," however.

Nicholson also suggested that local Brethren churches are lacking leaders who know God's Word well enough to have the gift of spiritual discernment. "May God give us more leaders who know how to study the Word for themselves, how to make decisions with it as the final authority, and how to teach the Lord's people by practice and precept."

The polarization and fragmentation that has developed among the assemblies owing to the "plethora of Bible versions, [diverse] hymnody, special interest divisions by age, [and] target-audiences selected by demographic studies, etc.," was another concern. Nicholson doubts that a "split" will occur because of the autonomy of local churches "unless a group of assemblies band together in some confederacy—which is advocated by some." He predicted, however, that on the local level "tensions will obviously increase when nearby churches take divergent views on what many consider key issues." Rejecting the concept of "agreeing to disagree," he argued that "one cannot continue in fellowship with a local church when constantly grieved by what is being practiced."

Finally, Nicholson was dismayed at the answers he got when asking young people "what the characteristics of a New Testament assembly are." He argued that "a true New Testament church *does* have a Senior Pastor—Christ." "We *do* have a name; we meet in the name of the Lord Jesus." Further, he took issue with the idea that "We don't let our women do much" by citing several passages from 1 Corinthians to illustrate the wide sphere of ministry that Paul assigned to women. "The woman's ministry is as high as the heavens; there is no restriction on her ministry to the heart of God as a *holy* priest . . . The only limitation is that in keeping with divine order she is not to represent the assembly to God or God to the assembly. But she certainly is not to be silent in her heart - [that is] what God hears!" (Abstracted from *Uplook*, February 1994, pp. 4-5)

25

Reaction to Change

A House Divided

The decade of the 1980s and on into the 1990s found the leaders of the Independent Brethren network in North America once again embroiled in a conflict. In some ways this resembled the earlier troubles (chapter 10) in that much of the contention revolved around the tendency of the more progressive brethren to change their methodology with the times, especially in view of developments in other evangelical congregations, and that of the more traditional brethren to view such change as compromise with the world and a threat to purity of doctrine.

A new element was present, however, (especially after 1985) in that this controversy took the form of a more or less organized reaction by the conservative brethren to the direction taken by Letters of Interest Associates, later Interest Ministries, to carry out the mandate of the Serious Call to Renewal. There is no question that the work of Interest Ministries from 1985 onward resulted in many new assemblies being planted (nearly 100), and in much encouragement to Brethren leaders through the Decade of Promise conferences and seminars. But in the eyes of the critics, Interest Ministries with the support of Stewards Ministries and Stewards Foundation was trying to introduce questionable church growth methodology as a replacement for the traditional Brethren pattern of gathering, long accepted as biblical. Also at issue: the role of women in leadership, including audible participation in public gatherings, the wearing of headcoverings by women, and the dominant role of residential full time workers in a number of assemblies.

Our purpose in this chapter is to try and give the reader the big picture by outlining what appear to be stages of development of what some refer to as the Stewards Controversy. Our sources include a very large number of documents, plus interviews and observations of events.

Stage One

Stage one was the time span beginning in the 1960s and early 1970s up to 1986. It includes the emergence of International Teams and its new approach to missions and youth ministry, the substantial changes in the style of *Interest* magazine made by Don Cole and his colleagues, the great impact of the youth culture on many assemblies, and the growing awareness fortified by statistical studies that the assemblies were declining in numbers and effectiveness (especially in contrast to the rise at the same time of other Bible-oriented evangelical churches).

In November 1980 (as documented in 23) a public statement of this concern, the "Serious Call," was made by fourteen leading brethren. In 1982 came the sale of the five hospitals, making available large sums of money both to Stewards Foundation and Stewards Ministries. Funding to Letters of Interest Associates (later Interest Ministries) enabled the directors in November 1983 to take decisive action toward renewal and to begin a search for a capable director. The appointment of Bruce McNicol as president of Interest Ministries came in 1985, and of Bill Conard as editor of *Interest* in 1986. Other leaders appointed were Mike Hamel and Andy Holloman.

Stage Two

Stage two began in 1986 with the publishing of Nate Smith's book, *Roots, Renewal and the Brethren* (chapter 23), documenting the exodus of many leaders from the assemblies and giving their own statements why. Attacks in writing by two well-known brethren followed, the opening guns of the broader public backlash to come later. That same year also saw the appearance of the first of several newsletters raising an outcry against (as one conservative brother put it) "an organized crusade which would change almost completely not only the structure but also the character of the assemblies as we have known them."

From 1986 to 1989 the backlash grew in intensity. Two brethren in the South began attending the previously routine annual Stewards Foundation board elections and publishing the minutes of the meeting, including their criticisms and accusations. As has been noted, Interest Ministries at this time was having considerable success with assembly-planting conferences and the consultation program (chapter 24). Likewise, significant changes had been made in the format and content of *Interest* magazine. Personal attacks on the brethren involved in those efforts were made both in the newsletters and publicly by commended workers.

Stage Three

Stage three, the period from January 1990 through September 1991, saw the attack on all three service organizations grow to a high pitch of intensity. Certain incidents and events added fuel to the fire of criticism. For example:

a. The April 1990 issue of *Christianity Today* carried a two-page paid ad consisting of a declaration entitled "Men, Women and Biblical Equality," and signed by a long list of prominent evangelicals including a few known to be among the Brethren.

b. In July 1990 a week-long conference on Brethren history was held at Regent College (itself the subject of much conservative criticism). The conference was organized by Ward Gasque of Granville Chapel, with the main lecturer Roy Coad of England. It drew a large number of delegates from Brethren circles in several countries, and an international network of Brethren historians was formed.

c. Also during 1990 a great stir was caused by the appearance of an anonymous paper satirizing the various polemical newsletters being circulated around the country. This was facetiously called *Truer Truth*, and since the conservative critics were the butt of most of the humor it was concluded that Interest Ministries was behind it. The brethren at Interest, however, denied it.

The climax of stage three was the Stewards Foundation board election in September 1991. A "Committee of Members" had been organized by some conservative brethren in the South and a slate of new candidates favoring the conservative position was announced to all the assemblies in a letter sent in July 1991. It was promised that if this slate were elected they would "bring an end to Interest Ministries' efforts to continue to associate themselves with Stewards Foundation." The election itself, preceded by a telephone campaign, drew a large crowd of supporters of the "Committee of Members." Although the incumbent Stewards chairman, Ken Murray, was able successfully to counter all claims of mishandling of funds, the new slate of candidates was elected, giving them a clear majority (they were referred to later as the "New Majority" trustees).

Stage Four

The ten months between the Stewards Foundation board election in September 1991 and the filing of a lawsuit in July 1992 can be considered stage four. The 1991 election had split the assemblies across the continent into two distinct camps. The Independent Brethren network in North America was now a house divided against itself. (We are speaking of the leadership, of course. Many people not in leadership are unaware of what goes on at the national level.)

Judging by the documents circulated by the brethren supporting the Committee of Members, the election was a mandate to control the funds both of Stewards Foundation and of Stewards Ministries and thus be in a position to cut off funding from Interest Ministries, perceived as the source of all the trouble. The brethren at Interest Ministries and Stewards Ministries, on their part, viewed the election as a ruthless hostile takeover. The tactics of the corporate business world had been used to wrest away control of funds from those whose dedicated service to the Lord had been the means of acquiring the money in the first place.

The chairman of the new Stewards Foundation board sent out a letter dated May 27 stating that the board was "seeking other approaches without going to law." Thus it was clear that a lawsuit was a distinct possibility. In June the president of Stewards Foundation circulated a letter offering *not* to sue if Stewards Ministries would agree to binding arbitration by a retired non-assembly Christian judge. Stewards Ministries, in the meantime, had proposed that the two organizations try to reconcile their differences by mediation and offered to contribute a large sum to the medical coverage for workers. The culmination came in July 1992, when a lawsuit against Stewards Ministries was filed in Chicago on behalf of Stewards Foundation and two local assemblies.

Stage Five

The period from the filing of the lawsuit to the Stewards Foundation election in September 1992 constitutes stage five. On July 9 there was a meeting of representatives of the boards of both Stewards Foundation and Stewards Ministries that evidently seemed hopeful at the time, but produced no results. On July 10 a letter was sent out by leaders of Stewards Ministries announcing the lawsuit and enclosing a copy of a letter dated June 24 to the new Stewards Foundation board urging mediation. The letter pointed out that arbitration would solve nothing, since the real problem "is a breach of trust, fellowship, cooperation and unity among Christians." On July 31 another letter went out from Stewards Foundation to member assemblies inviting them to the election meeting on September 26 and containing a slate of candidates and a proxy form.

The 1992 board election was scheduled to be held at Fairbluff Chapel in Charlotte, North Carolina, but the large number expected to attend led the conveners to change to the more spacious building of a Methodist church. Both the Committee of Members and the Grace Bible Chapel groups held receptions the previous evening at the nearby Marriott. Stewards Foundation reported later that "of the 464 member assemblies eligible to vote this year, 372 were represented . . . either in person or by proxy." They reported an attendance of at least 180, but there could have been over 200. For some two and a half hours the floor was continually occupied. Fifteen or more speakers addressed remarks to the chair, the vast majority speaking against the lawsuit and pleading for mediation and reconciliation. When the results of the vote were finally announced, however, the Committee of Members slate of candidates had won again, 215 to 156. Thus, instead of just a majority, the Stewards Foundation board was now comprised entirely of trustees representing the Committee of Members.

Stage Six

Stage Six is the period beginning with the 1992 board election. A letter from Stewards Foundation dated October 14, 1992, was sent to all member assemblies reporting objectively on the election, and also announcing an increase in the annual contribution to be made by health plan members. In that same month a letter was sent by Interest Ministries to all assemblies suggesting that a plan was in the making for a new type of Brethren inter-church fellowship. Another letter followed, dated November 10 1992, which asked for signatures to endorse a new ministry called The Partnership International (still on hold). The second Decade of Promise was held at the end of December 1992 in the O'Hare Airport Marriot. Attendance ran around 1,800 (chapter 24).

A most important development in the conflict during 1993 was a six-page Stewards Foundation letter to assemblies dated November 12, which constituted a "first" in Brethren history. Besides announcing a necessary increase in medical care contributions because of a loss of $1,140 in the last fiscal year, it specified "what type of churches are eligible for our services," and set up two categories of eligibility, #1 and #2. The second category was for workers commended by assemblies "who no longer meet our eligibility guidelines." Workers were required to sign the guidelines if they agreed with them.

The conclusion of this stage was a letter from Neil Glass of Stewards Ministries dated January 10, 1994, directed to All Brethren Assemblies and Commended Workers, reporting that the judge "ruled against [Stewards] Foundation on its motion for Summary Judgement and ruled in favor of [Stewards] Ministries on its Motions for Summary Judgement." The judge "emphatically and decisively declared that Ministries had not violated Illinois law as alleged by the Foundation." A copy of the judge's decision was attached.

Stage Seven

Stewards Foundation responded to the announcement of Judge Lewis's decision with a letter from president Barry Mahloy to member assemblies dated January 25 which denied that the judge "ruled on whether the transfer of the control of Stewards Ministries and over 28 million dollars was 'fair' or legal." Mr. Mahloy contended that the judgment concerned only the "first phase of the legal complaint" concerning conflict of interest. He stated that the "major aspect of our request for a declaratory judgment will now have to be determined through a trial."

On April 26, 1994, a letter from Stewards Foundation to its member assemblies signed by Barry Mahloy, president, and Kevin Cooper, chairman, reiterated their case against Stewards Ministries—i.e., "that the previous trustees . . . had secretly removed Stewards Ministries and its assets from the control of Stewards Foundation and the member assemblies." The letter announced the intention of Stewards Foundation to name in their lawsuit all of the seventeen men who voted for the severance. It was subsequently learned that nine of the fifteen Stewards

Foundation board members, including executive director Bob Chambers, had resigned rather than vote for this new move. They were replaced by three new members known to be sympathetic to the lawsuit, making a total of nine members.

Grace Bible Chapel of St. Louis again sent out a letter to both Stewards Foundation members and non-members urging them "to put this shameful episode behind us so that well-intentioned brothers may work toward peace and the faithful pursuit of our calling in Christ." Stewards Ministries also sent out a letter dated May 27, 1994, giving three specific quotes from the Stewards Foundation brethren pledging that they would not accuse their former board members of wrongdoing.

Stewards Foundation responded on June 30 pointing out that "our attorneys have told us that we can no longer pursue only Stewards Ministries, but must name as the defendants the trustees who served on the Stewards Foundation board in 1989--since Stewards Foundation trustees were responsible for the severance in 1989, and all but one of the individuals then on the Stewards Foundation board are no longer on the board, it was absolutely essential that the individuals responsible be named."

And finally, a letter dated June 1996 addressed to Member Assembly Delegates and signed by Kevin Cooper, Chairman, Board of Trustees, states as follows:

> The August 28, 1995, court ruling in favor of Stewards Ministries will now stand as the final legal resolution of this matter. We believe we have fulfilled our fiduciary responsibility to the members by pursuing the return of Stewards Ministries and its assets to this point. We now feel a responsibility to act upon the impact we have received from many of the member assemblies, to whom we are accountable by proceeding no further.

Is there a Solution to Schism?

Can a schism like that of the Stewards Foundation-Stewards Ministries controversy ever be resolved or healed? No and Yes. Once a feud among or between families or close associates gets under way, it is like an avalanche—it picks up momentum as it goes along. Pretty soon it destroys everything in its way. Historically, a solution is not often found in some kind of compromise or mediation after the trouble has gained momentum, because by then fellowship has already been irreparably broken. An attempt was made by the Darby assemblies in 1852 to woo Bethesda back into the fold, but George Müller and Henry Craik ignored it. Thus, in the minds of Exclusive Brethren at least, the Darby-Bethesda feud is still going on after nearly 150 years!

But the answer is also Yes. Among Christians, miracles *can* happen. The solution lies in the heart of every believer, and especially in the hearts of the "chief men" among us. Let us suggest that there are three keys to preventing bitter controversies and schisms, and all are shaped like the human heart:

The first key is *humility*. At the core of almost all quarrels and attacks against brethren is pride. Back in the seventeenth century the Puritan preacher Richard Baxter observed a similar dynamic going on among the various bodies that had broken away from the Church of England:

> I have ever observed the humblest men most tender of making separations, and the proudest most prone to it . . . There is a strange inclination in proud men to make the Church of Christ much narrower than it is, and to reduce it almost to nothing, and to be themselves the members of a singular Society, as if they were loth to have too much company in heaven.

Another side of this is the pride of the young or the liberal-minded, who are convinced that everything or everyone old or traditional must be swept aside to make way for the latest ideas. These, too, would "make the Church of Christ much narrower than it is."

The second key is *selflessness*. Invariably brethren enter into strife with one another because they want something for themselves: power, domination, money, etc. Harry Ironside once told the following story that well illustrates this point:

> Many years ago as a little fellow I attended a meeting in Toronto where some difficulties had come up between brethren. My dear mother took me along. "Little pitchers have big ears," and I well remember how horrified I was to see men I esteemed and had been taught to respect apparently so indignant with each other. I can remember one man springing to his feet and with clenched fist saying, "I will put up with a great deal, but one thing I will not put up with, I will not allow you to put anything over on me. I will have my rights!" An old Scotsman who was rather hard of hearing leaned forward, holding his ears, and said, "What was that, brother? I did not get that!" "I say, I will have my rights" said the man.

"But you did not mean that, did you? Your rights? If you had your rights you would be in hell, would you not? And you are forgetting, aren't you, that Jesus did not come to get His rights. He came to get His wrongs, and He got them." I can still see that man standing there for as moment like one transfixed, and then the tears broke from his eyes and he said, "Brethren, I have been all wrong. Handle the case as you think best." Then he sat down, his face in his hands, and sobbed before the Lord. Everything was settled in three minutes.

The third key consists of *wishing the best for our brethren*, of doing to them as we would have them do to us (even if we disagree with them). Jealousy is at the bottom of much of the trouble that is dressed up as preserving Brethren distinctives, or defending the precious truths we have always believed. The facts are that some brethren cannot stand to see the Lord blessing others. They convince themselves that somehow evil must have crept in, that there is compromise with the world, etc. They boldly sin by setting themselves up as judges of their brethren, loudly clamoring about the speck in the eyes of others when in fact there is a 2 x 4 in their own.

Thankfully, the Brethren movement, despite controversy at the national level, is continuing to play an important role in the ongoing history of Christ's church. But ironically, that role is being realized more fully in many countries less fortunate in material things than our own. The reason these dear saints are flourishing, growing in the Lord, reaching out to others, is because they are not impeded by the sad history of Exclusivism. They have gone back to the ten cardinal principles of the founders, and especially to the *spirit of the love of Christ*, which underlies those principles.

May God give *us* in North America the grace to restore the love of Christ among us, and to be spurred on by the achievements of our noble army of missionaries and pioneer evangelists to accomplish more great things for God until our Lord Jesus returns.

"Chief Men" Comment on Brethren Schisms

C.H. Macintosh

Macintosh, a loyal supporter of J.N. Darby, is probably the greatest writer on Old Testament typology of the nineteenth century. His works are still in print and sold worldwide.

> I say the Holy Ghost cannot approve the schisms in the professing
> Church, for He Himself has said of such, 'I praise you not.' He is grieved
> by them - - He would counteract them; He baptizes all believers into the
> unity of the one body, so that it cannot be thought, by any intelligent mind,
> that the Holy Ghost could sustain schisms, which are a grief and a dis-
> honor to Him.

W.H. Dorman

Dorman was one of the first clergymen in London to join the Brethren,
and he was an ardent supporter of J.N. Darby for many years. But
twenty years after Darby had cut off Bethesda, Dorman concluded that
Darby had been in the wrong and broke from the Exclusives. In 1916,
looking back over his long life, he wrote an essay called "Then and
Now," from which these words were taken:

> In humiliation and sorrow of heart I appeal to you all. For many years past
> I have urged Repentance, according to the Lord's word to Laodicea, on
> account of the evil and sinful spirit of division that has taken possession of
> us, that is so utterly and entirely contrary to the Word of God, and has
> paralysed the testimony committed to us by God.

R.C. Chapman

Robert Chapman was beloved by all the Brethren, even after the division of 1848. He was one of the most Christ-like figures in the history of
the Brethren movement.

> If there be but a shadow of disunion between us and any brother or sister,
> let us not give ourselves rest until we bring about a reconciliation; let us
> search out what in our ways may have caused the breach, and seek after
> communion with our brother like that of the Father with the Son. We
> should, moreover, watch against everything in us that may wound or
> grieve our brother, so that we may be wise to prevent breaches of fellow-
> ship; observant of 1 Corinthians xiii; our ways fashioned by the love that
> behaves itself not unseemly, and which faileth not.

With This We Close

At the end of his *Historical Sketch of the Brethren Movement*, Harry Ironside added several appendices, including the following (slightly edited
for clarity) by Harold St. John:

Liberty As To Methods

In many parts of the world I have come across Christians deep in
controversy of details such as the time and character of meetings, the

use of an organ or a solo, or an after-meeting. It is often quite seriously advanced that these matters can be settled by an appeal to the text of the New Testament, which only shows *how easy it is to become silly when we most want to be solemn.*

The state of society in the first century, when Christians were largely of the slave class, allowed of one meeting a week, usually at midnight or at an hour when they could be spared from their work. Our modern multiplication of meetings is the fruit of the more favorable conditions produced by the Providence of God. Such things as hymn books, Sunday schools, and Bible readings in the modern sense are as likely to be met with in the New Testament as motor cars!

The question may be asked, "Then by what rule shall our use of methods be governed?" To this our reply is simple: by precisely the same law as our general conduct. All things are lawful for us, but at every crossroad of life three points must be considered: (1) Will the proposed step "free my feet" for the race to God? (2) Will it tend to bring me into bondage? (3) Will it edify and help my neighbor (I Cor. 6:12; 10:23)? Any method that will pass the threefold test, Godward, selfward, and manward may safely be used as long as it serves its purpose.

Appendix I
As Others See Us

Because of their deep sense of being the called-out people of God, the Brethren in any local assembly tended, at least in earlier times, to be like an extended family. Conversely, Brethren families tended to be like miniature assemblies. Life centered around meetings and activities and the Lord's people. On the positive side, this generated a people who had their priorities straight and who were far more dedicated to Christian life and service than the average churchgoer. The negative side (though not altogether negative) was that Brethren young people were prone to find this lifestyle a bit too restricting and to move on to other Christian gatherings.

Not surprisingly, several of these dropouts have written about their experiences of growing up Brethren. One of these we have already reviewed (*Return to Old Paths*). Now we'll look at three more of these accounts, two of them still in print and quite well known: *Father & Son* by Edmund Gosse originally published in 1907, *The Brethren* by Anne Arnott brought out by Mowbray in 1969, and *Lake Wobegon Days* by the still popular author and entertainer Garrison Keillor. Through the eyes of these talented individuals, outsiders but still sympathetic, we may be able to gain some helpful insight on how others saw, and still see us.

Edmund Gosse

Edmund Gosse was a literary scholar and linguist in the England of Queen Victoria and Edward VII, a lecturer at Trinity College, Cambridge, chairman of the board of Scandinavian Studies at University College, London, and the author of more than twenty volumes of essays and literary criticism, the most famous of which is *Father and Son*. Edmund's father, Phillip, was a zoologist and biologist, a specialist in marine life and watercolor illustrator of same, who was widely known in his day. He was also something of an eccentric, a devoted though strict Plymouth brother, and a widower from early in Edmund's life. His greatest desire and the hope of his life was that his son and only child would grow up to serve the Lord as a Brethren preacher.

Shortly after the death of Edmund's mother, Phillip Gosse left London forever and took his son to a small village on the south coast of Devon. Here he continued his profession, close to the sea, and also shepherded a small Brethren assembly, of which there were a number in the south of England in those days. A keen and intelligent observer, young Gosse took in all that was going on around him as well as the mental and spiritual progress of his father. Outwardly Edmund became what his father wanted, a young believer of great insight and devotion—but internally he had another self, which gradually became dominant. Greatly though Edmund loved his father and respected his faith, he seems to have ended his life a skeptic.

As pointed out elsewhere in this history, the Brethren recognized no church holidays, but Phillip Gosse probably was more extreme on the subject than most, as the following will illustrate:

> On Christmas Day of this year 1857 our villa saw a very unusual sight. My Father had given strictest charge that no difference whatever was to be made in our meals on that day; the dinner was to be neither more copious than usual nor less so. He was obeyed, but the servants, secretly rebellious, made a small plum-pudding for themselves . . . Early in the afternoon, the maids—of whom we were now advanced to keeping two —kindly remarked that 'the poor dear child ought to have a bit, anyhow,' and wheedled me into the kitchen, where I ate a slice of plum-pudding. Shortly I began to feel that pain inside which in my frail state was inevitable, and my conscience smote me violently. At length I could bear my spiritual anguish no longer, and bursting into the study I called out: 'Oh! Papa, Papa, I have eaten of flesh offered to idols!'
>
> It took some time, between my sobs, to explain what had happened. Then my Father sternly said: 'Where is the accursed thing?' I explained that as much as was left of it was still on the kitchen table. He took me by the hand, and ran with me into the midst of the startled servants, seized what remained of the pudding, and with the plate in one hand and me still tight in the other, ran till we reached the dust-heap, where he flung the idolatrous confectionary onto the middle of the ashes and then raked it deep down into the mass. The suddenness, the violence, the velocity of this extraordinary act made an impression on my memory which nothing will ever efface.

Anne Arnott

Anne Arnott's background was also the Independent Brethren, but of a different era, that of the '20s and '30s leading up to and including World War II. Her father was a physician of some distinction in the city of Bath, and friendly association was maintained with Christians of other persuasions. Yet for Anne there was a long struggle to come to terms with a faith that was her own. Eventually her spiritual pilgrimage led her, together with her husband, into the Anglican communion. Her affectionate recollections of life among the Brethren give us a somewhat different perspective from that of Gosse:

> Sundays were to be regarded as holy days, a day of rest for those who worked, and a day of quiet for all, when the spirit of man could contemplate the things of God, and attendance at the morning meeting at eleven was obligatory . . . One day a worldly cousin accompanied us at her own request, out of kindness, I thought, or affection for my mother. Now any stranger had to be introduced to the 'Saints'. If one was 'in' the Brethren, a letter of commendation extolling our dear brother or sister, or commending them to the care of the meeting was received from the elder Brethren in the area to which the visitor belonged. If one was a member of 'one of the sects', always considered unsound in some particular or other, then one must have other recommendation.

> On this occasion my father murmured at length into the ear of the leading brother. What *would* they say, I wondered. Cousin Madeline was, deliciously, not 'one of us'. She wore a lot of colored wooden beads, and powdered her nose a good deal, and even ventured on a little lipstick . . . I listened with bated breath. The usual list of visitors commended from one Brethren 'Assembly' and another was read out, and now:

> 'Also, we have with us, Miss Dennis, known to be a believer.'

> Horrors! What would Cousin Madeline think of this? However, all was well. 'Dear Lou', she said with a giggle afterwards, gripping my mother's arm, 'do you know I was amazed to hear what they said about me. At first I thought that man said, "Also with us is Miss Dennis, known to have been in Geneva!'

Garrison Keillor

Garrison Keillor became known to the American public through his radio show, called the "A Prairie Home Companion," which he started in 1974. The immense popularity of that program was due in large measure to Keillor's gift for storytelling. His yarns revolved around his small town upbringing in Lake Wobegon, Minnesota, a place where nothing—and yet everything—happened, and whose characters he described with Dickensian wit. Out of these tales grew his second best-selling book, *Lake Wobegon Days*, in which his family's membership in the "Sanctified Brethren" is introduced as follows:

> We were Sanctified Brethren, a sect so tiny that nobody but us and God knew about it.

The facts are that Garrison Keillor *was* born in a small Minnesota town, Anoka, and his family *were* members of a tiny Exclusive Brethren splinter, called the Ames Brethren. The reason the stories he tells are so funny is because, like all gifted writers, he "holds a mirror up to life." Here is a sample:

> We were 'exclusive' Brethren, a branch that believed in keeping itself pure of false doctrine by avoiding association with the impure. Some Brethren assemblies, mostly in larger cities, were not so strict and broke bread with strangers—we referred to them as 'the so-called Open Brethren,' the 'so-called' implying the shakiness of their position—whereas we made sure that any who fellowshipped with us were straight on all the details of the Faith, as set forth by the first Brethren who left the Anglican Church in 1865 to worship on the basis of correct principles . . .

> Unfortunately, once free of the worldly Anglicans, these firebrands were not content to worship in peace, but turned their guns on each other. Scholarly to the core and perfect literalists every one, they set to arguing over points that, to any outsider, would have seemed very minor indeed . . . including the question: If Believer A is associated with Believer B who has somehow associated himself with C who holds a False Doctrine, must D break off association with A, even though A does not hold the doctrine, to avoid the taint?

Appendix II
Sources

The following are some books I found useful in writing *My People*. Special sources other than the titles listed below are referred to in the text and at the end of chapters. Unfortunately, most of the books and other materials referred to are out of print. The letters *OP* after the listing mean "out of print." The letter *A* means "available." If books are available, addresses of sources are given. Some out of print books can be found second hand. Others will only be available in private collections or a few libraries (see chapter 15).

Because *My People* is intended for popular reading, the only footnotes I included were to add some clarification to certain points, not to identify sources. I am of the opinion that for the general reader an abundance of footnotes in tiny print is often more of a threat than a help.

Histories of the Brethren

David J. Beattie *Brethren: The Story of a Great Recovery*. John Ritchie, Kilmarnock, 1940. OP This is primarily an account of how the work in various areas of Great Britain originated. Some very interesting old photos.

F. Roy Coad *A History of the Brethren Movement*. Paternoster Press, Exeter, 1968.OP To date, this is the only history of the Independent or "Open" Brethren in Great Britain (excluding Dr. Rowdon's work, which, however, covers only the origins of the movement). Coad has researched his sources meticulously. An authoratitive book.

F. Roy Coad *The Brethren Movement*. 5 lectures given at Regent College, Vancouver, July 1990. Unpublished. A summary of the above book in lecture form.

William W. Conard *Family Matters*. Interest Ministries, P.O. Box 190, Wheaton, IL 60189, 1992. *A* The author describes this new book as a "brief overview of . . . the Brethren Movement," and as such it is very well done and attractively presented.

Donald F. Durnbaugh *The Believers Church* "The Plymouth Brethren," pp. 161-172, Macmillan Co., NY, 1968.OP A very fair summary of Brethren history by an outsider.

H.A. Ironside *A Historical Sketch of the Brethren Movement*. Loizeaux Bros., Neptune, NJ, 1942, 1985. *A* Deals mainly with the squabbles of the Exclusives.

Ross H. McLaren *The Triple Tradition: the Origin and Development of the Open Brethren in North America*. 1982 Unpublished dissertation for Vanderbilt

University. Available from University Microfilms, 300 N. Zeeb Rd., Ann Arbor, MI 48106 Described in chapter 7. A seminal work. *A*

Ross H. McLaren *Will the Real Plymouth Brethren Please Stand.* 1975 Unpublished term paper for Vanderbilt University. This paper is an attempt, and quite a good one, by a young history scholar to indentify the Brethren through a summary of their history. Excellent research.

William B. Neatby *A History of the Plymouth Brethren.* London, Hodder & Stoughton, 1902, second edn. OP Neatby was the son of an Exclusive preacher, and had access to many in his day who knew the founders. An eloquent book.

Napoleon Noel *The History of the Brethren.* 2 vols., W.F. Knapp, Denver, 1936. OP These two volumes are a hotch-potch of history, biography, Exclusive doctrine, polemics, hero worship, etc., but valuable to the scholar as a kind of reference work. OP

Harold H. Rowdon *The Origins of the Brethren 1825-1850.* Pickering & Inglis, London, 1967. OP Dr. Rowdon wrote this as a doctoral dissertation. He was able to draw on extensive written resources, including a very important set of manuscript letters called the Fry Collection that had come to light not long before. An authoritative book.

Regional Histories of the Brethren

Keith & Alan Linton *I Will Build My Church: 150 Years Of Local Church Work In Bristol,* 1982. OP

Robert L. Peterson *Christian Assemblies On Mountain & Plain: A History of the Brethren in Colorado.* (Available from the author)

John S. Robertson *In His Name: A History of Assemblies . . . In the City of Toronto, Ontario.* "Food For the Flock," 1960. OP

Biographies and Autobiographies

Always Abounding: George Brearley, Evangelist of the Blackdown Hills, London, Morgan & Scott. n.d. OP

T. Baird *Back To the Beginning: A Miniature Manual of Missionary Memories.* The Book Stall, New York, 1919. OP

Chief Men Among the Brethren, compiled by Hy Pickering Loizeaux Bros., Neptune, NJ, (1918) 1986. *A*

J.N. Darby *Letters of J.N.D.,* 3 vols. Bible Truth Publishers, P.O. Box 649, Addison, IL 60101 *A*

John Trew Dickson *William J. McClure.* Privately printed, n.d. OP

E. Schuyler English *Ordained of the Lord: H.A. Ironside.* Loizeaux Bros., Neptune, NJ, (1946) 1976. *A*

A.N. Groves *Memoir of the late Anthony Norris Groves.* compiled by his widow. Second edition, London, 1857. OP

Frank Holmes *Brother Indeed.* (The life of Robert Cleaver Chapman) London, 1956. OP

G.H. Lang *Anthony Norris Groves: Saint & Pioneer*. The Paternoster Press, London, 1949. OP

George Müller *Autobiography of George Müller, or A Million and a Half In Answer To Prayer*, second edition, 1906. OP

Donald Munro: A Servant of Jesus Christ. John Ritchie, Kilmarnock, n.d. OP

Robert L. Peterson/Alexander Strauch *Agape Leadership: Lessons In Spiritual Leadership From the Life of R.C. Chapman* Lewis & Roth Publishers, Littleton, CO 80160. A

Donald Ross: *Pioneer Evangelist of the North of Scotland and the United States of America* Edited by his son (Charles Ross) John Ritchie, Publishers, Kilmarnock. OP

W.T. Stunt, et.al. *Turning the World Upside Down: A Century of Missionary Endeavor*. Echoes of Service, 1 Widcombe Crescent, Bath, England, 1972. A

Maksym S. Weremchuk *John Nelson Darby & the Beginning of the Brethren*. (Translated from German) Loizeaux Bros. New A

Church History

E.H. Broadbent *The Pilgrim Church*. Pickering & Inglis, London, (1931), 1981. A

J.D. Douglas, ed. *The New International Dictionary of the Christian Church*. Zondervan Publishing House, Grand Rapids, 1974. A

David L. Edwards *Christian England*, vol. 4, From the 18th Century to the First World War William B. Eerdmans Publishing, Grand Rapids, 1984. A

Andrew Miller *Miller's Church History*. Pickering & Inglis, London, 1974. OP

Works About the Brethren, Their Beliefs and Practices, etc.

Clarence Bass *Backgrounds To Dispensationalism*. Wm. B. Eerdmans, Grand Rapids, 1960. OP

J.N. Darby *Collected Writings*, 34 vols & index, Bible Truth Publishers, P.O. Box 649, Addison, IL 60101.

Arnold D. Ehlert *Brethren Writers*. Baker Book House, Grand Rapids. OP

A.N. Groves *Christian Devotedness*, 1825. OP

William MacDonald *Christ Loved the Church: An Outline of New Testament Church Principles*. Walterick Publishers, P.O. Box 2216, Kansas City, KS 66110-0216, 1956. A

Andrew Miller *The Brethren (commonly so-called): A Brief Sketch*. Bible Truth Publishers. A

Ernest R. Sandeen *The Roots of Fundamentalism: British & American Millenarianism 1800-1930*. University of Chicago Press, 1970. OP

R. Paul Stevens *Liberating the Laity: Equipping All the Saints For Ministry*. Inter-Varsity Press, Downers Grove, IL, 1985. A

The Jack Hozack Collection

The Jack Hozack Memorial Collection preserves historical photos of conferences, street meetings, picnics, evangelists, etc., graphics such as early meeting announcements, posters, Sunday school programs, etc., letters of earlyday workers and other memorabilia of an historic nature. We are also looking for North American Brethren periodicals dated before 1980. Contributions of the above to the Collection will ensure that these materials will be preserved for historical researchers in the future. Also welcome will be corrections, comments and questions regarding this book. Send to:

The Jack Hozack Memorial Collection
P.O. Box 33
Moraga, CA 94556

Photo Credits

Cover - Gift of Jack Young.

Part I Introduction Echoes of Service, Bath, England.

Part I Title Page Hozack Collection.

1. Dublin Tourist Authority.

2. *Chief Men Among The Brethren* by Hy Pickering.

3. *Chief Men Among The Brethren*.

4. *Chief Men Among The Brethren*.

5. National Portrait Gallery, London.

6. Engraving from *Memoir of The late Anthony Norris Groves*, 1857.

7. The Müller Foundation, Bristol.

8. The Müller Foundation, Bristol.

9. *Brethren: The Story of a Great Recovery* by David Beattie.

10. Gift of Mrs. R. Popplestone, Plymouth.

11. The author.

12. The author.

13. Copied from "Little Flock" hymnbook.

14. Rylands Library, University of Manchester.

15. *The History of The Brethren* by Napoleon Noel.

16. *Autobiography of George Müller*.

17. The author.

18. The author.

19. By The author.

20. The author.

21. *Brother Indeed* by Frank Holmes.

22. *Brother Indeed* by Frank Holmes.

23. *Back to The Beginning* by T. Baird.

24. *Chief Men Among The Brethren*.

25. *The se Seventy Years* by William Gilmore.

26. *The se Seventy Years* by William Gilmore.

27. The author.

28. *Henry Moorhouse: The English Evangelist* by Rev. John MacPherson.

29. The Hozack collection.

30. *Brethren: The Story of a Great Recovery* by Beattie.

31. *Baedecker in Russia* by R.S. Latimer.

32. *The History of The Brethren* by Napoleon Noel.

33. *Chief Men Among The Brethren* by Hy Pickering.

34. Echoes of Service.

Part II Title Page - Hozack Collection

35. Hozack Collection

36. The Hozack Collection

37. The Hozack Collection

38. *Alexander Marshall: Evangelist & Pioneer* by John Hawthorne, Pickering & Inglis.

39. The Hozack Collection

40. *Interest*

41. The Hozack Collection

42. Mr. & Mrs. Ernest Tatham

43. The Hozack Collection

44. The Hozack Collection

45. *Interest*

46. The Hozack Collection

47. *Our Record*

48. The Hozack Collection

49. Gift of Arthur Schnabel

50-54 The Hozack Collection

55. *The Barley Cake* (Part III title page) The Hozack Collection

56. Robert Mojonnier

57. The Hozack Collection.

58. Mr. & Mrs. Ernest Tatham

59. Tom & Pauline Parks

60. Leonard DeBuhr

61. Photo credit Mr. & Mrs. Cliff Smith

62. Wally Carroll (Dr. Arthur Hill)

63-65 *Interest*

C. Stacey Woods: IVCF

66. Faye Smart

67. *Interest*

68. Emmaus Bible College

69. (Cover of *Words In Season*)

70. (Cover of *Milk of The Word*)

71. (Cover of *Light and Liberty*)

72. (Cover of *Voices The Vineyard*)

73. (Cover of *The Fields*)

74. Jack Davies

75. The Hozack Collection

76. Irene Gallagher

77-81 *Interest* Magazine

82-85 Interest Ministries

86. Faye Smart

87. Interest Ministries

88. (Cover of *Assembly Annals*)

Part IV Title Page Photo cedit, International Teams

89-91 International Teams

92-97 *Interest* Magazine

98. William MacDonald

99. *Interest* Magazine

100. Regent College

101. *Interest* Magazine

102. Ibid.

103. James Stahr

104-107 *Interest* Magazine

Appendix III
Roster Of Commended Workers
Every 20 Years 1881-1995

The First Commended Workers Up To 1900

This list and others following have been gleaned from reports in periodicals published at the time, and may not be complete. No directories of workers were available until after World War II.

C.J. Baker
Bro. Beattie
Col. William Beers
G.O. Benner
S.W. Benner
William Beveredge
Samuel Binch
James Black
Thomas Black
F.W. Blair
Ben Bradford
Robert Bultmann
J.H. Burge
T.C. Bush
James Campbell
John M. Carnie
Dr. James N. Case
J. Coghlin
I.R. Dean
J.T. Dean
R.J. Dickson
Joseph Douglas
William Douglas
George Duncan
James Erskine
William Faulknor
R.N. Finch
John Gilcrist
John Gill

Alfred J. Goff
James Goodfellow
John Hallyburton
James Harcus
F.B. Haule
George Hicks
George Hunter
William H. Hunter
J. Hixon Irving
F. Jennings
W.B. Johnson
James Kay
L.L. Kendrick
William Kernohan
Dr. E.A. Martin
John Martin
Alexander Matthews
R.M. McClintock
William J. McClure
J.D. McFayden
Bro. McGeachy
Robert McJannet
A. McKellar
H. McWhirter
John Moffatt
A. Monkman
Thomas D.W. Muir
Donald Munro
George Nunn
A.N. O'Brien
David Oliver
J.A. Orton
William Paul
John Rae
Charles W. Ross
Donald Ross
J.J. Rouse
D. Scott
John Silvester
Allen Simpson
John Smith
William Sommerville
Robert Telfer
John K. Wilson
William Wilson

Workers 1920

L. Adams
S.B. Adams
W. Armstrong
Moses T. Barlow
R.A. Barr
William Beveredge
J. Black
Thomas Black
John Blair
Ben Bradford
G. Brandow
Sam Brennan
J.O. Brown
R.H. Bruce
T.C. Bush
Dr. H.A. Cameron
Lawrence Chambers
Don R. Charles
Robert Charles
Ronald Charles
N. Clark
H. Clifton
J.P. Conaway
H. Crone
Robert Curry
C.G. Davis
T.H. Dempsey
John T. Dickson
R.J. Dickson
T. Dobbin
W.P. Douglas
Bro. Duncan
James Erskine
Damon Fales
J.M. Farquhar
John Ferguson
Wm. H. Ferguson
Bro. Firth
O.C. Fish
Henry Fletcher
W. Foster
L.W. Gabler
Bro. Garrett

T. Bruce Gilbert
Bro. Gilespie
John Gill (d.Dec.)
James Goodfellow
Bro. Goodwin
John Govan
Roy Gratias
Samuel Greer
Wm. Grierson
F. Hanley
Bro. Harland
H.M. Harper(d.July)
H. Harris
Bro. Hillis
Bro. Hills
Charles Hoehler
C.F. Hogg
David Horn
J. Cecil Hoyle
J. Hunt
Wm. H. Hunter
W.B. Johnson
Charles R. Keller
Sam C. Keller
Bro. Kenny
Alex Livingstone
James Lyon
James Marshall
Dr. E.A. Martin
William Matthews
Philip Mauro
D. McClintock
Wm. J. McClure
R. McCracken
R. McCrory
Alex McDonald
Ian McDonald
R.R. McDonald
Hugh G. McEwen
Roy McEwen
Sam McEwenD.
  McGeachy
Isaac McMullen
J.B. McMullin
F.A. McNulty

W.H. McWhirter
R. Miller
R. Milne
John Moneypenny
A.G. Monkman
Harold P. Morgan
David Morrison
T.D.W. Muir
B.M. Nottage
Whitfield Nottage
A.N. O'Brien
David H. Oliver
Tom Olson
Cesare Patrizio
Joseph Pearson
George T. Pinches
John Pinches
William Pinches
Walter Purcell
John Rae (d. Mar.)
W.M. Rae
S.M. Ransome
Jose Rey
A.S. Rolph
Luigi Rosania
Charles W. Ross
J.J. Rouse
David L. Roy
E.B. Roy
Sidney J. Saward
D.R. Scott
Leonard Sheldrake
G. Shivas
J. Silvester
Oliver Smith
W.G. Smith
Bro. Steen
J. Stressenger
Charles S. Summers
G. Telfer
Robert Telfer
Hugh Thorpe
T.E. Touzeau
Filberto Trulli
James Waugh
A. Webb
Stanley Wells
J.H. White
T. Wilkie
C.H. Willoughby
Bro. Wills

William Wilson
Bro. Winemiller
Harold Wright

Workers 1940

This list was gleaned from reports by and references to workers that appeared in the various Brethren periodicals for the year 1940.

J.P. Anderson
Morton Ackerley
S.B. Adams
J. Altergott
Hector Alves
Conrad Baehr
E.K. Bailey
William Baillie
Joseph Balson
Sheldon Bard
Harry A. Becker
W.E. Belch
G.O. Benner
John Bernard
Bro. Bertell
Bro. Blackwood
John Bloor
Adam Bode
W.C. Bousfield
Charles O. Bowen
Ben Bradford
J.W. Bramhall
Sam Brennan
David Brinkman
Leonard E. Brough
J.O. Brown
Simon I. Brownson
William Bryson
E.A. Buchenau
C.E. Bulander
T.M. Busby
T.C. Bush
W.G. Calderhead
Rocco Cappiello
Tom Carroll, Sr.
Lawrence Chambers
Don R. Charles
J. Conaway
John Conway
Andrew Craig

E.B. Craig
Robert A. Crawford
A.R. Crocker
Robert Curry
Bro. Darling
Cyrus Davis
J. Dawber
Neal DeYoung
J.W. Deans
Dr. Northcote Deck
Edward Deffenbaugh
F.M. Detweiler
John Dickson
E.G. Dillon
H.G. Dobson
James Donaldson
Andrew Douglas
W.P. Douglas
H.K. Downie
A. Paul Duchesneau
Dan M. Dunnett
E.G. Dillon
Ervin D. Dresch
Roger B. Eames
Fred Elliott
J.M. Farquharson
Adam Ferguson
John D. Ferguson
William Ferguson
Allen Ferguson
Edwin Fesche
Frederick Fiss
Inglis Fleming
J. Harry Fleming
A. Foster
W.G. Foster
George Fraser
Neil M. Fraser
William Frew
Louis Germain
Alfred P. Gibbs
James Gibson
T. Bruce Gilbert
Bro. Glasgow
Bro. Glover
John Govan
Albert Graham
George Gray
Sam Greer
William Grierson
Lee Grisham

John Halliday
Samuel Hamilton
H. Hanis
Harold Harper
Bro. Hartsema
George Hatherly
Dr. Arthur Hill
Richard Hill
Owen Hoffman
Sidney Hoffman
Clara Holcomb
David Horn
John Horn
Robert Hoy
J.G. Humphrey
Dr. A.E. Hunt
G. Hunt
John Hunt
W. Fisher Hunter
William H. Hunter
William Hynd
J. Douglas Ibbotson
William Ingram
Richard Irving
B. Jamison
William Jelly
Torrey Johnson
Bro. Johnston
Clayton Jones
Harold S.B. Jones
A. Joyce
Hugh Kane
Charles R. Keller
Samuel Keller
Norman Kion
David Kirk
A.P. Klabunda
George M. Landis
David Lawrence
S. Ledyard
Troy Lee
George Leest
Leonard Linsted
Warren Lloyd
W.F. Logan
Lawrence London
James Lyttle
Thomas Lyttle
George MacKenzie
Alfred Mace
Harold G. Mackay

F.W. Marshall
John Martin
E.G. Matthews
Bro. McBain
William M. McBride
Fred McCleave
W.A. McClellan
Wm. J. McClure
R.M. McClurkin
Ross McConkey
Wilson McCracken
Robert McCrory
Tom McCullagh
James McCullough
Hugh G. McEwen
Bro. McGeachy
Oswald McLeod
James McMullin
Isaac McMullin
F.W. Mehl
Thomas Melville
Samuel Mick
W.J. Miller
Louis Montalvo
Howard Montgomery
George B. Morgan
Walter Munro
Lewis Music
Will Murray
Walter H. Nelson
Joe Nieboer
C.M. Nissen
B.M. Nottage
T.B. Nottage
Bro. Nugent
A.N. O'Brien
J.J. O'Brien
Tom Olson
C. Patrizio
Mervyn Paul
Joseph Pearson
Fred Peer
William Pell
Peter Pell, Jr.
Henry Peterson
Karl J. Pfaff
V. Phillips
Anthony Pierce
P.J. Pilon
George T. Pinches
Frank Pizzulla

Peter Rabey
William M. Rae
George Rainey
John Rankin
George Raust
John Rea
Gordon N. Reager
James Reid
R.J. Reid
William Reid
Edward Richmond
Victoriano Rivera
Richard Roberts
William Robertson
T. Robinson
Arthur Rodgers
J.J. Rouse
David Roy
John Ruddock
Leslie Sandberg
Winni Sandberg
Raymond Schuster
F.W. Schwartz
Leonard Sheldrake
J. Silvester
Mrs. M. Sinclair
John Smart
Arthur E. Smith
James Smith
Oliver Smith
A. Smyth
James F. Spink
Henry Stadt
J.G. Steel
A.R. Stephenson
Archie Stewart
Samuel Stewart
C. Ernest Tatham
Edwin J. Tharp
F. Thisse
Robert Thompson
H. Thorpe
Adam Trophy
August VanRyn
George A. Vigor
John Walden
William Warke
E.F. Washington
F.G. Watson
John Watt
James Waugh

Herbert C. Webber
Allison Welch
W.W. White
Albert Widdison
Tom Wilkie
Theo Williams
Lester Wilson
William Wilson
G. Winemiller
Russ Winslow
J. Wright
Robert Young

Workers 1960

This list was gleaned from worker's reports in *Letters of Interest* and other Brethren periodicals for the year 1960, together with a list of "Servants of the Lord Working In the United States and Canada" that appeared in the January, 1961, issue of *Letters of Interest*.

John E. Abernathy
John H. Adams
A. Aiken
Edgar Ainslie
John Y.M. Aitken
Hector Alves
Colin Anderson
W.F. Anderson
Donald M. Archibald
Robert M. Arthur
H.W.O. Atkins
Everett Bachelder
Kenneth R. Baird
George Baldwin
Lloyd Ballhagen
Joseph Balsan
George Barton
George Baxter
R.F. Bayles
Stanley T. Beasley
Ernest W. Belch
William E. Belch
Roy Beverly
Paul Bitler
James H. Blackwood
Paul Boeda
R. James Booker

Robert L. Booth
James K. Boswell
Charles E. Bouliane
Wm. G. Bousfield
Charles O. Bowen
R. Boyle
J.W. Bramhall
David Brinkman
Venus Brooks
William M. Brown
S. Brownson
Norman Buchanan
C.E. Bulander
Richard Burson
W. Roy Buttery
D.O. Calderhead
George Campbell
Rocco Cappiello
Frank Carboni
D.J. Carmichael
Tom Carroll, Jr.
L.T. Chambers
Don R. Charles
Svend Christensen
James Clark
Robert Clark
Charles Clohsey
John Collins
Allie Mae Coolidge
Godfrey W. Coombs
Charles Cox
Ernest B. Crabb
Andrew Craig
Norman Crawford
Robert A. Crawford
Wallace Cudmore
Joseph Darling
Ron Dart
Miss Elsie Davey
Vincent Davey
A. James Davies
W.M. Dawes
Neal DeYoung
Aubrey Dellandrea
Frank Detweiler
Welcome Detweiler
Arthur W. Dewhurst
John T. Dickson
Edward G. Dillon
H.G. Dobson
Chester Donaldson

My People

Andrew Douglas
H.K. Downie
Edwin D. Dresch
Roger DuPont
Joseph I. Duguid
Dan M. Dunnett
Kevin G. Dyer
David R. Ednie
O.W. Elder
Paul Elliott
R.F. Elliott
Worth Ellis
John Erwin
William Fairholme
Robert Fenty
Allen C. Ferguson
John Ferguson
William Ferguson
Edwin Fesche
Shockley Few
Leonard Fex
Archie Field
O.C. Fish
Clay C. Fite
Henry Fletcher
V. Paul Flint
T. Michael Flowers
Howard Forbes
Neil Fraser
O.F. Gall
Irene Gallagher
Sam Gallagher
Louis Germain
Murdy Getty
J.W. Gibb
Alfred P. Gibbs
T.B. Gilbert
John Gilchrist
A. Edwin Gill
Joseph Giordano
Fred Gladstone
W.J. Glasgow
E.B. Godfrey
John Govan
Albert Graham
George Graham
Albert W. Grainger
Arnold Gratton
Noah Gratton
J.A. Gray
Harold Greene

Ernest A. Gross
James Gunn
W. Gurnett
Don Gustafson
Roy W. Gustafson
Walter Gustafson
John A.W. Halliday
R.T. Halliday
Samuel Hamilton
R. Edward Harlow
Harold Harper
John Harper
Robert Harper
Herb Harris
Abe Hartsema
T.A. Hay
Colin Heath
George F. Heidman
John Hill
Richard Hill
Rowland Hill
Fred Hillis
George Hoekstra
Michael L. Hoffman
Owen Hoffman
Sydney Hoffman
Fred Holder
Thomas Holiday
E. Hollingsworth
Mun Hope
David S. Horn
John A. Horn
A.E. Horton
Douglas Howard
A.E. Hunt
Howard Hunt
John Hunt
Lionel A. Hunt
Wm. F. Hunter
William D. Hynd
J. Douglas Ibbotson
William Ingram
Alex Irvine
Dr. E.B. Jackson
Elgie B. Jamison
Walter Jensen
G.G. Johnson
Hesketh Johnson
Soren Jorgensen
A.W. Joyce
J.A. Joyce

Preston Keith
Timothy Kember
Harold Kessler
Stanley H. King
Norman L. Kion
David Kirk
A.P. Klabunda
Horace Klenk
W.L. Kosin
Chap. Gordon Kyl
Charles Lacey
Thomas Lacey
Roland LaCombe
George M. Landis
David Lawrence
W.J. Learoyd
David Leathem
Stanley M. Ledyard
Leonard Lindsted
James D. Lipke
Robert J. Little
Ralph Littlefield
Lawrence London
Milton Lovering
Clarence A. Low
Herman Luhm
Earl Lundin
Thomas J. Lyttle
William MacDonald
Fred MacKenzie
Oswald J. MacLeod
Harold G. Mackay
W.B. Mackie
O.E. Magee
H. Freeman Marks
John M. Martin
Herschel Martindale
Richard Matthews
Sydney Maxwell
Lorne E. McBain
Clark McClelland
Robert McClurkin
A. Ross McConkey
James McCormick
John McCracken
Harry McCready
Robert McCrory
T.R. McCullagh
Eric S. McCullough
J.M. McCullough
William McCullough

Ken McDonald
John McGehee
L.K. McIlwane
Mrs. Annie McKellar
Eric L. McKinley
George McKinley
Robert McLaren
A.A. McLaughlin
A.W. McLellan
Murray McLeod
Oswald McLeod
William McNeil
William McRae
Herbert Meeks
F.W. Mehl
Edward Meschkat
David Metler
Stephen Mick
Earl Miller
John M. Mills
Douglas B. Moffatt
Louis Montalvo
Howard Montgomery
George B. Morgan
William Morgan
Hayward L. Morrison
Walter Munro
Glenford Murphy
Woody Murphy
William Murray
Nazar Nazarian
Joshua Nelson
H.G. Newell
Donald L. Norbie
John Norris
T.B. Nottage
William J. Oglesby
Tom M. Olson
Albert H. Olton
Chap. Albert Otto
Cesare Patrizio
Wm. J. Patterson
Joe K. Paulick
R. Peacock
Frank Pearcey
E. Pearson
Fred R. Peer
Peter Pell
William J. Pell
Donald C. Perrault
Henry Peterson

David Petherick
Karl Pfaff
Leonard Phillips
Harry Pilkington
George T. Pinches
Frank Pizzulli
Matthew Pollock
Sydney O. Porteous
John Portman
Franklin Prestidge
Walter Purcell
John Rae
Miss Grace Rae
George Rainey
W. Ross Rainey
Emilio Ramos
G. Albert Ramsay
John Rankin
John Rea
Gordon Reager
John Reid
Arnold Reynolds
Harold A. Richards
Edward Richmond
V.M. Rivera
Miss Grace Roach
Douglas Robinson
Ermal A. Robinson
Arthur B. Rodgers
Charles J. Rolls
J.A. Ronald
Leslie Sandberg
Donald C. Sauer
R.L. Savage
Vernon Schlief
F.W. Schwartz
O.G. Shantz
David Sharp
Huron Sheppard
George L. Shivas
Cyril Shontoff
Stanley Simms
John Small
John Smart
Daniel H. Smith
James Smith
W.G. Smith
Daniel C. Snaddon
J. Sommacal
William Sommerville
Carl South

F.E. Spangler
J.H. Spreeman
Ernest B. Sprunt
James A. Stahr
Robert Staley
Tommy Steele
Arch T. Stewart
Sam Stewart
W.D. Stout
Stan Streight
C. Ernest Tatham
G.P. Taylor
Raymond Taylor
Samuel Taylor
Edwin J. Tharp
Thomas Thompson
John Todd
Ben Tuininga
August VanRyn
Charles VanRyn
Milo J. VandeKrol
Eric S. Vetters
Harold J. Wagler
John Walden
W.O. Walker
Lawrence Wallace
Charles Wallington
David Ward
Charles E. Waring
William Warke
F.G. Watson
William C. Watson
Allen Weber
John Welch
Stanley Wells
Ralph A. West
James White
Miss Dorothy Wick
B. Widdifield
Tom G. Wilkie
Theo Williams
George E. Wilson
Lester Wilson
Stuart Wilson
T. Ernest Wilson
William Wilson
Melvin G. Wistner
Ernest Woodhouse
Chester Woodring
C. Stacey Woods
Gordon Wornholtz

Chauncey Yost
Robert Young
Ray Zander
Ethel Zinn

Workers 1980

This list was taken from one printed in *Interest Magazine*, July/August 1980, exactly as it appeared.

John E. Abernathy
Alan Adams
John H. Adams
Robert F. Adcock
Brian T. Aggett
Stephen Allan
F. Edward Allen
David Allison
Randy Amos
Colin F. Anderson
Elmer Anderson
Verna Anderson
William F. Anderson
Nelson J. Annan
Carl Armerding
Robert Arthur
Ken Ashton
Kenneth Aston
Kingsley Baehr
James Baillie
Kenneth Baird
Charles Baker
Lloyd Ballhagen
Joseph Balsan
John Barclay
Doug Barnes
O.D. Batts
William L. Batts
Abner Bauman
George Baxter
Stanley Beasley
Richard Becker
Robert Beers
Clifford Beggs
Ernest Belch
William E. Belch
John J. Bell
Ronald G. Bennett
Gerrit Bergsma
Harold F. Bermel

Jean-Paul Berney
Byron Berry
Nelson Betoney
Keith Bidny
Arthur Billups
William Bingham
Richard Bishop
Paul Bitler
Jeff Bloom
John Bloom
Minna Gene Bollinger
Philip Bomberger
J. Lloyd Bone
R. James Booker
Robert L. Booth
James K. Boswell
Howard Bosworth
Charles-Eugene Bouliane
Frederick W. Bovey
Rennes (Butch) Bowers
Chet Boyd
John Bramhall
Dale Brooks
Leonard Brooks
Bill Brown
John Brown
Paul Brownson
Robert Bruton
Lawrence R. Buchanan
Richard Bunce
Lawrence Buote
Oliver Burns
W. Roy Buttery
George A. Campbell
George D. Campbell
Bernot B. Carlely
Kelvin (Bud) Carmichael
Signe Carter
David Cartwright
Donovan Case
Brian Catalano
James Catron
Marc Champagne
Svend Christensen
Heather Clark
James Clark
Ralph M. Clark
Robert Clark
Roger Cocking
Charles G. Coleman
David Collins

My People

Lois Comolli
James Compte, Jr.
Betty Conrad
Sharon Copeland
Sam Coppieters
Jack Correll
Gerard Couenhoven
Donald Cox
Venture Coy
Douglas Crabb
Ernest B. Crabb
Norman Crawford
Robert Crawford
David Crompton
Donald C. Crook
Wallace Cudmore
David J. Daley
Kamlaker N. Dandeker
Joseph Darling
E. Vincent Davey
Elsie Davey
Jack Davies
John M. Davies
William E. Davies
Lewis Dawes
William M. Dawes
Robert E. Deeds
Raymond Dell
Aubrey Dellandrea
Ernest Dellandrea
Robert Demster
Dandido Desousa
Frank Detrick
Frank Detweiler
Welcome Detweiler
Harry Deutchman
Loretto Dicesare
Peter Dillon
Michael Dingman
Lewis Doane
Herbert G. Dobson
Chester Donaldson
Joseph Doucet
Neil Dougal
Roger Drouyn
Robert Dryburgh
John Duckhorn
Donald Dunkerton
Laverne Dyck
Kevin Dyer
Clara M. Eccles

Ronald Edgecombe
David Ednie
John Elliott
Worth Ellis
Kenneth E. Engle
Bruce Ewing
William Fairholm
Robert Fenty
Allen Ferguson
Cathie Ferguson
William D. Ferguson
Edwin Fesche
Shockley Few
Len Fex
Jack Fish
Harold Fiss
Kenneth Fleming
Paul Fletcher
V. Paul Flint
T. Michael Flowers
Howard Forbes
A. Ray Fox
Bryan Fox
Gordon Fraser
Brent Freeman
Earle Fries
Irene Gallagher
Sam Gallagher
Arthur L. Garnes
Norman Gentry
Peter Gentry
Murdy Getty
Otis Jean Gibson
Doublas Gilmore
Joseph Giordano
Fred Gladstone
David Glock
Gaius Goff
Mariano Gonzalez
Philip Goodwin
Robert Gordon
George Graham
Vivian Grant
Dan Greene
Hal Greene
Louise Grindstaff
Virginia Gross
Andre Guay
Nicklaas Guikema
Phil Guikema
James Gunn

William Gurnett
Walter N. Gustafson
C. Russell Hadley
Van Hairgrove
J.A.W. Halliday
Mike Hamel
O.G. Hankins
Robert Hanks
Mike Hansinger
Gordon Haresign
R. Edward Harlow
John Harper
Robert Harper
Victor Harrington
B. Sam Hart
David Hausmann
Thomas Hay
Colin Heath
George Heidman
Sheila Henderson
Stuart Henrich
Jack Heseltine
Rowland H.C. Hill
Tom Hill
James G. Hislop
Owen Hoffman
P. Thomas Hoffman
Sydney Hoffman
Roger Hoffman
Fred Holder
W. Eugene
  Hollingsworth
John Hillmann, Sr.
George Honeycutt
Mun Hope
Robert Hostetler
John Hunt
W. Fisher Hunter
Robert J. Hutchinson
William Hynd
J. Douglas Ibbotson
Gary Inrig
Karen Isom
Hesketh Johnson
Robert Johnson
Ron Johnson
Gaston Jolin
J. Albert Joyce
Preston Keith
Timothy Kember
Harold E. Kesler

Jack Kimpel
John E. King
Stanley King
William E. King, Jr.
Tom Kirkpatrick
Richard Klein
Leroy Knowles
Rick Knox
Frederick Kosin
Wesley L. Kosin
Siegfried Krauss
Roland LaCombe
Serge LaFrance
Lorne Langfeld
Keith Lapsley
Brian Larmour
William C. Lavery
William J. Learoyd
David Leathem
Ethel Lee
Paul Lewis
Marcel Lightbourne
Glenn Lightfoot
Leonard Lindsted
Robert D. Lindsted
Rosetta Lingle
Wycliffe Livingston
LeRoy E. Lohre
D. Claude Loney
David B. Long
Patrick Long
Grant Love
Clarence A. Low
Bill Lowe
Herman Luhm
William MacDonald
Harold G. Mackay
David MacLeod
Murray MacLeod
Oswald MacLeod
O.E. Magee
Rex Major
George H. Mallone
G. Vernon Markle
Charles Marr
Ruch Marshall
Esther Martin
Gordon Martin
John Martin
Peter H. Mathews
Jim Matthews

Brian Maxwell	Robert Orr	V.M. Rivera	Dann Speichinger
Sydney Maxwell	Carl Ostertag	Marjorie Robbins	Jack Spender
James Mayer	Albert J. Otto	Thomas H. Roberts	Robert Spicer
Herbert McCaulley	Charles Oxendine, Jr.	Richard Robertson	John Spreeman
Clark McClelland	Harold S. Paisley	Douglas Robinson	J. Arthur Springer
A. Ross McConkey	Donald Paquin	Ermal Robinson	James A. Stahr
James W. McCormick	Ben F. Parmer	Garry Robinson	Ben A. Staley
Eric McCullough	Judy Patnaude	Willard Rodgers	Gregory Staley
Betty McGehee	John Mark Patterson	James A. Ronald	Robert T. Staley
Ted McKellar	Joseph Paulick	James W. Ronald	Tommy Steele, Jr.
Charles McKinnie	David Pavey	Ray Routley	Tommy Steele, Sr.
Robert L. McLaren	Carl Payne	William Ruckdashel	Stuart Steenmeyer
Gerald O. McLellan	Frank Pearcey	Gordon Rumford	Martin W. Steinberg
William McNeil	Fred R. Peer	Fernand Saint-Louis	Alexander Stephenson
Bruce McNicol	David Pegler	Raul Henry Sanchez	Julian Stephenson
William McRae, Jr.	Peter J. Pell	Leslie Sandberg	Gary L. Stewart
J.H. Herbert Meeks	Roy D. Pell	Hugo Santucci	Samuel Stewart
George Mercado	Donald Pelon	Donald Sauer	David Stiefler
Edwin Meschkat	Donald Perrault	Robert Scheid	Gerald Stiles
Virginia Metler	Frank Perry	Wayne Schlichter	Brooky R. Stockton
Earl Miller	Henry Peterson	Vernon Schlief	Stanley Streight
John Milton Mills	David Petherick	Herbert Schnabel	Gordon Strom
Ron H. Millson	Karl Pfaff	Cordell Schulton	Claire Strout
Claude Minkler	John E. Phelan	Glenn Schuman	Richard Strout
Don Mitchell	Les Picard	Raymond Schuster	Clara Suchard
Ronald Moeller	Gary Pickell	J. Eddie Schwartz	Everett Tarver
Helen J. Montgomery	Charles Pierce	David Sharp	Philip Tate
E. Raymond Moore, Jr.	Harry Pilkington	P. William Shatford	C. Ernest Tatham
George B. Morgan	George J. Pirie	Paul F. Shaw	Franklin Taylor
J. Philip Morgan	David Pollock	Victor Shaeffer	G.P. Taylor
T.S. Morgan	Matthew Pollock	Wes Shelman	Raymond Taylor
Raymond Morris	Alyce Procaccino	Huron Sheppard	Robert Taylor
Harry Morrison	Ramsey Quark	Liddon Sheridan	Gary Thompson
Hayward L. Morrison	Claude Queval	Joseph Sherlock	Hartley Thompson
Leslie Muirhead	Grace Rae	Cyril Shontoff	Robert I. Thompson
Joseph J. Muller	John T. Rae	Carl Simmons	Thomas J. Thompson
Wilfred Munnings	Lawrence Rae	Edith M. Simmons	Bill Thrall
F.W. (Woody) Murphy	George Rainey	Cecil E. Simms	Robert Thrall
Nazar Nazarian	W. Ross Rainey	Stanley Simms	Otis Tillman
Lewton Neilly	Robert F. Ramey	John Small	Glenn C. Tompkins
David Nelson	Gordon Reager	Ken Small	Glendall Toney
John Nelson	James Redling	Daniel Smith	Sidney Tordoff
Michael Nelson	David R. Reid	Daniel H. Smith	Joseph Tremblay
J. Boyd Nicholson	John Reid	Harold Smith	Litizia Trulli
J.B. Nicholson, Jr.	Robert Remley	Hubert Smith, Sr.	Norman Tucker
Janet Nickel	Arnold J.M. Reynolds	James N. Smith	Ben Tuininga
Donald L. Norbie	David Richards	Nathan Smith	Alma Turnbull
John J. Norris	Harold A. Richards	Dan Snaddon	Ed Turner
Alfred Nottage	Edward Richmond	William Snyder	Arnold Usher
William Oglesby	David Rickert	John M. Sommacal	James VanDuzer
Albert H. Olton	Merle Ridlen	Franklin Spangler	Keith VanHolst

My People

Milo VandeKrol
Elliot VanRyn
Margaret VanRyn
Russell VanRyn
Harold Wagler
Jack E. Wagner
Phillip Wagner
George Walker
Lawrence Wallace
David Ward
Ron Ward
Fred Warnholtz
Ann Warris
Grace Watson
Robin Weatherford
Robert Webb
Allan R. Weber
Neil Weir
Donald Welborn
William A. West
Dorothy Wick
E.J. Wickert
Wilfrid G. Wight
David B. Wilkerson
Don Williams
Harry Williams
John Williams
Richard Williams
Theodore Williams, Sr.
Aubrey N. Wilson
Lester Wilson
Stuart Wilson
T. Ernest Wilson
William R. Wilson
Melvin G. Wistner
William Wolitarsky
Ernest Woodhouse
James Wright
LeRoy L. Yates
Jean Young
Robert (Bert) Young
George Yphantides
Ray Zander

Workers 1995 in U.S. and Canada

Bob & Susan Abegg
Paul and Joanne Abrahams

Fabio and Dorothy Abreu
David and Agnes Adams
John H. Adams
Robert and Ruby Adcock
Ken and Sonia Additon
Brian and Jenny Agett
Steve and Karen Allan
Brian and Carla Alldredge
F. Edward and Velma Allen
Tom and Joyce Allen
David and Lorraine Allison
Marlene Allyn
Randy and Sylvia Amos
Carl and Cathy Anderson
Colin and Joan Anderson
Don and Dorothy Anderson
Miss Miriam Anderson
William & Virginia Anderson
Dick and Donna Andrews
Michael and Diane Andrews
Bill and Joy Armerding
Ken and Evelyn Ashton
Kenneth Aston
Timothy & Yvonne Ayers
Christo and Laura Ayoub
Eugene Badgley
Kingsley and Holly Baehr
Eldred C. & Shirley Bagley
Kenneth & Ruth Baird
Charles and Carol Baker
Jack & Adele Baker
Joseph and Lois Balsan
Ernie and Rhonda Baptiste
Richard and Nora Barada
Bruce & Janice Barbour
Samuel Barkat
Doug and Morven Barnes
Philip and Marilyn Barnes

Ron Barnes
Anthony & Judith Barone
Harold & Dorothy Barrington
William & Barbara Batts
Abner and Rosie Bauman
Mark & Carrie Baumgardner
Phil and Carol Baxter
Richard and Zoanna Becker
Thomas and Kristine Beeghly
Richard and Carol Beers
Robert & Betty Lou Beers
Clifford and Shirley Beggs
Ernest and Evelyn Belch
Ken and Carol Belch
John and Mary Ann Bell
Ronald & Sharon Bennett
John and Delayne Berglund
Gerrit and Mary Bergsma
Harold and Irene Bermel
Jean-Paul & Eglantine Berney
Paul and Carol Beverly
Keith and Judi Bidne
Arthur and Georgia Billups
Fred and Sheila Binns
Richard and Betty Bishop
Scott & Melodie Bissell
John and Ann Bjorlie
Scott and Marsha Blair
Ray and Becky Blais
Michelle Blakeburn
Daniel & Bonnie Blanchet
Gerrit and Susan Blok
Jeff and Alyce Bloom
John and Ruth Bloom
Roy & Lonita Boettcher
Gerald and Marilyn Boisvert
Minna-Gene Bollinger
Vera Bollinger
Philip & Phyllis Bomberger
Mr. J. Lloyd Bone
David & Marybeth Booker
Ken and Patty Botton

Derrick & Beryl Bourne
Rennes & Julie Ann Bowers
Kenneth Bowles
Margaret Bowman
Chet and Bonnie Boyd
Jay Brady
John & Margaret Bramhall
Bob and Gwen Bramhill
Thomas Brammer
Horen and Virginia Brasov
Craig Braun
Jennifer Bregand
Brent and Jill Brooks
Leonard and Esther Brooks
Steven and Jane Brotherton
Jonathan & Elizabeth Brower
David and Ann Brown
Donald Brown
Duane and Alice Brown
Robert and JoAnne Brown
Paul & Carol Brownson
Simon and Olive Brownson
Dean and Cristy Bruns
Robert & Jean Bruton
Robert and Sherry Bryant
Lawrence & Doreen Buchanan
Wilfred and Sheila Buchanan
Miss Alice Buckland
Lawrence Buote
Edward and Peggy Burdick
Frank and Tammy Burgess
Colin and Natalie Burnett
Bob and Evelyn Burns
Dave and Terri Burns
David and Nancy Burrows
George and Eunice Butcher
Roy and Evelyn Buttery
Mr. & Mrs. Wayne Byrd
George and Judy Byrum

Charles and Lydia Cade

Bruce and Sue Calder-
wood

David and Ann Calder-
wood

Gina Caldwell

Clifford and Norlene
Campbell

Donald & Elizabeth
Campbell

Wilson and Joy Cam-
poverde

James and Barbara Car-
rington

Signe Carter

David & Mary Cart-
wright

Donovan and Carolyn
Case

Carlos Castaneda

Edgardo and Nelly Cas-
tro

James and Lillian Catron

Carlos Cerqueira

Bob and Mary-Lynn
Chambers

Marc and Lise Cham-
pagne

Warren and Betty Chas-
tain

Pye Chew

Ron and Lorene Chin

Paul & Vonda Chipman

Les and Emma Chopard

Phil & Cynthia Christen-
sen

Rob and Cheryl Christen-
son

Jim and Wanda Cichy

Ralph Clark

Robert & Mary Joyce
Clark

Jean-Pierre & Lucie Clou-
tier

John and Margaret Clu-
nas

Bill and Jill Cobb

Brian and Wanda
Coburn

Herbert and Ruth Cock-
ing

Bruce and Isolene Cofer

William & Elizabeth Cof-
fey

Don and Naomi Cole

Charles & Katherine
Coleman

Mrs. William James Cole-
man

John and Flo Coles

Bruce and Geneva Col-
lins

David and Meryl Collins

James and Heather
Comte

William and Ruth Con-
ard

Rodney and Judy
Conover

Garnet and Gwen
Cooney

Robert and Martha Coo-
per

Samuel and Ida Cop-
pieters

Jack and Mae Correll

Keith and Gay Coss

Jerry and Pat Couen-
hoven

Tom and Harriet Cowan

Venture Coy

Douglas and Jeanne
Crabb

Helen Crabb

David and Patti Cramer

Norman and Lois Craw-
ford

Don and Bunny Crook

Dean and Antonia
Crossley

Joseph and Marion Cum-
ming

Miss Barbara Cummings

Ron and Joan Curtin

Karl and Linda Dalen-
berg

Robert and Patty Daley

Claude and Sheila Dallas

Gerald and Esther Dalli-
more

Kamlaker and Sheela
Dandeker

John and Marilyn
Daniels

Lawrence and Maria
Darling

Kenneth and Carol
Daughters

Ms. Elsie Davey

Vincent Davey

Peter and Judith Davids

Barry and Bev Davidson

Theron and Barbara
Davidson

Jack and Florence Davies

Candido and Celina
DeSousa

Jimmy and Martha Dean

Don and Jan Debaere-
maeker

Cheryl Debanne

Mary Decker

Steve and Patricia Decker

Robert & Carol Deeds

James and Trenda De-
Graw

Aubrey and Ena Dellan-
drea

Gerard and Mickie De-
Matteo

Ingimar and Ivete DeRid-
der

Frank and Thelma
Detrick

Michael and Linda B.
Deur

Rick and Gail DeVaul

William David & Norma
Dewhurst

Ovilio and Delia Diaz

Kurt and Marsha Dibble

Dick Trevor

Edward Dickinson

James and Linda Difino

Pablo and Amy Dillon

Pedro and Lucy Dillon

Michael and Barbara
Dingman

Dave and Cheryl Dirks

Douglas Dixon

Roy and Mildred Dombo

Chester & Marion Don-
aldson

Neil Dougal

Clayton and Isobel Dou-
gan

David and Leona
Douglas

Nathan Douglas

Richard and Martha
Douglass

Marshall and Kelly
Drake

Paul and Beth Drechsel

Bob Drumm

Alex Dryburgh

John and Dona Duck-
horn

David and Sharon Dun-
bar

Douglas and Gail Dun-
can

Warren and Florence
Dunham

David and Martha
Dunkerton

Donald and Diana
Dunkerton

James and Carolyn
Dunkerton

David and Faith Dunlap

Bruce & Glenda Dunning

Joe and Bonnie Duran

Craig and Lacey Dyer

Kevin and Eloise Dyer

Mark and Sue Dyer

Vida Eardley

Jack and Pennie Earls

Thomas and Laura Ebert

Thomas and Mei-chu
Edilinski

Daniel and Amy Eernis-
see

Worth and Dorothy Ellis

Paul and Sue Emery

Kenneth and Mary Lou
Engle

Garry and Connie Engler

Francisco and Maria Es-
carraman

Grace Eustace

Anthony and Lois Evans

George and Gail Farber

Stan and Joan Farmer

Dann and Nancy Far-
quhar

Dr. Arthur Farstad

Dan and Teri Faulkner

Jack and Karen Faulkner

John and Mary Faulkner

Steven and Gail Faulkner

Bill and Mary Fear

Ron and Linda Felton

Robert Fenty

William D. & Elizabeth
Ferguson

Dorothy Ferrett

Edwin and Garland Fesche

Shockley and Dottie Few

Len and Madeleine Fex

Jacqueline Fierman

Jay and Dorothy Fippinger

Jack and Nancy Fish

Harold and Molly Fiss

John and July Fitzgerald

Charles and Darlene Fizer

Ken and Helena Fleming

Paul and Dorothy Fletcher

T. Michael and Ella Flowers

Mr. Howard Forbes

James Fred & Cheryl Forester

Lawrence and Rita Fors

Lawrence and Lucille Fortin

Mark and Deb Foshager

Jordan and Mary Foster

Kent and Kim Fraser

Owen and Sybil Fraser

Ronald and Lynn Fraser

Steven and Sharon French

Earle and Julie Fries

Robert and Alice Fryling

Gord and Mary Fuller

Bryan and Elizabeth Funston

Craig and Gwynne Funston

Brad and Debbie Gaasrud

Sam and Dorothy Gallagher

Grant and Carol Galpin

Gregg Garman

Arthur and Vivian Garnes

Ward and Laurel Gasque

Robert and Winnie Gay

Rodney and Durinda Geiger

Peter & Margaret Gelderbloem

Norman and Margaret Gentry

Peter and Barbara Gentry

Lew and Barbara Gervais

Murdy and Eileen Getty

Charles and Mary Gianotti

Diane Gibb

Richard and Marjorie Gibson

Joseph and Connie Giordano

Fred and Mattie Gladstone

Clyde and Jillian Glass

Craig and Beryl Glass

Gil and Sue Gleason

oe and Cindy Gliori

David and Melvina Glock

Jonathan Glock

Benjamin and Bertha Glover

Neale and Barbara Goetsch

Richard and Peggy Goetze

Gaius and Linda Goff

Mariano and Pearl Gonzalez

Ray and Laura Gonzalez

John and Anne Gordon

Normand and Jeannine Gosselin

Joseph and Diane Gould

Tom and Ruth Gould

Albert and Isabel Grainger

Vivian Grant

James and Shirley Gray

James M. & Maxine Gray

John and Linda Green

Dan and Tempa Greene

Harold and Norma Greene

Stuart and Karen Greene

Leroy and Barbara Griffiths

Kevin and Zoe Grimes

Mrs. Lois Grindstaff

George and Mary Groezinger

Mrs. Virginia Gross

Randy and Donna Gruber

Andre and Louise Guay

Phil and Edna Guikema

George Guillont

Jay and Margie Gurnett

Tim and Elizabeth Gurnett

Daniel Gustafson

William & Barbara Gustafson

Mr. & Mrs. Roger Haber

Charles and Joann Haley

Ronald and Bonnie Hall

John and Marjorie Halliday

Mike and Susan Hamel

David and Rose Hammond

Ken and Ellen Hampton

John and Pat Hand

Johnny and Linda Hands

Gordon and Nancy Haresign

R. Edward & Getrud Harlow

David & Karyl Lynn Harper

Robert and Jeanette Harper

Carmen Harris

Dean and Virginia Harris

Mark and Adrienne Harris

Charles and Dilys Hart

John and Linda Hayden

Reed and Anne Heckman

George and Frances Heidman

Rob and Helen Heintz

John and Roberta Heller

Angus & Ruth Henderson

Sheila Henderson

David and Janet Hendry

Stuart and Hilda Henrich

Vivene Heron

Laurie Herrington

Steven and Alice Herzig

Jack and Irene Heseltine

Robert and Evelyn Hess

Clifford Hicks

Eugene and Nancy Higgins

Henry & Barbara Hildebrandt

Todd And Shelley Hiller

James and Beverly Hislop

Zane Hodges

Paul Thomas and Suzanne Hoffman

Gail Hogan

Andy and Danielle Holdsworth

R. Douglas Holiday

William Engene & Carrie Hollingsworth

Andrew and Pamela Holloman

Henry & Shirley Holloman

Miss Lisa Holloway

Curtis and Mavis Holmes

Mun and Adeline Hope

Karen Hopkins

Peter and Laurie Horton

Douglas and Muriel Howard

William and Karen Howell

Ron & Debbie Hughes

Stephen and Nancy Hulshizer

Dave and Diane Hultgren

Georgia Hunter

David and Judy Hyland

Clifford and Lee Ice

Yolanda Moreno Imperio

Gary and Elizabeth Inrig

Robert and Norma Irvine

William Isaac

Bob & Suzanne Jackson

Jake and Linda Jackson

Kevin and Tanya James

Hanes and Brenda Jarvis

Curtis and Katherine Jenkins

James and Elizabeth Jenkins

Samuel and Maud Jeremiah

Benjamin and Louise Johnson

Brian and Ruth Johnson

Hesketh and Dawn Johnson

Nathan and Regina Johnson

Mrs. Nedra Johnson

Stefan and Linda Johnson

Wayne & Nancy Jane Johnson

Willie and Emma Johnson

Robert and Sharon Johnston

Ron and Gloria Johnston

Gaston and Marguerite Jolin

Gerard and Angeline Jolin

Dick Jordan

Peter and Donna Ruth Jordan

J. Albert and Emily Joyce

Andrew and Helen Joye

Leroy and Debra Junker

Goerge and Mari Kaim

Teus and Maria Kappers

Martha Karam

Paul & Jacqueline Kaschel

Preston and Katie Keith

Stephen and Patricia Reed Kempf

Paul & Rebecca Kersey

Mark and Carol Kieft

Jack and Grace Kimpel

Kevin and Christy King

Stanley and Eileen King

William and Mary King

Tom & Betty Kirkpatrick

Richard and Roanne Klein

David and Mary Lynn Knight

Dwight Knight

Miss Rebecca Knopf

Mr. & Mrs. Leroy Knowles

Rick and Beth Knox

Howard and Marie Kohrmann

Rex and Joan Koivisto

Mark and Cynthia Kilchin

Paul and Becky Koppen

Miss Karen Kraemer

Siegfried and Morag Krauss

Keith Kris Krispin

Ron and Helen Kroeker

ark Lacey

Roland Lacombe

Orlando and Stephanie Lafica

Michel and Diane Lafleur

Allen and Barbara LaMorey

Lyman and Doris Lancaster

Lee and Ellen Landeck

Len and Carol Lane

Bruce and Debbie Langevin

Lorne and Ruth Ann Langfeld

Jonathan and Tawana Lansa

David and Marion Lanum

Steven and Laura Larink, Sr.

Rick and Cheryl Larman

Chuck and Kathy Larsen

Daniel and Alinda Latchman

William C. & Margaret J. Laverty

Rene Lavoie

David and Shirley Lawrence

Michael and Cyndy Lax

Glenn and Marjorie Layton

J. Wade and Lynne LeBlanc

Jim and Linda Leaptrot

Malcolm and Jo Lee

Michael and Deanna Lee

Ethel Lee

Jean and Liliane Lepine

William and Della Letkeman

Keith and Betty Leverentz

Art and Lisa Levy

Thomas and Laura Lewellen

James and Sherry Lewis

Paul and Gertrude Lewis

Walter and Olive Liefeld

Don and Jean Liesemer

Marcel and Leila Lightbourne

Glenn and Elizabeth Lightfoot

Dan and Mary Lindsted

Robert and Sharon Lindsted

Rosetta Lingle

Kirk and Paula Lithander

Lee and Viginia Lohre

Dick and Nancy Ann Loizeaux

Claude and Marion Loney

George and Carol Loney

Patrick and Gael Long

Rick and Shelley Long

Eliseo and Jane Lopez

Thomas and P. Kay Lopez

Pellam and Marion Love

Doug and Ruth Loveday

Clarence Low

Ed and Cathy Lowe

Elizabeth Lowe

Mr. Herman Luhm

John and Stacey Lynch

William MacDonald

Robert & Margaret Macgregor

Tim and Sarah Macintosh

Kiernan and Barbar Mack

Robert & Lauren Mackay

Mildred MacKenzie

Barry and Anne Mackey

John and Heather Mackie

David and Linda Macleod

Marray and Sarah Macleod

James and Jean Mader

David and MaryLo Main

Rex Major

Josephine Makill

Alfred Mallory

Edward and Isabel Maltman

Timothy and Mary Malyon

Tito and Sandy Mantilla

Tom and Patti Marinello

Phillip & Mary Cathryn Marquez

Charles Marr

David and Eleanor Marshall

Gordon and Heather Martin

John and Melissa Martin

Mahlon and Marjorie Martin

Robert and Susan Martin

Dr. & Mrs. G.V. Mathai

Mr. & Mrs. P.G. Mathew

Peter and Blanche Mathews

Greg and Gwen Matthews

Jim and Connie Matthews

John and Alison Matthews

Robert and Ruth Matthews

Brian and Heather Maxwell

Gary McBride

Jim and Jean McCarthy

Herbert and Marybeth McCaulley

Clark and Jean McClelland

Tim and Vicki McClelland

Bill and J. Faith McConnell

James and Janet R. McCormick

Bob and Joanne McCoy

John and Karen McCubbing

Eric and Jean McCullough

Ian and Eleanor McDouall

Maurice and Lois McElrea

Mrs. Betty McGehee

Fred and Lisa McHugh

Arnot and Helen McIntee

Ted and Lucille McKellar

Dennis and Donna McKendrick

Jim and June McKendrick

Brian and Grace McLaren

Robert and Helen McLaren

Warren and Beverly McLaren

Linden & Marcia McLaughlin
Ruth McLellan
Rick and Alice McLeod
Timothy and Liz McNeal
William and Janet McNeil
Bruce and Janet McNicol
Dennis and Grace Medeiros
Blane and Kathy Meier
Lance and Heather Meiners
Bruce & Bertha Merritt
Edwin & Mary Ellen Meschkat
Kelton and Sharon Meyer
Ata and Salwa Mikhael
Jonathan and Sharon Miller
Dean and Sandra Mills
Rick and Maree Mills
Ron and Verna Millson
Darryl and Carrie-Anne Milne
James and Claudette Mitchell
John and Susan Mitchell
tuart and Linda Kay Mitchell
Steve and Lauren Mizel
Greg and Sharon Monroe
John and Evelyn Montgomery
Doug and Joy Moore
Hal and Mary Moore
Ron and Lori Moore
Michel and Monique Morency
J. Phillip and June Morgan
T.S. and Catherine Morgan
William and Mary Morgan
Ralph and Helen Morris
Raymond and Dorothy Morris
Harry and Jean Morrison
Cleve and Dona Mugford
Leslie and Louise Muirhead
Joseph and Helen Muller

John and Gudny Munro
F.W. (Woody) Murphy
James and Margaret Naismith
Dorothy Neeley
Lewton and Ivorine Neilly
Craig and Grace Nelson
David and Lois Nelson
Bruce and Bev Newkirk
Michael and Nancy Nichols
Ralph and Dorothy Nichols
J. Boyd and Bernice Nicholson
Miss Janet Nickel
Michael Niehaus
Tim and Sue Nielsen
Jerry Nininger
Donald and Marie Norbie
Untra Northern
Dwane Norton
Alfred and Alice Nottage
Michael and Reiko O'Donnell
Marc and Germaine Oden
Lary and Beverly Offner
William Oglesby
David Oliver
Sumner and June Osborne
Neil & Yvonne Ostrander
John and Kathleen Ottley
Peter and Maureen Oulton
Charles and Mabel Oxendine
Jesse and Karen Padgett
Gordon and Irene Parks
Alan and Carol Parks
Ben Parmer
Mrs. Nora Paterson
David and Mary Patterson
Peter Patton
Jim and Elizabeth Paul
Thomas and Sylvia Paul
Joseph Paulick
Edward (Ted) and Jo Payne

Homer and Margaret Payne
Bill and Brenda Pearson
Heather Peat
Michael and Diane Pedneault
Pierre and Claudette Pellerin
Donald and Frances Pelon
Lawrence and Ruth Perkins
Donald and Nona Perrault
Frank and Emily Perry
Clifford and Charlene Peterson
Karl and Glynn Peterson
Mark and Debbie Petke
Jim and Janice Pettifer
Karl and Alice Pfaff
John and Mary Lou Phelan
Fred and Grace Phillips
John and Jean Phillips
Frank and Helen Pianki
John and Debra Pianki
Les and Margaret Picard
Charles and Gretchen Pierce
Howard and Barbara Pierucki
Lawrence and Linda Pile
Harry and Joan Pilkington
George and Nancy Pirie
Henry and Ruth Pitman
Leslie and Sandra Plett
Richard & Mary Beth Plowman
David And Ann Pollock
Bert and Muriel Poole
Dan and Elaine Pope
Mark and Carol Porter
Joel Portman
Harold and Vena Preston
Douglas and Jean Price
Keith and Rosemary Price
Larry and Wanda Price
Gerald and Janet Pryor
Ramsey and Audrey Quark
Peter and Sandy Rabey

Eleanor Rae
W. Ross and Lillian Rainey
Henry and Iva Ralston
Robert F. Ramey
Salvador and Elba Ramos
Rahlyn and Betty Ramsaran
Ken and Tascha Raymond
Gordon Reager
David and Connie Redekop
Mark and Inge Redka
Joe and Jane Ann Reese
John and Cheryl Reeves
David R. & Margeret S. Reid
Kim and Sylvia Reid
Andrew and Hilary Rennie
Arnold and Janet Reynolds
Mike and Sandy Rice
David and Elizabeth Richards
Edward & Evie Richardson
David and Doris Rickert
Omar and Dora Noemi Rios
Marj Robbins
Tom and Les Roberts
Don and Krista Robertson
Frank and Ruth Robertson
Boyd and Patti Robinson
Douglas and Marion Robinson
Garry and Janet Robinson
Harvey and Ruth Rodger
John and Lydia Rodgers
Woody and Susan Roland
Craig and Nancy Rolinger
William and Doreen Roller
Derrick and Eileen Rollerson
Harley and Deborah Rollins

Don and Susan Romphf

James A. and Anne Ronald

James W. and Florence Ronald

Ruth Doyle

Harry and Helen Roundtree

Ray and Laura Routley

Harold and Jean Rowe

Carl and Colleen Ruby

Bill and Jayne Ruckdashel

Jeffrey and Deanne Rush

Denise Russell

Michael and Michelle Sacco

Fernand & Yolande Saint Louis

Donald and Martie Salmans

Henry and Sara Sanchez

Richard and Betty Sanders

Hugo and Kathleen Santucci

Paul and Elaine Sapp

Enrique (Henry) & Lisa Sardina

Joel and Joanna A. Sasscer

Russ and Pat Sasscer

Mac and Mindy Sauerlender

obert and Carol Scheid

Wayne and Betty Schlichter

Vernon and Gladys Schlief

Daniel and Susan Schmidt

Mr. and Mrs. Dale Schrag

Chris and Barbara Schroeder

Stan and Rhonda Schultz

Glenn and Ruth Schuman

Douglas & Marianne Schuster

J. Eddie and Louise Schwartz

Dennis and Olive Scott

Edwin and Phyllis Scott

Brian and Sally Seim

Ronald and Cindy Serpliss

Gary and Bonnie Sharp

Rod and Amy Sharp

Bill and Joyce Shatford

Paul and Joan E. Shaw

Richard and Frances Shaw

Lamont and Willie Shazier

Mark and Kim Shelley

Wesley and Ruby Shelman

Liddon and Hellen Sheridan

Miss Maureen Sheridan

Joseph and Isobel Sherlock

Cyril and Marjorie Shontoff

Robert and Beverly Shorten

Barbara Shull

David and Marian Shull

Grace Sidebotham

en and Vicki Sidey

Bob and Janet Sieker

Mark and Linda Siersma

Ion and Silvia Sima

Denis and Donna Simard

Carl and Eloise Simmons

Rick and Gayle Simmons

Jeff and Lynda Simunic

John and Suzanne Sinclair

Ernest and Lovie Singleton

Roy and Agnes Sixto

Stan and Pat Skees

Billy and Christine Skelton

John and Earlene Small

Betty Smith

Daniel and Martha M. Smith

Gary and Karen Smith

Glenn and Sandra Smith

Harold and Erma Smith

Hubert and Wilma Smith

James and Margaret Smith

Jonathan and Maybelle Smith

Nathan and Ann Smith

Stuart and Mary Smith

Daniel and Lily Snaddon

William and Marian Snyder

Mark and Jennifer Soderquist

Carl and Iris South

Rodney and Carole Ann Spade

Dann and Linda Speichinger

John and Ruth Spender

Robert and Willene Spicer

Robert and Janis Spiro

Myrue and Patricia Spivey

John and Lorraine Sproule

James and Betty Stahr

David and Cynthia Staley

Gregory and Kathy Staley

Ken and Sandy Stanton

Lee and Carol Stauff

Tommy and Golda Mae Steele

Mr. & Mrs. Fred Steenmeyer

Spencer and Carol Steenmeyer

Martin Steinberg

Alex and Jean Stephenson

R. Paul and Gail Stevens

Billy and Mary Stevenson

Gary and Melinda Stewart

David and Ruth Stiefler

Gregory and Debra Stier

Gerald and Judith Stiles

Constance Stimpson

Lorraine Stirneman

Bernice Stocker

Brooky and Jo Ann Stockton

Graham and Margaret Stokes

Mr. & Mrs. Al Stoltzfus

Alexander and Marilyn Strauch

Stanley and Marjorie Streight

Gordon and Margaret Strom

Mark and Laurie Strout

Richard and Virginia Strout

Harvey and Janie Stuart

Stan and Victoria Surbatovich

Robert and Wilda Surgenor

Ben and Sarah Sutton

David Swan

Jay and Rosalie Swisher

Jeff Tackes

John and Karen Tardonia

C. Ernest and Louise Tatham

Daniel and Evelyn Taylor

Dr. Franklin D. & Patricia Anne Taylor

Robert and Annetta Taylor

Denis and Debora Thompson

Gary and Kay Ann Thompson

Hartley and Maria Thompson

John and Dawn Thompson

Randy and Linda Thompson

Steven and Felecia Thompson

homas & Marjorie J. Thompson

Allen and Ellen Thrall

Bill and Charlotte Thrall

Bill and Grace Thrall

Robert and Carolynn Thrall

al Threadcraft

David and Barbara Throndson

Jim Tice

Jeffrey and Beth Tichelar

Otis and H. Geraldine Tillman

Bob and Nanci Tissot

George and Heather Tompkins

Glenn and Helen Tompkins

Glendall and Janet Toney

Sidney and Betty Tordoff

My People

Ed and Jean Tracey

Joseph and Jessie Tremblay

Keith and Rebecca Trevolt

Rex and Nancy Trogdon

Carlton and Georgiana Truax

Letizia Trulli

Norman and Priscilla Tucker

Ben and Margaret Tuininga

Stephen and Deb Tulloch

Geoff and Jewel Tunnicliffe

Alma Turnbull

Ed and Cilla Turner

Donald and Dwyla Unruh

Arnold Usher

Claude and Louise Vachon

Jim and Kathy VanDine

James and Ruth VanDuzer

Lee and Loier VanDyke

Gerrit and Cathy VanEssen

Carroll and Roberta VanRyn

Elliot and Joan VanRyn

Russell VanRyn

Milo and Gladys VandeKrol

Mr. & Mrs. Stan Vaninger

Steven and Carol Vanslyke

James and Anita VarnHagen

Douglas and Ellen Virgint

Robert and Alice Vogel

Rick and Ellen Volgarino

Anthlone and Jennifer Wade

Jack and Ruth Wagner

Phillip and Carole Wagner

Raymond and Elaine Wald

Christopher Walker

George Walker

Timothy and Arlene Walker

Mrs. Barbara Walton

Craig and Bonnie Ward

Ronald and Laura Ward

Fred and Jean Warnholtz

Gordon and Charlotte Warnholtz

Richard and Carla Warnholtz

Mrs. Anna C. Warris

George and Frances Washington

Douglas and Jewell Watson

Grace Watson

Robin and Myrna Weatherford

James and Muriel Webb

Allan and Joyce Weber

Roy Weber

Neil and Genevieve Weir

James and Alice Weisbecker

Donald and Gloria Welborn

William & Winnifred West

Dean and Cindy Westacott

Mrs. Jean Wetherbe

Bob and Debbie Whattoff

Steve and Marguerite Whitten

Dorothy Wick

Christine Wigden

Wilf and Connie Wight

David and Kathleen Wilkenson

Dan and Sharon Williams

Harry and Jean Williams

John and Audrey Williams

Terry and Mary Joanne Williams

Aubrey & Josephine Wilson

Doug and Terri Wilson

Jeffrey and Mary Wilson

Ken and Mary Wilson

Rod and Bev Wilson

Rolland and Flora Wilson

Stuart and Jacqueline Wilson

T. Ernest and Elizabeth Wilson

Thomas and Ruth Wilson

Terry and Joan Winter

Melvin and Helen Wistner

Steven and Cary Witter

William and Karen Wolitarsky

Ernest and Joyce Woodhouse

Jim and Louise Wright

Richard and Nancye Yarrall

Leroy and Beverly Yates

Jack and Lilian Yocum

James and Roma Yorgey

Alfred & Glen Marie Young

Dr. Jean M. Young

Robert and Cynthia Young

Stephen and Alison Yuille

Ray Zander

Workers' Reports Over 120 Years

From *THE BARLEY CAKE*, DECEMBER 1881.

JOHN SMITH and C.W. ROSS have had a series of good meetings at Galesburg. Ill. The word was doing its work.

D.F. HUGHES has been at Hamilton and St. Catherines, Ont., Canada. He had large Gospel meetings in the former.

JOHN M. CARNIE has been at Sparta, and had good meetings.

J.K. McEWEN has been at Mattoon, Ill., and at Crown Point, Ind.

E. RONAYNE has been in Whiteside Co., Ill., and has had interesting times giving forth the word of truth. He is returning.

J. BAIN is at Watford, Ont., Canada, and has had some good meetings in the Music Hall. Brethren KERNOHAN and GOODFELLOW were, or are, with him.

W.P. DOUGLAS, writing from Lawrence, Mass., says "- - Just a line. Bro. KING, recently from Glasgow, and who left his nets a few weeks ago to follow the Lord in service. He and I go together. Large open-air meetings during the week, and a hall capable of seating over two hundred is usually filled on Lord's day evenings. We purpose having an all-day meeting on 24th, at this place. We expect some of the saints from the Boston, Byfield and Lowell meetings, to be present with us. Some sinners seem troubled."

T.D.W. MUIR is working in his usual way at Detroit.

THE *BARLEY CAKE*, DECEMBER 1887

Brn. Marshall and Case have just finished a month's meetings in Belleville, Ontario, and Bro. Case is now in Toronto with Bro. Munro.

Richard Irving has again gone forth to preach Christ, taking nothing of the Gentiles. He makes Belleville his centre.

Brn. Smith and Rae are seeing some blessing in Manitoba. We believe Bro. Smith has it somewhat on his mind to come to the United States for tent work during the summer.

Brn. Kernohan and R.R. McDonald are in Ravenswood, Ontario, where the Lord has been graciously been giving them to see some fruit. We understand that there have been some manifestations of blessing in Forest also.

Brn. Campbell and Matthews are still in Philadelphia seeking to make Christ known throughout that large city. Some have already received Him, but the vast majority there, as elsewhere, prefer the world.

Brn. Telfer and Crook are in Elgin, Ill., and have been in that vicinity for some little time.

J.M. Carnie is preaching in a new hall rented by the South Side assembly in this city [Chicago].

T.D.W. Muir is in Detroit. He reports good open-air meetings there. He left Bro. Reich in Au Sable, where they are having good times.

For news of San Francisco tent see our California letter.

We subjoin a letter just received from our brother Faulknor

[William Faulknor was, to our knowledge, the first Independent Brethren foreign missionary from North America. He had joined Frederick Arnot, Appendix IV]

Charles Swan and other workers in Central Africa earlier in 1887. As we pointed out in chapter 16, Ross was the first to publish missionary letters, preceding *Voices From the Vineyard* by several years. Below is an excerpt from the long letter that Ross refers to:]

"When Bro. Swan came to the coast to see Peter Scott off to England, Br. Swan was sick himself and seems to be so now, and from all accounts Br. Arnot is on the sick list, so I will need to be careful of my health. On the steamer we heard of the death of two missionaries on the Congo lately. If the Gospel is going to be preached in Africa it will be at great cost."

OUR RECORD, JULY 1894

R.G. Benner and A. Monkman pitched a Gospel Tent on the Red River, Manitoba, Canada. They "had a baptism at St. Andrews on June 10th. Twelve were buried." About 500 were present as onlookers. A number of brethren preached the Gospel, and there were some earnest listeners. It was a "good day and trust there will be fruit to God as the result."

Mr. D. Munro is giving prophetic lectures in the Gospel Tent in this city [Oakland, Calif.]. The meetings are fairly well attended.

The tent of Homestead and Munhall, Pa., is pitched on the very site on which the stump orators vented their grievances before the terrible strike of two years ago. We look for better results from this new departure. Brethren Oliver and Crook preach.

The Kansas City tent has been pitched at the corner of Cherry and 6th Sts. on June 1st. All the meetings in the hall 1333 Grand Ave. have been suspended while the tent meetings were in progress, excepting the Lord's day morning meeting and the Sunday school and Bible class at 3 p.m., conducted by Mr. Baker.

OUR RECORD, NOVEMBER 1900

Colorado Springs, Col. - Since taking down the tent, Bro. McKellar has been devoting his time to street preaching and cottage meetings. A little company now gather to remember the Lord there. Our brother is looking longingly toward some needy places still farther west.

Punxsutawney, Pa. - The conference meetings here were well attended, and the ministry helpful. Brethren W.P. Douglas and Kendrick were the only ones of those given exclusively to the ministry of the Word who came to help, but God was with them.

Standish, Mich - The conference here well attended, and the meetings good. Brethren Munro, Smith, Douglas, Muir, Kay, and A. McDonald were the preachers present. The town was crazy over politics, but God brought out quite a few unsaved, and we trust results for eternity will follow.

Victoria Road, Ont. - Brother Binch has been spending some time here with the Two Roads chart. He says, "The testimony in this place is the result of the labors of

Brethren McClure, Telfer, Faulknor, Douglas, and others during the past fourteen or fifteen years. I purpose going on as long as the roads continue favorable, three nights during the week and twice on Lord's day, visiting the saints around, as the Lord gives strength and opportunity. Will value much the prayers of the Lord's people for the work in these parts."

OUR RECORD, MAY 1906

[An excerpt from a letter from Dr. J. Norman Case, now in China. He describes the martyrdom of Mr. & Mrs. Kingham and their little girl] - "As we view things, Mr. Kingham could ill be spared from the groups of workers known to us in Kiangsi. Some in the States and Canada will remember our martyred friends. He was a young man of exceptional grace and devotion, and Mrs. Kingham was a devoted wife, mother and missionary. . . Many fear that a time of special trial is at hand for Christians and missionaries in China."

Texas - Special efforts are to be made this summer in tents. The season is longer here than in more northerly climates. It was expected that this month there would be a tent pitched in Waxapachie, and also one in Dallas. Other places are in view, too, before the close of the season. Bro. Bush will be helped in the one tent by D.R. Charles and Bro. Dean, in the other by J.G. Charles. May the Lord give much blessing in all places visited.

OUR RECORD, DECEMBER 1911

London, Ont. A letter from here says they had helpful ministry at the conference, held at Thanksgiving. "Training the young and reaching them with the Gospel," and such like subjects were taken up, it is said, with help and profit. There was a good attendance Sunday and Monday.

Peterboro, Ont. The annual meetings here, while not large, were good. The laboring brethren who came were helped of God in the Word ministered. Our esteemed brother, W.P. Douglas, is far from being strong yet, and we bespeak the continued fellowship in prayer for his full restoration.

Hamilton, Ont., Conference. The 37th annual convention of Christians gathered to the Name here, will (D.V.) be held on January 19, 20 and 21, 1912. Prayer meeting, Thursday, 7:30 p.m., and Friday all day will be held in Gospel Hall, 140 McNab Street. On Saturday and Lord's Day meetings will be held in Association Hall, James Street South. Circulars from W. Duncan, Dundurn Park.

Kansas City Conference. As noted last month the annual conference will be held here at Christmas time. The exact dates are as follows: Prayer meeting on Saturday evening, December 23rd, at 7:45. Meetings Sunday, Monday and Tuesday, December 24th, 25th and 26th, three times daily as usual. Meetings will be held in the Midland Building, 711 Walnut Street. Strangers take Independence Avenue car from Depot to Walnut Street, and walk one block north. Further information may be had by addressing "Conference," 617 Wyandotte Street.

OUR RECORD, JANUARY 1913

Kinde, Mich. Messrs. Dobbin and McGeachy had a few weeks' meetings in the hall seven miles from here. Bad roads hindered the people getting out. But those who did attend enjoyed the Word. Mr. Dobbin has gone to Saganaw, and purposes, D.V., later joining Bro. Touzeau in work in Canada. - Los Angeles. "Brethren

Hunter and McClure are expected here for our four days' conference at Christmas and will go on for the two days' meetings at Monrovia. We also hope to see our young brethren, Hillis and Greer. Pray for California." - Port Angeles, Wash. Messrs. W.M. Rae and C.H. Willoughby have had some fairly good meetings here. Have found a few of God's people, and so go on for a little while. May rent a hall for a few meetings at the other end of the city.

OUR RECORD, FEBRUARY 1919

[Following World War I an epidemic of influenza or "flu" swept through Europe and North America and thousands died. The following notices show the effect on the Brethren:]

Berry Creek, Alta. - Leonard Swan, son of Mr. G.A. Swan of Portugal, died of influenza in the military camp at Sarcee. We also parted with our young sister, Mrs. H. Collings, who fell asleep in Jesus, leaving a husband and young babe.

Everett, Wash. - Our brother, Walter Cuttle, died here, aged 36, after but a few day's illness of the "flu." Leaves a widow and two little girls. Dr. Martin spoke at the funeral.

Hamilton, Ont. - On Dec. 24 our brother, Hubert Wilmot, died, aged 26. Saved five years ago, and in fellowship at Rosslyn Ave. Gospel Hall, he left a good record. Remember his unsaved relatives, to whom he preached the Word ere he died.

Hastings, Ia. - Our young brother, Clarence McClary, went home to the Lord, aged 25, on Dec. 18. Saved only September last, he witnessed a good confession. Leaves wife and child. Brn. Charles and Lindeman spoke at funeral.

Corona, L.I., N.Y. - On Jan. 6th our young brother, Inkerman Collins, aged 15, after about 24 hours' illness, went to be with Jesus. Saved while W.H. McWhirter was reading God's Word to him five years ago, he has been a bright case. Bro. J. Lyon spoke at his burial.

OUR RECORD, MARCH 1920

Kenora, Ont. Our brother, J.J. Rouse of Vancouver, has been here and held a number of weeks of meetings. There is a small assembly and they have had a few gospel meetings, but the people come out well, and although the cold was intense, ranging from 20 to 45 below zero, and several of them got frosted toes and ears, still they came, and God saved a number of them and they are a happy, rejoicing lot.

OUR RECORD, NOVEMBER 1921

E. Orange, N.J. - Eleven were baptized who professed to get saved in the tent at Bloomfield, N.J., conducted by Bro. James Marshall and four others with them, who had already been baptized, were received into the E. Orange assembly.

Kansas City, Mo. - C.W. Ross was at Omaha, and has gone on to Texas for the conferences.

Los Angeles, Calif. - W.J. McClure is again in these parts. 1834 W. 41st place will find him.

Palisade, Neb. - Bro. J.O. Brown has moved here to help in the Lord's work. The Horn Bros. keep plodding on in the Gospel.

Our brother Jose B. Rey, saved in Spain . . . has now removed to Albuquerque, N.M., where he is laboring among the Spanish-speaking people, giving them Spanish tracts and preaching the Word to them.

OUR RECORD, OCTOBER 1924

Kanorado, Kans. - This place is in the extreme western part of Kansas, near the border of Colorado, while Perry is on the east side of the state. A few years ago a brother moved into Kanorado from another part of the state. Gospel meetings were held and God worked, so that now a company gather to the Name there. They have built a hall, and the conference this year "opened" it. At these meetings were Brn. Jas. Erskine, C.W. Ross, John and David Horn, and D.R. Charles. Saints came from Denver and Longmont, Colo., Palisade, Neb., and from points in Kansas, and the meetings are reported as "helpful and wholesome."

Astoria, N.Y. - A new Gospel Hall was "opened" by having a three day conference, Aug. 30 to Sept. 1. The hall is situated at 4th and Astoria Aves., Astoria, and all surface cars transfer to Flushing Ave. cars from 2nd St. Ferry or Steinway Ave. cars from 59th St., New York. All subway cars transfer to Astoria subway, get off at Hoyt Ave. Station. Three minutes walk to Fourth Ave. Hall.

The Gospel Car in which our Brethren Sheldrake and Mehl are going from place to place in Northern Michigan with the Gospel is proving useful. They visited Rudyard, where they had the tent last season, and went on, calling at Trout Lake. They're passing through "new" territory as they go, and found opportunity to preach to tourists at the camping grounds by the way.

Los Angeles, Calif. - Bro. W.J. McClure (c.o. 5444 Hillcrest Dr.) is holding forth in the tent still, having at present put up his dispensational chart. The meetings are continuing large, in fact increasing in size, and the brethren are exercized to get a hall in which to continue the work so auspiciously begun, as it is ten miles from the Gospel Hall, 1225 Jefferson St. It may be needful to build.

OUR RECORD, AUGUST 1926

Ferndale, Mich. - The tent used last year in Ferndale is pitched in Pontiac, Mich., this season, and being worked by Br. A. Stewart and D. McGeachy. There has been help in the attendance by friends from Ferndale and Royal Oak, with occasionally some from Detroit, but the people of the town have not responded very heartily. Our brethren are moving the tent to Ferndale.

The Bible Carriage worked by Brn. W. Ferguson and Geo. Smith has been visiting some outlying places for the distributing of Gospel tracts and the holding of meetings in the open air, as well as in schools, homes, etc. Remember such work before the Lord.

Michigan City, Ind. - Our brethren, Charles R. Keller and Robt. Curry, are here under canvas, and have been going on nightly (except Saturday) at the corner of Michigan and Jackson Streets. They get a good hearing on Sunday nights, with a smaller crowd other nights. Altogether, by printed page and otherwise many hear the Gospel.

Scotch Plain, N.J. - Brn. C. Patrizio and L. Rosania have their tent pitched here among a number of Italian families, and their hope is to see God's hand at work among them. They are all Catholics and by virtue of the teaching of that corrupt system, idolators - but God's gospel is the remedy.

OUR RECORD, SEPT. 1928

Philadelphia, Pa. - Copies of letters have been sent us from here, telling of mutual confessions and much prayer, leading to reconciliation between assemblies of God's people, meeting in various parts of Philadelphia and Collingdale, who have been estranged for six years. In all such efforts to nulify the enemy's work all saints loyal to the truth will rejoice, and pray that the stamp of divine reality may be manifestly upon it. Two meetings at Hammonton, J.J., also who have walked apart for some time, have become one in their testimony for God. For all this we thank God! To divide God's people, and foster a spirit of division is Satan's work. To heal the breaches among the saints is of God. "Behold how good and how pleasant it is for brethren to dwell together in unity."

WORDS IN SEASON, MARCH 1929

Toronto - A. Livingston had meetings in the West Toronto Hall, Bro. Steweart in the Swanwick Hall. Bro. Telfer had his "Two Roads" chart up in Pape Ave. Meetings were large; some professed; but the meetings were closed because of a breakdown in health. The Dr. ordered a complete rest.

LIGHT & LIBERTY, MARCH 1931

Bro. Alfred Gibbs had ten days of children's meetings at Waterloo, Iowa, closing Feb. 13. He used lantern slides of Bible subjects. The attendance and interest were good.

Everett, Washington - Brother Neil Fraser has been conducting nightly meetings for three weeks. His meetings have been well attended and there is evidence of considerable blessing. Christians have been refeshed, some restored to fellowship and four or five of the young folks have confessed Christ. We have not had such good meetings since 1920 when our Brethren C.W. Ross and William Rae had tent mewetings on the site where our hall now stands.

Knox, Ind. Meetings go on here with interest and blessing. The attendance has greatly increased in our regular Gospel meetings. About 35 strangers were out last Sunday night; three professed faith in Christ the week before. Our Sunday school has increased 150% and a number of scholars have been saved since last fall.

West Palm Beach, Florida - A Christian assembly was formed here about five years ago and there has been a steady work of grace all these years, nothing spectacular, but a slow, steady, solid growth. A Sunday school has been formed with fifty children on the roll.

ASSEMBLY ANNALS, MARCH 1934

Sault Ste. Marie, Ont. Luigi Rosania writes: "Thank God, the Lord's work among the Italians is still going on good. In spite of all the opposition from the Italian Catholic priest (who in his preaching told the people not to come to the meetings and to burn all the books and calendars I have given them) we see new ones come in every night to hear the gospel. The Russellites are also trying to hinder the people from coming. Like Herod and Pilate . . . so it is with these people. They seem to be working with the Catholics. A few more souls have professed to be saved, and others are very much interested. The weather is intensely cold, sometimes 24 below zero, but still the Italians come out well."

LIGHT & LIBERTY, DECEMBER 1935

Wm. Ingram writes: "Have been holding forth in the gospel to appreciative audiences in school houses and farm houses on the prairie. The last week of October the snow came and it has been blowing a blizzard for about a couple of weeks now, and temperatures gone down to twenty below. It was difficult carrying on in the blizzard, as the winter came so suddenly and unexpectedly. Usually one is several miles from a school house and the trip has to be made in an open sleigh drawn by horses.

"The soul of the people is much discouraged in these parts, because of the way. Crop conditions have been poorer than ever, and it is sad indeed to see many so ill prepared for the long cold winter. Little children with broken shoes and not properly clothed is a most unfortunate condition in a cold climate like this."

ASSEMBLY ANNALS, JUNE 1937

Missouri - "On Saturday afternoons the country people all go in town and in Marionville they have a big drawing from tickets which the merchants give out so there is a large anxious crowd. Before the drawing we have opportunity to give out hundreds of gospel papers and after the drawing have an open air meeting. The tracts are received with readiness and people thank you for them. They have a similar drawing in another little town called Billings, and if we get through with meetings in time in Marionville we go there and have another meeting. It takes a big supply of tracts to keep up this work. It might be that some Christians have boxes or drawers full in their homes they would like to put in use; if so we would be glad to put them to work for them. We desire your prayers on behalf of the work here."

Thomas R. McCullagh, Springfield, Mo.

LIGHT & LIBERTY, MAY 1940

We are glad to hear . . . of a work carried on by brother J. C. Thompson of North Bay, Ont. Mr. Thompson is manager of a lumber mill but finds many opportunities to serve the Lord. Besides a Sunday school at North Bay he conducts a service in the jail. He visits the Old People's Home regularly. During each week he conducts meetings in the rural communities. We thank God for numbers of business men in the Assemblies who are exercized and are reaching out with the gospel as does this brother.

Oswald MacLeod and Wm. M. McBride were in their fifth week of meetings at Hickory, N.Carolina. The attendance and interest has been quite varied, the children's meetings are a source of encouragement. A noonday meeting which has been convened at a factory for some weeks is very encouraging, the interest here seems to be greater than at the hall. In these days when it appears so hard to get sinners to come in, it may be well for all of us to follow the example of these and other breathren and "go" out into the highways and byways and compel them to partake of the gospel "feast."

WORDS IN SEASON, JULY 1943

Brawside, B.C. - Alex McGaughey expects to follow up the work begun in this place. About 26 persons who came to his previous meetings gather every Lord's Day for a Bible reading and Sunday school for children. Some have expressed a desire to be baptized, so our brother hopes to return to lead them on in obedience to the Word of God. He also purposes to open up new work in Prairiedale where a man promised him the community hall to preach the Gospel. This work deserves the full fellowship of the Lord's people.

WORDS IN SEASON, OCTOBER 1945

Washington, Pa. - J. Govan and A. Klabunda had a tent pitched here. They visited 500 homes with announcements and tracts without much response and a good deal of opposition, but did a good work among the children, teaching them the Scriptures.

Maryland - W.F. Hunter visited Cumberland and Frostburg; five were baptized in Frostburg and one in Cumberland. Since then he has had a week of meetings in Camden, N.J., and one week in Barrington, N.J.

Lynden, Wash. - Hector Alves and Wallace Cudmore are having the first series of meetings in the new hall here. The attendance is beyond their expectations and they look to see a visitation of the Lord at this time.

Los Angeles, Calif. - Mr. Whiteman, who has been for some years a missionary in Manila, and who has recently been released from a Japanese internment camp, is visiting the assemblies in this city telling of his experiences while there.

Sault Ste. Marie, Ont. - Gordon Johnston and F. Carboni closed their tent meetings August 26th. After seven weeks plodding they were able to rejoice over a few souls who had professed faith in our Lord Jesus Christ and seemed to have some desire to please Him.

LETTERS OF INTEREST, JAN. 1947

Brother Theodor Williams, Sr., who has come to Chicago to labor among the colored people, is still unable to find a home for his family. He labors here while his family remains in Michigan. A young colored boy of 19 attended the Chicago conference with brother Williams. He was in the colored assembly morning meeting the next Sunday and looked on for the first time as the Christians remembered the Lord. At the close of the meeting he said, "I have been longing and looking for the truth . . . Someone told me about the A. church and I went there, but could not find what my heart longed for . . . The Lord kept me from joining them and brought me here from St. Paul, Minn., to find the truth."

LETTERS OF INTEREST, JUNE 1948

Brother Harold Harper was in Kenilworth, N.J. in April, seeking to help the young believers in the assembly. Quite a number professed here when brother

L. Wilson had meetings in January. We understand the assembly in Kenilworth have their Sunday morning meeting at 9:15 a.m. - - at 11:00 a.m. they have a meeting especially for the neighborhood called the Family Bible Hour. The Gospel is preached and the Word ministered. On Sunday, April 21, there were 300 at this meeting by count. Some assemblies are finding that neighborhood people come out in the mornings more readily than in the evenings. Brother Harper, writing to a friend, says regarding the assembly at Kenilworth, "The Lord hath done great things here, for His name's sake."

LETTERS OF INTEREST, FEB. 1950

Ruth H. Valentine writes from Immanuel Mission, Shiprock, N.M. - "Our school has doubled in number this year over last. Fourteen youngsters live with us for six days in the week. We have a new teacher, too. A fine Christian young lady from Pennsylvania, Miss Lucille Frey. Then there are two Indian babies we are raising. Miss Varder's little Mary is now age two. And little Priscilla, age seven months, has fallen to me to raise. Her mother did not want her and gave her to me. She's been sickly since birth but is now growing strong. It is our desire they be special lights for Him.

LETTERS OF INTEREST, MARCH 1953

Ernest Woodhouse writes - "The past months have been busy with meetings as far apart as Spanish Wells in the Bahamas to North Bay in Ontario. Two young people who came 200 miles for the metings in North Bay were soundly saved and are brightly progressing. A middle-aged woman professed faith in Christ at conference meetings in Sea Cliff, N.Y. Series on Philippians and Jude were given over a period of a few weeks in Toronto. In the weeks that lie ahead campaigns are planned for Greenwood Gospel Chapel in Toronto and for Durham, N. Carolina, God willing."

LETTERS OF INTEREST, MARCH 1954

David Brinkman reports, "We continue to seek to reach out with the gospel by means of public address system, Bible signs on the highways, film evangelism, tract distribution, and going into new towns with gospel efforts. Recently we placed 112 more Bible signs on the highways. In a small sawmill town in south Georgia we preached by public address system and then showed our gospel films to both colored and white. I was also able to show the pictures to 250 school children, and to preach the gospel to them. On this trip I cooked and slept in my little tent, but due to the cold and swamps all around took sick. My age makes it hard for me to rough it."

LETTERS OF INTEREST, OCTOBER 1958

Anchorage, Alaska - Our meetings are now held in the Northern Lights Boulevard Gospel Hall, corner of Northern Lights Boulevard and Blueberry Lane, Spenard, Aanchorage.

North Atlanta Gospel Chapel - We had Woody Murphy with us for a week of DVBS during which five boys and girls professed to be saved. Recently we baptized a teenage girl, also a newly saved young married man. After the baptism his wife was saved. The same week a young girl, also in her teens, accepted Christ.

Odessa (Texas) Bible Chapel - The Daily Vacation Bible School was held at the chapel with about 150 children registered and an average attendance of 110. We closed the school with a Saturday picnic for 107 of the children at the sand hills and a program at the chapel Sunday night at which many of the parents were present. We believe some of the children were saved.

Bro. O.C. Tillman reports from Buffalo, N.Y. - The Lord answered prayer in the procuring of a store front for Gospel preaching to the colored people of this area.

Rent on this store front is taken care of for three months through God's people at Elmwood Chapel. Pray that the Lord will supply the necessary equipment: piano, platform, pulpit, material for curtains, and paint. The classes in the home continue, two for children and one for adults. There have been professions of the Lord Jesus as Savior among some of the older children. Mr. T. Michael Flowers of Sevannah, Ga., visited recently and is coming back to give us some help.

LETTERS OF INTEREST, MARCH 1959

Len Galpin reports from Prince Rupert, B.C. - Since September our Sunday school has grown steadily from 40 to 79, putting a heavy strain on the few teachers we have. We ask prayer for more workers. A young couple from West Vancouver is desirous of moving here but have not as yet been able to sell their home. Pray for them. The Gospel meetings have been well attended. We have a good group of teen-age young people who attend meetings regularly and show much interest. We are looking to the Lord for our own building as the union hall used for Sunday school is fast becoming too small. Pray that the work of the Lord will continue and that souls will be saved.

LIGHT & LIBERTY, APRIL 1960

Milo VandeKrol - I am beginning a series of meetings at the Gospel Hall in Ottumwa, Iowa, using the Scene-O-Felt as a drawing attraction for the young folks. Following this we plan to have the same kind of meetings in Eddyville, Albia, and Waterloo, Iowa. We are having weekly Bible classes in our home in Oskaloosa, and interest has been encouraging. We are exercized about a further Gospel effort in this city, and are looking to the Lord to provide a suitable building or meeting place.

John A.W. Halliday (El Paso, Texas) reports real encouragement in the work among Mexicans near the Mexican border. Permission has also been granted to distribute Christian literature at the U.S. Reception Center for Mexican farm workers.

David Ward (Mystic, Conn.) - During the month of February, just finished, I have been ministering in connection with the local assembly at Groton. Interest has been good in the regular meetings and much valuable work accomplished in the visitation. This past week-end we held our annual winter retreat for young people and the Lord gave us a profitable time together.

ASSEMBLY ANNALS, SEPT. 1960

New Brunswick - During July and August our brethren Blackwood and Wilkie had a wooden tent pitched in Riverview, a new town across the river from Moncton. The meetings were poorly attended by adults from that community, but the Monday night meetings for children brought in a fair number. Several professed to be saved.

Our brother E.B. Sprunt has spent some time in California. He purposes to have meetings for children in some of the gatherings in Michigan this fall. A communication received Aug. 24 states James Stewart from India is in Toronto. Pearcy and Dart are seeing blessing in Milton, Ont., R. Crawford and G. Wilson are still in Hopewell, Virginia. F.W. Schwartz had appreciated meetings in Victoria, Va.

LETTERS OF INTEREST, APRIL 1962

J.W. Gibb, Belmont, Mass., reports: "On ships bearing the Liberian or Panamanian flags is found very often a rather mixed crew. This was the case on the Cities Service Traveler which consisted of Finnish, Norwegian, Italian, Spanish and Americans. With the help of my emergency kit (carried at all times for just such cases as this), these men were all given some portion of the Word or message thereof in their own language. I also had some fine opportunities to speak to individuals."

Ketchikan, Alaska - "For a few months last year we sought to help a little with the work in Anchorage. In November my wife and I came to Ketchikan in the S.E. Panhandle where there is no assembly testimony. We trust the woek will be prospered by the Lord and soon we may see a little company gathered together in His Name." - John E. Abernathy

Arkona, Ontario - "We ministered here in the assembly in Arkona from the 1st of October to the end of December. During that period at the regular meetings a series of messages were given with the chart 'Eternity To Eternity.' We have also been able to start a teen-agers group on Saturday nights, and a boys and girls hobby class on Monday nights for the 10-14 age group. Through these avenues we are reaching a goodly number of young people outside the assembly with the Gospel." - Ernie Belch.

LETTERS OF INTEREST, APRIL 1964

"An unusual opportunity was mine recently with an alcoholic who had sought to end her life with an overdose of sleeping pills. She seemed to respond to the message of a Saviour's power to break her thralldom. As is too frequetly the case, she has no help from a husband who has the same failures; though he too has been our patient for serious stomach surgery and should be impressed by the near call that he had." - Robert Arthur, Tacoma, Washington.

Paul Bitler reports from New York - "A baptism is to be held this week. One of those to be baptized is a daughter of a sister in our Spanish Manhattan assembly. The Mother had been saved some years ago through reading the Sunday school papers that the children brought home. She has gone on faithfully for the Lord despite opposition at times in her home. Now she has the joy of seeing her sixteen-year-old daughter baptized. A man from the Bronx assembly will be baptized also."

Cochrane, Ont. - "A young Indian man for whom we've been praying came to our house at 10:30 one night seeking salvation, and we pointed him to the Lord. Pray for this young Indian as he is gifted in music and it will be hard for him to break away from the old world. He is also very popular among the young people." Lawrence Buchanan

WORDS IN SEASON, APRIL 1965

Waianie, Hawaii - Our brother Francis Vendetta, who moved here recently seeking to further the work of the Gospel, continues with the children's work. They have had over fifty children's meetings, interest good. He has built an 8 x 10 Bible trailer which will seat 30 people and hoped to commence here five nights a week. Pray for him.

Clyde, Ohio - Bre. Norman Crawford and John Slabaugh have had seven weeks of meetings here of late - nice interest and a few have professed. Bro. Slabaugh just did this in connection with his daily work. He is from Akron. We feel this is very commendable and this sort of thing should be encouraged.

Garnavillo, Iowa - Bre. Brandt and Wahls saw a few profess at Bloomer, Wisc. Bre. Elliot and Orr of Hitesville were to try again in Graettinger. Bre. Mick and Hamilton were in Blue River, Wisc, sowing the good seed.

LETTERS OF INTEREST, DECEMBER 1967

Fernand St.Louis, Montmagny, Que. - We are occasionally holding meetings in a village 70 miles east of Montmagny - St.Pascal de Kamouraska. At least three people have come to know Christ. Itinerant work is also part of my ministry since there are quite a few assemblies without a "full-time" worker. Please also remember continually in your prayers our French radio ministry, La Foi Vivifiante, that we intend to carry on as the Lord leads. More than ever before will this ministry be important as so many French people need to be followed up.

Dan Smith, Vancouver - Besides the privilege of seeing some saved, this itinerary has afforded me these special joys. One is the new assembly at Golden, Tex., now housed in a remodeled barracks given by R.G. LeTourneau. It's commodious and comfortable enough. The singing there is lively and wholehearted to the Lord. The believers know the truth of grace, the sweetness of the Lord Jesus, and are in love with Him and with one another.

Another special was hearing a young man burst out in a truly annointed expression of worship following a wee message I had given. It is many a day since I heard such a spirit-energized word, such bubbling spontaneity, in worship. May the Lord give us much more of this among young and old.

Still another special was to see a broken family reconciled to the indescribable joy of the children.

WORDS IN SEASON, JUNE 1968

Iowa - There is talk of bro. Paisley, with bro. Warke, working a large tent again in the Waterloo - Cedar Falls area near U.S. 20, Pray about this, as well as any other tent efforts, etc. We regret that we have had NO reports of any pioneer work being attempted in these United States this past Winter of a definite kind. Assemblies have had many preachers but the country lies wide open. This is a pity.

Huntsville, Ont. - Brethren here ask us to inform visitors to bring proper Letters of Commendation, as many Summer visitors come here. They also request "modest apparel" as in 1 Tim. 2:9,10. We welcome brethren walking in the "old paths." Have enjoyed visits recently from brethren brethren Ramsay, Steele of Japan, Paisley and Gray.

INTEREST, JANUARY 1971

Lawrence Darling, San Antonio, Tex. - Recently we started working one night a week at a clinic for dope addicts. These are all hard-core heroin addicts. The Christian doctor puts them on methadone, a non-habit forming drug, to help them off the addiction. Margaret has a group of ladies, some of them addicts and some of them wives of the addicts. I have a Bible study with the advanced ones who are most promising. We take a simple lesson in What the Bible Teaches. We have found the work both depressing and rewarding.

Henry Sanchez, Brooklyn, NY - One week recently I had both a happy and a sad experience. I had the joy of baptizing a teenage boy who was saved through our youth work at Pine-bush Camp two years ago. He is now in fellowship and helping in our childrens work. In the same week I spoke at the graveside of a teenage girl who died of an overdose of drugs. She too went to camp and had made a profession of faith but could not break loose from the devil's trap in which she found herself.

Jack Heseltine, Cosmopolis, Wash. - In October I conducted two weeks of meetings in Boise, Idaho, with meetings on the subject, "That I May Know Him." This assembly has just completed a remodeling program with many beneficial improvements. Already an increase in the Sunday School is indicated and a real desire to see God's blessing is evident. These meetings were climaxed by a baptism of six young people on Sunday afternoon.

INTEREST, MAY 1973

D.Claude Loney, Agincourt, Ont. - We are continuing to study the scriptures with two of our neighbors who were saved last November. They have recently experienced some difficult times and they realize more than ever the need to fellowship with other Christians and the necessity of daily reading and praying. We are discovering other neighbors who are showing a little interest in the Bible. We hope that we can encourage that interest and eventually begin to study the scriptures with them.

Peter Foggin, Chicoutimi, Que. - I continue my work of teaching and reaching students as a professor of geography in the Universite du Quebec a Chicoutimi. We believe that for the present time at any rate this is definitely the Lord's will. Although time is most certainly at a premium, there are some definite advantages in serving the Lord in this capacity. For one thing, Christians and unbelievers alike are unable to say or think that "he is doing it because it is his job" as they sometimes do when they talk or think of the activity and efforts of the "full-time worker." In addition, we have the opportunity to have very natural relationships with professors and students that it would be impossible to have otherwise. Beth and I meet with two other professors and their wives, for example, every two or three weeks for supper followed by a Bible study (we're in John's gospel). Please pray with us that these friends might come to know Christ personally as Savior and Lord.

INTEREST, SEPTEMBER 1975

C. Gordon Kyle, Chaplain, APO N.Y. - The Bible conference for service people at Berchtesgaden was a blessing to many. We had over 400 in attendance, most being single soldiers. It was plenty of work, and I'm still completing after-action matters re. the conference. I have been asked to be the conference director in 1976.

W. Rick Knox, Prospect Heights, Ill. - July 1 we shall be joining the staff of Literature Crusades. Our primary responsibility is to be houseparents for young people in the Christian Life Development program. That means that from September to April we will have up to six new members in our family. These newest additions will be post-high school fellows and/or girls who desire to learn how to make biblical teaching and principles an integral part of their daily lives.

LeRoy Beverly, Ellsworth, Maine - Praise the Lord with us for five who followed the Lord in baptism last Sunday, and for their growth in Him. There were two young men from the Navy base, two ladies and our youngest son, David. It was a time of joy and fellowship, as well as testimony. There were some unsaved relatives there.

WORDS IN SEASON, JUNE 1976

Glen Ewen, Sask. - Saints here carry on in godly ways - we can continue to pray for these more or less isolated assemblies that God shall help them in their testimony to His Name.

Thunder Bay, Ont. - Bro. A. Thompson had two weeks recently, three professed, others were interested. Also had a previous visit from bro. Robert Boyle with helpful ministry.

Barrington, N.J. - Saints here had visits from bre. Saward, also McCann (en route to S.A.), also bro. Harding. The monthly ministry meeting well attended, bre. William Ferguson and William Oliver helped in ministry. Saints of Pennsahken nearby attended. They have had some good visits from brethren enroute also. One professed at their recent meetings.

INTEREST, OCTOBER 1976

Arthur Billups, Buffalo, N.Y. - Ellicott Center ("Inner-City Christian Services") has been in existence for six years. During that time we have experienced success, failure, discouragement and frustration. In inner-city work there is a particular set of obstacles that must be overcome. Black Americans have been despised, rejected and neglected both socially and spiritually. When any person has been rejected as worthless he will have a difficult time receiving or giving love, or even loving himself. Most of the young people have never experienced a father/mother family relationship, which results in lack of parental discipline and leads to many social problems. Even in our work we have not been able to bridge this lack of parental guardian concern and involvement. God and Christianity are viewed in terms of whiteness and establishment, producing an almost anti-God segment of our American society. God has placed us here to represent Him. Our aim is to give a visual, verbal display of what New Testament Christianity is all about.

Wayne Schlichter, Hamilton, Ohio - We are encouraged to see the hand of the Lord in our midst at Ross, and are grateful for what has taken place since moving into this converted farmhouse. We can seat 60, and last week, with several families gone, we had to send the small children out during the opening of Family Bible Hour. If this situation continues we are going to have to extend the meeting room. There is good interest in the Bible study and prayer meeting. A number of individuals are involved in one-on-one discipling.

INTEREST, MARCH 1977

Cyril Shontoff, Lennoxville, Que. - We've been having some encouraging times in the French work. Four brethren have opened a coffee bar in Sherbrooke where people come in for free coffee and are given the gospel by personal testimony, film, music, etc. It is very informal and many young people come and several have been saved.

George Rainey, Plymouth, Mich. - I thank my Father for His care and for open doors during the past year. While we saw larger meetings here and there than in former days, we see fewer coming to Christ.

Gordon Strom, Seattle - We are in our third year in the Seattle area and are very much aware of the ministry needs of the area. We have given ourselves to assisting the elders of two Vancouver local churches to evaluate and shape their perspective on shepherding - including evangelism on a personal level and the establishing of young believers in the basic biblical roles in their respective families and in the body of Christ.

David Pollock, Mullens, West Virginia - We have lived in this coal-mining area of West Virginia almost seventeen years, doing pioneering. The past few years have evidenced considerable growth. Attendance at the Family Bible Hour averages 100 or so, with several unsaved attending. There are many younger families and there seems to be interest, if not hunger, in several lives. We have had the joy of seeing a good number saved and desire now to see them go on in the things of the Lord.

INTEREST, JANUARY 1979

Henry Peterson, Inglewood, Calif. - Fifty-one elders from 14 southern California assemblies met for our first Elder's Retreat at Verdugo Pines Bible Camp on Sept. 22 & 23. All felt the messages, panels, discussions and warm fellowship were very worthwhile. In the informal prayer time, under the blue mountain sky, we came to know each other and our Lord just a little better.

John Williams, Vancouver, B.C. - We are building quite a large extension onto our facility at Lambrick Park Church. The work is growing and we need more room. We are especially encouraged in almost a doubled enrolment in our Sunday School. This gives good community contact.

Charles G. Coleman, Falls Church, Virginia - After a summer of youth camp work for both my wife and me, we have launched into a busy fall schedule of teaching in local assemblies, speaking at youth retreats and adult meetings, and writing. We also find ourselves involved in fostering and coordinating a needed "gift development" program in our local chapel.

Van Hairgrove, San Diego, Calif. - The migrant work is still a joy to do. The people who come over from Mexico to work on farms in southern California are very kind to take our literature. We are giving out more and more English tracts. I don't know if it is curiousity or hunger for the Word.

INTEREST, JANUARY 1980

Donovan Case, Wentzville, Missouri - On October 7, after speaking at the Walnut Park assembly in St. Louis, a 17-year old man came forward and accepted Christ. I was told that the next Sunday his sister came to the assembly and said she wanted what her brother got the week before, for he was a changed person. Praise the Lord! During September and October we taught a series on Nehehiah at a small black church. It was encouraging to see so many young people taking notes and so keen on studying God's Word.

Arnot P. McIntee, St. Catharines, Ont. - "The Living Word For the Dying World" was the theme of the twentieth annual Radio Conference of the Family Bible Hour held October 27. During afternoon and evening sessions the Lord's voice was heard with clarion clearness as the desperate need of the dying world was presented by J. Boyd Nicholson, Alan Adams and Audley McLean.

Don Dunkerton, Oak Park, Illiois - Emmaus is to be represented at URBANA 79 this December. Two students will join me at the booth as we seek to make contacts with many young people, both for the Correspondence School and for the Day School.

Candido DeSousa, Ossining, N.Y. - The Portuguese work at Harrison, New Jersey, is going well. Recently four believers were baptized and a lady has made a profession of faith.

INTEREST, OCTOBER 1981

David Ward, Mystic, Conn. - We would appreciate prayer for an area-wide crusade, November 1 to 8, here in the Groton area. I have been asked to serve as general chairman and our chapel will be heavily involved. The evangelist is Ralph Bell, a Billy Graham associate. We are looking to see many people reached and saved. We are thrilled that Billy Graham will be coming to New England for a three-week effort in May 1982. God is doing a mighty work in these states and it is exciting to be on the cutting edge.

Peter Dillon, Cupertino, Calif. - Twenty to twenty-five come regularly to the Spanish Sunday School class and to our week-night study. Many are new believers and five were baptized in May. At a retreat in May Daniel Lozano of Grace Community Church was the speaker. Two persons came to know the Lord at that time. Theme of the retreat was consistency. Pray that we will be consistent and faithful Christians.

Doug Crabb, Helena, Montana - I just got back from Wilderness Camp. Rick Norman spoke at evening campfires on the life of Moses and I took up the subject of Consequences and Rewards. There was an excellent attitude and good feedback. Pray for one of the fellows who was in his fourth year at camp. He goes into the navy this fall, is still not saved and is nervous about some spiritual considerations.

INTEREST, APRIL 1983

Betty McGeehee, Cincinnati, Ohio - In December the bank granted [the use of their auditorium for a downtown Bible class]. We were delighted to have two consecutive lunch hour studies with business and professional women. Again in January we were granted one Tuesday, and we had a combined attendance of one hundred. It is a joy to see Christian girls - some quite new in the Lord - bringing their fellow workers to hear the Word of God. But we feel we have only touched the fringe of the needs of "downtowners" with their job pressures and uncertainties, in addition to the void within where the living Lord is not known.

Glen & Elizabeth Lightfoot, Burlington, Colo. - We have been "live," except on rare occasions, on KNAB radio here every Sunday, 9 to 9:15 a.m., for three years and we still hear good reports. We have heard of one person being saved and two families have come into the assembly as a direct result of the program.

INTEREST, JUNE 1984

Bob & Marie Weadge, Prospect Heights, Ill. - Two weeks ago we returned from a visit to Fall River, Nova Scotia where, Lord willing, we will begin our church planting ministry in late June. Our prayer concern at this point is for adequate housing. I have just attended an Evangelism Explosion clinic. What a positive learning experience it turned out to be. Many new tools were gained that will prove helpful in Fall River and wherever else we go.

William & Nadine Learoyd, Montreal, Que. - Last Sunday we baptized two young men before the worship service. What was unusual and encouraging about one of them was that his parents and three other relatives who had never seen the morning meeting were present. Unusally there is opposition in a family when one of them takes a stand. The father does not profess to be a Christian, but I have never seen a parent who seemed more happy than he on such an occasion.

Don & Krista Robertson, San Leandro, Calif. - Easter Sunday marks the kick off day for our new facilities at San Lorenzo Bible Chapel. After 18 months of meeting in homes, we have now gained access to Redwood Christian High School for our meetings. When we began in October 1982, there were just a few families, barely filling a living room. We prayed for the salvation of many of our friends and contacts. The Lord expanded our numbers until we filled the living room and other rooms besides. Each Sunday we moved out all the furniture to make more and more room until we were just bursting at the seams.

INTEREST, JUNE 1986

Tim & Yvonne Ayers, Milford, Mich. - Attendance continues to grow at Grace Countryside Church. Attendance at the two Easter morning services totaled 340 people. Evangelism Explosion teams plan to call on each new visitor. The assembly is investigating options for larger facilities.

Arnold & Janet Reynolds, Lennoxville, Que. - Arnold has been ministering both in French and English assemblies in Quebec. The French assemblies in Sherbrooke and Cookshire joined with other French evangelical churches in the district for a Gospel campaign May 9-21.

David Collins (Sea Cliff, N.Y.) led a discussion on the subject, "Marriage and Divorce." Various interpretations were analyzed, and participants were challenged to re-examine their own positions. Some emphasized the responsibility of local assemblies. Advance teaching and good examples are needed, they said, to help individuals avoid divorce.

WORDS IN SEASON, SEPT. 1987

Marysville, WA - Tent meetings held here in connection with the Arlington assembly, conducted by brethren Gaius Goff and Jonathan Procopio, ended on July 15 with a nice number professing, including three outsiders.

Garnavillo, IA - The young brethren of this assembly are having encouraging children's meetings in some of the surrounding towns, using a Bible Van. Children from the poor or broken homes have responded well, proving the truth of Scripture - "The poor have the gospel preached unto them."

Fergus Falls, MN - Brethren Robert Orr and Lloyd Ballhaged, Sr. finished tent meetings on July 28, in which a 12-year old professed. This gave the assembly, where only nine are in fellowship, a real lift.

Fort McMurray, Alta. - Brother Bryan Funston is busy with visitation among some of the Indian reservations in the district.

INTEREST, DECEMBER 1988

Stan & Joan Farmer, Hillsboro, NH - We continue to receive calls and letters about the Pressing Onward support groups for alcoholic, addicted and affected loved ones. These support groups constitute a key evangelistic tool for reaching hundreds in every community.

Mun & Adeline Hope, Aldergrove, B.C. - The Lord blessed richly during my recent visit to the Northwest Territories. I distributed tracts and Gospel booklets at Yellowknife and Inuvik. Over 100 people, mostly Inuit, greeted me in Inuvik and asked me to preach. Three adults confessed the Lord Jesus Christ afterward.

Cheryl Smith, Montreal, Que. - Much of my time is devoted to working with unreached segments of Montreal's 1.4 million women. Last year I began a Bible study group at a home for unwed pregnant teenagers. Recently I was also invited to help at a home for young prostitutes. The challenges in these ministries are great, but so are the rewards.

WORDS IN SEASON, SEPTEMBER 1989

LaCrosse, WI - Brother Richard Bruley of the LaCrosse Assembly and brother Calvin Erickson of the Mt. Sterling Assembly have been working among the H'mong children here, with between 60 to 80 children in each Monday night. There are around 2000 H'mong people in the LaCrosse area.

Taylorside, Sask. - Gospel meetings held in the Gospel Hall with brethren Robert Neill (South Africa) and Robert Boyle ended on July 30, without any known results in salvation.

Dawson Creek, B.C. - The recent conference was a encouragement to the saints and one of the largest in recent years with a number of brethren sharing in the ministry and gospel. Following the conference, 10,000 gospel texts and tracts were distributed throughout Dawson Creek and other neighboring towns, allowing further follow-up of interested contacts.

INTEREST, FEBRUARY 1990

Graham & Margaret Stokes, Okanagan Falls, B.C. - Roy & Lonita Boettcher from Bothell, Washington, joined us here for a week of special meetings. Services held at the local prison were attented by 25% of the convicts. A Prison Ministries Night at Preston Avenue Bible Chapel, Penticton, challenged the believers to prayer and activity in this area. A series of Bag Lunch Concerts also reached out to local business people.

John & DeLayne Berglund, Eagle Grove, IA - Faith Community Church had dwindled to four people when we moved here. But with an overhaul, including gearing the morning service to be seeker-oriented and changing the name, it's grown to about 50 adults and 20 children. Every Sunday unsaved people walk through our doors, and during the past few months four were saved - - that's how many there were total just a few years ago!

Marc & Germaine Oden, Philadelphia, PA - God has done some great things here! At our basketball tournament at LaSalle University 95 souls came to Christ. Our largest Youth Worker's Conference brought blessing to us as B. Sam Hart ministered the Word; nearly 250 participants from sixteen churches attended the Teen

Convention in Camden, New Jersey, and many dedicated their lives to Christ as a result of the large Youth Spectacular activities.

George & Betty Walker, N. Miami, FL - We have a "foreign mission field" right on our very doorstep, as there are over a million exiles here, all fleeing from different parts of Latin America. The five Spanish assemblies have fo;und enco;uragement as spiritual gifts are raised up and numbers added. Ovilo Diaz's work has been a great asset; his injury hurts the whole body of believers.

WORDS IN SEASON, JULY 1991

Clinton, Ont - Joseph St. Gospel Hall - As of the beginning of this month, brethren Alexander Dryburgh and Yvon Poirier have had five weeks of gospel meetings. They are continuing, and one young girl has professed. On May 31 three teenage girls obeyed the Lord in baptism.

Saugus, MA - Bible readings were held on the first weekend of June. Brethren Norman Crawford, A.M.S. Gooding, Harold Paisley, Thomas Meekin and David Oliver opened the readings with helpful exposition of the prophetic portions in Matthew 24 and 25. Brother Gooding was with the assembly for a number of nights taking up the seven parables of Matthew 13.

Punxsutawney, PA - Brethren William Seale, Jr. and John Dennison started tent meetings on May 19. Attendance has been encouraging. A man in his seventies is concerned. They are continuing into the fourth week.

UPLOOK, SEPTEMBER 1991

Brother Harold Preston of Lexington, KY, sends this news: . . . At present we are sending Bible study courses to about 165 jail and prison inmates in 20 institutions in East-Central and Eastern Kentucky. Many have professed to be saved through this ministry. Virginia Frasher, Vena and I do most of the work in getting these courses out. Pray that the Lord will send us some good, mature help to give me more time to visit inmates, and hopefully, get a Bible class started for inmates as they are released.

Brother Bill Bush of Claremont writes: The California Bible Conference's unique program combines a profitable Bible conference and an ideal vacation in one of our country's most popular and beautiful National Parks - Yosemite. . . This year, our brethren Boyd Nicholson, Sr., and William MacDonald treated us to profitable ministry and excellent, old-fashioned Gospel preaching. We know of four young people who trusted the Lord Jesus Christ.

Donald Norbie reports [from Colorado]: We are seeing some encouragement in the work here, but we long to see more being saved. And some who have professed Christ are struggling in their Christian growth. We long to see young believers develop into strong, stable Christians. Some have lived such undisciplined lives before conversion. The devil is constantly working to discourage and thwart the work of God. We realize we are in a spiritual battle. Do pray for these young believers.

INTEREST, FEBRUARY 1992

Tim & Sue Nielsen, Winnipeg - We had our annual Intertribal Christian Communications (Intercom) Banquet in November. About 600 people attended and we were powerfully challenged to be praying people as Vincent Yellow Old Woman spoke to us. . . . It is difficult to distinguish between Intercom and church life since much of our church ministry involves native people. The scenarios are different, but the basic needs of these people are all similar. They come from very dysfunctional families where Christian values were not taught, and as a result life has bee very harsh for them. Sue is having regular Bible studies with three native ladies, all of whom have given up a child in the last year.

Michael & Cindy Lax, Ventnor, NJ - In December we rejoiced to have over 120 Jewish people attend one of our Friday night services. A group called "Sound of Joy" sang and the Gospel was presented. Four professions of faith were made, and two couples prayed to ask God to show Himself to them as the Messiah! The previous week two people were baptized.

Gary & Melinda Stewart, Hampton Roads Community Church, Newport News, VA - We are encouraged to have seen several people saved recently. One man came for six months with his wife who is a Christian. He played on our church softball team and was friendly to be around. He approached me at a church hayride and said that he was ready to "do it." I asked him what he was ready to do and he replied that he was ready to trust Christ . . . One of the aspects of Hampton Roads that he liked the most was that he could come and listen and not be pressured. He commented that people were friendly, even though his dress was casual. Those are the comments we love to hear! Please pray for us that we will keep a heart for loving lost people like this man.

Ed & Carmen Harris, Willingboro, NJ - Early in December our only car was totaled when a branch from a large tree was blown onto it while Ed was driving. Miraculously, Ed was not hurt, and we are thankful to God for sparing him. We're also grateful to Interest Ministries for sending a check within a few days to allow us to put a down payment on another car.

Index